Studebaker
Ultimate Portfolio
1946 - 1966

Compiled by R M Clarke

ISBN 9871855207752

BROOKLANDS BOOKS LTD.
P.O. BOX 146, COBHAM,
SURREY, KT11 1LG. UK
sales@brooklands-books.com

Discarded

Brooklands Books

ROAD TEST SERIES

Abarth Gold Portfolio 1950-1971
Alfa Romeo Giulietta Gold Portfolio 1954-1965
Alfa Romeo Giulia Berlina Lim. Edit. Extra 1962-76
Alfa Romeo Giulia Coupes Lim. Edit. Ultra 1973-76
Alfa Romeo Alfasud 1972-1984
Alfa Romeo Alfetta Gold Portfolio 1972-1987
Alfa Romeo Spider Ultimate Portfolio 1966-1994
Alfa Romeo Spider & GTV Perf. Port. 1995-2005
Alpine Renault Ultimate Portfolio 1958-1995
Alvis Gold Portfolio 1919-1967
AMC Rambler Limited Edition Extra 1956-1969
AMX & Javelin Gold Portfolio 1968-1974
Armstrong Siddeley Gold Portfolio 1945-1960
Aston Martin Gold Portfolio 1921-1947
Aston Martin Ultimate Portfolio 1948-1968
Aston Martin Ultimate Portfolio 1968-1980
Aston Martin Ultimate Portfolio 1981-1993
Aston Martin Ultimate Portfolio 1994-2006
Audi Quattro Gold Portfolio 1980-1991
Audi Quattro Takes On The Competition
Audi TT Performance Portfolio 1998-2006
Austin-Healey 100 & 100/6 Gold Port. 1952-1959
Austin-Healey 3000 Ultimate Portfolio 1959-1967
Austin-Healey Sprite Gold Portfolio 1958-1971
Bentley & Rolls-Royce Portfolio 1990-2002
Berkeley Sportscars Limited Edition
BMW 6 & 8 Cyl. Cars Limited Edition 1935-1960
BMW 700 Limited Edition 1959-1965
BMW 1600 Collection No. 1 1966-1981
BMW 2002 Ultimate Portfolio 1968-1976
BMW 6 Cylinder Coupes & Saloons Gold P. 1969-1976
BMW 316, 318, 320 (4 cyl.) Gold Port. 1975-1990
BMW 320, 323, 325 (6 cyl.) Gold Port. 1977-1990
BMW 3 Series Gold Portfolio 1991-1997
BMW M3 Ultimate Portfolio 1986-2006
BMW M5 Gold Portfolio 1980-2003
BMW 5 Series Gold Portfolio 1988-1995
BMW 6 Series Ultimate Portfolio 1976-1989
BMW 7 Series Performance Portfolio 1977-1986
BMW 7 Series Performance Portfolio 1986-1993
BMW 8 Series Performance Portfolio
BMW X5 Limited Edition Extra 1999-2006
BMW Alpina Performance Portfolio 1967-1987
BMW Alpina Performance Portfolio 1988-1998
BMW Z3, M Coupe & M Roadster Gold Port. 1996-02
Borgward Isabella Limited Edition
Bristol Cars Portfolio
Buick Performance Portfolio 1947-1962
Buick Muscle Portfolio 1963-1973
Buick Riviera Performance Portfolio 1963-1978
Cadillac Performance Portfolio 1948-1958
Cadillac Performance Portfolio 1959-1966
Cadillac Eldorado Performance Portfolio 1967-1978
Cadillac Allante Limited Edition Extra
Impala & SS Muscle Portfolio 1958-1972
Corvair Performance Portfolio 1959-1969
El Camino & SS Muscle Portfolio 1959-1987
Chevy II & Nova SS Gold Portfolio 1962-1974
Chevelle & SS Gold Portfolio 1964-1972
Camaro Muscle Portfolio 1967-1973
Blazer & Jimmy Limited Edition Extra 1969-1982
Blazer & Jimmy Limited Edition Extra 1983-1994
Camaro Performance Portfolio 1993-2000
Chevrolet Corvette Gold Portfolio 1953-1962
Chevrolet Corvette Sting Ray Gold Port. 1963-1967
Chevrolet Corvette Gold Portfolio 1968-1977
High Performance Corvettes 1983-1989
Chrysler Imperial Gold Portfolio 1951-1975
Valiant 1960-1962
PT Cruiser Performance Portfolio
Citroen Traction Avant Limited Edition Premier
Citroen 2CV Ultimate Portfolio 1948-1990
Citroen DS & ID 1955-1975
Citroen DS & ID Gold Portfolio 1955-1975
Citroen SM Limited Edition Extra 1970-1975
Shelby Cobra Gold Portfolio 1962-1969
Crosley & Crosley Specials Limited Edition
Cunningham Automobiles 1951-1955
Datsun Roadsters Performance Portfolio 1960-71
Datsun 240Z & 260Z Gold Portfolio 1970-1978
DeLorean Gold Portfolio 1977-1995
De Soto Limited Edition 1952-1960
Dodge Limited Edition 1949-1959
Dodge Dart Limited Edition Extra 1960-1976
Dodge Muscle Portfolio 1964-1971
Charger Muscle Portfolio 1966-1974
ERA Gold Portfolio 1934-1994
Facel Vega Limited Edition Extra 1954-1964
Ferrari Limited Edition 1947-1957
Ferrari Limited Edition 1958-1963
Ferrari Dino Limited Edition Extra 1965-1974
Ferrari 308 & Mondial Ultimate Portfolio 1975- 85
Ferrari 328 348 Mondial Ultimate Portfolio 1986-94
Ferrari F355 & 360 Gold Portfolio 1995-2004
Fiat 600 & 850 Gold Portfolio 1955-1972
Fiat Dino Limited Edition
Fiat 124 Spider Performance Portfolio 1966-1985
Fiat X1/9 Gold Portfolio 1973-1989
Ford Consul, Zephyr, Zodiac Mk. I & II 1950-1962
Ford Zephyr, Zodiac, Executive Mk. III & IV 1962-1971
High Performance Capris Gold Portfolio 1969-1987
Capri Muscle Portfolio 1974-1987
High Performance Fiestas 1979-1991
Ford Escort RS & Mexico Limited Edition 1970-1979
High Performance Escorts Mk. II 1975-1980
High Performance Escorts 1980-1985
High Performance Escorts 1985-1990
Ford Thunderbird Performance Portfolio 1955-1957
Ford Thunderbird Performance Portfolio 1958-1963
Ford Thunderbird Performance Portfolio 1964-1976
Ford Fairlane Performance Portfolio 1955-1970
Ford Ranchero Muscle Portfolio 1957-1979
Edsel Limited Edition 1957-1960
Ford Galaxie & LTD Gold Portfolio 1960-1976
Falcon Performance Portfolio 1960-1970
Ford GT40 & GT Ultimate Portfolio 1964-2006
Ford Torino Performance Portfolio 1968-1974
Ford Bronco 4x4 Performance Portfolio 1966-1977
Ford Bronco 1978-1988
Shelby Mustang Ultimate Portfolio 1965-1970
Mustang Muscle Portfolio 1967-1973
High Performance Mustang IIs 1974-1978
Mustang 5.0L Muscle Portfolio 1982-1993
Mustang 5.0L Takes On The Competition
Ginetta Cars Limited Edition Ultra 1958-2007
Goggomobil Limited Edition
Honda S500 • S600 • S800 Limited Edition 1962-1970
Honda CRX 1983-1987
Honda S2000 Performance Portfolio 1999-2008
Hudson Performance Portfolio 1946-1957
International Scout Gold Portfolio 1961-1980
Isetta Gold Portfolio 1953-1964
ISO & Bizzarrini Limited Edition Ultra 1962-1974
Jaguar and SS Gold Portfolio 1931-1951
Jaguar C-Type & D-Type Gold Portfolio 1951-1960
Jaguar XK120 • 140 • 150 Gold Portfolio 1948-1960
Jaguar Mk. VII, VIII, IX, X, 420 Gold Port. 1950-1970
Jaguar XJ6 Series I & II Gold Portfolio 1968-1979
Jaguar XJ6 Series III Perf. Portfolio 1979-1986
Jaguar XJS Gold Portfolio 1975-1988
Jaguar XJ-S V12 Ultimate Portfolio 1988-1996
Jaguar XK8 & XKR Performance Portfolio 1996-2005
Jeep CJ-5 Limited Edition 1960-1975
Jeep CJ-5 & CJ-7 4x4 Perf. Portfolio 1976-1986
Jeep Wagoneer Performance Portfolio 1963-1991
Jeep J-Series Pickups 1970-1982
Jeepster & Commando Limited Edition 1967-1973
Jeep Cherokee & Comanche Pickups P. P. 1984-91
Jeep Wrangler 4x4 Performance Portfolio 1987-99
Jeep Cherokee & Grand Cherokee 4x4 P. P. 1992-98
Jensen Interceptor Ultimate Portfolio 1966-1992
Jensen-Healey Limited Edition 1972-1976
Kaiser-Frazer Limited Edition 1946-1955
Lagonda Gold Portfolio 1919-1964
Lancia Aurelia & Flaminia Gold Portfolio 1950-1970
Lancia Fulvia Gold Portfolio 1963-1976
Lancia Beta Gold Portfolio 1972-1984
Lancia Stratos Limited Edition Extra
Lancia Delta & integrale Ultimate Portfolio
Land Rover Series I, II & IIA Gold Portfolio 1948-71
Land Rover Series III 4x4 Perf. Portfolio 1971-1985
Land Rover 90 110 Defender Gold Portfolio 1983-94
Land Rover Discovery Perf. Port. 1989-2000
Fifty Years of Selling Land Rover
Lamborghini Performance Portfolio 1964-1976
Lamborghini Performance Portfolio 1977-1989
Lamborghini Gold Portfolio 1990-2004
Lincoln Gold Portfolio 1949-1960
Lincoln Continental Performance Portfolio 1961-1969
Lincoln Continental 1969-1976
Lotus Sports Racers Portfolio - covering 1951-1965
Lotus Seven Gold Portfolio 1957-1973
Lotus Elite Limited Edition 1957-1964
Lotus Elan Ultimate Portfolio 1962-1974
Lotus Elan & SE 1989-1992
Lotus Europa Gold Portfolio 1966-1975
Lotus Elite & Eclat 1974-1982
Lotus Elise & Exige Gold Portfolio 1995-2005
Marcos Coupés & Spyders Gold Portfolio 1960-1997
Maserati Cars Performance Portfolio 1957-1970
Maserati Cars Performance Portfolio 1971-1982
Maserati Cars Performance Portfolio 1982-1998
Maserati Cars Ultimate Portfolio 1999-2007
Matra Limited Edition 1965-1983
Mazda Miata MX-5 Performance Portfolio 1989-1997
Mazda Miata MX-5 Performance Portfolio 1998-2005
Mazda Miata MX-5 Takes On The Competition
Mazda RX-7 Gold Portfolio 1978-1991
McLaren F1 • GTR • LM Sportscar Perf. Portfolio
Mercedes 190 & 300 SL 1954-1963
Mercedes S & 600 Limited Edition Extra 1965-1972
Mercedes S Class 1972-1979
Mercedes S Class Limited Edition Extra 1980-1991
Mercedes 230 • 250 • 280SL Gold Portfolio 1963-1971
Mercedes-Benz SLs & SLCs Ultimate Port. 1971-89
Mercedes SLs Performance Portfolio 1989-1994
Mercedes G-Wagen Gold Portfolio 1981-2005
Mercedes 190 Limited Edition Extra 1983-1993
Mercedes CLK & SLK Limited Edition 1996-2000
Mercedes AMG Gold Portfolio 1983-1999
Mercedes AMG Ultimate Portfolio 2000-2006
Mercury Gold Portfolio 1947-1966
Mercury Comet & Cyclone Lim. Edit. Extra 1960-75
Cougar Muscle Portfolio 1967-1973
Messerschmitt Gold Portfolio 1954-1964
MG Gold Portfolio 1929-1939
MG TA & TC Gold Portfolio 1936-1949
MG TD & TF Gold Portfolio 1949-1955
MGA & Twin Cam Gold Portfolio 1955-1962
MG Midget Gold Portfolio 1961-1979
MGB Roadsters 1962-1980
MGB MGC & V8 Gold Portfolio 1962-1980
MGC & MGB GT V8 Limited Edition
MGF & TF Performance Portfolio 1995-2005
Mini Gold Portfolio 1959-1969
Mini Gold Portfolio 1969-1980
Mini Gold Portfolio 1981-1997
High Performance Minis Gold Portfolio 1960-1973
Mini Cooper Gold Portfolio 1961-1971
Mini Moke Ultimate Portfolio 1964-1994
Mini Performance Portfolio 2001-2006
Starion & Conquest Performance Portfolio 1982-90
Mitsubishi 3000GT & Dodge Stealth P.P. 1990-99
Morgan Three-Wheeler Gold Portfolio 1910-1952
Morgan Plus 4 & Four 4 Gold Portfolio 1936-1967
Morgan Cars Portfolio 1968-2001
Morris Minor Collection No. 1 1948-1980
Nash Limited Edition Extra 1949-1957
Nash-Austin Metropolitan Gold Portfolio 1954-1962
NSU Ro80 Limited Edition
NSX Performance Portfolio 1989-1999
Oldsmobile Muscle Portfolio 1964-1971
Cutlass & 4-4-2 Muscle Portfolio 1964-1974
Opel GT Ultimate Portfolio 1968-1973
Opel Manta Limited Edition 1970-1975
Pantera Ultimate Portfolio 1970-1995
Panther Gold Portfolio 1972-1990
Plymouth Limited Edition 1950-1960
Plymouth Fury Limited Edition Extra 1956-1976
Barracuda Muscle Portfolio 1964-1974
Plymouth Muscle Portfolio 1964-1971
High Performance Firebirds 1982-1988
Firebird & Trans Am Performance Portfolio 1993-00
Pontiac Fiero Performance Portfolio 1984-1988
Porsche Sports Racing Cars UP 1952-1968
Porsche 917 • 935 • 956 • 962 Gold Portfolio
Porsche 912 Limited Edition Extra
Porsche 365 Ultimate Portfolio 1952-1965
Porsche 911 1965-1969
Porsche 911 1973-1977
Porsche 911 SC & Turbo Gold Portfolio 1978-1983
Porsche 911 Carrera & Turbo Gold Port. 1984-1989
Porsche 911 Ultimate Portfolio 1990-1997
Porsche 911 Takes On The Competition 1990-1997
Porsche 911 Ultimate Portfolio 1998-2004
Porsche 914 Ultimate Portfolio
Porsche 924 Gold Portfolio 1975-1988
Porsche 928 Gold Portfolio 1977-1995
Porsche 928 Takes On The Competition
Porsche 944 Ultimate Portfolio
Porsche 968 Limited Edition Extra
Porsche Boxster Ultimate Portfolio 1996-2004
Railton & Brough Superior Gold Portfolio 1933-1950
Range Rover Gold Portfolio 1970-1985
Range Rover Gold Portfolio 1985-1995
Range Rover Performance Portfolio 1995-2001
Range Rover Takes on the Competition
Riley Gold Portfolio 1924-1939
Rolls-Royce Silver Clould & Bentley S Ultimate Port.
Rolls-Royce Silver Shadow Ultimate Port. 1965-80
Rover P4 1949-1959
Rover 2000 & 2200 1963-1977
Studebaker Ultimate Portfolio 1946-1966
Studebaker Hawks & Larks Lim. Edit. Premier 1956-66
Avanti Limited Edition Extra 1962-1991
Subaru Impreza Turbo Limited Edition Extra 1994-00
Subaru Impreza WRX Performance Port. 2001-2005
Sunbeam Alpine Limited Edition Extra 1959-1968
Sunbeam Tiger Limited Edition Extra 1964-1967
Suzuki SJ Gold Portfolio 1971-1997
Vitara, Sidekick & Geo Tracker Perf. Port. 1988-1997
Toyota Land Cruiser Gold Portfolio 1956-1987
Toyota Land Cruiser 1988-1997
Toyota Supra Performance Portfolio 1982-1998
Toyota MR2 Gold Portfolio 1984-1997
Toyota MR2 Takes On The Competition
Triumph TR2 & TR3 Gold Portfolio 1952-1961
Triumph TR4, TR5, TR250 1961-1968
Triumph TR6 Gold Portfolio 1969-1976
Triumph Herald 1959-1971
Triumph Vitesse 1962-1971
Triumph Spitfire Gold Portfolio 1962-1980
Triumph 2000, 2.5, 2500 1963-1977
Triumph GT6 Gold Portfolio 1966-1974
Triumph Stag Gold Portfolio 1970-1977
TVR Performance Portfolio 1986-1994
TVR Performance Portfolio 1995-2000
TVR Performance Portfolio 2000-2005
VW Beetle Gold Portfolio 1935-1967
VW Beetle Gold Portfolio 1968-1991
VW Bus, Camper, Van Perf. Portfolio 1954-1967
VW Bus, Camper, Van Perf. Portfolio 1968-1979
VW Bus, Camper, Van Perf. Portfolio 1979-1991
VW Karmann Ghia Gold Portfolio 1955-1974
VW Scirocco 1974-1981
VW Golf GTI Limited Edition Extra 1976-1991
VW Corrado Limited Edition 1989-1995
Volvo PV444 & PV544 Perf. Portfolio 1945-1965
Volvo 120 Amazon Ultimate Portfolio
Volvo 1800 Ultimate Portfolio 1960-1973
Volvo 140 & 160 Series Gold Portfolio 1966-1975
Forty Years of Selling Volvo
Westfield Performance Portfolio 1982-2004

RACING & THE LAND SPEED RECORD

The Land Speed Record 1898-1919
The Land Speed Record 1920-1929
The Land Speed Record 1930-1939
The Land Speed Record 1940-1962
The Land Speed Record 1963-1999
Can-Am Racing 1966-1969
Can-Am Racing 1970-1974
Can-Am Racing Cars 1966-1974
The Carrera Panamericana Mexico - 1950-1954
Le Mans - The Bentley & Alfa Years - 1923-1939
Le Mans - The Jaguar Years - 1949-1957
Le Mans - The Ferrari Years - 1958-1965
Le Mans - The Ford & Matra Years - 1966-1974
Le Mans - The Porsche Years - 1975-1982
Le Mans - The Porsche & Jaguar Years - 1983-91
Le Mans - The Porsche & Peugeot Years - 1992-99
Mille Miglia - The Alfa & Ferrari Years - 1927-1951
Mille Miglia - The Ferrari & Mercedes Years - 1952-57
Targa Florio - The Porsche & Ferrari Years - 1955-1964
Targa Florio - The Porsche Years - 1965-1973

RESTORATION & GUIDE SERIES

BMW 2002 - A Comprehensive Guide
BMW 02 Restoration Guide
BMW E30 - 3 Series Restoration Bible
Classic Camaro Restoration
Engine Swapping Tips & Techniques
Ferrari Life Buyer's Portfolio
Land Rover Restoration Portfolio
PC on Land Rover Series I Restoration
Lotus Elan Restoration Guide
MG 'T' Series Restoration Guide
MGA Restoration Guide
PC on Midget/Sprite Restoration
PC on MGB Restoration
Mustang Restoration Tips & Techniques
Practical Gas Flow
Restoring Sprites & Midgets an Enthusiast's Guide
SU Carburetters Tuning Tips & Techniques
PC on Sunbeam Rapier Restoration
The Great Classic Muscle Cars Compared
Weber Carburettors Tuning Tips and Techniques

MILITARY VEHICLES

Complete WW2 Military Jeep Manual
Dodge WW2 Military Portfolio 1940-1945
German Military Equipment WW2
Hail To The Jeep
Combat Land Rover Portfolio No. 1
Land Rover Military Portfolio
Military & Civilian Amphibians 1940-1990
Off Road Jeeps Civilian & Military 1944-1971
US Military Vehicles 1941-1945
Standard Military Motor Vehicles-TM9-2800 (WW2)
VW Kubelwagen Military Portfolio 1940-1990
WW2 Allied Vehicles Military Portfolio 1939-1945
WW2 Jeep Military Portfolio 1941-1945

ROAD & TRACK SERIES

Road & Track on Aston Martin 1962-1990
Road & Track on Austin Healey 1953-1970
Road & Track on BMW Cars 1966-1974
Road & Track BMW M Series Portfolio 1979-2002
R & T BMW Z3, M Coupe & M Roadster Port. 96-02
R & T Camaro & Firebird Portfolio 1993-2002
R & T on Cobra, Shelby & Ford GT40 1962-1992
Road & Track on Corvette 1968-1982
Road & Track on Corvette 1982-1986
Road & Track on Corvette 1986-1990
Road & Track Corvette Portfolio 1997-2002
Road & Track Dodge Viper Portfolio 1992-2002
Road & Track on Ferrari 1975-1981
Road & Track on Ferrari 1984-1988
Road & Track Ferrari V-12 Portfolio 1992-2002
Road & Track Ferrari F355 360 F430 Portfolio 95-06
Road & Track on Fiat Sports Cars 1968-1987
Road & Track on Jaguar 1950-1960
Road & Track on Jaguar 1961-1968
Road & Track on Jaguar 1968-1974
Road & Track on Jaguar 1974-1982
Road & Track on Jaguar 1983-1989
R & T Jaguar XJ-S - XK8 - XKR Portfolio 1975-2003
Road & Track MX-5 Miata Portfolio 1989-2002
Road & Track on Mercedes 1952-1962
Road & Track on Mercedes 1963-1970
Road & Track on Mercedes 1971-1979
R & T Mercedes SL - SLK - CLK Portfolio 1990-2003
Road & Track on MG Sports Cars 1949-1961
Road & Track on MG Sports Cars 1962-1980
Road & Track Mustang Portfolio 1994-2002
Road & Track Nissan 300ZX & 350Z Portfolio 1984-03
Road & Track on Porsche 1951-1967
Road & Track on Porsche 1968-1971
Road & Track on Porsche 1972-1975
Road & Track on Porsche 1975-1978
Road & Track on Porsche 1979-1982
Road & Track on Porsche 1985-1988
Road & Track Porsche 928 Portfolio 1977-1994
Road & Track Porsche 911 Portfolio 1990-1997
R & T on Rolls Royce & Bentley 1950-1965
R & T on Rolls Royce & Bentley 1966-1984
R & T on Toyota Sports & GT Cars 1966-1984
R & T on Triumph Sports Cars 1967-1974
R & T on Triumph Sports Cars 1974-1982
Road & Track on Volkswagen 1951-1968
Road & Track on Volkswagen 1968-1978
Road & Track on Volvo 1957-1974
Road & Track on Volvo 1977-1994
Road & Track - Best of PS
Road & Track - Peter Egan Side Glances 1983-92
Road & Track - Peter Egan Side Glances 1992-97
Road & Track - Peter Egan Side Glances 1998-02
Road & Track - Peter Egan Side Glances 2002-06

CAR AND DRIVER SERIES

Car and Driver on BMW 1957-1977
Car and Driver on Corvette 1978-1982
Car and Driver on Corvette 1983-1988
Car and Driver on Ferrari 1955-1962
Car and Driver on Ferrari 1963-1975
Car and Driver on Mustang 1964-1973
Car and Driver on Porsche 1955-1962
Car and Driver on Porsche 1963-1970
Car and Driver on Porsche 1970-1976
Car and Driver on Porsche 1977-1981
Car and Driver on Porsche 1982-1986

HOT ROD 'ENGINE' SERIES

Chevy 265 & 283
Chevy 302 & 327
Chevy 348 & 409
Chevy 396 & 427
Chevy 454 thru 512
Chrysler Hemi
Chrysler 273, 318, 340 & 360
Chrysler 361, 383, 400, 413, 426 & 440
Ford 289, 302, Boss 302 & 351W
Ford 351C & Boss 351
Ford Small Block
Ford Big Block

MOTORCYCLES

To see our range of over 70 titles visit www.brooklands-books.com

15/12Z7

Contents

Brooklands
Books

Contents - Continued

Acknowledgements

We published our first portfolio on post-war Studebakers in the early '90s and it went out of print some years ago. Because of the popularity of these inovative cars we have been persuaded to check our archive for new material and the result is this enlarged *Ultimate Portfolio* with a section in color. The series however would not have been possible without the help and understanding of the worlds leading motoring journals, who have supported us for many years. We are sure that Studebaker owners will wish to join with us in thanking the managements of the following magazines: *Auto Age, Autocar, Automobiles, Automobile Topics, Auto Sport Review, Car and Driver, Car Life, Car South Africa, Complete Road Tests, Modern Motor, Motor, Motor Life, Motor Manual, Motorcade, Motor Age, Motor Sport, Motor Trend, Motor World, Popular Science, Road & Track, Science and Mechanics, Speed Age, Sports Car Illustrated, Track & Traffic, Wheels* and the *World Car Catalogue.*

R.M. Clarke

Studebaker really started something when they released their coming or going sedans in 1947. Styled in collaboration with the famous Raymond Loewy Studios the company was the first in America to come out with a completely new postwar style of automobile. This boldness set Studebaker apart from the Big Three as well as the other independents in the industry and set production records at South Bend. The fact that they were prewar in their mechanical specifications made absolutely no difference to a car-starved America, it was the style that counted!

These sedans, badged Commander, Champion, Regal and Land Cruiser, names that would later appear on rival cars' models, would see Studebaker rise to eighth among the US manufacturers with production of 228,402 units built in 1949 rising to 268,099 in 1950. Sadly it would go downhill from there. Model changes would come and go during the 50s, all based around the work done for the impressively styled 53s. The ancient side-valve six was joined by the company's first-ever V8 in 1951; available in one capacity only at first, 232-cubic inches, or 3.8-litres that produced 120bhp, it was the US industry's first compact V8. By 1955 it had been enlarged to 259-cid and to 289-cid the following year. In 1963 Studebaker shocked the industry with their release of the Super Lark and Super Hawk fitted with the R1 and R2 supercharged 289 V8s that produced 240bhp and 300bhp respectively courtesy of a Paxton centrifugal supercharger. These cars garnered much media attention but sadly for the company few were sold; they are much sought after today.

In 1953 Studebaker introduced their Starliner series of convertibles, cars that have gone down in history as the nicest styled American car of the 50s. So well received was the series that subsequent saloons would adopt its styling theme. From these coupes the company developed the Silver and Golden Hawk coupes and, at the end, the Grand Turismo Hawk. All these coupes are now eminently collectible today. Studebaker's boldest move was the introduction in 1959 of the compact Lark. At a stroke it brought a fresh new style to the company's product range as well as some excitement performance wise from the V8 engined versions, long before Detroit ever thought about offering similarly hot sedans! A Lark V8 with a manual gearbox could accelerate from 0-60mph in 10.7 seconds and run to a maximum of around 100mph, for 1960 that was really something!

And then there was the stunning Avanti, the company's last desperate attempt to break the mould and establish itself as a maker of cars for those who appreciated and understood something different from the behemoths that Detroit was building. Unfortunately, less than 5,000 of the fiberglass-bodied Avantis were made, each one at a loss. This money could well have been invested in a major upgrade of the Lark that famous consultant Brook Stevens had developed but remained, sadly, on the drawing board. Unfortunately for the automobile world the company was never able to generate sufficient profit to finance the design and development of the next model cycle and so the Lark became the last of a famous automobile line when the company closed its doors in Hamilton, Canada in 1966. It ended a 117-year history of manufacturing transportation equipment by the Studebaker brothers.

Gavin Farmer

New Styling on Studebaker

New grille and bumper are among a few of the features in the Studebaker Champion series.

"Skyway" motif is featured by Studebaker in four body types in the 1946 Champion series

FRESH new styling, improved riding qualities and luxury appointments mark the new automobile models announced by Studebaker.

Four body types in the Champion series, will be manufactured in 1945. Production schedules promise a complete sampling for dealers within the next month.

The first passenger cars to be built by Studebaker since plant facilities were converted to war manufacture carry more numerous advances than the four-year blackout of research on civilian products would indicate.

New styling introduces the "Skyway" motif in a wide variety of colors to the lowest price field. A bright, new grille, with horizonal members extending virtually full-width across radiator and fenders, complements the lines of the car. Rugged bumpers with vertical guards are also new.

Both in exteriors and interiors the new models include many interesting features. Now standard are such features as de luxe steering wheels; automatic dome lights in all models; automatic rear compartment lights in four-door sedans; and bright metal for body sill finishing strips, windshields, and rear and side window moldings. Twin air-tone horns, dual sun visors and windshield wipers, and arm rests on both front doors are

other features. Interiors are made additionally notable by the use of a rich wool Bedford cord as the upholstery cloth.

The Champion six-cylinder engine, that as the power unit for the war-famous Weasel is continued substantially unchanged. Worthy of comment among engine changes is the return of aluminum alloy pistons which were discarded in 1941 due to the scarcity of aluminum as a war material. The substitution of aluminum for cast iron reduces piston weight by more than half.

Chief among chassis advances are the newly designed springs. Spring action has been improved by tapering the ends of the leaves and the introduction at both front and rear

of oil-impregnated, full-length inserts known as Flex-o-liners. These inserts tend to reduce interleaf friction and to assure smooth, soft spring action. Combined with the planar front springing, the development provides improved riding qualities. Shot peening has been continued for all of the spring leaves.

Automatic choke, floto oil screen, large capacity air cleaner are features. A 15-plate battery replaces the previous 13-plate. Transmissions have helical, silent gears throughout. Overdrives, assuring more gas mileage at higher speeds, hill-holders, and the Climatizer, which gives forced air circulation for both winter and summer driving, are among the accessories available at extra cost.

ADVANCED STYLING.—The new Studebaker "Champion" Sedan is a creation of Raymond Loewy, well known for his futuristic body designs. Special features are much increased width, and seating of all passengers well forward of the rear axle.

FIRST DETAILS OF
The New Studebakers

JUST announced are the 1947 Studebaker models, entirely new in appearance and with a considerable number of mechanical changes. Among the oldest manufacturers in the American automobile industry, the Studebaker Corporation now returns to car production, with futuristic looking models styled by Raymond Loewy.

Engines used in the new models are six-cylinder side-valve types in two sizes, developing 80 b.h.p. and 94 b.h.p. respectively. Basically similar to existing units, the new engines incorporate such improvements as interchangeable big-end bearings. The complete power plant has now been moved a long way forward, so that the oil sump now comes ahead of the front-suspension.

Clutch operation is lightened by a spring-loaded toggle mechanism, and an overdrive is an optional feature of the transmission system. A divided propeller shaft has been combined with a hypoid bevel rear axle to enable the propeller-shaft tunnel to be eliminated.

Front suspension is still independent, by wishbones and a rubber-mounted transverse leaf spring, location of the wheels being entirely by the wishbones. The frame is of rigid box-section throughout, and, with the extremely forward engine position, it has been found possible to move the rear seat 19½ ins. forward of the rear axle.

An important advance is the employment of automatically self-adjusting brakes on these cars. The adjusting mechanism is controlled by a graphite bronze pad incorporated in one brake shoe, and takes up excess clearance by steps of 0.005 in.

Wide-base tyres are used, in the interests of greater stability and reduced wear, on rims of only 15 ins. diameter. Tyre sections vary from 5.50 ins. to 6.50 ins., according to the model.

Wheelbases of the new Studebakers range from 9 ft. 4 ins. on the Champion model up to 10 ft. 3 ins. on the largest Commander "land cruiser." The full-width bodies provide a rear seat 58 ins. wide.

AWAY AHEAD.—The Studebaker engine is placed so far ahead in the chassis that the oil sump is now ahead of the front suspension assembly.

STUDEBAKER DATA

	Champion	Commander		Champion	Commander
Present tax ..	£27 10s.	£33 15s.	Suspension ..	Independent front (transverse leaf)	Independent front (transverse leaf)
Cubic capacity ..	2,780 c.c.	3,700 c.c.		Semi-elliptic rear	Semi-elliptic rear
Cylinders ..	6	6			
Valve position ..	Side	Side	Steering gear ..	Variable ratio	Variable ratio
Bore	76 mm.	84 mm.	Wheelbase ..	9 ft. 4 ins.	9 ft. 11 ins.
Stroke	102 mm.	111 mm.	Track, front ..	—	—
Comp. ratio ..	6.5 (optional 7.0)	6.5 (optional 7.0)	Track, rear ..	—	—
			Overall length ..	16 ft.	—
Max. power ..	80 b.h.p.	94 b.h.p.	Overall width ..	5 ft. 9¾ ins.	—
at ..	4,000 r.p.m.	3,600 r.p.m.	Overall height ..	5 ft. 0¾ in.	—
H.P.: Sq. in. piston area ..	1.89	1.82	Tyre size.. ..	5.50 × 15 ins.	6.50 × 15 ins.
Ft./min. piston			Wheel type ..	Bolt-on disc	Bolt-on disc
speed at max.			Electrical system	6 volt	6 volt
h.p.	2,670 ft./min.	2,630 ft./min.	Battery capacity	100 amp.-hr.	100 amp.-hr.
Carburetter ..	Downdraught	Downdraught			
Ignition	Coil	Coil	**Top Gear Facts :**		
Fuel pump ..	Mechanical	Mechanical	Engine speed per		
Oil filter make			10 m.p.h. ..	550 r.p.m.	510 r.p.m.
(by-pass, full			Piston speed per		
flow)	Optional extra	—	10 m.p.h. ..	365 ft./min.	370 ft./min.
Top gear.. ..	4.10	4.09	Road speed at		
Prop. shaft ..	Divided	Divided	2,500 ft./min.		
Final drive ..	Hypoid bevel	Hypoid bevel	(piston) ..	68 m.p.h.	68 m.p.h.
Brakes	Self-adjusting	Self-adjusting			

As an approximation, 2,800 litres per ton-mile enables a car to climb a gradient of 1 in 10 in top gear. Similarly pro rata—a gradient of 1 in 9, for example, requires 3,100 litres per ton-mile.

THE POST-WAR CAR

1947 CHAMPION SEDAN

The Surprise Car of the Year

STUDEBAKER.

Just announced in Australia are the 1947 Studebakers, in two models: the Champion and the Commander. They are probably the world's most advanced post-war designs.

This review features the Champion, the smaller of the two. The Commander will be reviewed in a later issue.

The Studebaker Champion is entirely new in appearance and incorporates a considerable number of mechanical changes. Among the oldest manufacturers in the American automobile industry, Studebaker quickly switched from war production, which included the famous Weasel, to production of a really post-war car.

DESIGN.

The model available in Australia is the entirely radical four door sedan, designed by Studebaker in conjunction with the famous designer Raymond Loewy. It is much lower than normal cars, and wider, with wings almost completely absorbed into the body. The engine is mounted further forward, giving a much lower body and consequently a longer rear decking, and greater luggage space. Passengers are now seated further forward (rear seat 19½ inches forward of axle) and well down between the wheels allowing a much lower centre of gravity. Much more glass is used in a deeper, wider windscreen and a beautifully curved rear panel, giving almost un-interrupted visibility all around.

Almost the whole design of the car contributes to greater safety, extra width, lower centre

of gravity, greater visibility, wide rim wheels, even down to rotary door locks and new "pull" type door handles.

Also a feature of the new design, are the 15 inch steel disc wheels with new 5 inch wide safety rims. They are also fitted with smart coloured plastic covers.

INTERIORS.

The interior is beautifully appointed and the wide leather seats accommodate three people comfortably. There is a big two-spoke wheel with a neat gear lever, and the well laid out instrument panel uses black lighting for illumination. Doors are opened from the inside by pressure on a thumbpiece and the rotary latches shut without slamming. Ventilation is well provided for and the body is completely insulated against heat and sound.

POWER LAYOUT.

The engine is the well-known Champion 6 cylinder, side valve unit of 21.6 h.p., but incorporates numerous minor improvements. The whole power plant has been moved a long way forward, so that the oil sump now comes ahead of the front suspension. Clutch operation is lightened by a spring loaded toggle mechanism and an overdrive is an optional feature of the transmission system. A divided prop. shaft and a hypoid bevel rear axle enable the prop. shaft tunnel to be eliminated.

Front suspension is independent with Planar type wish-bones and a rubber mounted transverse

Studebaker sets the coming style . . .

leaf spring. The frame is of rigid box section throughout. An important advance is the employment of automatic, self-adjusting brakes which take themselves up in steps of 0.005 ins. at a time.

The steering is of the direct action "Shockless" type with variable ratio cam and twin-lever gear. This dual ratio provides a normal gear for driving and a larger one to supply more leverage when parking.

THE OVERDRIVE.

There is an overdrive transmission provided as an optional feature on Studebaker cars, and this briefly consists of an automatic higher gear that cuts in at 30 m.p.h., and reduces the engine speed 30 per cent. This is an economy factor as it not only saves petrol, but decreases wear and tear on the engine.

PERFORMANCE.

The road performance of the car is outstanding, it is quiet and comfortable and the steering is firm and positive, even at high speed. Again the most appealing feature is the all round visibility and the feeling of safety.

The Champion is also extremely economical and up to 30 m.p.g. can be obtained on a run even at comparatively high cruising speeds. This is indeed tomorrow's car today!

The aircraft influence on instrument paneling is pronounced. Unique "cockpit" lighting illuminates the dials. This lighting, now known as "black light," was developed during the war when scientists took over the study of aircraft instrument panel glare.

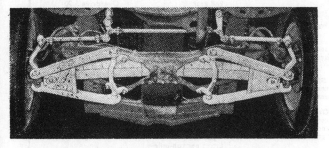

THE PLANAR SUSPENSION, which Studebaker pioneered, is re-engineered with a revised front mounting that enhances riding comfort. In earlier design, the spring served as a structural member. The ends of the laterally mounted springs were anchored to shackle pins. With the new type, spring ends "float" on rubber cushions.

SPECIFICATIONS

ENGINE.
Six cylinders, L head engine of 21.6 h.p., with side valves, developing 80 b.h.p. at 4,000 r.p.m. 3 in. bore x 4 in. stroke and compression ratio of either 6.5:1, or 7:1 (optional).

TRANSMISSION.
Three speed synchro-mesh gearbox with helical cut gears and optional overdrive. Remote control lever on steering column.

SUSPENSION.
Independent Planar type front suspension, long semi-elliptic springs at rear. Houdaille shock absorbers.

BRAKES.
Hydraulic self-adjusting brakes. Pull type hand-brake and automatic hill-holder (optional).

STEERING.
Cam and twin lever shockless steering gear with variable ratio.

WHEELS.
15 inch steel disc wheels with wide base rims, 5.50 x 15 in. tyres.

DIMENSIONS.
Wheelbase—112 inches.
Overall Length—192¾ inches.
Height—60¾ inches.
Width—69¾ inches.

The Motor Continental Road Test No. 7C/48

Make: Studebaker. **Type:** Champion 5-seater Coupe.

Makers: The Studebaker Corporation, South Bend, Indiana, U.S.A.

Dimensions and Seating

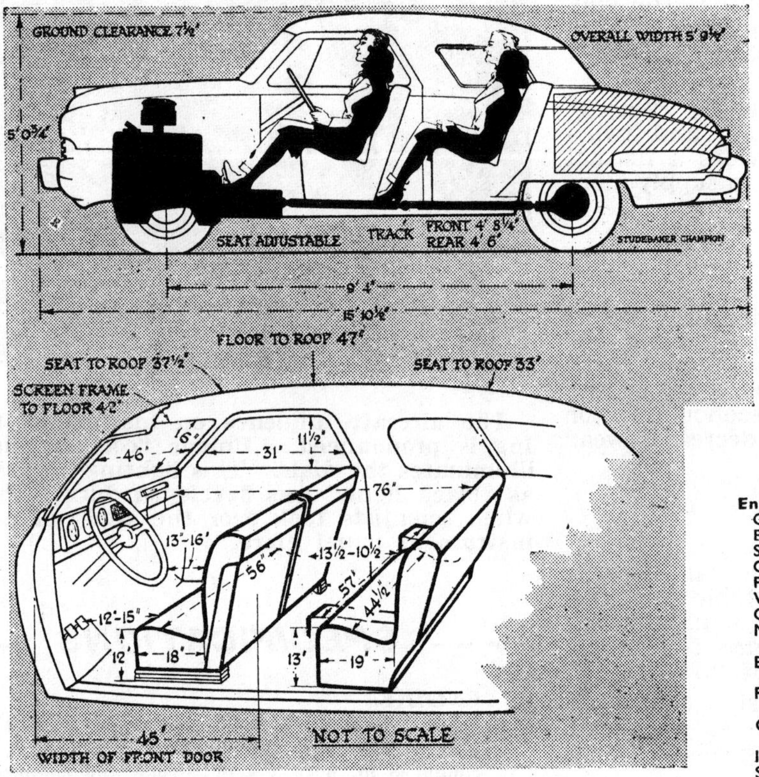

Test Conditions

Mild weather, little wind, wet concrete surface, Belgian pump fuel.

Test Data

ACCELERATION TIMES on Upper Ratios

	Overdrive Top	Direct Top	Overdrive 2nd	Direct 2nd
10-30 m.p.h.	—	8.8 secs.	—	5.8 secs.
20-40 m.p.h.	—	9.1 secs.	—	6.3 secs.
30-50 m.p.h.	18.0 secs.	11.4 secs.	10.6 secs.	—
40-60 m.p.h.	23.2 secs.	15.5 secs.	16.0 secs.	—
50-70 m.p.h.	32.0 secs.	—	—	—

ACCELERATION TIMES through gears

0-30 m.p.h.	5.1 secs.
0-40 m.p.h.	9.6 secs.
0-50 m.p.h.	18.0 secs.
0-60 m.p.h.	26.6 secs.
0-70 m.p.h.	41.7 secs.
Standing quarter-mile	23.1 secs.

MAXIMUM SPEEDS

Flying Quarter-mile

Mean of four opposite runs	78.5 m.p.h.
Best time equals	80.4 m.p.h.

Speed in Gears

Max. speed in direct top gear	69 m.p.h.
Max. speed in overdrive 2nd gear	61 m.p.h.
Max. speed in direct 2nd gear	43 m.p.h.

BRAKES at 30 m.p h.

Best deceleration on wet concrete surface, 0.71g (=42½ ft. stopping distance).

FUEL CONSUMPTION

Overall consumption, driven hard, 19 m.p.g.
30.0 m.p.g. at constant 30 m.p.h.
28.5 m.p.g. at constant 40 m.p.h.
24.0 m.p.g. at constant 50 m.p.h.
21.5 m.p.g. at constant 60 m.p.h.
18.0 m.p.g. at constant 70 m.p.h.

HILL CLIMBING

Max. direct top gear speed on 1 in 20.. 62 m.p.h.
Max. direct top gear speed on 1 in 15. 56 m.p.h.
Max. direct top gear speed on 1 in 10.. 41 m.p.h.
Max. gradient climbable on overdrive top gear, 1 in 18 .. (Tapley 125 lb. per ton)
Max. gradient climbable on direct top gear, 1 in 8¾ .. (Tapley 255 lb. per ton)
Max. gradient climbable on overdrive 2nd gear, 1 in 9½ .. (Tabley 235 lb. per ton)
Max. gradient climbable on direct 2nd gear, 1 in 5¾ .. (Tapley 390 lb. per ton)

STEERING

Left- and right-hand lock .. .. 41 ft.
4 turns of steering wheel, lock to lock.

In Brief

Price:	$1,437, at factory.
Equivalent at £1=$4.03,	£356.
Capacity	2,780 c.c.
Road weight unladen	26¼ cwt.
Front/rear weight distribution	57/43.
Laden weight as tested	29½ cwt.
Fuel consumption	19 m.p.g.
Maximum speed	78.5 m.p.h.
Maximum speed on 1 in 20 gradient	62 m.p.h.
Maximum top gear gradient	1 in 8¾.
Acceleration, 10-30 on top	8.8 secs.
0-50 through gears	18.0 secs.
Gearing,	23.2 m.p.h. in overdrive top at 1,000 r.p.m. 87 m.p.h. at 2,500 ft. per minute piston speed.

Specification

Engine	
Cylinders	6
Bore	76.2 mm.
Stroke	101.6 mm.
Cubic capacity	2,780 c.c.
Piston area	42.4 sq. ins.
Valves	Side
Compression ratio	6.5 (Optional 7.0)
Max. b.h.p. (Bare engine)	80
at	4,000 r.p.m.
B.H.P. per sq. in. piston area	1.89
Piston speed at max. b.h.p.	2,665 ft./min.
Carburetter	Carter downdraught WE661S
Ignition	Auto-lite coil
Sparking plugs	14 mm. Champion J7
Fuel pump	AC Mechanical
Oil filter	Fram (Optional extra)
Transmission	
Clutch	8-in. s.d.p. Borg & Beck
Top gear	Overdrive 3.19 Direct 4.56
2nd gear	Overdrive 5.20 Direct 7.43
1st gear	11.88
Propeller shaft	Spicer, divided
Final drive	Spicer, hypoid
Chassis	
Brakes	Wagner hydraulic
Brake-drum diameter	9 ins.
Friction-lining area	148 sq. ins.
Tyres	5.50 x 15
Steering gear	Ross, Cam and twin lever
Performance Factors (At laden weight as tested)	
Piston area, sq. ins. per ton	28.8
Brake lining area, sq. ins. per ton	100
Litres per ton-mile— overdrive top	2,420
direct top	3,470

Maintenance

Fuel tank: 14 gallons. **Sump:** 8½ pints, S.A.E. 30 Summer, S.A.E. 20 Winter. **Gearbox and overdrive:** 2 pints, S.A.E. 90. **Rear axle:** 2 pints, S.A.E. 90 Hypoid oil. **Radiator:** 16½ pints. **Chassis lubrication:** by grease gun every 1,000 miles to 30 points. **Ignition timing:** 2° before T.D.C. **Sparkplug gap:** 0.025 in. **Contact-breaker gap:** 0.020 in. **Tappets (cold):** inlet and exhaust 0.016 in. **Valve timing:** I.O., 15° B.T.D.C. I.C., 49° A.B.D.C. E.O., 54° B.B.D.C. E.C., 10° A.T.D.C. **Front-wheel toe-in (9 ins. above floor):** $\frac{1}{16}$ to ⅛ in. **Camber angle (no load):** ½° to ¾°. **Castor angle (no load):** 1½°. **Tyre pressures:** front 30 lb., rear 28 lb. **Brake fluid:** Wagner Lockheed. **Battery:** Willard 6-volt 100 amp.-hour. **Headlamps:** sealed beam.

Ref. U.S./28/48.

THE STUDEBAKER CHAMPION COUPÉ

Well-executed Detail Work a Feature of the Smallest American Popular Automobile

PERHAPS the most striking impression left by the Studebaker fixed-head coupé which was recently submitted for "The Motor" road test was of a car in which mass production has enabled low cost to be combined with an amazing standard of detail refinement. The general quality of interior furnishing, on a car which is small by American standards and inexpensive on any basis of comparison, is quite astonishingly high.

In external appearance the saloon models of the Studebaker range launched an original fashion which has since been followed, to a substantial extent, by many other manufacturers. The car submitted for test, by arrangement with the Studebaker Export Corporation, was the slightly less roomy two-door coupé model, which carries even further the idea of a short bonnet, vast rear bay window, and long tail. Striking appearances are not obtained by undue sacrifice of body space, however, and entry to the rear compartment is quite easy, thanks to wide doors and diagonal tilting of the front seat squabs.

Happy Medium

Internally, this striking-looking car is finished in a style which, without being unduly conservative, is in no way offensive to European tastes. There is considerable use of light-coloured plastics, but these are set off against cloth, leather, and really good artificial woodwork. The steering wheel is a simple two-spoke design carrying a thin horn ring, and the instruments are in three unashamedly circular dials directly facing the driver. On the car tested, woven plastic washable loose seat covers, with a somewhat prominent check pattern, were a serviceable extra, but rather slippery.

ALL-ROUND VISION.—The expanse of glazing at the rear of the Studebaker Champion coupé is matched by a wide windscreen of bent glass.

In mechanical specification the Studebaker is generally in line with present-day American practice, with a six-cylinder side-valve engine, set above a transverse wishbone independent front suspension system, operating in conjunction with a three-speed gearbox and automatic overdrive gear. An unusual feature, however, is that a transverse leaf spring, with its extremities acting between rubber pads, is incorporated in the front suspension instead of the more usual coil springs.

With the slightly stiffer front spring supplied to many European markets, but without the oversize tyres fitted to cars assembled in Belgium, the Studebaker gave a ride which was very satisfactorily comfortable, even if falling slightly short of the highest standards of freedom from bump and pitch. The most striking characteristic of the suspension layout used, however, was the absolute stability of the car on straight

going at any speed within the car's range.

On corners, the stiffened suspension and the wide build of the car combine to keep the angle of roll within reasonable bounds even when the car is handled in forceful fashion. We never encountered any tendency for bumps to put the car off its course on bends, and in a considerable amount of driving on wet cobbles noticed singularly little of that tendency to wheelspin and tail—sliding sometimes associated with powerful engines set far forward in the chassis.

The steering itself, geared at four turns of the wheel from full left to full right lock, was precise and strongly self-centring but transmitted appreciable reaction to the driver's hands—though some of this was of a type suggesting that a front tyre which had obviously undergone repair was somewhat out of balance. The white plastic steering wheel was set rather high, and the absence of very definite finger-grip mouldings induced a driver to grip it with rather tiring firmness.

Self-adjusting brakes are used on the Studebaker, and they give a driver complete confidence. Pedal pressures were moderate for normal retardation, becoming fairly high for emergency conditions, but even with the wheels locked by violent braking on the wet roads encountered almost throughout our test the car showed only the slightest deviation from its straight path.

The engine had the most desirable of characteristics, in that it utterly failed to attract any attention to itself. In the morning it was simply a case of operating the starter once, manœuvring out of the garage, and driving off; there was no choke to be operated, no delay in starting, and no uncertainty of pulling or tick-over evident at any stage in the warming-up process. When the engine was normally warm, its idling with the car at rest in traffic was so smooth as to

TWO-DOOR DETAIL.—The bench-type front seat has a divided backrest, the halves of which fold diagonally to facilitate entry to the back of the car.

INTERIOR STAND-
ARD.—A two-spoke
steering wheel and
neatly simple instru-
ment panel are pro-
vided for the driver.

EXTERIOR EXTRAS.-
The test car carried a
radio aerial retract-
able from inside the
car, a spotlight, and
a neat rear view
mirror.

be entirely imperceptible by either feeling or hearing.

Linked with the power unit was a Borg and Beck clutch and Warner three-speed gearbox with overdrive. This transmission, in effect a three-speed manually controlled gearbox plus an automatic two-speed gear, gives, in fact, five useful and distinct ratios, these being 1st, 2nd, high 2nd, 3rd and high 3rd. The gap between the direct and overdrive ratios, between which changes are made automatically, is narrower than the gaps between ratios on the main gearbox, so that a really comprehensive choice of ratios is on call for the enthusiastic driver.

The three-speed gearbox works very pleasantly indeed, with effective synchromesh mechanism to simplify engagement of the two upper gears, and a steering column control which is light and smooth in action. First gear is recommended for starting from rest, but the car will, in fact, take off smoothly and surely in second gear— even on the tick-over with no opening of the throttle.

The automatic overdrive unit is of the usual type, set to make the upward change so soon as the throttle is released at a speed above 35 m.p.h., and to change down either when the speed sinks below 30 m.p.h. or when

the driver presses the throttle fully open at any higher speed. The ordinary driver will find the normal and over-drive top gears together meet most of his driving requirements: he can drive in the most effortless fashion by using the accelerator pedal alone to control speed and to obtain overdrive or direct gear as suits his need for acceleration.

For the hurried driver, it is convenient to be able to run up to, say, 35 m.p.h. in second gear, release the throttle momentarily before going on accelerating briskly to perhaps 50 m.p.h. or so in overdrive second gear, then changing into top and either settling down to cruise in overdrive top or opening the throttle fully to accelerate further in low top gear. The pleasantest cruising speed is a genuine mile a minute, but although higher speeds are accompanied by some wind and other noise, they do not in the least distress the car.

Night motoring in the Studebaker reveals an extremely effective " black light " system of instrument lighting. A lamp with an infra-red screen is used in conjunction with luminous painted instrument pointers and figures, the effect being that no actual light is visible, but the vital features of the facia glow strongly luminous. Another night motoring subtlety is that, the huge

expanses of rear window being almost incapable of coverage by a blind, the central rear vision mirror is of a special type which, at the touch of a button, is dimmed out without being put out of adjustment. Driving lights are the standard U.S. sealed beam pattern, with separate parking lamps above them.

Wet weather which predominated during our tests showed up one source of irritation, the windscreen wipers being of vacuum type with no booster pump or reservoir and consequently inoperative at the car's ordinary open-road cruising speeds. With the throttle closed sufficiently for them to function, however, the wipers gave good vision through a steeply raked single-piece windscreen which was unusual in comprising two flat panels joined by a curved section on the centreline of the car.

With a bench-type front seat which, even if set rather low, is readily adjustable fore and aft, driving vision over the short bonnet with its backbone motif was very satisfactory. The car tested had left-hand drive, to suit the continental " keep right " rule of the road, and the one condition under which visibility was bad was on right-hand corners, when roll on the springs, the high scuttle, and the location of the large driving mirror combined to obscure vision of most of the kerb to the right of the car.

Luggage accommodation in the rear locker of the coupé body is very generous, even allowing for the presence of a spare wheel and tools. Inside the car there are no door pockets, and the cubby hole (with a light inside) is of modest size, but lockers of immense capacity are incorporated in the two rear seat side armrests.

Instruments are very adequate in number, and are of types which read steadily, the kilometres speedometer exaggerating by approximately 10 per cent. at 80 m.p.h. One large dial incorporates the oil pressure gauge, fuel contents indicator, ammeter and radiator thermometer, while matching dials beside this one are clock and speedometer respectively.

Special Equipment

The test car carried a considerable number of items of equipment which, although extras not included in the basic price quoted for the car, are special Studebaker fitments. The radio was accompanied by a telescopic aerial which could be wound out or retracted from the driving seat. An external mirror was very neatly installed on one front door to give a clear view of overtaking traffic. A controlled spotlight, mounted on the windscreen pillar, was most useful for reading signposts at night, and a two-way switch linked the horn ring to flash the headlights as a silent warning signal for town driving.

In sum, the Studebaker is an extremely well turned out automobile, unusual in appearance but entirely practical and pleasing to many eyes, with eminently satisfactory all-round behaviour.

Underside view of the front end of the Champion chassis showing the suspension mounting and steering linkage.

The Champion suspension from above, showing the new steering gear arrangement with the cross link to the rear of the engine.

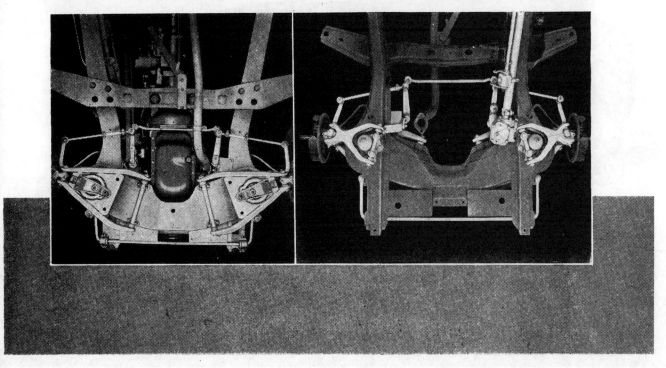

STUDEBAKER
Restyles for 1950

Major mechanical improvement is in the

redesigned front suspension on all models

IN making its bid for the 1950 market, the Studebaker Corporation has restyled its models both inside and out. Fenders, hood and front end appearance have been redesigned to give the cars an entirely new appearance.

The front suspension has been redesigned, now using coil springs instead of the previous planar

system. The coil springs have unusual deflection characteristics which, in combination with new shock absorbers, are said to provide a smoother ride than previous models.

The major elements of the running gear remain fundamentally unchanged with the exception of the two-piece propeller shaft line which

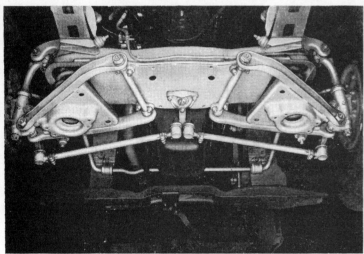

View of the underside of the Commander front end showing the center point steering linkage and front stabilizer bar mounting.

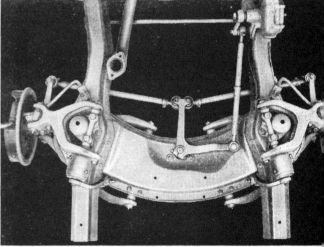

Top view of the Commander front suspension showing the simplified steering linkage with the reach rod and bellcrank.

now features improved center bearing design.

Wheelbase has been increased one inch on all models, the Champion up to 113 in., the Commander to 120 in., and the Land Cruiser to 124 in.

An interesting feature of the new front suspension is the fact that both upper and lower control arms are so pivoted as to rake to the rear about 15 degrees with respect to the transverse axis. This is said to have the effect of cushioning

front wheel shock on rough pavement. Another feature of the front mounting is that the coil springs are cushioned top and bottom in rubber within the tower to prevent telegraphing of shock into the chassis.

Coming to the mechanical features of the Champion, direct acting airplane type shock absorbers are employed both front and rear, the front shocks being mounted within the coil

Studebaker Restyles

springs, the rear being mounted in "sea-legs" fashion, inclined inwardly at the top.

A front sway bar has been added to provide lateral stability and this has had the effect of improving stability as compared with previous models.

Although the steering linkage is of the same type used in previous models it should be noted that the gear has been relocated with the result that the center reach rod now is back of the engine. While overall steering ratio is unchanged, the change in steering linkage in the new model makes for a noticable improvement in handling and steering ease. The steering gear is of greater capacity, the Model TA 12 Ross gear being specified for the '50 models.

Front end alignment specifications remain the same except for caster. This has been made zero (0) deg. The turning radius of the car too, has been decreased.

An important design change has been effected in the propeller shaft support on both Champion and Commander models. The bearing inner race is mounted directly on the machined outer end of the front propeller shaft end fitting. The universal joint end for the rear propeller shaft is then splined and slip-jointed within this fitting. This arrangement has simplified the construction of the center support as well as joint ends materially, has reduced weight and mechanical complication as well. This is said to result in better balance and greater assurance of balance. The new design also simplifies the assembly problem on the final line since the entire joint assembly now is installed as a unit including the support member.

The only significant change in the engine is the adoption of a standard compresion ratio of 7 to 1, with compression pressure of 120 lb at 150 rpm. Auto-Lite ignition units are standard on the Champion.

An improvement in cooling is effected on both Champion and Commander models by the introduction of a radiator shroud. In addition, on the Commander only, the radiator core is tilted to take advantage of wind sweep.

Coming to the Commander chassis, the front suspension is of coil spring type, similar in all details to that on the Champion. However, the Commander retains the double-acting Houde shock absorbers front and rear, the mounting being as illustrated, the rear mounting linkage being of "sealegs" type. The major change in this respect is that front shock absorbers are of larger size and greater capacity than before.

Steering gear is the same as last year and front end alignment specifications are unchanged. However, the steering linkage has been changed materially, using a simplified center-point linkage with bellcrank. Not only is the linkage simpler mechanically, but it has fewer joints and less back-lash, with the result that steering effect is noticeably better and more responsive although no change has been made in overall ratio.

Another major improvement is the introduction of sway bars, both front and rear on Commander models. This has improved road stability markedly.

It may be noted that the rear suspension on all models remains the same as before. On Commander models front spring rate has been made higher.

Only significant change in the Commander engine specifications is the adoption of a standard compression ratio of 7 to 1, with an increase in compression pressure to 120 lb at 150 rpm. The ignition system, however, is changed, all electrical units being supplied by Delco-Remy.

Tire size has been upped on Commander models, standard equipment being 7.60 x 15 mounted on 6L rims. Inflation pressure is 24 lb front, 20 lb rear.

On the Land Cruiser Studebaker has introduced diagonal struts which run from the cowl downward to the front fender aprons. This serves to tie the body structure more firmly to the chassis.

White sidewall tires and wheel discs available on all models at extra

Presenting the "next look" in cars

NEW 1950 STUDEBAKER

Success breeds success! The car that led in modern design now moves still more spectacularly out ahead!

The new 1950 Studebaker is here—and you can see at a glance that it's America's "next look" in cars.

Here's the dramatic and unexpected sequel to the tremendously popular "new look" in cars that Studebaker originated three years ago.

Here's a truly inspired 1950 Studebaker—dynamically new in form and substance—America's most advanced new car—styled ahead and engineered ahead for years to come.

Paced by a breath-taking new Studebaker Champion in the low-price field, this is a complete line of completely new 1950 Studebakers.

Each one is increased in wheelbase length and over all length—thrill-packed with the new performance of higher compression power—comfort-cushioned with self-stabilizing new Studebaker coil springs.

Discriminating America is giving the 1950 Studebaker an enthusiastic welcome. Stop in at a nearby Studebaker showroom the first chance you have. See the 1950 Studebaker —the "next look" in cars!

16

STUDEBAKER CHAMPION SALOON

As striking as they come, even in 1950. The latest Studebaker Champion is similar in body shape to the design which has become familiar, but has this restyled front. Among extras, over the basic price, seen are the white wall tyres, wheel trim rings and bright hub plates, fog lamps and mirror.

DATA FOR THE DRIVER

STUDEBAKER CHAMPION

PRICE, (at factory) with Regal de luxe saloon body, $1,647 = £588 at £1 = $2.80. Plus extras $318 = £113 10s. Total, as tested, $1,965 = £701 15s approx.

RATING : 21.6 h.p., 6 cylinders, side valves, 76.2 × 101.6 mm, 2,779 c.c.

BRAKE HORSE-POWER : 85 at 4,000 r.p.m. COMPRESSION RATIO : 7.0 to 1.

MAX. TORQUE : 138 lb ft at 2,400 r.p.m. 16.9 m.p.h. per 1,000 r.p.m. on top gear; 24 m.p.h. on overdrive top.

WEIGHT: 26 cwt 3 qr 7 lb (3,003 lb). LB per C.C.: 1.08. B.H.P. per TON: 63.40.

TYRE SIZE : 6.40 × 15in on bolt-on steel disc wheels. LIGHTING SET : 6-volt.

TANK CAPACITY : 14.9 Imperial gallons : approx. fuel consumption range, 18–21 m.p.g. (15.7-13.45 litres per 100 km).

TURNING CIRCLE: (L) 39ft 4in; (R) 40ft 8in. MIN. GROUND CLEARANCE: 8in.

MAIN DIMENSIONS : Wheelbase, 9ft 5in. Track, 4ft 8¼in (front) ; 4ft 6in (rear). Overall length, 16ft 5½in ; width, 5ft 9¾in ; height, 5ft 1½in.

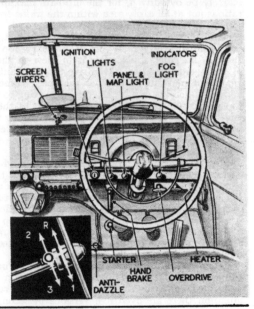

ACCELERATION

From steady m.p.h. of 30 to 50

Overall gear ratios	10 to 30 sec	20 to 40 sec	30 to 50 sec	O.D. sec
4.56 to 1 ..	9.9	10.3	11.3	17.5
7.43 to 1 ..	6.2	7.3	10.0	10.5
11.86 to 1 ..	5.1	—	—	—

O.D. = Overdrive

From rest through gears to :— sec

30 m.p.h.	..	..	..	7.0
50 m.p.h.	..	..	..	17.7
60 m.p.h.	..	..	..	25.9
70 m.p.h.	..	..	..	38.8

Steering wheel movement from lock to lock : 4 turns.

Speedometer correction by Electric Speedometer :—

Car Speedometer	Electric Speedometer	Car Speedometer	Electric Speedometer
10	= 9	50	= 46.25
20	= 18	60	= 55.75
30	= 27.5	70	= 65.5
40	= 36.5	80	= 74.75

Speeds on gears (by Electric Speedometer)

	M.p.h. (normal and max.)	K.p.h. (normal and max.)
1st	18—32	28.9—51.5
2nd	40—54	64.4—86.9
Top (4.56 to 1)	77.5	124.7

Overdrive

	M.p.h.	K.p.h.
1st (8.30 to 1)	46	74
2nd (5.20 to 1)	70.5	113

WEATHER : Dry, mild ; light wind.

Acceleration figures are the means of several runs in opposite directions.

BEFORE the war, when it was possible to include in this series a wider range of American cars than is available similarly nowadays, the Studebaker displayed some noticeable and worth while differences in some respects from its contemporaries, but conforming in the main, of course, to the general pattern. Today there is the added interest among a range of U.S.A. cars which has tended to increased engine size that the Studebaker Champion is of no more than about 2¾ litres engine capacity. It is therefore in this matter closely in line with a number of British cars and is probably considered small in this respect in the U.S.A., where 3½ and 4 litres is the rule. It is not noticeably cut down in body capacity, however, having a four-door saloon which provides three-seater width at front and rear and which is not cramped in other dimensions.

External appearance may enter more into opinions on the car than is usual even in these days of striking "styling." When the post-war Studebaker was introduced in 1947 it created something of a furore because of the low build for an American car ; and the approximately similar lengths of the bonnet and tail, and the large curved rear window resembling a windscreen, caused it to become known in lighter comment as the car which was deceptive as to whether it was coming or going ! The 1950 model overcomes that point by a front-end treatment which as a whole is almost startling at first impact.

In its general road behaviour the Champion is characteristic of the present lower-priced American car in that the six-cylinder side-valve engine is quiet and smooth, without attaining to superlatives, and has plenty of power for its load. Indeed, the power-to-weight ratio is decidedly favourable. So much does this fact show itself that an average day's motoring, taking in town driving and a main-road journey on which there is opportunity to hold high cruising speeds, is likely to cause the driver to pay the implied tribute to it of forgetting that the engine is not of the bigger size usually associated with American cars. There is plenty of acceleration, a gradient is scarcely noticed, and top gear or overdrive nearly all the time is the manner of motoring provided.

As regards the easy fast cruising, the overdrive trans-

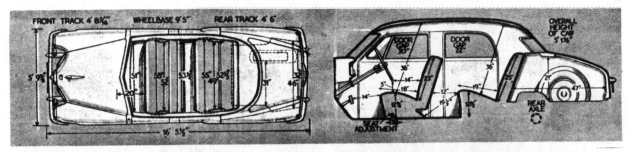

Measurements in these scale body diagrams are taken with the driving seat in the central position of fore and aft adjustment and with the seat cushions uncompressed.

mission is a very important factor. This is a valuable item among the many extras which are available, as on U.S. cars in general. It is certainly worth having, both for the quietness and lack of effort it brings, and for the economy aspect of reduced engine speed.

Ordinary top gear is 4.56 to 1, in other words a comparatively low ratio, and one which serves extremely well for town driving. Then, automatically, in one position of the overdrive control within the driver's reach, and at approximately 30 m.p.h. as a minimum, overdrive top is engaged upon brief release of the throttle pedal and the final drive is stepped up to the quite high ratio of 3.19 to 1, representing a reduction in engine revs of approximately 30 per cent.

In an English motoring phrase involving a clash of terms which an American might not find easy to understand, the result is that on the overdrive the car can scarcely be overdriven, for the ultimate maximum on this ratio is not at all easily seen within the traffic-free stretches of main road normally found in England. It lies at certainly around 80 m.p.h., a speed at which the engine feels comparatively fussy on its ordinary top gear, and there is no point in so using it in view of the existence of the overdrive ratio. Overdrive top goes out of action, again automatically, whenever the speed comes down to approximately 24 m.p.h., the drive reverting to the normal top gear, and a free wheel, which is part of the overdrive addition, then functions unless it is cut out by the control previously mentioned. This control is desirable for retaining the overrun braking effect of the engine for use on a prolonged or particularly severe descent.

Key feature of the application of an overdrive to the current American cars is the kick-down control through the throttle pedal, whereby at any speed practically instantaneous return can be made to the ordinary top gear for overtaking purposes or fast climbing. In effect the car has four speeds, and movements between top and overdrive, and vice versa, are foot controlled and rapid. The change from top to overdrive is virtually undetectable, and the reverse action only barely noticeable.

The overdrive is obtained by a compact unit carried behind the main gear box and incorporating a free wheel and a single epicyclic gear. By accident rather than intention there are overdrive versions of second and first gears. These scarcely come into ordinary driving reckoning, but overdrive second, of which the ratio (5.20 to 1) is lower than that of normal top gear, though appreciably higher than the normal second gear, has some practical

interest for sustained climbing in mountainous districts.

One may gain an initial impression of a very soft suspension—independent in front by coil springs—but it is regulated effectively by telescopic dampers. There is very little side sway, the car riding level in a very satisfactory way, and to an extent perhaps not expected in advance of actual road experience. There is an unusual proportion of total weight in front. Very rarely is there any

A luggage compartment interior of somewhat irregular shape but unquestionably valuable capacity. Specially designed suitcases to make the best use of the space are obtainable in the U.S.A. The lid is spring balanced to stay in this position without a strut and there is an interior light. Sound-deadening material is applied to the wheel arches and panels. The twin rear and stop lamp units embody the American pattern of " winking " traffic signals, which are not recognized in Great Britain. These are extras.

The upholstery is in cloth, concealed by the tailored covers fitted to the car tested. There are elbow rests but a central arm rest is not provided. A check device retains the doors in the fully open position.

Radio controls at the centre of the facia board increase impression of a multiplicity of minor controls, which in fact normal in number. The steering column gear lever is oper by the left hand. At an average position of seat adjust the driver is placed a considerable distance from the faci windscreen. The British Clayton interior heater seen tak place of the American system disturbed by conversion to hand drive.

A central motif, borrowed from aircraft practice, which can claim the functional purpose of a subsidiary air inlet, is the eye-catching feature of the front view. The bumper is carried on tubular outrigger horns, not seen here.

Lengths of bonnet and " rear deck," enclosing a very big luggage compartment, are about equal. Rear window area is very considerable and the driver's view behind is correspondingly good. The rear wheels are not spatted, it will be observed. The petrol filler cap is behind the panel in the left rear wing, which is not lockable.

vertical movement of the body. It can be said that rear seat passengers travel as comfortably as those in front, and they sit unusually far ahead of the rear axle even at a time when the principle of bringing the rear seats forward has become almost universal.

The steering has a variable ratio, lower towards the full locks, which serves to retain a light movement throughout the turning range. Accuracy on the straight is satisfactory and no road-wheel movements are noticed through the steering wheel. There is castor return action, and a satisfactory course can be steered on fast bends, aided by the good suspension traits already mentioned and the car's low centre of gravity.

The hydraulically operated brakes do an average day's work without cause for special comment. The pedal pressure required for a quick pull-up is not heavy, and in the general run of driving they are brakes that are unobtrusively present to a satisfactory degree when wanted. Fading occurred during the more severe part of the test, involving a series of rapid decelerations from 60 and 70 m.p.h., but efficiency quickly returned after cooling off.

Among the considerable list of extras fitted to the car as tested was a feature found on pre-war Studebaker cars, which it is surprising has not been more widely adopted— a "hill-holder." This device, by introduction of a ball valve in the hydraulic brake pipe line, causes the car to be held on an up gradient upon operation of the brake pedal, and released as soon as the clutch pedal is depressed for moving away, without any need for using the hand brake. A more valuable feature to an inexperienced driver, or in face of the frequent awkward placing of modern hand-brake controls, as here, is hardly to be imagined. There is little gear changing to do, but the synchromesh for second and top is effective; the clutch need not be used for changing in the traffic range of speed over which the free wheel operates. The starter switch is foot operated and can be used without removing the foot from the clutch pedal; there is some chance of depressing it unintentionally when the engine is running, but it has points of convenience.

The seating is low, in conjunction with which fact the mounting of the steering wheel is higher than is liked. Lowering the wheel or raising the seat by about an inch would make a very considerable difference to confidence and comfort of control—preferably the seat rise, as this would improve driving vision as well. A view is obtained fairly close on to the road immediately in front of the car, but at times the peak of the bonnet is obstructive, as also are the windscreen pillars.

There is a good deal of chromium ornamentation of the facia board, but the instruments are placed in a good position immediately in front of the driver and are effectively but not too brightly illuminated at night; on the opposite side is a useful compartment which can be locked and which has an interior light (as an extra). An excellent rearward view is given by the non-glare type of driving mirror, though it forms a blind spot at times in vision towards the left side, being mounted near the bottom of the screen. Neither seat has a central arm rest, a provision which would be an advantage, as the seats are excessively wide for two people. Elbow rests on the doors also act as hand grips for closing purposes from inside.

The provision of right-hand controls on this particular car involved the replacement of the American interior heating and windscreen de-misting and de-icing installation by a British unit, which, not being built in as part of the design, could scarcely be expected to be as effective in this instance as the original. Again among the valuable extras is a windscreen sprayer for clearing mud, working from a water container under the bonnet. The suction-operated screenwipers are noisy and dry up almost at once at full throttle, a tendency of this otherwise efficient pattern which can be overcome by use of a vacuum tank or a booster pump; the latter expedient is available at extra cost on the Champion.

The head-lamp beam is quite good for about 70 m.p.h. and fully up to the average standards of built-in head lamps. The start from cold was instantaneous by means of thermostatically controlled choking, and the car went straight off without a trace of hesitation. A useful light is provided for map reading and illuminating the front interior when passengers are getting in and out, and to show the ignition keyhole. In addition to the normal function of the ignition key it can be turned in the opposite direction to allow electrical auxiliaries to be used without the ignition being switched on.

The car was made available to *The Autocar* for Road Test by Studebaker Distributors, Ltd., 385, Euston Road, London, N.W.1.

Seemingly a bonnetful of auxiliaries to which, from at all events the camera's angle, the engine appears secondary. The battery—six-volt but well up to its job by reason of its amperage—could hardly be more accessible, the oil filler, of which the cap is seen behind the battery, is handy, too; the dipstick is convenient enough when discovered. The flexible control for the bonnet release from the driving seat is seen running behind the radiator cap; there is the usual safety catch, operated from the front. Extras again come into the picture in the shape of the Fram oil filter, the windscreen washer equipment, of which the water container and connections are seen to the right of the battery, and the oil-bath type of air cleaner.

19

ROAD and TRACK ROAD TEST No. A-1-51

Make: Studebaker **Model: Land Cruiser**

HEIGHT 61¾"

TREAD 56¼"
REAR 54"²

CLEARANCE 8"
WHEELBASE 119"

kimzey

Price: $2380 F.O.B. South Bend
Horsepower: 120 at 4000 rpm
Displacement: 232.6 cu. in.
Bore: 3.375 in.
Stroke: 3.250 in.

Weight: 3293 lbs.
Overall length: 201.5 in.
Overall width: 70.7 in.
Front seat width: 59.25 in.
Rear seat width: 58.25 in.
Tire size: 7.10 x 15

PERFORMANCE FIGURES

ACCELERATION	MAXIMUM SPEED
Standing ¼ Mile - 21.1 sec.	Flying ¼ Mile - 90.91 mph
0-50 mph - 11.8 sec.	Opposite Direction - 94.74 mph
0-60 mph - 15.4 sec.	
0-70 mph - 20.6 sec.	Average - 92.83 mph

Fourth of a series of road tests of foreign and American automobiles from the American driver's viewpoint

—PHOTO BY JACK CAMPBELL

"Mr. B" takes a sharp turn on sandy desert trail while testing Studebaker Land Cruiser.

MR. C REPORTS

The Studebaker Land Cruiser is a "typical American car" .... with all the qualities that are implied in that phrase. Good points are: Plenty of power, silent, smooth ride, low price, and effortless driving. Not so good: "Women's steering ratios" (6 turns, lock to lock), considerable roll while cornering, and easily faded brakes.

The new Studebaker ohv engine is one of the best your writer has tried. Complete silence at cruising speeds up to 70 mph, no detonation at any time (premium fuel was used, however), instant starting, smooth idling, excellent cooling .... as far as we could determine, no faults at all.

The new Borg-Warner torque converter—automatic transmission was very interesting to sample, as it is reputed to be relatively easy to build and service. In drive position, the acceleration from a standstill is more than adequate, and on a slightly damp or loose surface, will spin the rear wheels. On low ratio starts, wheelspin is the rule rather than the exception. No clutch pedal is fitted, yet shifts between low and high range are smooth and instant.

Biggest selling point of the Studebaker automatic transmission is the direct drive feature. At varying speeds from 20 to 70 mph (according to pedal pressure) the transmission shifts into direct drive, with solid mechanical connections from engine to rear wheels. What this means in terms of speed and economy is self-evident. A kickdown into lower gear, plus torque converter, provides additional acceleration when needed below 60 mph. Other noteworthy features of this drive are an anti-creep device (which worked satisfactorily) and a park position (which locks the drive shaft positively when standing still).

The performance test verified the belief that the "Stude" was one of America's faster cars. A timed calibration check of the speedometer revealed it to be 3.6 mph fast at 50, 4.0 mph fast at 60 and 4.8 mph fast at 70. .... a remarkably small error. At an indicated 100 mph the car was clocked at 94.74 mph, and made a two-way average over the flying ¼ mile of 92.82 mph.

The acceleration figures listed in the table are self-explanatory, except to note that the test area is above 3000 feet elevation, which probably produced somewhat slower readings than could be expected at sea level.

During the several hundred miles to and from our desert testing area, cruising speeds were kept near 70 mph with complete comfort, except for considerable wind noise due to open windows and ventilators.

Minor points of criticism include the glove compartment which is small, hard to open and close, and gives a "tinny" sound when pushed out. The instrument panel is recessed far below the windshield and well forward, which is excellent for reducing glare, but reaching the various knobs, particularly the radio, while in motion is difficult without removing one's eyes from the road.

The faults mentioned at the beginning are typical of practically all American cars, and can be corrected by: (1) power steering, and (2) air-cooled or larger brake drums and greater lining area.

MR. B REPORTS

Studebaker has always paid more attention than most other manufacturers to weight saving and this commendable policy accounts for the excellent acceleration of the

Land Cruiser, whose 120 hp is lower than some of the other cars in its price class. The weight of the test car (3440# with full fuel load) is extremely low when one considers that the Land Cruiser is Studebaker's big long-wheelbase model, and that the test car was equipped with radio, heater, underseal, etc. It would be interesting to compare the acceleration figures of the heavier Land Cruiser with the lighter models equipped with the same engine.

The new over-square overhead valve V-8 engine gives fast, smooth acceleration and quiet cruising at high speeds.

The very forward location of the engine results in a weight distribution which places nearly 60% on front wheels. This, in conjunction with the low pressure tires fitted, results in considerable tire squeal. (35 lbs. pressure was maintained thruout our test, reducing this to a minimum.)

On a 32% grade, the Studebaker climbed easily in low range and was able to stop and restart at any point. However, as with most modern cars, it was unable to back up the hill, not due to a lack of power but because of the shift of predominant weight to the front wheels.

At Road and Track's secluded test area some extremely rough and winding desert trails are available for bringing out the best (or worst) of cars' suspension qualities, and the Studebaker earned plaudits for its smooth ride. The weather sealing is excellent and very little dust worked into the interior or trunk compartment. Early morning temperatures were low and provided a work-out for the well-designed heating system fitted by Studebaker .... it furnished an adequate flow of warm air to all parts of the car and kept the windshield free of fog.

In spite of 500 hard miles while in our possession, the Studebaker still had remarkable absence of rattles at the conclusion of the test.

For the typical American buyer, the Studebaker can be considered an excellent value. Such details as center arm-rest, "black-light" instrument panel, interior finish in good taste, and Nylon cord upholstery should prove powerful selling points for the American woman, who, after all, usually has the final say.

MR. X REPORTS

It is only fair that prejudices be admitted —I like *small* cars, ones which hold the road like a leech and have quick steering—I own and drive such a car because I like it. Big cars just don't interest me. With that off my chest, I'll tell you about the Studebaker.

The Studebaker climbed the 32% hill at 12 mph in Low range, failed half-way up in Drive. Hills such as this are not easy for automatic transmission equipped cars of any make.

The original post-war Studebaker was a harmoniously designed car with an appealing personality. From the cowl aft the 1951 model is still pleasing.

Having driven the automatic transmission equipped Studebaker Land Cruiser, I now know how an ex-steam locomotive engineer feels the first time he takes over a diesel. You release the brakes, select the wizz-o-matic position, advance the throttle and after a very slight lurch, you are moving! It is easy to understand why people who find no enjoyment in shifting are so happy with automatic transmissions. To me, it is like the promise of replacing food with vita-energy pills—it may be more scientific and require less effort, but the pleasure is gone.

A little practice soon develops a technique for squeezing the last ounce out of the transmission for acceleration. Start in low range, foot to floor board and keep it there while changing to high range at the "wound-up" speed. This procedure will keep the overdrive unit in low until considerable speed has been reached. The mechanism operated so smoothly that times on acceleration tests

came as a surprise indeed to the test driver.

The sound of the new V-8 closely resembles that of the Olds Rocket powerplant. It is responsive, quiet, and brisk. Valve-float was audible at flat-out speed but quickly disappeared when relaxing to top cruising speed. Fuel consumption was good, averaging slightly over 20 mpg during the entire test. (A Land Cruiser averaged 27.66 mpg in the recent Mobilgas Economy Run.)

Considering the wide variety of surfaces over which the Studebaker was tested, the ride was very smooth altho the seat seemed a bit firm on long runs.

The interior should please those with large families, as the recessed position of the dash leaves standing room for kids — me . . . I get agoraphobia. A light over the instrument panel lights up when the door opens, thus giving you a chance to find the necessary firing-up gadgets. For driving, the black-lighted instruments can't be beaten. Even the automatic transmission indicator has a self-contained light.

This car was furnished by courtesy of War-ren Biggs, Los Angeles Studebaker dealer.

—PHOTOS BY JACK CAMPBELL

CONTROLLABILITY of the Studebaker (above) is remarkable. Steering is positive and accurate

CUTAWAY of the Studebaker V-8 (left) shows the remarkably good "straight-through" manifolding, which makes for fuel/air flow with comparatively little friction loss. Wedge-shaped combustion chamber focuses expanding gases directly on piston head. Valves slightly slanted

IF YOU'RE the kind of person who likes his cars fast, when you get behind the wheel of an "economy car" you resign yourself to a boring ride. The Studebaker line of cars has always been known as an economy line, but—if you haven't taken a ride in the new Studebaker Commander V-8, you're in for a big surprise.

If we—Associate Editor Griffith Borgeson and I, of MOTOR TREND Research—hadn't heard of some of the capabilities and prowess of the Studebaker V-8 prior to the three-day Motor Trial, we probably would have planned for an "economy ride," too. As it was, we were mentally prepared for some outstanding performance from the car. And we weren't disappointed!

The Studebaker Commander four-door sedan delivered to us by the Los Angeles factory was well broken in, registering

DEMONSTRATING roadability of the Studebaker is Griffith Borgeson. On asphalt roads there was no need to correct for wandering tendencies

3650 miles on the odometer. It wa equipped with the Studebaker Automati Drive (optional automatic transmission) By the time we had returned the car t the Studebaker Corporation we had pu 900 miles on it, undoubtedly the rugged est mileage put on the car in its shor life span.

According to all indications, the Stude baker Corporation should be able t sell all the V-8s they can build. The can't miss, offering the public such package of power and comfort for th money. We were so impressed with th performance of the Commander that w feel no qualms whatsoever in making th prediction.

Test Report

FUEL CONSUMPTION: This featur has always been a selling point wi Studebaker. It was thought by many th with the advent of the V-8 engine, Stud baker had at last thrown in the spong on this score. However, in the rece Mobilgas Economy Run and accordi to the exhaustive tests which we pe formed on the car, Studebaker is bett off than before. For proof of this y need only look at the figures in t Table of Performance; the *overall avera* on the Motor Trial was a phenomen 21.41 mpg! Between 30 and 45 mp the consumption remains quite consta

STUDEBAKER V-8 A TERRIFIC SURPRISE

by Walter A. Woron

PHOTOGRAPHS BY FELIX ZELENKA

increasing as 60 mph is approached. However, even with the disadvantage of automatic transmission (which can mean from one to three mpg less) fuel economy remained quite good.

.TOP SPEED: With Automatic Drive, the Studebaker Commander uses a high-speed rear axle—3.54:1. This axle ratio made it possible for us to hit a highest one-way top speed of 93.55 mph and a four-way average of 92.78 mph, a truly commendable performance. Even though you'll probably never travel at these speeds, it's good to know that if you have to you will be able to control the car with no difficulty. Through all these top speed runs the car held the road very solidly. The acceleration curve is quite flat—the Commander reaches top speed smoothly and quickly.

STEERING: The steering wheel has a good feel and is at the proper location for fast control. The center-point steering is accurate and positive. Taking a sweeping curve at 60 or 70 mph, it was only necessary to turn the front wheels to the desired amount—that angle of turn was easily maintained. There was no need for constant rocking of the steering wheel to correct for wandering tendencies in the rear end. Oversteer and understeer were notable by their absence. A minor point of criticism is that if the car is taken into a sharp corner at high speed, the body leans considerably. At all times, however, you can maintain good control, although it is necessary to pull the wheel back to a "neutral" position—the wheel does not "return" itself.

RIDE: The Studebaker holds the road very ably, even with the speedometer needle pushed up near the 100 mph mark. We took a severe dip at an indicated 90 mph (unintentionally, of course) and proved to ourselves that the shock absorbers were put there for a definite purpose. There was no bounce and no bottoming. Over an "ocean-wave" road there is some pitching motion, which is the case with most cars. The important thing to us was that this motion did not affect control in any way. The overall suspension system seems to us to have struck a perfect balance between softness and comfort on the one hand and stability and safety on the other.

ACCELERATION: This factor of the Studebaker V-8 is not its outstanding feature, but it is quite good. The combination of the 120 bhp V-8 engine and a conventional transmission would undoubtedly give any average driver more than enough acceleration. As it is, the V-8 with automatic transmission is more than adequate to cope with all traffic conditions. As with most automatic-transmission-equipped cars, we found that elapsed times for all tests through the gears could be improved by using LOW range, then later shifting to HIGH. A speed of 45 mph seemed to be the best shift point for maximum acceleration.

TRANSMISSION: The test car for this Motor Trial was equipped with Studebaker's "Automatic Drive," a combination of cork friction clutch, conventional hydraulic torque converter and planetary gearing. Two forward speed ranges (LOW and DRIVE) and a reverse are provided by the planetary transmission. All normal driving is done in DRIVE range, although for added acceleration, LOW range can be used, followed by a shift into DRIVE.

We found that automatic gear changes were made with good speed and smoothness, with very little slippage between the driving and driven components. The hill-holding device is positive and a great convenience, although the anti-creep braking feature on the test car was not found to be always reliable. The rear brakes are equipped with an electric solenoid valve that retains pressure in the lines after the brakes have been applied. Pressure on the throttle releases the brakes . . . in our case, a minor adjustment would probably have restored the reliability of this feature.

A downshift to the intermediate range (in DRIVE) by depressing the throttle gives the power necessary for passing. This full-throttle downshift can be made at any speed up to 60 mph. The transmission will stay in this range until you momentarily relieve pressure on the pedal, or until you reach a speed of 70 mph. Braking is possible with this transmission by merely flicking the selector lever to the LOW range, but should only be done at speeds below 40 mph.

BRAKING: A feature of the brakes that definitely appears to be a trend in the industry is that of the widened brake pedal. After a few hours behind the wheel it became quite normal to hit the pedal with the left foot. This is probably the best thing that could happen to cars with automatic transmissions; up to now the left foot has had increasingly less work to do. A right-foot-throttle, left-foot-brake operation makes for quicker co-ordination through traffic and practically eliminates the possibility of the foot slipping off the brake and onto the throttle. We look for the pedal to move farther and farther left, still remaining wide, however.

We gave the Studebaker self-adjusting, self-centering brakes a brutal workout and managed to get a loss of efficiency through fade during our braking tests. However, it took severe testing to reduce the brakes to this state and only drivers in stock car races and cross-country rallies need concern themselves with this detail. Our test car was equipped with special chromium wheel covers which obstructed the cooling vents in the wheel discs. Cooling of the drums would be considerably better without these fancy covers.

Mechanical Features

The box-section, double-flanged frame remains substantially unchanged except for some minor front end modifications to allow for the new V-8 engine. Front suspension is of the independent, coil spring and wishbone variety, with rear suspension being by four-leaf, 2½-in.

POSITION of starting lever (being pulled for engagement) could be improved. Its location alongside hood release lever caused latter to be pulled unintentionally several times during Motor Trial. The brake pedal has been widened

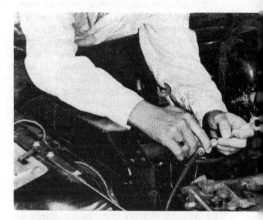

CONNECTING fuel line from tank line to fuel testing device. Studebaker engineers have provided remarkable accessibility for the mechanic

TRUNK space is adequate; accessibility to spare tire is good. Here, Associate Editor Borgeson is seen removing nuts holding tire in place

Studebaker Motor Trials

semi-elliptics. These rear springs have polyethylene liners to keep out dirt and moisture. Direct-acting shocks are used at all four wheels.

The appearance of the Studebaker causes an immediate reaction in the minds of most persons: they either like it or have a positive distaste for it. It is not for us to state whether or not the lines are good or bad from an esthetic point of view: however, they do possess strong originality. The entire body is functional: it includes good headlight placing, excellent access to the engine, easy and economical replacement of body sections, minimum intrusion of powerplant and propeller shaft on passenger and luggage space, and visibility that is about tops.

Although both front and rear seats are ample to accommodate three people with ease, the transmission tunnel reduces the middle passenger's legroom in the front seat. Legroom in the rear seat for all passengers is excellent, thanks to the two-piece driveshaft, which eliminates the tunnel in the rear floor. This two-piece shaft is used primarily for additional legroom, although, because of its shortness, it does have the added advantage of being less susceptible to vibration and whip periods at high speeds.

Studebaker has followed its established pattern of providing easily legible instruments, these being illuminated at night with "black light." Another good feature for night driving is the use of "black light" for showing the setting of the automatic transmission gear selector.

An improvement in controls could be made in the hood latch and starter handle. These are identical in appearance, both being T-handles, and to confuse the issue, are side-by-side. On the Motor Trial the hood latch was pulled a minimum of four times instead of the starter. This necessitates getting out of the car and closing the hood before attempting another start. The controls could be painted sharply contrasting colors or one of them could have a different shape.

Other minor points for improvement: inside door handles with a more positive grip (the door is sometimes difficult to open); and, relocation of the window handle on the driver's side (it is too close to the steering wheel for convenience).

More than anything, it's the upper end of the new V-8 engine that fascinated us most. It was here that we saw another manifestation of the welcome, long-due trend in American engine design toward greater efficiency. Increased power goes with the greater economy of such engines and it's in the "upper end" that the big results are being gained. Studebaker's approach to the problem involves the use of overhead valves inclined slightly away from the cylinder axis, in a wedge-shaped combustion chamber. Remarkably good "straight-through" porting completes the layout, enables the engine to breathe more freely and produce much greater

power for a given amount of fuel.

Trend Trials Number

The Studebaker Commander, Automatic Drive equipped, falls in the $1951-2200 price bracket, and has been given a Trend Trials No. of 29.1. This number is remarkably low, bearing out our contention that the car is a good buy (the lower the number, the better the buy).

The TT No., as with previous cars we have tested, was arrived at by totaling the cost per bhp (which tells you how much it costs for the power of the automobile), the fuel cost per year (based on the overall fuel consumption average obtained on the Motor Trial), the normal maintenance upkeep and average depreciation percentage. The depreciation percentage is arrived at as follows: The average used car price of each model from the five previous years is subtracted from the new model's price. When this is averaged, it gives the average depreciation percentage, projected over a one-to-five-year period. This *should not be* construed as the *average yearly* depreciation.

Inside and out, both mechanically and style-wise, the '51 Studebaker Commander is a well-conceived and well-finished product—it's a lot of car for the money.

TABLE OF PERFORMANCE
DYNAMOMETER TEST
1200 rpm (full load) 30 mph		32 road hp
2000 rpm (full load) 49 mph		53 road hp
3000 rpm (full load) 72 mph		76 road hp (max.)

ACCELERATION TRIALS (SECONDS)
Standing start ¼-mile	:22.11 (D)*; :20.67 (L-D)**
0-30 mph (no gear change)	:07.44 (D); :05.91 (L)
0-60 mph through gears	:21.22 (D); :18.15 (L-D)
10-60 mph in DRIVE (downshift to intermed.)	:18.29
30-60 mph in DRIVE (downshift to intermed.)	:12.48

TOP SPEED (MPH)
Fastest one-way run	93.55
Average of four runs	92.78

FUEL CONSUMPTION (MPG)
At a steady 30 mph	25.73
At a steady 45 mph	25.58
At a steady 60 mph	21.79
Through light traffic	22.68
Through medium traffic	18.49
Through heavy traffic	14.21

BRAKE CHECK
Stopping distance at 30 mph	43 ft. 6 ins.
Stopping distance at 45 mph	98 ft. 5 ins.
Stopping distance at 60 mph	191 ft. 8 ins.

*Shift using drive only
**Shift from low to drive

GENERAL SPECIFICATIONS
ENGINE
Type	Overhead valve, V-8
Bore and Stroke	3⅜ x 3¼ ins.
Stroke/Bore Ratio	0.96:1
Cubic Inch Displacement	232.6
Maximum Bhp	120 @ 4000 rpm
Bhp/ Cu. In.	.516
Maximum Torque	190 ft. lbs. @ 2000 rpm
Compression Ratio	7:1, Optional 7.5:1

DRIVE SYSTEM
Transmission—Conventional three-speed. Ratios:
Low—2.57:1, Second—1.55:1, Third—1:1, Reverse—3.48:1
Automatic drive, torque converter.* Ratios:
Low—2.31:1, Intermediate—1.44:1, Direct—1:1, Reverse—2.01:1, Max. torque converter torque ratio—2.16:1
Rear Axle—Spicer, semi-floating. Standard—4.09:1, Overdrive†—4.56:1, Automatic Drive—3.54:1

DIMENSIONS
Wheelbase	115 ins.
Overall Length	197½ ins.
Overall Height	61¾ ins.
Overall Width	70 11/16 ins.
Tread	Front—56½ ins., Rear—54 ins.
Turning Radius	Right—19 ft. 9 ins., Left—19 ft. 4 ins.
Turns, Locks to Lock	5½
Weight (Test Car)	3280 lbs.
Weight/Bhp Ratio	27.3:1
Weight/Road Hp Ratio	43.2:1
Weight Distribution (Front to Rear)	55.5/44.5%

*Optional, $201.25   †$97.85 extra

THE STUDEBAKER CORPORATION
South Bend, Indiana

THE LAND CRUISER

COMMANDER
STATE
CONVERTIBLE

COMMANDER
STATE
STARLIGHT
COUPE

CHAMPION REGAL
4-DOOR SEDAN

CHAMPION CUSTOM
2-DOOR SEDAN

'52 STUDEBAKER COMMANDER

By Walt Woron

PHOTOS BY CARL TUVESON, STUDEBAKER

CLEANER STYLING, MECHANICAL REFINEMENTS, GUARANTEE THE FINE NEW STUDE V-8, A COMMANDING POSITION AMONG THE NEW CARS

AS I LEFT the semi-tropical climate of Southern California, flying eastward toward the chilly snows of the Midwest, I began to wonder how much effect the weather would have on the performance of the '52 Studebaker I was to test. Much to my *personal* discomfort, I was soon to find out, for when I arrived at the Studebaker Proving Grounds (in South Bend, Ind.) the temperature had nosedived to 28°F., with the air crisp, but clear.

As it turned out, the Studebaker Commander V-8 performed every bit as good, and slightly better (in some respects) than last year's car. The reason for some of the improved performance was that the last Studebaker "Motor Trial" (June '51 Motor Trend) was done with a Commander equipped with Automatic Drive; this year's test was made with a Commander equipped with standard transmission and overdrive. (A test of the '52 V-8 fitted with the *same* drive system would have proved little. since last year's model and this year's car have basically the same engine and drive train.

If you recall last year's "Motor Trial," you'll remember that we predicted that "the Studebaker Corporation should be able to sell all the V-8s they can build." After having pounded the car for three consecutive days, that prediction was easy to make—happily (for Studebaker) it came true. It wasn't their best year, be-

cause production was limited, but it was their *second* best year. It's not hard to see that this year's car should meet with even greater approval. Improvements, engineering- and style-wise, have made the Studebaker V-8 an even better car.

Standard Transmission Is Faster

The Studebaker V-8 still isn't the fastest go-job of stock American cars, but it is among the top five. As shown in the chart with the MOTOR TREND Engineering Award (Feb. '51) the Stude with Automatic Drive was fifth fastest in average acceleration, fourth fastest in the standing ¼ mile.

The car I had at the proving grounds would have held fourth in both categories. This could be used to strengthen the argument that speed-shifting a conventional gearbox is faster than letting a fluid coupling do the shifting for you (with which I'm inclined to agree); on the other hand. different rear axle ratios are used in each case—standard with overdrive is 4.55:1, automatic is 3.54:1. Since a lower gear normally gives you more acceleration, this is probably the reason for the added oomph.

All acceleration checks through the gears were made by speed-shifting, with
(Continued on next page)

SECOND DAY of Motor Trial was made after a four-in. snowfall had blanketed the ground

CAR ON 40 per cent slope shows amount of give in springs and shocks, tire deflection

TO INDICATE body lean and to see if Stude in this position would cause tires to rub on fenders, steering was cramped hard over, gearshift placed in low, full throttle used

all possible combinations being used: revving up to 2000 rpm, popping the clutch and letting the rear wheels spin; revving up to 2000 rpm, popping the clutch to only where it would take hold so as not to spin the wheels; shifting to second at 25-35 mph; shifting to third at 50-60 mph; and, trading the driving job between J. H. ("Mac") McIntyre, Experimental Engineer, and myself. You can see why we're sure that we got the best performance out of the car. The right combination for this machine was to spin the rear wheels, shift to second at 32 mph and to third at 58 mph. After we hit on this, we were able to do the ¼ mile at an average of :20.49 and were hitting from 67 to 70 mph at the end of the ¼ mile.

"Automatic Drive" Optional

There's not much to say about the standard transmission except that with overdrive and a 4.55:1 rear axle, you're pulling a 3.19 gear, which makes a good high-speed cruising gear. Standard gear ratio without overdrive is 4.10:1. Automatic Drive provides you with two forward speed ranges (LOW and DRIVE) and a reverse, with all normal driving in DRIVE position.

Steering Is Good

The center-point steering system of the Studebaker is a peculiar combination of good, responsive control, a fairly fast ratio, too many turns from lock-to-lock (six), no understeer nor oversteer, and no wandering tendencies. When you slam into a corner at 65-75 mph the body leans considerably, but you don't have to fight against mushiness—control is easy, even though the wheel does not return itself.

Later on I had the opportunity to ask some of the engineers why the body leaned as it did on corners, and if customers had found it objectionable. "What you like about the way it steers and object to in lean is due to the spring rate and positioning of the front shocks, giving what we believe to be the best compromise be-

tween cornering stability and ride. The front end uses an anti-sway bar and we recommend to owners who'll drive in mountainous country that they equip their cars with a rear anti-sway bar (optional on Commanders). Do you think that our car leans any more than other cars and that the public objects to the *amount* of lean, or to the *rate* of lean?"

My reply was that I thought their car does lean more than some cars but that the second part of the question stumped me. I'd like to hear from our readers on this score: Do you care how much a car body leans over, providing it approaches that angle gradually, or would you rather sacrifice some softness in ride to keep the car as level as possible around corners?

My next comment was that they had achieved a good balance between comfort and stability, except on an "ocean-wave" road where the car had some tendency to pitch. Engineering's answer: "We feel that the pitching motion is less than most cars (which I concur with). This, again, is a compromise of ride and stability."

Fuel Economy Lowered by Cold

In all previous "Motor Trials" performed on the West Coast, the temperature has seldom, if ever, dipped below 50°F. At the Studebaker Proving Grounds the fuel consumption checks were made in crisp, clear weather, with the temperature varying between 27.5° and 34°F. (For the difference this makes in fuel economy, see the accompanying chart which shows our tests and those conducted by Studebaker test engineers this summer in 67°F temperature.) Even so, fuel consumption averages were good, but not, unexplainably, as good as those we obtained last year with Automatic Drive.

Two things were against us in getting fuel consumption checks in traffic: all test had to be performed on the proving grounds because it was prior to car announcement time; the second day of my stay in South Bend it began to snow, and it snowed all week long. In order to get you the quickest report possible, we had to go to press without this information but we will publish it as soon as possible.

Storming Up Hills

Both as a test of the Studebaker's hill climbing ability and as a check of the hill holder, I took the car up a concrete-surfaced, 30 per cent grade. Half-way up I stopped the car, pushed in the clutch pedal, switched the ignition off, took it out of gear, and took my foot off the brake. The car stayed right there, the hill-holder having securely locked the brakes. I then started the car again, placed it in low, pushed in the clutch pedal, revved the engine and slowly let the clutch out. The rear wheels slipped on some loose gravel o

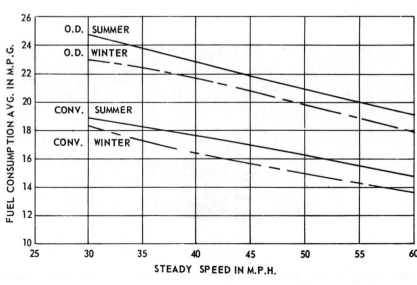

DIFFERENCE IN fuel consumption using over drive and conventional, both winter and sum mer, are indicated in mpg and steady mp

28

the hill, smoking rubber before we got traction, but we plowed right on up the steep grade. If you apply enough pressure to the throttle to overcome the inertia of the car on the slant, then ease out the clutch to release the hill-holder, you'll have no difficulty starting on the severest slope.

Brake Improvements Made

Brakes on the Studebaker Commander are adequate, with improvements on this year's model giving us better stopping distances than we got last year. The one objection we had on the '51 car—brake fade —has been reduced to a great degree. When I brought up the subject of brake fade to Harold Churchill, Director of Research, his reply was, "We have new lining now and a trailing reverse shoe (no return spring) which gives the effect of a self-adjusting shoe and compensates for expansion due to heat. This helps to reduce the fade. We've also changed the ratio of connecting arms to give the same braking effect with less pedal pressure." Continuing research on brakes—drum cooling, possibly power braking—is now going on at Studebaker.

The parking brake is just that—as an emergency brake I doubt if it would be sufficient, since several times with the parking brake lever all the way out we were able to start from a standstill, using no noticeable engine effort. If it actually was designed to be an emergency brake, it should be moved further to the right, where the front seat passenger could also reach it, if necessary. This emergency brake problem is one common to almost all production cars.

Top Speed, 97.85 Mph

It was fortunate that we completed the majority of the tests on the first day, for on the second day it began to snow. We had left the top speed runs and chassis dynamometer checks for the last—but a run around the three-mile, banked track at 50 mph convinced us that no top speed runs could be made on *that* glazed surface. An attempt to keep from slipping and sliding on the snow-packed, icy asphalt, and a crack at climbing a gravel-surfaced 28 per cent grade packed with four inches of snow convinced us the test was through.

What we did then was to compute the top speed from many acceleration graphs made on test Studebakers, all overdrive-equipped. Plotted on these graphs were the acceleration curves up to 80 mph. From these curves we extrapolated the top speed figures, both for third gear and overdrive, then averaged these up (a total of eight was used). Where there was any doubt, we used the low side. Average speed in third was 87.57 mph; average in overdrive, 97.85 mph. I don't believe these figures are at all out of line, for on the

clear day I had the car up to 90 mph on the backstretch of the track and there was still plenty of throttle left. Then, too, the '51 Stude with Automatic Drive and a 3.54 axle did 92.78 mph. It's safe to assume that the same car with overdrive, giving it a *higher* gear of 3.19 *should* go faster.

Engine Is Well Designed

Few stock cars on the road today can match Studebaker's fine V-8 engine. Although it winds up fairly tight (4000 rpm) to achieve its bhp of 120, its piston speed is well below the theoretical "top reliability" limit of 2500 fpm. Bhp/cu. in. (.516) is one of the highest in the industry. It is easy to see that many man-hours of research went into the development of this overhead valve V-8, including toying with overhead cam designs. Studebaker Engineering explained that although this type of system would be desirable, the cost and production problems in mass-produced engines make its use highly unlikely.

As far as higher compression ratios and output are concerned, Engineering went on to explain, experimental pistons are available that come up flush with the top of the cylinder, which in conjunction with 7.5:1 heads, give a compression ratio of 9:1 with a proportionate rise in bhp. Domed pistons of the same type will take the compression ratio up to approximately 14:1. These types of pistons can conceivably be made available for production whenever higher octane fuels also become available.

Topside improvements in the accessible and conveniently arranged engine include: an internal vent carburetor (to prevent dirt from entering the engine); relocation of the choke stove from the exhaust manifold (where it picked up dirt) to the in-

WORON STORMS Studebaker around three-mile Stude track. Calculated top speed: 97.85 mph

LAST YEAR we complained about starter and hood latch both being identical T-handles on automatic transmission-equipped cars. This year Stude changed to pushbutton starter

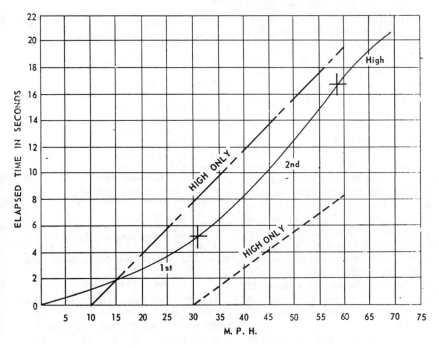

CURVES SHOWING acceleration in high only and in all gears are indicated in elapsed time against mph. Crossmarks indicate shift points

'52 Studebaker Motor Trial

take manifold, where it provides a faster warm-up; and, a seven-psi pressure water cooling system, to compensate for the reduced copper content core and to give the same cooling as before.

Body Changes

No changes have been made either in the box-section, double-flanged frame, or in the coil-spring, independent front and semi-elliptic rear suspension systems; however, several obvious style changes have been made in the body: new grille, new hood, different tail lights. Another change, undoubtedly at the women's request, is the relocation of the tension spring in the trunk hinge to lessen the lifting effort.

Interior Comments

An improvement made in the starter control is one that we asked for last year.

GENERAL SPECIFICATIONS
ENGINE

Type	Pushrod ohv V-8
Bore and Stroke	3⅜ ins. by 3¼ ins.
Stroke/bore ratio	0.96:1
Cu. in. displacement	232.6 ins.
Maximum bhp	120 @ 4000 rpm
Bhp per cu. in.	.516
Maximum torque	190 lbs.-ft. @ 2000 rpm
Compression ratio	7:1, 7.5:1 optional

DRIVE SYSTEM
Conventional synchro-mesh, three-speed transmission

Ratios:	First—2.57	Second—1.55
	Third—1.00	Reverse—3.48

Rear Axle: Semi-floating, Hotchkiss drive, hypoid gears. Ratios: Conventional—4.09 Overdrive—4.55

DIMENSIONS

Wheelbase	115 ins.
Overall length	197 ⁹⁄₁₆ ins.
Overall width	70¹¹⁄₁₆ ins.
Overall height	61¾ ins.
Tread	Front—56½ ins. Rear—54 ins.
Tread/wheelbase ratio	1:2.08
Turns, lock to lock	.5
Weight (test car)	3293 lbs.
Weight/bhp ratio	27.4:1
Weight/road hp ratio	37:1
Weight distribution (front to rear)	58.5/41.5

CHASSIS DYNAMOMETER TEST

1200 rpm (full load) 22 mph	34.5 road hp
2000 rpm (full load) 35 mph	57 road hp
4100 rpm (full load) 70 mph	(max) 89 road hp

At that time the hood latch and starter control (on Automatic Drive cars) were both T-handles, located side-by-side below the dash, causing frequent annoyance when pulling the wrong handle. This has now been taken care of by means of a starter button on the dash. (Cars with standard transmission still have the starter located under the clutch.)

Two other minor criticisms we made last year concerned the closeness of the window crank to the steering wheel and the sometimes-difficult-to-operate door handles. These points were discussed with Engineering, with these answers: "In order to change the window crank we'd have to shorten the handle, which would increase the turning effort, or relocate the mechanism, which would necessitate die changes. Apparently most owners get used to this, because we've received very little complaint. Door handles are not a source of irritation, except on new cars where it takes more effort to open the door until the door seats."

Entry into the fairly wide front seat of a four-door sedan is quite easy; but with an overcoat and hat on, it becomes somewhat difficult to enter the rear, due to the fact that the door does not open wide enough. Leg room and head room, both front and rear are adequate. Steering wheel position is good and all dashboard controls are within easy reach. Vision, since the first of the post-war Studebakers, is one of this car's best features.

Interior Safety Check

As editorialized in previous issues of MOTOR TREND, we are quite concerned about car safety. Some things can be checked with figures (brake stopping distances), others are hard to pass on with-

MAJOR CHANGES in rear of Stude Commander are tail lights. Bumper extensions are extra

out a highly technical research lab (possible collapse of front suspension units, possible wheel breakage, etc.), still others are easy to overlook (dangerous knobs on the dash, blind spot to right rear, etc.). We give you the pertinent figures in our report of the car's performance and with this issue, we inaugurate a convenient "Interior Safety Check," consisting of questions about the car's safety and our answers. For each "yes" answer, the car receives 12.5 points, 100 points being ideal.

QUESTION	YES	NO
1. Blind spot at left windshield post at minimum?	X	
2. Blind spot to right rear at minimum?	X	
3. Positive lock to prevent doors from being opened from inside?		X
4. Does adjustable front seat lock securely in position?	X	
5. Minimum of projections on dashboard face?	X	
6. Is emergency brake an emergency brake and is it accessible to driver and passenger both?		X
7. Are cigarette lighter and ash tray both located conveniently for driver?		X
8. Is rear vision mirror positioned so as not to cause blind spot for driver?	X	

TOTAL FOR STUDEBAKER COMMANDER: 62.5

And in Conclusion

This year we have even more respect for the prowess of the Studebaker Commander V-8, a really great performer. It's safe, it cruises nicely, has good accelera-

tion, is comfortable and economical to operate. Proof of our point will be found in the Stude V-8's Trend Trials No. 1, which we expect to be very favorable and which will be printed in a forthcoming issue. Lack of sale price data as we go to press keeps us from computing the figure at this time.

TABLE OF PERFORMANCE
ACCELERATION TRIALS (SECONDS)

Standing Start ¼-mile	:20.49
0-30 mph (low gear only)	:04.96
0-60 mph (through gears)	:17.16
10-60 mph in high	:19.30
30-60 mph in high	:08.04

TOP SPEED (MPH)

Calculated average of eight test cars (overdrive)	97.85
Calculated average of eight test cars (conventional)	87.57

FUEL CONSUMPTION (MPG)

	Conv.	O.D.
At a steady 30 mph	18.14	22.95
At a steady 45 mph	15.65	20.75
At a steady 60 mph	13.70	17.90

SPEEDOMETER CHECK

At 30 mph indicated 32 mph	6.7% error
At 45 mph indicated 49.5 mph	10.0% error
At 60 mph indicated 65 mph	8.3% error

FROM SMALL BEGINNINGS.—Today's Studebaker Corporation employs 23,000 people and has sales annually reaching the 500-million-dollar mark. This picture shows the main works at South Bend, Indiana, where the two-man business was originally founded to build wagons, in 1852.

From the Days of the Covered Wagon

100 YEARS OF STUDEBAKERS

FIVE BROTHERS shared in the establishment of the business which carries their name. They were, left to right: Clem Studebaker, Peter E. Studebaker, Henry Studebaker, J. F. Studebaker and J. M. Studebaker.

THE Studebaker Corporation, world's fourth largest manufacturer of automobiles, is celebrating its 100th Anniversary this year. The only automobile maker with a vehicle manufacturing history that antedates the automobile itself, Studebaker began in 1852, with Henry and Clem Studebaker, $68 worth of capital, two sets of blacksmith's tools, and a small wagon-building shop in South Bend, Indiana. That first year the Studebaker brothers made three wagons.

In its one-hundredth year, the Studebaker Corporation sold more than 285,000 vehicles; working capital stands at $65,000,000. Plants at South Bend, Indiana, Los Angeles, Calif., New Brunswick, N. J., and Hamilton, Ontario, Canada, for making automobiles, trucks and jet aircraft engines are carried on the company's ledgers at approximately $50,000,000; there are 23,000 employees; sales in the 100th year were in excess of $500-million.

The story of the growth of Studebaker Corp. is the story of the growth of the automobile industry itself. And although the product, personalities, factories and customers have changed, Studebaker owes its initial success and a great deal of its continuing prominence to its founders and their manufacturing policy, which has in large part

been the mainspring of this century of progress. In the early days of H. & C. Studebaker that policy was expressed in the motto of the Studebaker brothers: "Always give a little more than you promise."

In the beginning the brothers in South Bend prospered mildly. Profits were too small to permit expansion, or the building of wagons except to customers' orders. Capital was needed if the little business was to grow. A younger brother, John, was to provide that capital.

John had taken one of the original three wagons produced by the infant H. & C. Studebaker shop in its first year, and given it to a California-bound wagon train in payment for his passage across the plains and Rockies. In California John divided his time between prospecting for gold and building wheelbarrows. In the long run he found wheelbarrows were more profitable than gold-digging, and in five years saved $8,000. The day John Studebaker decided to leave California for South Bend was the day destiny separated Studebaker from the hundreds of other small and struggling wagon makers in the era.

Inspired by the growing America he had seen on the way home, and convinced that transportation was the key to that growth, John decided to invest his capital in his brothers' wagon business. So, in 1858, John Studebaker bought the half interest of Henry in H. & C. Studebaker; and Henry Studebaker bought a farm near South Bend that he long had wanted. The rest of the $8,000 John had saved became working capital for the expansion of H. & C. Studebaker.

A fourth brother, Peter, was a merchant in nearby Goshen, Indiana. With expanded capital the company was able to build wagons without waiting for customers' orders, but soon found it was waiting for customers. Peter was persuaded to "stock" three Studebaker wagons in 1860. These he sold with little difficulty, and in the three years that followed he made many trips to South Bend for more. This success, coupled with military orders from the Union Army and an expanding civilian output made the time ripe for developing a sales organization. In 1863 a contract was made:

TRACING PROGRESS.—In 1904, Studebaker sold its first gasoline-powered vehicle. This was the Model 9502, seen on the left, which had seats for five, a two-cylinder, 16 h.p. engine, and sold for $1,750. Below is the first Studebaker to bear the name "Champion." Introduced in 1939, this car was the Corporation's challenge in the low-price field, a challenge which was successful and sent Studebaker's sales soaring. Modern example of the concern's products is the 1952 Starliner (*bottom left*), a five-passenger hard-top design produced on both Champion and Commander chassis.

"I, Peter Studebaker, agree to sell all the wagons my brother Clem can make.—Peter Studebaker."

"I agree to make all he can sell.—Clem Studebaker."

In 1865, at St. Joseph, Missouri, gateway to the expanding West, Peter set up the first branch office and showroom—a "repository" as it was called in those days. And a new era of Studebaker expansion was born.

In 1868, H. & C. Studebaker ceased existence and The Studebaker Brothers Mfg. Co. was organized with Clem as President, John, now called "J.M.", as treasurer, and Peter as secretary—each paying in one-third of the $75,000 capital. In 1870 the fifth and youngest Studebaker brother, Jacob, came into the company as a salesman, and later directed the carriage business until his death in 1887. Studebaker "repositories" opened in major cities throughout the eastern United States. A new factory was built. And in 1875 sales reached $1-million for the first time. By 1887 they crossed the $2-million mark.

Studebaker vehicles wore deep tracks in the roadways of the world. Sales went over $3 million in 1898, a year when both the British and United States governments placed orders for vehicles to be used respectively in the Boer and Spanish-American wars.

In 1904 Studebaker Brothers Mfg. Co. sold its first gasoline-powered vehicle, and for four years marketed the Studebaker-Garford. In 1908 the Studebaker-E.M.F. was introduced—produced by the Everitt-Metzger Flanders Co. of Detroit.

Salesman Peter had left the company an invaluable heritage in the nation-wide, world-wide, wagon and carriage distributing organization. In an era when new automobile makers were having to learn about distributing organizations, Studebaker had one already.

By 1910 it appeared that automobiles would be big business for Studebaker. So in 1911 the Studebaker Corporation was organized, incorporating the assets of the Studebaker Brothers Mfg. Co. and the E.M.F. Co.

The nation-wide depression of the '30s also affected Studebaker. Then for the first time in the history of the company, Studebaker lost money—and in 1933 the directors consented to a receivership. At that time no auto company had ever survived such a financial trial. By March of 1935, however, Studebaker had once more been reorganized and put in the black.

To re-establish its permanent place in an industry now dominated by the "big three," the new leaders of the 1935 Studebaker company felt accomplishment would depend on one thing: successfully entering the low-price field. The 1939 Studebaker "Champion" grew out of that insight, and Studebaker's climbing sales figures—from $43 million in 1938, to $81 million in 1939, to $84 million in 1940—testified that Studebaker had now established itself more firmly than ever in the auto industry. In addition to the South Bend plants, Studebaker acquired an assembly plant in Los Angeles, Calif., to supply the booming Pacific Coast market. Assembly plants were later added in Hamilton, Ont., Canada, and New Brunswick, N.J.

The daring new post-war Studebaker that hit the market after the Japanese surrender in World War II completely scooped the auto industry. Car-hungry Americans bought heavily, and Studebaker sales figures, up to $267 million from the previous pre-war high of $84 million, attested to management wisdom in retooling for a new model for a time when other manufacturers were "freezing" all pre-war car designs into post-war offerings.

As it ends its first century, Studebaker Corp. is tooling up for jet plane engines, and military trucks roll off its production lines. The Korea war has caused cutbacks in automobile output, but the designers and engineers are at work, as they were in the closing days of World Wars I and II, to bring the buying public a vehicle built in keeping with the policy handed down from the Studebaker brothers—". . . a little more than you promise."

PRESENT HEAD of Studebaker is Harold S. Vance, Chairman of the Board and President of the Corporation.

Surprising Studebaker

With continental styling and mechanical power steering, this auto firm sets new pace in American car design

WHEN Studebaker introduced its famous design back in 1946, it set a pattern—or at least preceded a trend—which was taken up by most major U.S. auto manufacturers in the immediate postwar years. This week the 100-year-old firm again set a new standard as it pulled the wraps from its 1953 models, which are as startlingly different in body styling. Shown above is Commander coupe against a Parisian background.

Designated as the Centennial line, the cars strongly reflect continental European influence, although t h e style was created by Raymond Loewy, f a m o u s American industrial designer. Studios of other auto builders undoubtedly are humming as effect of the '53 Studebakers on the future is weighed.

Of almost equal interest is the introduction by Studebaker of mechanical power steering—the first time it has been offered for passenger car use. Developed by Borg-Warner, the system differs from others now in use in that it is mechanical and obtains its power directly from engine, rather than through hydraulics.

THE body style has been achieved through use of basic horizontal lines, modified by a concave motif which flows from the "shovel-nose" front end, somewhat reminiscent of the German Porsche, to the back angle rakish trunk lid. The cars, particularly the hardtops and coupes, have an unusually low silhouette.

In fact, the hardtop convertible and five-passenger coupe are lower in overall height than any other stock U. S. production car. They are a mere 56 and 5/16 inches high, less than five feet. Yet overall length is 201 and 5/16 inches, longer than corresponding '52 Studebakers by 4

New instrument panels are Champion model (left) and Commander Series (right), designed for visibility and convenience.

and 3/8 inches. Height of Champion and Commander sedan models is 60½ inches. Width has been increased one inch from previous years and wheelbase is 5½ inches longer, 120½ inches for the hardtop and coupe.

Glass area of the new Studebakers, which was subject of many jokes when first postwar design appeared, has again been increased. On a four-door sedan, for example, it is 33 per cent greater than 1952 model.

The frontal design, about which most of the controversy probably will center, incorporates a functional engine-cooling air scoop just below the bumper. Despite the emphasis on continental lines, however, absence of wire wheels, either as standard or optional equipment, is significant. Only concession made in this direction are wheel discs with cone-shaped concave centers from which extend three small, ridge-like fingers.

Designing engineers report that elimination of "squarishness' in style drastically reduces wind noise. The body fairing performs the function of washing air over the cowl fillets and past the sloping one-piece curved windshield.

CHIEF elements in the mechanical power steering system are power unit mounted on the steering gear, a power input shaft and a pulley assembly. Heart of the innovation is the power unit, which is a compact six-inch square device weighing only 22 pounds. Inside it are a gear train and two multiple disc clutches rotating in opposite directions, one for turns to the left, the other for turns to the right.

Power comes to steering unit direct from engine by means of a V-belt pulley on a small auxiliary shaft which runs parallel to engine and back to mechanism. Ring gears in the power unit revolve constantly while engine is running, but only at one-fourth of engine speed.

When driver turns steering wheel to the right, the lower ring gear and clutch transfer power from engine and reduce, by 75 per cent, the effort of steering. Upper ring gear and clutch perform same function for left turns.

The system is simple in construction, uses no valves, hydraulic lines, pump or fluid reservoir. A gear lubricant is needed periodically and can

Operational setup (above) of mechanical power steering unit. Power is delivered direct from engine by V-belt pulley at left, through auxiliary shaft to gear assembly at right which contains two multiple disc clutch assemblies rotating in opposite directions—one for left turns, the other for right.

be provided during normal servicing. If the power steering becomes inoperative, conventional manual control is immediately available.

OTHER innovations on the '53 Studebakers are minor, such as recessed floors and new instrument panel. Steering wheels on hardtop and coupe models are slightly more vertical than in the past, a theme Studebaker confesses it borrowed from sports cars. The new trend in division of front seat, noted in other '53 cars, appears in Studebakers with seat separated off center.

Chassis changes are merely refinements. Frame has been altered to accommodate new body, but is structurally the same. Radiator is wider and shorter. Carburetors were re-designed to fit lower hood line and dry-type air cleaners replace cartridges that were standard.

Center of gravity has been lowered and shocks have new type of valving to improve ride. Clutch pedal inkage was changed to obtain softer pedal

New rear-end treatment of Studebaker includes fin-type fenders and V-shaped bumpers recessed to protect license plates. Moldings emphasize "rake" angle of tail lights.

pressure and front suspension now has rubber bushing in inner ends of upper and lower support arms.

In the past, drastic changes in design of new car usually has been accompanied by price increases. Studebaker, however, reported this week that it is holding the line and, in some instances, lowering cost. The hardtop is $100 less than last year and there was a $46 reduction in price of V-8 Land Cruiser sedan. Only the five-passenger coupes were raised by $10 to $12.

Bottom factory list price is for Champion custom two-door sedan which stars at $1,585. Most costly is the Commander hardtop Regal, previously called the "State," which now starts at $2,175.

Studebaker made no changes in its engines, which it considers highly successful. The Champions still are powered by the six-cylinder L-head, which develops 85 hp. The Commander line has a 120-hp V-8 and a similar engine powers the Land Cruiser models.

European influence illustrated (below) in contour of Champion hardtop model which has low silhouette. Car is only 57 inches in height but is 202 inches long. Engine is 85-hp six.

The 1953 Studebaker Champion hardtop reflects the European styling influence

STUDEBAKER PIONEERS A NEW STYLE

By Harry Cushing

STUDEBAKER has done it again! Just seven years ago—in 1946—the firm in South Bend, Indiana, brought out a line of cars which kicked off a major style trend! Now, for the second time in less than a decade. this doughty independent boldly introduces a series of cars which is sure to shake the styling sections of every other American company right down to their last blueprint and full-color rendition!

If the U.S. car buyer *really* wants the low, clean lines of the post-war European school of design, then here it is! Gone is the impression of great masses of steel, highlighted with chrome and other ersatz ornamentation.

In its place are motion and beauty created brilliantly by the form of the metal itself. Grace and fleetness of movement are implied by line and contour. Yet with

it all, Studebaker retains the comfort, stamina, and roadability characteristics of larger American cars designed for motoring conditions found primarily in this country.

There is no doubt that every other car manufacturer will eye the public's acceptance of this advanced styling. All firms have been timidly toying with such a concept for some time, as evidenced by the rash of "experimental" jobs during the last year. Should it click overwhelmingly —and Studebaker is betting its life it will —watch the Detroit concerns jump aboard this bandwagon!

The new car was designed by internationally famous Raymond Loewy, who has come up with a package which is lower than any other standard American-built automobile. There is no doubt that Studebaker's 1953 offerings are an audacious at-

tempt to capitalize on the growing sports car rage from an appearance standpoint.

Coupes and hardtops are a mere 56⅚ inches high—just two inches higher than an MG-TD with its top up! Their overall length is 4⅜ inches greater than that of the corresponding 1952 models. or 201¹⁵⁄₁₆ inches as compared with 197⁹⁄₁₆ inches. Height of Champion and Commander sedan models is 60½ inches Overall length of these cars is 198⁹⁄₁₆ inches, and that of the Land Cruiser. 202⁹⁄₁₆ inches.

Maximum overall width has been increased slightly, and the wheelbase of the hardtop and coupe is 120½ inches vs. 115 inches for last year's models. Wheelbase of the Champion and Commander two- and four-door sedans is 116½ inches, and that of the Land Cruiser, 120½ inches. Rear tread width on all models has been

The side view of the '53 Studebaker Land Cruiser emphasizes its overall length by a concave motif which flows from the front fender and ends in a back angle rake in the rear door panel. Front wheels are fully exposed. Note hubcap styling

increased from 54 to 55½ inches. Front tread width remains 56½ inches.

Glass area, with resulting improved visibility in all directions, has been greatly increased on all models, ranging from a boost of 133 square inches on hardtop convertibles to an increase of 819 square inches on the Land Cruiser. The total glass area of a four-door sedan, for example, is 33 per cent greater than on the corresponding 1952 model.

From an engineering standpoint, power steering will probably claim Studebaker's spotlight this year. It is a mechanical unit, the first such adaptation in the industry. It was developed by Borg-Warner, and is reported to be much simpler in construction than hydraulic systems. For a complete description of Studebaker's new mechanical power steering system, see "Spotlight on Detroit," page 10.

Chassis changes on both the Champion and Commander consist for the most part of refinements and modification, a number of them due to the jaunty changes in style and design. Frames have been altered to conform to the new bodies, but structurally they remain unchanged. Radiators are wider and shorter, but cooling capacity remains the same. New engine mounts provide smoother engine operation and vibration absorption. Carburetors have been redesigned to fit the lower hoods and at the same time provide greater efficiency. Dry-type air cleaners with replaceable cartridges are now standard on all models.

As the result of lower centers of gravity, greater road-hugging stability and improved weight distribution are achieved. Contributing to better riding characteristics and roadability are improved rear springs, shock absorbers with a new type of valving which improves the cushioning action, and anti-roll sway bars.

A revised carburetor on the Champion incorporates an exhaust-heated flange to eliminate engine stalling due to icing in the unit during warm-up on cold and damp days.

There are no important engine changes in the 1953 lines. The economical six-cylinder 85 bhp powerplant is installed in the Champion series. Commander Series features the potentially potent 120 bhp ohv V-8 introduced a year ago. Bore and stroke of this engine is 3⅜ x 3¼ inches. It displaces 232.6 cubic inches, and develops 190 lbs.-ft. torque @ 2000 rpm. Compression ratio is 7:1, with 7.5:1 optional. Peak horsepower is achieved at 4000 rpm.

As may be gathered from the above figures, this engine is purposely held back, but it is one of the most satisfactory mills for souping to be found.

Another item of interest regarding Studebaker is the oft-repeated rumor that this manufacturer is coming out this year with a true sports car. That rumor is hereby squelched; closest thing to it will be a convertible model of their regular series.

Low height of hardtop is seen with H. S. Vance, Studebaker pres., standing alongside

Champion series instrument panel has clear visibility; toggle switches are convenient

Commander panel is different. Note the extremely wide opening doors of this model

Rounded slope of the trunk lid accentuates the fin-type rear fenders. Bumpers are V-shaped; rear bumper is recessed to protect license plate. Hood slope gives better vision

36

IS THE STUDEBAKER PRACTICAL?

**An MT Research Road Test Report
By Walt Woron**

Photos by Jack Campbell

Most people are impressed with its style, but if you want to know how practical it is, read about it here in our road test report

TO OUR MINDS the new Studebaker is the most refreshing, stimulating, and progressively styled car to emerge from a stock car manufacturer's factory since the days of the Lincoln Continental and the coffin-nosed Cord. Yet, it may be *too far advanced* in styling concept for the public to accept. This we doubt, but it's something that the Studebaker Corporation is probably sweating out. After placing this body style on 43 per cent of their total production, if they wind up with the same result that Chrysler did with their 1934 Airflow, they'll have a rough row to hoe.

Whether or not the radically styled Studebaker will meet with public approval is hard to determine. A quick poll of people caught looking at our test coupe (as if anyone didn't!) during our test week would seem to indicate that the public might approve. This sampling (hardly an adequate amount to base an opinion on) liked the style in the ratio of five to one. And since the Studebaker definitely follows the Italian concept of styling, it would appear that it has supporters ready to hop on the bandwagon: thousands of foreign-car advocates in this country. The majority of them will like the car and will like its price: compared to other projected U.S. sports and semi-sports cars, the Studebaker is priced low.

The Studebaker has more feeling of a sports car than any other stock car today: the wheel practically sits in your lap, the low seats and high transmission tunnel give you the illusion of bucket seats, and you sit close to the windshield. You slip behind the wheel, and in just a few blocks

you feel you know the car; before too long you find that it's actually *fun* to drive (which you can't say about too many cars these days).

Of course, style isn't the only thing that sells a car. In fact, according to a recent poll of new car owners, appearance is well down the list of reasons why they bought the car they did. "All right," you say, "I'll agree that it's a pretty car. But, what about the way it's built, its performance, and its economy of operation?"

Is it economical to operate? Based on fuel economy, our operating cost per mile and the maintenance-and-repair-cost analysis, the answer would appear to be yes. It is a little better than average. Are you particularly concerned with fuel economy? The Stude will rate above average. This year's car (using Automatic Drive and a 3.54 rear axle) gave us poorer economy than last year's car (with overdrive and 4.55 axle). The test of the '52 was at the Studebaker Proving Ground with the temperature between 27.5° and 34° F., while

the test of the '53 was made with the thermometer hovering in the 70s. Under identical conditions the overdrive-equipped car would have given even better mileage, mainly because the final ratio is higher (3.19 *vs.* 3.54), and also because of less drive-line loss than through the torque converter (this loss is not a factor over 18 mph, when the torque converter is locked out).

And how does this "little beauty" perform? If it feels like a sports car, and the car you tested looks like a sports car, does it act like one? Hardly, but we don't think that Studebaker intended it to. It's no "bomb" in getting away from a signal or in passing another car on the highway. (The Automatic Drive-equipped '53 is equal to the overdrive-equipped '52 in ¼-mile acceleration; from 0-60 it is a bit faster.) Neither will it stay with an MG or a Jaguar in a corner. Its handling *has* been improved over last year and it has a top speed high enough (95.6 mph) for any of our highways.

Compare this Italian Lancia with the stock Studebaker above

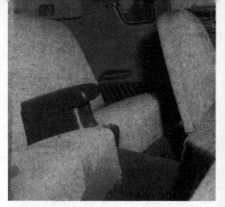

Among those drawn to the Stude will be the people who have looked longingly at some of the imports from across the Atlantic. Here, the V-8 takes the measure of an MG

Armrest in rear seat of the coupe is permanent, opens for storage of odds and ends

What about the way it handles? Speaking for the car with conventional steering, we found the Studebaker to be vastly improved over previous years in this category. No corrective action is required on a straight road, nor is any wind wander noticed. This year, they've cut down the number of turns lock-to-lock (to 5¼ from 6, and down to 4¼ with power steering). Steering is still not fast enough for quick control. If you drive normally you'll find it to be adequate. We found that the car was quite easy to correct when going through a corner. You can make the rear end break loose on tight turns taken at well above average speed. Even so, you can keep it in control. Under normal conditions, you won't get crossed up. You feel steering wheel vibration (no shock) on ruts and on rough road surfaces. About the only time you will notice wheel hop is when accelerating over streetcar tracks.

Is it easy to drive and to park? Yes. It doesn't take much steering effort when it's moving, and remember, this is not power steering we're talking about. Parking is no problem at all. It's a little stiff to steer, but you can practically see the front bumper, and vision toward the rear is exceptional (even though you cannot see the rear fenders).

What about the position of the steering wheel? This is right in your lap, and on more of a vertical plane than in any other stock car. You don't ever have to hunch forward to grip the wheel (at a "10:10" position). It has a good feel: the entire underside has fingergrips and the topside (upper portion) is grooved to prevent your hands from slipping. The wheel knob and horn ring are both well recessed below the wheel rim.

Are the brakes good? About four per cent better than the average of all '52 cars; stopping distances were close to what we got with the '52 Commander. During our tests we were unable to lock the wheels until the last few feet. With a full load this could result in increased distances (only one person is in the car during braking tests). The pedal is wide enough for left foot operation and is fairly soft in operation. It takes time, however, to get used to the closeness of the pedal to the steering column, because your foot can easily strike the column in applying the brake.

What about ride? Overall, the ride is one of the best in its price class; it is not a soft ride. It smooths out normal dips, and over bad dips taken at high speeds (70-80 mph) the car did not bottom, nor did it become airborne. It will

bottom over a deep drainage dip, but you do not lose control of the car. There is very little oscillation (up-and-down movement of the body after going over a dip) and recovery is rapid. Over washboard roads at low speeds (10-20 mph) there is not much shock. It is not until you take such a road at considerably faster speed that the car begins to skip. Body lean in previous Studebakers has been quite noticeable; in the '53 models, it is low (even on sharp curves taken at speeds up to 50 mph). The combination of low center of gravity, minimum spring travel, good shocks, and sway bars both front and rear keeps the car well tied down around any corner.

Is it noisy inside the car while you're driving? Noise level inside the car is not high; undercoating, however, would help. On normal road surfaces you can hear and feel a certain amount of vibration (it's evident in the mirror to such an extent as to make it virtually useless). There is very little wind noise until you get up to high road speeds of 70-80 mph. Twice, however, when bucking a diagonal crosswind a peculiar "drumming" sensation was noted inside the car. It was necessary under these conditions to close the driver's window. There are no drafts with the windows closed.

THE CAR AT A GLANCE	POOR	AVG	GOOD
ACCELERATION			
Standing start			
¼ mile		X	
30-60 mph		X	
BODY WORK	X		
BRAKES			
Stopping distance average @ 30, 45, 60 mph		X	
EASE OF HANDLING			X
FUEL ECONOMY			
Averages @ 30, 45, 60 mph			X
INTERIOR		X	
RIDE			X
ROADABILITY			X
TOP SPEED		X	

This rating is based on the average of all '52 cars tested (see February '53 MOTOR TREND).

MT Research clipboard (on seat) recorded more definite opinions than for any other '53 car. Driving position brought pleased smiles to most faces. Note toggle switches

Editor Walt Woron has to bend low to sight across the Commander's smooth, low hood

From every angle, the new models show an eye-catching result of the designer's knowing when to sculpture a radical line, and—most important—when to show restraint

Is the body style a practical one? Generally, yes. The sloping hood provides a good view of the road immediately ahead and helps you to judge distance in traffic; the lowness of the car contributes to its good handling characteristics and its high resistance to roll; the high percentage of glass gives you exceptionally fine vision. Other good features include a pleasing absence of chrome (from the esthetic viewpoint); fully exposed rear tires that allow for easy tire changing; a low-cut deck lid that permits easy removal of luggage or the tire; wide-opening doors that allow for easy entry into the front seat (although it is a difficult task getting in and out of the rear of this two-door coupe). On the other hand, there are certain disadvantages: if you get caught in traffic behind most stock-height cars, you'll have trouble seeing ahead; neither the bumpers nor the guards are designed to give the grille and rear deck much protection (the guards are too small to prevent overriding, vertical movement of the bumpers will damage the fenders); the luggage space is limited vertically for the sake of the sloping rear deck. The doors on the test car did not open easily, nor did they close soundly. Body panels fitted well; there were no noticeable ripples. Finish at the seams was not too good and

there was some "orange peel" in the paint. The car gave the impression of being hastily put together, which it probably was, since this was one of the first cars built. Although later models probably will be built better, these are points you should look for before buying *any* car.

How did they get the body so low? The frame is lower on the coupes than on other Studebakers. In addition, their seats are lower. Longitudinal frame rails on all models are fairly close together (with room for the drive train to pass through) and transverse hangers are used for body attachment. It is not a step-down or channeled design; the front floor is still level with the top of the frame rails.

With such a body style, is there any room inside? Actually, the Studebaker is like a sectioned-body car: the top is low (cutting down on headroom) and the seats are placed practically on the floor (so that your knees are high or your legs are straight out). The car seats only four people comfortably, five cramped (three in front, two in the rear). The rear center armrest is a permanent one. Shoulder room is adequate both front and rear. If you are doing much mountain driving, you will have to move away from the door, since the armrest will sometimes interfere with your elbow. There is not

an excessive amount of legroom either front or rear. For the driver, there is just enough room with the seat all the way back; it's not easy to find a comfortable resting place for the left foot. In the rear seat of the coupe, wells are provided for the feet between the frame rails and the driveshaft; they are not wide and it is necessary to keep your feet uncomfortably in the same position, close together. All of the above comments are made on the basis of an average-sized person; if you are larger than average, you will have some difficulty in driving this car.

Are the seats comfortable? For the driver, extremely so. Even around the sharpest turns, you don't bounce or slide from side to side. The airfoam-padded seats are firm, giving the body comfortable and adequate support. The manual seat adjustment does not provide for easy positioning of the seat; the seat does not move swiftly and easily on its track. If you ever lean against the door, you will meet the sharp edge of the plastic-covered, metal-frame armrest.

Are the upholstery material and workmanship good? Material is a combination of cotton and wool, while panels are a combination of plastic and fabric. Both should be fairly durable. Workmanship is fair—some loose ends were showing and

Continued on next page

Stowing your luggage in the new car's deck may take some getting used to. Suitcases will be placed horizontally for '53

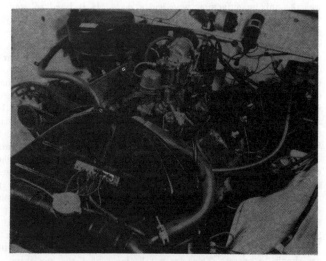

Studebaker's V-8, introduced in 1951, is anachronistically modest with its 120 horsepower. You can hop it up if you like

Is the Studebaker Practical?

some bad seams were in evidence on our test car. The back of the front seat is devoid of a stiffener under the upholstery to protect both the passengers and the material.

What about the rest of the interior? Floor mats are carpeting material and not of particularly good quality. The door handles, of die-cast, chromed metal, are positioned where they're easy to grip. MT Research is sorry to see the change in window cranks. The ends used to flatten against the lever arm by a spring arrangement, being then well out of the way. Now arrow tips stick out and will bother your leg if you rest it against the door. No handgrips or assist cords are provided for rear seat passengers; either would be a welcome aid in getting in or out of this particular car.

Is the instrument panel good looking? Actually, it is not a panel in the usual sense: the instruments are located in an "accessory panel" that is suspended from the top of the narrow cowl. This makes it fairly simple and gives you somewhat the impression that you're driving a sports car (a tachometer is missing, however). Controls for starting, wipers, lights, etc., are operated by toggle switches, further completing the illusion. Each of the four instruments is easy to read by itself, but they are spread out in a single row. If they were grouped as two rows of two, they would be vastly easier to read at a glance. They are also fairly low, making you drop your eyes further than you should while driving. The door-type glove compartment, located on the far right side of the panel, is not particularly large. For night driving, a two-position toggle switch is provided to dim the dash lights. The tops of the instruments are shielded to prevent distracting reflections from being thrown on the windshield. The cane-type emergency brake is located to the right of the steering column, and is easily operated.

Would you rate the interior as safe? This is mainly answered in our Safety Chart; however, there are a couple of points worth enlarging upon. For a long while, Studebaker was the only manufacturer who had a rear view mirror mounted in a position (on top of the cowl) where it *did not* interfere with vision. Now, unfortunately, it is suspended from the top of the windshield, where it creates a blind spot to the right front under certain conditions. The windshield wipers operate smoothly and have a good average-sized swipe, but not sufficient to eliminate all blind areas during stormy weather. From a safety standpoint, the Studebaker is to be commended for minimizing all projections on the dash and for eliminating the chrome divider between the vent window and the main window in the front door. This metal strip can cause serious injury to either driver or front seat passenger in an accident. **How does the heat and vent system work?** Satisfactorily for heating, fair for cooling. The controls are convenient to the driver and are simple to operate. They are not lit for night operation, although this system does not require much manipulation.

What changes had to be made to the engine to allow the hood to slope? Two things had to be done. The air cleaner was repositioned to the side and rear of the engine, with a duct leading to the carburetor. The radiator was cut down in height, but widened to give the same cooling capacity. **Is the engine easy to work on?** With the hood up, it's easy to get at any part of the engine or the components packed in around it. Adjustment of the overhead valves necessitates only the removal of the air cleaner (for access to the right bank); then the valve covers can be removed. There is enough working area. The use of the correct socket extension makes the job of removing plugs a comparatively easy one. The generator (at the right front, well up), fuel pump (at the side of the oil filler neck), and distributor (at the rear center between the two banks) are all easily accessible for servicing or removal. For the service station attendant, the oil dipstick could be located more conveniently than underneath the new-type air cleaner. **Are there any internal changes in the V-8 engine?** None. This compact (232.6 cubic inch) engine, with a 7:1 compression ratio, puts out a good 120 bhp at 4000 rpm, and 190 foot-pounds of torque at 2000 rpm. It's a highly efficient engine overall, giving .516 bhp per cubic inch displacement. As pointed out last year (March '52 MT), an optional ratio of 7.5 to 1 is provided, while compression can be taken up to 9 to 1 with the use of special pistons (flush with the top of the cylinder) and up to 14 to 1 with domed pistons. These could conceivably be made available, but it would only be logical when the higher octane fuels are available. Octane requirement is now 83 with the 7 to 1 head, which was satisfied by the use of Mobilgas Regular on our test car. Over the past years, Studebaker has done a good job of keeping octane requirements well within the range of available fuels, as contrasted to other makes which recommend but cannot operate on regular gas, and a few that the best premiums will not satisfy. **Is it hard to start and noisy like some V-8s?** It starts easily, and with the use of the toggle switch on the dash (next to the key) it is reminiscent of airplane controls. You can release the starter at once when the engine begins to run. With Automatic Drive, you have to place the lever in either P or N position before the starter will operate. With the engine running, there is a certain amount of engine and chassis noise, including a few creaks and "clunks" when starting. **What about Automatic Drive—what are its advantages?** Like any automatic transmission, its advantages are in ease of driving: there are no gears to shift, no clutch to operate. This transmission has an additional advantage over other automatics in the combined anti-creep and hill-holder. When you come to a stop on level ground or on a slight grade, the anti-creep device will prevent the car from moving ahead, without the necessity of keeping your foot on the brake. When stopping on normal upgrades,

as long as the engine is running, the hill-holder will keep you from rolling backward. Normal driving is done in the D (DRIVE) range, except when you want more power and then you use L (LOW), shifting to D below 40 mph. Using this method, you can improve your 0-60 mph speed by from two to three seconds. In L, the transmission is operating on torque converter plus a 2.3 to 1 gear ratio. **What about its disadvantages?** We feel that they are these: in upshifts from the torque converter (in DRIVE) to direct drive, there is a definite slackening of speed (during normal shifts). It shifts to direct drive at too low a speed (unless the throttle is held nearly wide open), below the engine rpm that develops good torque for pulling in direct drive. The torque converter operates with a 1.4 to 1 ratio, while direct drive is 1 to 1 (and the torque converter is out of operation). You can downshift from direct drive to torque converter for passing acceleration anywhere below 60 mph, but when you do, there is a definite "clunk" in the Hotchkiss drive. At idle, when in P or N, the transmission is noisy. **Would the Studebaker be a durable car?** This is one of the most difficult questions MT Research has to answer. We attempt to give you some kind of guide by pointing out what went wrong with our car during our tests. This cannot be construed as what might happen to each and every car of this make, since we treat cars rougher than the average owner will. On the basis of the 1400 miles that we put on the Studebaker Commander V-8, it would appear that it is a fairly durable car. The *body* was in good shape, except for a sticking door latch. The *chassis* appeared to be in good order. The noisy transmission and the "clunk" that actually jarred the body were the two things that were noticed in the *engine-transmission*. **What is your overall opinion of the Studebaker?** Here we'll revert back to our first statement in this appraisal. But, you can't have both a terrifically stylish car and all the comforts of home; the Studebaker is definitely the best compromise between the two. If you like style, you'll have to sacrifice some interior room, luggage convenience and ease of getting in and out. The car is economical to operate, has good (not outstanding) performance, handles exceptionally well (for a stock car), is easy to drive, has one of the best rides in its price class, has comfortable seats, has only fair workmanship, has a dependable, easy-to-work-on engine, has an automatic transmission that needs some improvements, has average brakes, and should be durable. The rest is up to you.

—Walt Woron

"Dig that crazee rhythm!"

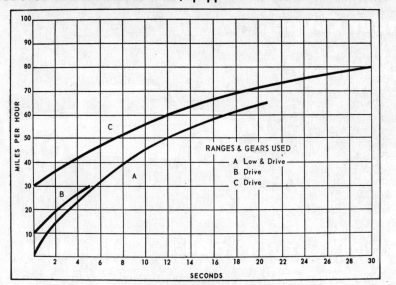

RANGES & GEARS USED

A Low & Drive
B Drive
C Drive

ACCELERATION

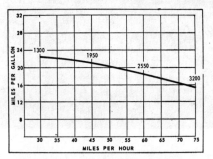

FUEL CONSUMPTION

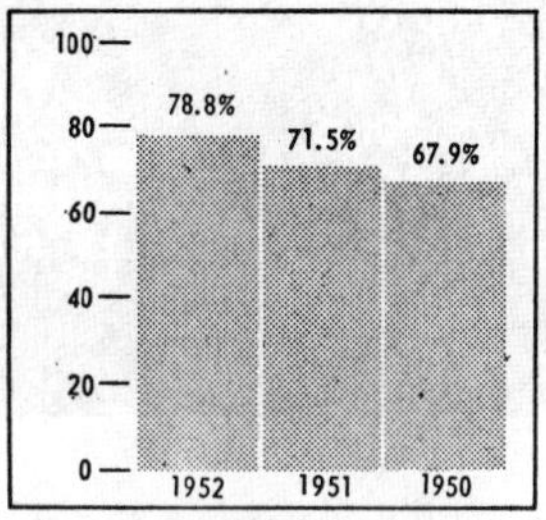

DEPRECIATION

	CUSTOM	DELUXE	REGAL	LAND CRUISER
COMMANDER:				
Four-door sedan	———	2121.15	2207.54	2315.64
Two-door sedan	———	2088.90	———	———
Club coupe	———	2126.52	2212.91	———
Hardtop coupe	———	———	2374.16	———

SAFETY CHECK

DRIVER SAFETY:	YES	NO
Blind spot at left windshield post at a minimum?	X	
Blind spot at rear vision mirror at a minimum?		X
Vision to right rear satisfactory?	X	
Windshield free from objectionable reflections at night?	X	
Dash free from annoying reflections?	X	
Left side of dash free of low projections?		X
Cigarette lighter, ashtray, and glove compartment convenient for driver?		X
DRIVER AND PASSENGER:		
Front seat apparently locked securely at all adjustment points?		X
Metal strip eliminated between front quarter window and main door window?	X	
Rear view mirror free of sharp corners?	X	
Right side of dash free of projections?	X	
Adequate shock-absorbing crash pad?		X
REAR SEAT PASSENGERS:		
Back of front seat free of sharp edges and projections?	X	
Rear interior door handles inoperative when locked?	X	
Adequate partition to keep trunk contents out of passenger compartment on impact?		X

(MOTOR TREND constantly improves its test procedures. Because of this, we are dropping percentage ratings on the Safety Check to avoid seemingly inaccurate comparisons between cars from month to month.)

OPERATING COST PER MILE ANALYSIS

(In this portion of the test table, MOTOR TREND includes those items that can be figured with reasonable accuracy on a comparative basis. The costs given here are not intended as an absolute guide to the cost of operating a particular make of car, or a particular car within that make. Depreciation is not included.)

Cost of gasoline (regular)	$132.40
Cost of insurance	116.00
Maintenance:	
Wheel alignment	5.25
½ brake reline	7.35
Major tune-up	9.45
Automatic transmission (change lubricant)	7.50
First year of operation cost per mile	2.8c

MAINTENANCE AND REPAIR COST ANALYSIS

(These are prices for parts and labor required in various repairs and replacements. Your car may require all of them in a short time, or it may require none. However, a comparison of prices for these sample operations in various makes is often of pertinent interest to prospective owners.)

	COST	LABOR
Distributor	$ 19.03	$ 1.75
Battery	20.95	.70
Fuel pump	5.66	1.40
Fan belt	2.31	1.05
Valve grind	5.40	38.15
One front fender	38.50	13.30
Two tires	51.36	———
One bumper	24.50	1.75
TOTALS	$167.71	$58.10

PERFORMANCE

ACCELERATION (SECONDS)
(Checked with fifth wheel and electric speedometer)

Standing start ¼ mile (67 mph)	20.5
0-30 mph (0-32, car speedometer)	5.4
0-60 mph (0-67, car speedometer)	16.9
10-20 mph (DRIVE range)	2.1
10-30 mph (DRIVE range)	5.1
30-40 mph (DRIVE range)	3.3
40-50 mph (DRIVE range)	3.9
50-60 mph (DRIVE range)	4.7
60-70 mph (DRIVE range)	6.7
70-80 mph (DRIVE range)	11.2

TOP SPEED (MPH)
(Clocked speeds over surveyed ¼ mile)

Fastest one-way run	98.1
Slowest one-way run	92.6
Average of four runs	95.6

FUEL CONSUMPTION (MILES PER GALLON)
(Checked with fuel flowmeter, fifth wheel, and electric speedometer)

Steady 30 mph	22.4
Steady 45 mph	21.1
Steady 60 mph	17.9
Steady 75 mph	14.7

BRAKE STOPPING DISTANCE
(Checked with electrically actuated detonator)
Stopping distance at:

30 mph	47 ft. 4 in.
45 mph	102 ft. 4 in.
60 mph	196 ft. 11 in.

GENERAL SPECIFICATIONS

ENGINE

Type	Overhead valve V-8
Bore and stroke	3⅜x3¼
Stroke/bore ratio	0.96:1
Compression ratio	7.0:1
Displacement	232.6 cu. in.
Advertised bhp	120 @ 4000 rpm
Piston travel @ max. bhp	2166 ft. per min.
Bhp per cu. in.	.516
Maximum torque	190 lbs. ft. @ 2000 rpm
Maximum bmep	123.18 psi

DRIVE SYSTEM

Automatic Drive:
Hydraulic torque converter with gears

Ratios:
Drive, torque converter plus 1.43:1 gear ratio into direct drive.
Low, torque converter plus 2.31:1 ratio.
Reverse, torque converter plus 2:1 ratio.
Maximum torque ratio at stall 2.15 at 1600 rpm.
Mechanical lockup from 18 mph up.

Conventional Transmission:
Synchromesh, three-speed
Ratios:
Low, 2.57; second, 1.55; third, direct; reverse, 3.48.

Rear Axle:
Semi-floating hypoid drive.

Ratios:
Automatic 3.54
Conventional 4.09
Overdrive 4.55

DIMENSIONS:

Wheelbase	120½ in.
Tread	Front 56½, rear 55½ in.
Wheelbase/tread ratio	2.1:1
Overall width	71 in.
Overall length	201¹⁵⁄₁₆ in.
Overall height	56⁵⁄₁₆ in.
Turning diameter	44 ft.
Turns lock to lock	5¼
Weight (test car)	3350 lbs.
Weight/bhp ratio	27.9:1
Weight/road hp ratio	49.2:1
Weight distribution	Front 55.5%; rear 44.5%
Weight/sq. in. brake lining	20.9 lbs.

PRICES

(All prices are factory delivered prices and include retail price at main factory, provisions for federal taxes, and delivery and handling charges.)

	CUSTOM	DELUXE	REGAL	LAND CRUISER
CHAMPION:				
Four-door sedan	$1767.40	$1862.83	$1949.17	———
Two-door sedan	1735.12	1830.58	1916.92	———
Club coupe	———	1868.21	1954.55	———
Hardtop coupe	———	———	2115.80	———

"Dig that crazee withdrawal!"

ROAD and TRACK ROAD TEST No. A-3-53
Studebaker Commander Coupe

SPECIFICATIONS

Wheelbase	120.5 in
Tread—front	56.5 in.
rear	55.5 in.
Tire size	7.10 x 15
Curb weight	3340 lbs.
weight on rear	44.7%
Test weight	3690 lbs.
Engine	V-8
Valve system	ohv
Bore & stroke	3.38 x 3.25 in.
Displacement	232.6 cu. in.
	(3813 cc)
Compression ratio	7.0
Horsepower at 4000	120

Torque at 2000	190 ft./lbs.
Gear ratios (overall)	
overdrive	3.19
direct	4.55
2nd od.	4.95
2nd	7.06
1st	11.7
Mph per 1000 rpm	25.5
Mph at 2500 fpm—	
piston speed	118
Seating capacity	5
List price /od	$2379

PERFORMANCE

	mph
Top speed (avg.)	95.30
fastest 1 way	97.82
Max. speed in gears	
direct	87.6
2nd od	83
2nd	59
1st	35
Shift points from—	
direct	73
2nd	48
1st	28

ACCELERATION

0-30 mph	4.4 secs.
0-40 mph	6.7 secs.
0-50 mph	10.8 secs.
0-60 mph	14.9 secs.
0-70 mph	20.8 secs.
0-80 mph	31.6 secs.
0-90 mph	54.0 secs.
Standing 1/4 mile	
average	20.05
best	19.80
Mileage	15/19.0 mpg

TAPLEY READINGS

Pulling Power	Gear	mph
540 lbs/ton	1st	17
380 lbs/ton	2nd	26
230 lbs/ton	2nd od	35
245 lbs/ton	direct	38
130 lbs/ton	od	51

COASTING
(wind & rolling resistance)

40 lbs/ton	at	10 mph
65 lbs/ton	at	30 mph
100 lbs/ton	at	60 mph

SPEEDO ERROR

Indicated	Actual
10 mph	11.2
20 mph	19.6
30 mph	29.4
40 mph	38.5
50 mph	47.8
60 mph	56.6
70 mph	65.0
80 mph	74.1
90 mph	83.1

"The American Car With the European Look"

Photographs by Peggie and Al Lee

Interior of the Commander coupe shows the windshield located close to the wheel, which we liked, and the low mounted instruments which were small and hard to read.

Although *Road and Track* tests only an occasional, more interesting domestic manufactured car, the interest generated among sports car enthusiasts toward the new Studebaker coupes prompted us to run a full scale road test to see whether the performance would live up to the appearance. Although not a sports car, it gives the American public a chance to prove whether they really want style and individuality.

Studebaker has never accepted the bath tub school of design, and the '53 model shows more Italian influence than a certain manufacturer's cars who admits Italian design. There is no doubt that this car marks a milestone in American car manufacturing.

We particularly wanted to test the manually shifted model equipped with overdrive, because, in most cases, performance of this combination is better than is the automatic drive model. Although it is difficult to arrive at the exact percentage of automatic drives that Studebaker is building, it must be quite high because it is practically impossible to find a coupe that isn't so equipped. After numerous phone calls, it was discovered that the Burbank Studebaker dealer, Phil Rauch, Inc., was in possession of the exact model in which we were interested and that they were more than willing to place it at our disposal for a road test.

Handling . . .

The ride of the Studebaker is slightly more firm than any of its contemporaries, and we felt that it was an excellent compromise for an American car both in desirable firmness of suspension and cornering ability.

It has a moderate amount of understeer which is generally considered to be desirable in the interest of safety since an understeering vehicle requires a steady pull on the steering wheel to hold the car into a constant radius corner. People who are used to driving the cars of Studebaker's competitors will discover when they first drive this car that the steering is quite different to what they are accustomed.

For the first few miles we didn't care for the lack of "caster return action" but after 500 miles of experimenting with it, we found to our amazement that we were quite keen on the idea. It improves handling and definately is less tiring to drive. The abnormally high ratio steering of 6 turns lock to lock is necessary because of the high percentage of weight on the front wheels and can be modified, if desired, by using the Saginaw gear parts from the Champion 6-cylinder model, built on the same wheel base.

It might be well to explain that the high amount of lock to lock turns is occasioned by the varible ratio. When the wheels are pointing straight ahead, the gearing is 19 to 1; however, near the end of the turning action the ratio has increased to 24 to 1. If the 19 to 1 ratio was employed throughout the entire action, the lock to lock turns would drop to 5.

This car corners better than any of the cars in its class, but, as usual, we objected to the squeal of the ELP tires. Underhood inspection disclosed that the engine was installed fairly well back in the frame, which certainly helps the handling characteristics.

Top Speed . . .

From the chart it is seen that this car is capable of a genuine 97.82 mph. During the high speed runs, the car felt extremely stable and the uncanny engine smoothness contributed to ease, and inasmuch as the engine, at 95 mph, operates at a piston speed of 2,000 feet per minute (well under the generally accepted maximum of 2500 feet per minute), the top speed of this car is certainly an ultra safe cruising speed, as far as mechanical component reliability is concerned.

Acceleration . . .

That the manually shifted transmission with overdrive is faster on acceleration than the automatic drive is shown by the 0-60 time, 14.9 seconds against 16.5 seconds for the automatic drive when it is started in "low" range. The automatic drive takes over 18 seconds when using the "drive" range only. It was interesting to note that despite the claim of many salesmen that their automatic transmission models are equal or better in performance than manually shifted models, it is not true of the Commander. Valve bounce was experienced at 5150 rpm, or 59 mph in 2nd gear, and at 35 mph in 1st gear. We found that for faster times through the gears, shifting to 2nd at around 28 mph and into high at 48 mph, gave us much better results.

Actually maximum speeds of 40 mph in 1st and 66 mph in 2nd are possible with the non-overdrive car with the 4.09 axle ratio. The transmission ratios should be altered on the overdrive equipped cars (4.55 axle) so as to eliminate the "buzz box" effect, as well as the early "fade" in acceleration as valve bounce rpm is approached.

"Hop Up" Possibilities . . .

For the person who is content with good performance the stock Studebaker V-8 is the answer. Those who think they need the ability to burn rubber will find that it doesn't have quite the urge that will satisfy them. The standard car is a nice compromise of brisk performance combined with good economy. However, there are a number of alternatives available. The hop up kits available from Stu V, 3495 East Pico Boulevard in Los Angeles, will add a respectable amount of energy to the car and still have it remain docile enough for traffic driving. Frick Motors on Long Island have available the Studebaker equipped with Cadillac engines. The "Studillacs" are described as having a 125 mph top speed with acceleration to match, and people fortunate enough to have driven one of these conversions report absolutely phenomenal performance.

An "all out" conversion, for those with the amount of money neccessary, would be the Utzman double overhead cam heads as used on the Indianapolis car built for Agajanian. This outfit is reputed to develop 370 brake horsepower and performance should be fantastic, although the cost would be well over $5000 extra.

Of the three alternatives the mild hop up would be the least expensive, but probably the Cadillac conversion would be the most satisfactory as the Cadillac engine weighs only 13 pounds more than the stock Commander engine and has 331 cubic inches as compared to 232.6 for the stock Studebaker. Perhaps Studebaker has something of this nature in mind, as the Commander engine has the same size bearings and nearly the same hole center dimensions as the Cadillac. If the horsepower race persists, Studebaker can increase the capacity of their sturdy V-8 engine to enable them to compete.

(Continued on next page)

good share of the credit for the coupe's low roof line is due to the permanent center rest which conceals the driveshaft tunnel. This is not a Lancia Aurelia with body by Farina, but the similarity is certainly striking. Note the effective window ventilator.

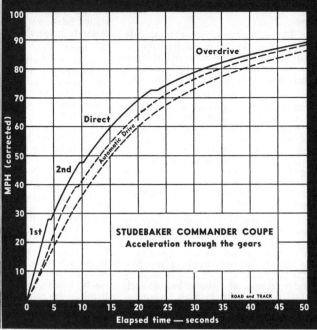

Front end styling of the 1953 Studebaker gives quick identification and driver visibility which many other cars should copy.

The two dotted curves show the acceleration of the automatic drive Studebaker V-8 using Lo and Drive, and Drive only.

General Comments . . .

The seats are a trifle skimpy and begin to get uncomfortable on long trips. A touch more foam rubber should fix this. The low driving position seems to be subject to controversy. In our test of well over 500 miles, we personally felt that both front and back seats were adequate. The back seat has a permanent arm rest in the middle to provide propeller shaft clearance occasioned by the extreme lowness of the car. On the coupe, which is merely the "austerity" version of the hard top convertible, the rear windows swing open to provide ventilation.

The trunk space is somewhat restricted in that the height is inadequate for the tire to be mounted vertically as on the sedans.

The shift mechanism had a lot of play, yet seemed "sticky," making fast low to second shifts virtually impossible. However, usage and adjustment might overcome this fault.

The car ran uncomplainingly on regular grade gasoline and on long, hot desert stretches cooled better while in overdrive than it did in direct drive, confounding the Technical Editor no end. The cooling was ex-

cellent under all of the conditions encountered despite the rather small radiator. Fan noise at higher rpms was considerable although not unpleasant. The instruments were poorly located and were rather difficult to read.

Altogether South Bend has come up with a terrific first step toward a sensible new American concept of motoring. They have the body, the chassis is acceptable and the engine provides good sturdy performance. It is possible that with this start Studebaker has the potential to force the other manufacturers to follow suit. Let us hope so. •

ROAD TEST: Studebaker Commander V-8 Coupe

Exterior styling of Studebaker coupe blends the best elements of Italian design.

**By Barney Clark
and
Austin Chaney Jr.**

EVER SINCE the new Studebakers were introduced last January the question has been: "Are they as good as they look?"

The millions who have been moaning about Detroit's barrage-balloon school of styling were greatly cheered by Stude's bold decision to gamble on the chance that the public really did want a car designed along the muchly-admired Italian lines—one that was shorn of chromium pastry-icing, lean-looking and clean-lined. It was a big gamble, and the really risky part of it was that the cars would have to sacrifice some degree or interior size, seating capacity and luggage room to get that European look.

The major interest, of course, focused on the coupes, since these were even lower and more dramatic than the sedans (and made an even stronger break from Detroit's conventions). So it was with considerable curiosity that Auto Sport Review's road test crew descended on the Studebaker branch plant in Los Angeles to pick up a Commander V-8 five-passenger coupe. (This was the five-window "Starlight," not the hard-top.) It was equipped with Borg-Warner torque converter transmission but didn't have Studebaker's new mechanical power steering.

AFTER A TEST that was necessarily limited in time (Studebaker's coupe body-builder—Budd has been struggling with a strike, and coupes with miles on them have been rarer than two-headed calves), the ASR crew arrived at a number of conclusions—some of them regretfully.

(1) Studebaker has done the American car-buying public a considerable service: it has produced one of the best-conceived, cleanest and handsomest exterior shapes ever put on any production car anywhere.

(2) Despite the sleek Italian lines, this is NOT a sports car, either in responsiveness, roadability or handling.

(3) The seasoned Studebaker overhead-valve V-8 engine is a rugged, well-engineered powerplant that is satisfactory as it now stands —and is easily adaptable to soup-

45

Commander's dashboard has hooded dials topped by a row of toggle switches. Glove compartment is small because dash is undercut.

ROAD TEST: Studebaker Commander V-8 Coupe

Handsome rear of Studebaker coupe shows the angle assumed under really hard cornering. However, body roll is not disturbing.

ing-up for really sparkling performance.

(4) The body shell is beautiful—but the interior finish, seating and general quality of construction leave a good deal to be desired.

(5) The *basic* stability of the car has been considerably improved by the lower center of gravity and this is particularly noticeable at high speed. Studebaker has an excellent start toward a top-grade road car. If the company is willing to concentrate on some easily-made improvements—correcting the mushy steering, alerting the chassis balance and steering geometry to reduce the tendency to drift in high-speed turns, revising the seating, rearranging the instrument panel to suit the driver's eye instead of the stylist's, bringing up the general quality of the construction—then they'll have one of the world's best production cars.

THE FIRST impression is that the car is low—really low. At 56-5/16 inches the coupe is far lower than any other American car—and only some three inches higher than the Jaguar hard top coupe.

Sliding in behind the wheel—and that's not as easy as it might be due to the lowness—you find yourself sitting on a rather thinly padded and somewhat lumpy seat placed close to the floor. The transmission hump and driveshaft tunnel are enormous, but the position of the throttle and the ultra-wide brake pedal is good. The leg room is sufficient, though your legs are stretched out almost horizontally and that means a tiring position for long drives. (Any seat under 1. inches in height tends to fatigue the driver.)

The steering wheel position is good as far as rake and vertical angle are concerned, though it is rather close to the driver's chest and comes rather too near his thighs (on fast turns you tend to bump your knuckles into your legs). Ignition switch and emergency brake are in the center, between driver and passenger, which is good and there is the usual drive selector with quadrant on the top of the steering post.

The instrument panel shows the touch of the stylist. There are four dials across the bottom of the panel, with ammeter and gas gauge in No. 1, speedometer in No. 2, clock in No. 3 and oil pressure and heat indicator in No. 4. These each have little individual hoods, which prevent light being thrown up on the windshield at night, but they are

Even on dirt corner rear end showed no tendency to break loose easily, but the slow steering made recovery from slides a real acrobatic feat. There was no rain, hence no report on wet weather characteristics.

oo low—the pilot has to drop his eyes a long way from the road to read them. Above these is a long row of toggle switches in recesses —a cute idea but a confusing one. These read (from left) "fog," "lights," "panel lights," "defroster," "air," "starter," with ignition key on far right. Control for the two-speed electric windshield wiper is a little knob stuck on as an afterthought in the middle of the dash header bar.

Visibility is excellent; that dramatically-sloping hood really lets you see the road ahead close up and the fenders are in view, front and rear. Also, the windshield is closer to the driver than is normal nowadays. The windshield corner posts could be slimmer, but aren't likely to be on a production car 2-1/8 inches, the width between the pupils of the eyes, is the ideal, but that takes special construction, not just folded body metal).

The armrests are cleverly designed—a thin shelf with a hunk of padding that also serves as a convenient hand grip for pulling the doors closed—but the one on the driver's side thumps his elbow as he spins the wheel and also interferes with the window winder.

So you flick the starter toggle—and a really appalling tinny racket breaks loose under the hood, ending only when the engine comes to life. Shift the lever to "Drive" range and you move smoothly off—not like a rocket but with a good solid push and no feeling of excessive slip in the torque converter transmission. "Low" range starts give a lot faster takeoffs, as the acceleration table shows, and you can perform the usual trick of pushing up into "Drive" range at about 40 mph, full throttle.

Now we come to the steering—and that's the real black mark. The wheel takes 6¼ turns from lock to lock and that is bad enough, even by American standards. But the steering also is soft and rather sticky in feel and you just aren't going to be able to do any serious correcting if you should happen to lose the rear end. The self-return action could be better.

ASR would have liked to try Studebaker's new mechanical power steering, which cuts down the *ratio* as well as the effort, but, at the time this test was made, Studebaker L.A. just didn't have a coupe with that device—and miles—on hand. Maybe that would be a partial an-

swer to the problem, but ASR contends that you have to start with good geometry *first*, even so.

ON THE ROAD, the car tracks pretty well and sits fairly solid and true at high speed. The lowered center of gravity certainly helps in this and also cuts out a considerable proportion of the body roll. On fast turns, however, such as Los Angeles' famed Sepulveda Boulevard, the car drifts sideways alarmingly, even when you try to compensate for it by aiming *two* lanes inside of where you want to place the car. This can be partially corrected by higher tire pressures, but the tendency remains.

However, the Studebaker's *stability* in a turn is pretty good. The back end doesn't tend to break away and the front end doesn't "wash out," though there is an understeer characteristic. The *position* of the car remains okay—it's just that it corners like a mechanic's creeper as far as sideways movement is concerned.

To accommodate front and rear seat passengers and the long, graceful body on the same chassis Studebaker had to lengthen the wheelbase of the coupes to 120½

Studebaker Road Test

inches. That's four inches longer than the sedans, and it compensates for being four inches lower. This gives a better ride and Studebaker purchasers won't have any complaints in this department.

The engine, as we've mentioned before, is an excellent powerplant. You burn ethyl, of course, but the overhead-valve V-8 doesn't seem to be at all fussy. Through a long series of fast acceleration runs, plus long periods of idling in traffic, it failed to show any signs of overheating, indicating that the new Italian shape and small grille have been well thought out from the cooling standpoint. There was no carburetion lag or flat spot and the engine noise level was low.

RIGHT HERE the ASR test crew would like to pat Studebaker on the back for not plunging into the horsepower race. There obviously is a lot more to be gotten from the engine, but Studebaker has held to 120 horsepower with a mere 7-to-1 compression ratio This doesn't provide startling acceleration, but it does provide maximum reliability—and for those who want the extra horses they can be had easily. If Stude can change the concept of the American car, reversing the trend toward bigger, fatter bodies, plus bigger, thirstier engines, then it will have done Joe Motorist a real service, not only through the sales of its own cars but also through its effect on all Detroit design.

While we're on the subject of the engine, it's interesting to note that the lower coupe models, which you'd expect would tend to crowd the engine compartment, actually provide a good deal more accessibility

The coupes are penalized when it comes to trunk space, however. The trunk is shallower than on the sedans and the spare tire, which is vertical on the family models, has to be laid flat on the coupes. Rear seats also suffer on the coupes. Two passengers are the absolute limit here, because the driveshaft tunnel comes up so high. As a matter of fact, Studebaker provides an immovable armrest in the center of the rear seat. Passengers get a real sports car bucket-seat effect, which is good, but the little footwells for their brogues hold them in pretty much one position.

A car as sleek as this, with bumpers brought right back against the body, is fairly vulnerable to injury Studebaker has compensated, in part, by making grille and fender repairs easy. Despite the smooth shape the front body metal is designed in small sections that can be easily removed and replaced. And the fenders are bolt-ons—not part of the body shell.

IN CONCLUSION, we'll point out again that Studebaker has made a significant change, one that could easily alter the trend of U.S. design and scale-down our present rolling boudoirs to human size again. Studebaker's reasonable attitude toward engine displacement and horsepower (and over-all weight) are a hopeful signpost for Detroit, pointing the way to a compromise that would combine the American virtues of durability, cheapness and power with the European qualities of good taste, roadability, response and practical size.

South Bend has the basic ingredients—the body shell and the motor. A little hard work by the engineering department on the problems of handling, steering and road-holding and some real thinking by the body department on the details of seating, positioning of controls, and general quality of finish—and you couldn't ask for a sweeter road car.   •••

STUDEBAKER STATISTICS
(1953 Commander V-8 Starlight Coupe)

ENGINE SPECIFICATIONS

Type	ohv V-8
Bore and stroke	3 3/8 by 3 1/4
Compression ratio	7 to 1
Displacement	232.6 cu. in.
Advertised bhp	120 at 4000 rpm

DRIVE SPECIFICATIONS

Transmissions Borg-Warner torque converter (optional); standard: manual three-speed column shift (overdrive optional). Maximum torque converter ratio, 2.16 to 1. Rear axle ratio: 3.54 to 1 (automatic drive); 4.09 to 1 (standard); 4.55 to 1 (overdrive).

DIMENSIONS

Wheelbase—120 1/2 in.	Road Clearance—7 1/4 in.
Tread—56 1/2 in. front	Steering—6 1/4 turns,
55 1/2 in. rear	lock to lock
Length—201 15/16 in.	Turning circle—40 ft.
Width—71 in.	Gas tank capacity—18 gals.
Height—56 5/16 in.	Weight—approx. 3300 lbs.

PERFORMANCE
(Fifth-wheel speedometer and stopwatch)

Standing start	Low Range & shift	High Range only
0-30 mph	6.2 sec.	7.8 sec.
0-50 "	12.2 "	14.6 "
0-60 "	16.4 "	14.6 "
0-70 "	25.4 "	28.9 "
0-80 "	33.8 "	36.0 "
Standing 1/4 mile	26.4 "	Top speed 93.4 mph

CONSTANT SPEED START

10-30 mph—6.2 sec.   30-50 mph—7.2 sec.   50-70 mph—12.6 sec.

SPEEDOMETER COMPARISON

Studebaker speedo	5th-wheel	Studebaker speedo	5th-wheel
10 mph	10 mph	50 "	47.5 "
20 "	19 "	50 "	55 "
30 "	29.5 "	70 "	64 "
40 "	38.5 "	80 "	72.5 "

Factory delivered price (with excise tax, etc.) $2212.91

The Studebaker has long, low lines and, by American standards, a surprisingly small amount of chromium plate. The car tested had several optional extras such as exterior mirrors and special wheel nave plates.

STUDEBAKER COMMANDER COUPÉ

THE idea in the minds of many people that an American car is by design and of necessity bulbous and ostentatious is strikingly upset by the latest model produced by the Studebaker Corporation, the Commander coupé. One of the lowest and certainly one of the best-balanced and beautifully styled cars to come off the production lines of a factory in the United States, this close-coupled four-five-seater reflects the Italian styling influence that is becoming increasingly popular in that country as well as in Europe. It is styling that results from true beauty of line and does not require excessive ornamentation in an attempt to correct or distract from bad basic design.

The outstanding beauty of the body and its sleek, sporting appearance tend to result in this car's being judged as a sports model as distinct from the fast normal saloon which it is intended to be, propelled by an engine developing 120 b.h.p., a figure considerably lower than that for a number of saloon cars from the same country of origin. The model of the car made available to *The Autocar* for test purposes on the Continent, by courtesy of the Regional Director for Europe of the Studebaker Corporation, was provided with a 7 to 1 compression ratio engine and Borg-Warner hydraulic transmission. An optional engine with a 7.5 to 1 compression ratio is also available, as well as a normal synchromesh gear box and overdrive transmission and alternative axle ratios to suit the various requirements of the alternative systems.

A 7 to 1 compression ratio engine and Borg-Warner transmission represent a good all-round combination, offering a lively performance, no doubt less thirstily than the more highly tuned power unit, and perhaps slower than the model would be with an overdrive transmission. The car tested was shod with Belgian tyres of a type designed to grip the slippery *pavé* and in consequence had a slightly higher drag by comparison with the tyres fitted in the U.S.A. Yet in spite of all this the Studebaker recorded a mean maximum speed of 93.5 m.p.h., so that, although it did not reach the three-figure mark, as its lines suggested it might, it performed very well and was certainly more than fast enough to meet the needs of most people.

Transmission Characteristics

The transmission consists of a single-stage torque converter and an epicyclic gear box arranged to provide a Drive and Low range. Normally the car is started in drive range, when the overall ratio in intermediate gear and with the torque converter at stall is 10.96 to 1, and as the car accelerates the torque converter ratio is reduced until it is acting as a fluid coupling. At a speed between 20 and 38 m.p.h., depending on the throttle position and loading, a plate clutch locks up the mechanism and provides a direct drive. An over-riding kick-down switch is also incorporated and if the throttle is depressed past the normal full open position the plate clutch is freed, provided that the car speed is below 62 m.p.h.; consequently, if the throttle pedal is held in the kick-down position as the car is being accelerated the lock-up speed is increased from 38 to 62 m.p.h. For extra acceleration when starting from rest, or to obtain extra engine braking, low range can be used at speeds below 49 m.p.h. In this range the overall gear ratio will vary between 17.61 and 8.16 to 1.

Another feature of this transmission is an anti-creep device which prevents the car from moving slowly forward in traffic when it is left in drive range; this device is brought into operation by applying the brake pedal and releasing it

The auxiliaries are conveniently grouped around the overhead valve V eight engine. The coil is mounted on the bulkhead alongside the windscreen wiper electric motor, and the six-volt battery is housed on the left-hand wing valance.

In spite of the low build, the Studebaker has a generous luggage compartment, which is of a very convenient shape.

The air intake is very wide to help in cooling the brakes, and extends below as well as above the bumper, which is well styled into the design. There is a slight depression in the side of the body panel running from the front wing almost to the rear edge of the door, which accentuates the high lights. The sides of the body are swept in at the bottom to give increased kerb clearance, and a splash plate is fixed to the rear of each front wing to keep the body sides clean. A small trap door encloses the fuel filler cap in the left-hand rear wing.

again. The brakes are then automatically held on until the car is accelerated by opening the throttle. Yet another mechanism prevents the car from rolling in a direction opposite to that of the selected gear, so that the car will not run back when it is being started from rest on a hill. A parking position is also provided for the selector lever and the engine cannot be started unless this lever is in either the park or the neutral position.

Perhaps the most important disadvantage is that it is not possible to change down for a corner (unless it is taken at a speed low enough for low range to be engaged), and, like all mechanisms of this type, this transmission works on the cause and effect principle and cannot think ahead. Yet, in spite of this criticism, under normal driving conditions this transmission is likely to provide the average driver with all that he wants for general purpose motoring and also eliminates the effort required for declutching and gear changing. The automatic change from intermediate to top is very smooth and there is very quick response when the kickdown switch is operated. All normal driving is done in the drive range, although the selector lever can be operated as a two-speed gear change if extra acceleration is required. There is, however, a certain amount of overlap between the ratios provided in the two ranges.

Suspension and Steering

A relatively long wheelbase and inter-axle seating complement the general riding qualities of the suspension, which gives a comfortable ride over all types of road surface, ranging from *autobahn* to *pavé*. The general low build improves stability and there is very little roll on corners even if the car is driven quite quickly. The steering is accurate, there is no lost motion, and road shocks are not transmitted back through the mechanism. The chief criticism of the steering is of the very large number of turns required from lock to lock, and that, owing to the layout of the steering gear in the straight ahead position, the general feel gives the impression that there is a much smaller number of turns than the five and three-quarters provided. This impression must be disregarded when the car is cornered quickly, as it has to be wound into the bend, requiring much more steering wheel movement than would be expected. Driving with two up there is a slight amount of understeer and the car feels very stable, although it should be recorded

that it is possible to make the rear end slide on a slippery surface.

The brakes have a good overall efficiency, although it is necessary to apply quite heavy pedal pressure for maximum braking. For normal check braking the required pressure is quite satisfactory. Over the test mileage very little brake fade was experienced, nor was there any loss of balance in the system or noticeable increase in free pedal travel.

The general noise level is very low. There is noticeably little wind noise, while the mechanical components are well insulated from the driving compartment. On the other hand, quite a lot of tyre squeal was experienced when cornering at comparatively low speeds on dry concrete.

The very low build has not adversely influenced the arrangement of the driving position and controls; in fact, the Commander coupé is particularly comfortable to drive. Although there is a bench-type front seat the back rest is divided and hinged a third of the way along, to allow access to the rear compartment, as is necessary in view of the body being a two-door style. Both the steering wheel and the pedals are well placed relative to the seat. The steering wheel itself is rather more forward than is usual in an American car, yet its position is not uncomfortable. Because automatic transmission was fitted on the car tested, no clutch pedal was provided, and in its place a double-width brake pedal is used, which can be operated with either the left or the right foot—while in cases of emergency the pedal is large enough to accommodate both feet!

From the driving seat there is particularly good all-round visibility. The low bonnet enables both front wings to be clearly seen, while because of the very large rear glass area it is possible to see the driver's side rear wing from the driving seat. The windscreen pillars are fairly thick, but they are placed so that they do not unduly obstruct the driver's general angle of vision. The rear view mirror is also well positioned and has a useful range.

Although the general body styling is very clean and simple, the layout of the facia panel and instruments is quite complicated, with four large dials, each separately cowled, placed below a row of switches. However, all these items are centrally grouped near the steering column and can be clearly seen or operated by the driver. In four groups of instruments, from left to right, are a combined ammeter and fuel gauge, speedometer and clock, and a combined oil pres-

A wide single door at each side provides easy access to both front and rear compartments. The divided front seat back rest is hinged so that the section on the driver's side can be moved forward without disturbing front passengers.

50

sure and water temperature gauge. Two-speed electric windscreen wipers are fitted and although they appear to be quite powerful they did not produce a very clean wipe on the screen. The windscreen itself, and in fact all the glass on the car, was of a blue-tinted variety—an optional extra. Its use appeared to reduce glare slightly without noticeably reducing visibility under adverse conditions. The twin sun vizors are very well placed so that they will pivot forward when necessary, to mask a small portion of the glass at the top of the screen. In place of a rheostat control, two-position instrument lighting is provided and the large cowls prevent instrument reflections in the windscreen at night.

Because of the low build of the car there is a quite large tunnel over the transmission casing in the front compartment and a smaller tunnel to provide clearance for the propeller-shaft in the rear compartment, but in spite of this it is possible to seat three persons in front, while the rear compartment is arranged to seat two and has a fixed arm rest in the centre of the seat cushion. There is a satisfactory amount of head room and leg room for the rear passengers even when the front seat is well back.

Again because of the car's shape, the luggage locker is long and shallow and, although it contains the spare wheel, it has useful space for luggage. The head lamps have a useful spread of light in the dipped position, and also a satisfactory range for normal main road operation, but an even longer range would be useful for high-speed driving on roads of the *autobahn* type. The chassis has 23 lubrication points which require attention at intervals of 1,000 miles.

The 1953 Studebaker Commander coupé is a particularly attractive American car which provides very pleasant transport for up to five persons. It has a useful turn of speed, lively acceleration, and, within its class, a satisfactory fuel consumption.

STUDEBAKER COMMANDER COUPÉ

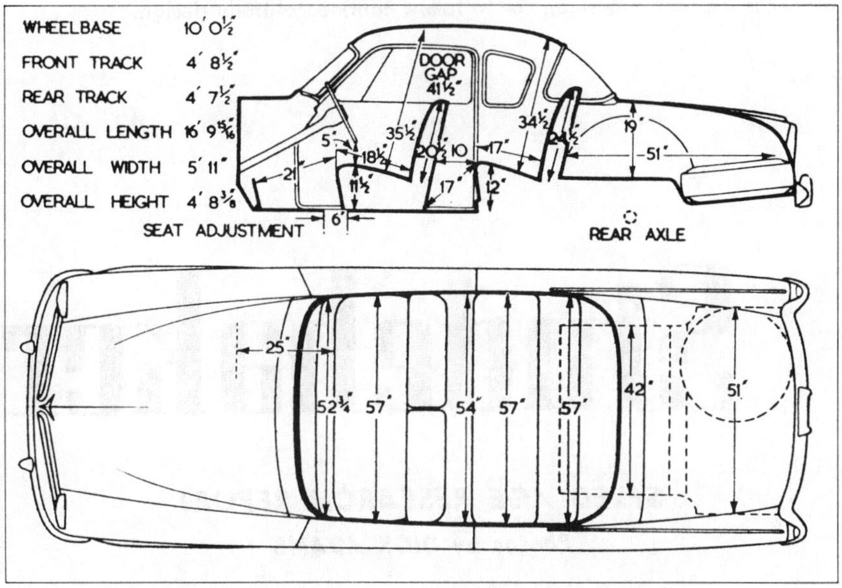

WHEELBASE 10' 0½"
FRONT TRACK 4' 8½"
REAR TRACK 4' 7½"
OVERALL LENGTH 16' 9 15/16"
OVERALL WIDTH 5' 11"
OVERALL HEIGHT 4' 8 3/16"
SEAT ADJUSTMENT
6"
DOOR GAP 41½"
REAR AXLE

Measurements in these ¼in to 1ft scale body diagrams are taken with the driving seat in the central position of fore and aft adjustment and with the seat cushions uncompressed.

PERFORMANCE

ACCELERATION : from constant speeds. Speed, *Gear Ratios and time in sec.

M.P.H.	Drive Range	Low Range
10—30	5.9	4.6
20—40	7.2	5.5
30—50	7.4	—
40—60	8.8	—
50—70	11.1	—
60—80	15.2	—
70—90	26.0	—

From rest through gears to :

M.P.H.	sec
30	5.3
50	12.1
60	16.9
70	23.1
80	32.0
90	51.0

*Gear Ratios : Drive Range 3.54—10.96 to 1. Low Range 8.16—17.61 to 1.
Standing quarter mile, **20.4** sec.

SPEED ON GEARS :

Gear		M.P.H. (normal and max.)	K.P.H. (normal and max.)
Top	**(mean)**	**93.5**	**150.5**
	(best)	**94.0**	**151.3**
Low Range		**40—49**	**64—79**

TRACTIVE RESISTANCE : 22.5 lb per ton at 10 M.P.H.

TRACTIVE EFFORT :

	Pull (lb per ton)	Equivalent Gradient
Drive Range	380	1 in 5.8

BRAKES :

Efficiency	Pedal Pressure (lb)
80 per cent	130
60 per cent	100
40 per cent	70

FUEL CONSUMPTION :
19 m.p.g. overall for 180 miles. (14.9 litres per 100 km).
Approximate normal range 16-22 m.p.g. (17.7-12.8 litres per 100 km).
Fuel, Belgian first grade.

WEATHER : Fine, dry surface, moderate wind.
Air temperature 75 deg F.
Acceleration figures are the means of several runs in opposite directions.
Tractive effort and resistance obtained by Tapley meter.
Model described in *The Autocar* of April 10, 1953.

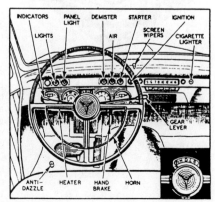

SPEEDOMETER CORRECTION : M.P.H.

Car speedometer	10	20	30	40	50	60	70	80	90	96.3
True speed	9	19	29	38.5	48.5	57	66.5	76.5	87	94

DATA

PRICE (basic), with coupé body and automatic transmission, 194,000 F. Belgian. = £1,405 at 138 F = £1.
Not available in Great Britain.
Extras : Radio 8,500 F = £63 10s 0d (approx.).
Heater 6,500 F = £47 (approx.).

ENGINE : Capacity : 3,812 c.c. (232.6 cu in).
Number of cylinders : 8.
Bore and stroke : 85.73 × 82.55 mm (3⅜ × 3¼in).
Valve gear : Overhead ; push rods.
Compression ratio : 7.0 to 1.
B.H.P. : 120 at 4,000 r.p.m. (B.H.P. per ton laden 72.3).
Torque, 190 lb ft at 2,000 r.p.m.
M.P.H. per 1,000 r.p.m. on top gear, 22.9.

WEIGHT (with 5 gals fuel), 30¼ cwt (3,380 lb).
Weight distribution (per cent) 54.5 F ; 45.5 R.
Laden as tested : 33¼ cwt (3,730lb).
Lb per c.c. (laden) : 0.98.

BRAKES : Type : F, Two-leading shoe. R, Leading and trailing.
Method of operation : F, Hydraulic. R, Hydraulic.
Drum dimensions : F, 11in diameter, 2in wide. R, 9in diameter, 2in wide.
Lining area : F, 88 sq in. R, 72 sq in. (96.3 sq in per ton laden).

TYRES : 7.10—15in.
Pressures (lb per sq in) : 26 F ; 22 R (normal).

TANK CAPACITY : 15 Imperial gallons.
Oil sump, 10 pints.
Cooling system, 29 pints (plus 2 pints if heater is fitted).

TURNING CIRCLE : 41ft 0in (L and R).
Steering wheel turns (lock to lock) : 5¾.

DIMENSIONS : Wheelbase : 10ft 0½in.
Track : F, 4ft 8½in ; R, 4ft 7½in.
Length (overall) : 16ft 9 15/16in.
Height : 4ft 8¾in.
Width : 5ft 11in.
Ground clearance : 8 3/16in.
Frontal area : 22.3 sq ft (approximately).

ELECTRICAL SYSTEM : 6 volt ; 100 ampère-hour battery.
Head lights : Double dip, 45-35 watt.

SUSPENSION : Front, independent, coil springs and wishbones ; anti-roll bar. Rear, Half-elliptic springs.

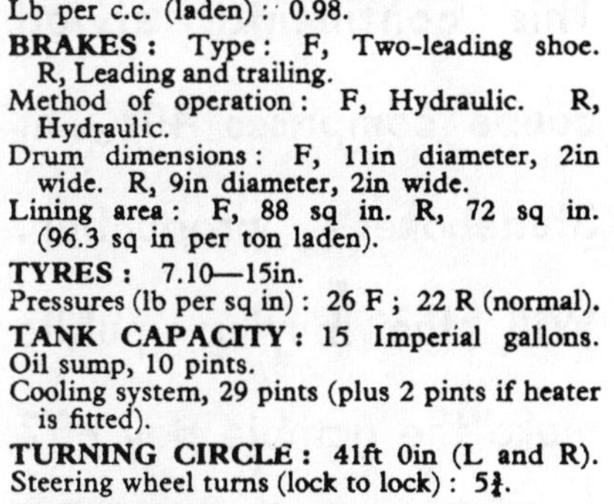

INDICATORS
PANEL LIGHT
DEMISTER
STARTER
IGNITION
LIGHTS
AIR
SCREEN WIPERS
CIGARETTE LIGHTER
GEAR LEVER
ANTI-DAZZLE
HEATER
HAND BRAKE
HORN

Only 56 inches high, the Starliner is the first American car to follow continental body design.

ROAD TEST:

This continental styled coupe comprises 40% of Studebaker's production. Will the buying public make the gamble pay off?

Studebaker

SPEED AGE RESEARCH REPORT
Photos by DICK ADAMS

STUDEBAKER has never been bashful about calling attention to the periodic stodginess of the automotive world.

There have been factory sponsored racing teams at Indianapolis, countless speed records, cross-country tours and the 'double-enders' of the 1947-49 era that gave rise to considerable mirth and—the competition admits—considerable sales.

Then this year came the *coup de grace* —Studebaker unveiled the Starliner. This was the gauntlet, design-wise, that overnight made everything else on the highway an antique.

Ever since 1852 when the Studebaker brothers, Henry and Clem, went into the wagon business at South Bend, Ind., with $68 and their tools, this firm has taken calculated risks which, for the most part, have paid a handsome return.

From their wagons, which were the standby of troops in the Civil War, Studebaker kept pace with progress and turned out battery powered horseless carriages and bodies for the Studebaker-Garford gasoline vehicle until their first year of marketing the E.M.F. motorcar proved so successful they bought the company in 1909 and went into the automobile business in earnest. Later they slashed prices yet managed to retain the previous value of their product and joined in the pioneering of the small car with the Erskine, Rockne and Champion. The first two fell by the wayside, victims of the times. The company's interests also have included the Pierce-Arrow and the White Truck Company.

In the '40s Studebaker hitched their 20th Century wagons to the pencil of designer Raymond Loewy and the trend turned from the conservative. Other manufacturers have occasionally been bold enough to introduce a radical design only to meet with public rejection. Notable in this instance was Chrysler's Airflow models of the '30s.

Disregarding the lessons learned by others appears to be the first Studebaker tenet to win buyers and influence competitors. The industry's trend to the wrap-around glass which followed Studebaker's Starlight coupe of 1947 is one example.

The company's faith in the current, streamlined coupe is backed up by scheduling more than 40% of production for those models in the Champion 6 and Commander V8 series.

And the gamble will probably pay off. The car-buying public is less reluctant to plunk down its cash for the unusual than in the '30s and the ever-increasing number of sleek, foreign imports combined with the mushrooming of the hotrod

Air scoop protrudes below bumper.

Steel skid, at left, protects rear.

Door cranks hit driver's leg.

Foot well is uncomfortable.

Starliner

and custom car fad has whetted John Q's appetite for similar transportation—appearance-wise at least.

Studebaker undoubtedly wasn't alone in recognizing the potential appeal of such an automobile but, being an independent and probably not in a position where orders exceeded production, they took the plunge.

And, having plunged, they kept the price tag within reason. For approximately $3,000, Mr. Average Buyer can have a reasonable facsimile of the European handiwork he has admired plus all the comfort and driving aids to which he has become accustomed.

The mass appeal of Loewy's design was evident at auto shows throughout the country when the Starliner was unveiled. Those handbuilt models outdrew every other car displayed and Studebaker dealers reported a terrific response. They had a car which they believed would sell itself.

And it does, although registrations for the first four months of the year, plus 19 states for May, quoting from *Automotive News,* indicates Studebaker dropped from eighth place in 1952 to eleventh in total sales this year. Having registered 63,209 automobiles in the same period of '52, sales were down more 8,000 units at the time of the report.

Those figures can be misleading for Studebaker dealers, due to factory production problems and labor troubles in the Borg Warner gear works, didn't begin receiving cars in quantity for delivery until late in March and early April.

In July, a canvass of dealers in the Baltimore-Washington area revealed orders were still running far ahead of deliveries and none of the '53 Starliners had turned up on the 'new-used' car lots although many other '53s could be found.

The purchaser however is buying only the European 'look' for the handwork of foreign plants can't be duplicated on the production line. The early models of the Starliner inspected by SPEED AGE staffers in February and March were a disappointment viewed close-up. Body seams were ragged and workmanship was so inferior it was a sacrilege of the beautiful lines that had come from Loewy's drawing board. Many individual dealers sensibly took unto themselves the responsibility of cleaning up that poor workmanship before putting the cars on their showroom floors.

The test car, which was delivered to SPEED AGE through Robert Fleigh's in Baltimore, still had some imperfections although the majority had been rectified. The paint job of synthetic enamel was excellent but the seams in the area between the grille and body panels had a too generous caulking of putty. Still soft on the test car, it will eventually dry and drop off—leaving unsightly gaps.

Studebaker has retained the bolt-on fender, holding down the cost of repairs if Madame misjudges the width of the garage door. Bumpers appear to be flimsy and offer scant protection in event of front or rear-end jostling. However, Studebaker representatives contend the bumperettes are designed to ride over another bumper, damaging the victim but leaving the Starliner unscathed. In the rear, a semi-circular steel skid protrudes from the chassis to prevent damage to the underpan. Without factory okay, SPEED AGE test jockeys were reluctant to attempt to prove the logic of this argument.

Accompanying the European 'look' is that concept of space for the Starliner is actually a 4-passenger automobile. The rear seat is permanently split with a shallow compartment in the dividing armrest.

This armrest reportedly was an afterthought resulting from the discovery that the chassis design necessitated a hump in the floor to accommodate the up-and-down movement of the differential which is positioned directly beneath that point.

The rear seats also provide little legroom for the two passengers and long trips would be tiring. A well, approximately three inches deep and 12 wide, is located on each side of the driveshaft tunnel but the entire layout of the rear passenger compartment is not too practical.

Legroom is sufficient in the front and the ride there more comfortable than first appearance indicates. The seat is not high enough at its leading edge for many persons, forcing the passenger to sit with the legs straight out with chin on knees.

A pair of bucket seats in the true continental tradition would be a vast improvement for the idea of riding three in the front is little more than an illusion. The drive-line tunnel is so high only a midget could sit there comfortably.

From the driver's standpoint things are better. The wheel is almost vertical and its height can be adjusted by adding or removing shims although this must be done by the dealer's service department. Several drivers complained it was positioned too far off center from the conventional position and the third spoke, pointing downward, doesn't contribute to safety in event of an accident but the wheel is thin and ribbed on top with finger grooves on the underside.

The overall 'feel' is one of a sport car and the front fenders are easily visible. The hood drops away to reveal more of the road than most current models and the single-piece windshield is free of distortion. The majority of the test crew liked the design of the hooded instruments but their placement, a considerable distance below the cowl line, makes more than average eye movement necessary for scanning.

The introduction of toggle control switches is reminiscent of an airplane control panel—the instruments also contribute to this effect—but their location with-

Body roll on curves at 50 MPH is not excessive.

out provision for night lighting calls for a trial and error procedure until one has memorized the sequence.

The glove compartment and ashtray are beyond reach of the driver and the mirror, suspended from the front and top of the headliner, develops a bad case of St. Vitus dance when the car is in motion. In addition, its position creates a serious blind spot for a driver who is more than five feet, eight inches tall and the unwary passenger who leans forward in haste also feels its presence. The built-in armrest on the door cramps the driver and is an annoyance when driving on winding roads.

The necessity of stiffening the windows on the Starliner returned the divider in the windwings and this, in conjunction with the sloping windshield profile, is so far back on the door as to be responsible for serious injury in a crash deceleration.

Although the chassis of this model is new and has been engineered for great stability, the possibility of a rollover can never be entirely eliminated. Such an accident in this car would probably be most unpleasant for the corner posts in the front provide little strength and those in the rear are equally as scant. Nor is there any depth to the body; it's virtually impossible for an average size passenger to wear a hat and ride and anyone taller than average should have a crew haircut to fit with comfort.

Apparently because it has become a habit, the hood retains the prop-up tenure that has characterized Studebaker products for a number of years. It reduces cost but is a minor inconvenience. However, lifting the hood won't unduly tire the service station attendant for it is a single piece of metal, quite flexible and without bracing other than a rod at the rear. The trunk lid, on the other hand, is well braced and counterbalanced.

In this particular model, with the spare tire of necessity in a flat position, trunk space is not too great but sufficient lug-

Tall drivers have little headroom in Starliner.

With spare wheel flat, trunk room is restricted.

a standard transmission and overdrive.

The power steering machinery on the test car crowded the engine room. With the battery at the rear of the left bank and the generator at the front of the right, the home mechanic will find it necessary to first remove those accessories before he can locate two spark plugs on each side. Studebaker has made it 'convenient' for their own servicemen by devising a specially shaped wrench for this chore. Other than this, the vital parts needing adjustment can be reached without trouble.

To the uninitiated, the carburetor linkage appears complicated for springs are stretched in all directions. Studebaker discovered, apparently belatedly, that the Starliner had the habit of taking the throttle in its teeth so to speak on hard left turns.

This peculiar trait of automatically accelerating is due to the soft mounting of the powerplant. Although the car rides reasonably flat, the engine shifts on its mounting, resulting in a pull on the throttle linkage. The springs are designed to counteract this force.

Those soft mountings also complicate things in another direction and make a screwdriver essential motoring equipment. On two occasions SPEED AGE test drivers found themselves marooned in 'Park' on a grade. A screwdriver in the hand of a mechanic freed the car. This peculiar immobility results, according to mechanics who claim they have answered numerous calls, from the engine and transmission shifting backward slightly but enough to bind the linkage so that it is impossible to move the shift lever from 'Park' into 'Drive.'

The screwdriver is inserted between the linkages and this extra leverage snaps it out. Studebaker servicemen at Dealer Fleigh's, who also admitted having had a number of calls for similar trouble, argue the high and dry position is caused by a pawl in the transmission not being sufficiently worn-in. Take your pick but park at your own risk on a grade.

Due to the low frontal area, the engine runs hot in heavy traffic but does not boil. The radiator has been dropped below the level of last year and a wide air scoop extends across the lower part of the grille. The fan is shrouded also and this contributes to keeping the powerplant from simulating a percolator.

This engine is the only one of the numerous overhead valve jobs to retain solid lifters. In part this holds production costs down and contributes a bit of tappet noise but makes the souping addict's job that much simpler. And there's plenty here for the hot-rodder—remember that Aggie Agajanian's mechanics turned up to 7000 RPM with an overhead cam conversion on the Stude block and lower end in an Indianapolis car this year.

SPEED AGE's test crew, interested in the early-in-the-year announcement of Studebaker's mechanical power steering had been looking forward to trying this latest addition to the 'make-it-easy-for-the-driver' school.

They are still waiting the opportunity to test this gismo for the Starliner was equipped with the Saginaw hydraulic linkage used on GM products.

gage for the ordinary trip can be carried if it is stowed properly. This feature, with the corresponding lack of interior room, will discourage the buyer with a large family.

The lightness of construction, noted elsewhere, is carried over in the doors. With the windows rolled down, you won't have to reach for the vitamin bottle to squeeze the top sill together on the glass. There obviously is an absence of bracing at this point and rigidity suffers; a possible source of future squeaks and rattles.

Not all of the poor workmanship is on the exterior. The under-the-cowl lining was poorly matched on the test car, the metal door sill had sharp edges, mats were trimmed shy for the area they were intended to cover and windshield moldings were warped out of position on fastening. The latter criticism applies to numerous Starliners inspected at various dealers' showrooms.

Upholstery is serviceable but doesn't create the impression of lasting the lifetime of the car. The vinyl door panels and simulated leather headliner, however, are striking and go far to add to the custom appearance.

Studebaker, since the introduction of the slightly oversquare V8 engine in 1951, has been content to go along with the original 120 HP. This horsepower rating, out of 232 cubic inches is more than adequate to move the Starliner over the road at reasonable speed—in fact, the average of four high-speed runs in opposite directions over a 5-mile stretch of test road without traffic interference, gave an average of 101 MPH.

The Champion 6 is, of course, the economy car in the Studebaker line but the V8 compares favorably with others in its price range although it may prove disappointing on the basis of displacement and weight. Traffic mileage figured out to only 15 miles per gallon with a steady 60 giving only two miles per gallon more. One or two miles more could reasonably be expected if the Starliner was equipped with

Sweeping lines bring fenders above trunklid.

It seems that in pilot models with a handbuilt mechanical device, everything worked fine. When the linkage was placed on a production line basis, however, assorted noises developed—it went back to the laboratory for further development and Studebaker adopted the older Saginaw type to avoid disappointing customers.

Actually, with an automobile of this weight, power steering is not essential. With slightly more than four turns required lock to lock, the steering ratio is still too slow and, on first acquaintance, the uninitiated can get into trouble. A few miles behind the wheel and the ease of handling makes one look on the tug-of-war of non-power as archaic. And getting back behind a conventional wheel is literally backbreaking.

Coupled with the V8 in the test car was the Borg-Warner automatic transmission, at $231, just about the most expensive in the industry and not exactly the biggest ball of fire. The cost undoubtedly is due to the fact Studebaker isn't as large a customer as other manufacturers who use BW self-shifting boxes at lower prices.

This transmission is an improvement over last year's but BW and Studebaker have no reason to rest on current laurels in this department. An indication the factory is not unaware of shortcomings was had in the assurance of one Studebaker representative that a much improved version is in the works for '54.

Operation of the BW resembles Hydra-Matic from behind the steering wheel but there the resemblance ends. All normal driving is done in Drive range with a Low range included for emergency and braking. Starting in L and shifting to D improves acceleration somewhat. Below 60 MPH, additional power and acceleration may be obtained by pressing the throttle to the floor to obtain an intermediate gear which continues until the throttle is released or the speed exceeds 70 MPH.

This gearbox is also inhabited by a variety of noises and clunks, all of which

Mirror creates blind spot.

apparently have nothing to do with its operation.

Considering the powerplant only puts out 120 HP and 190 foot pounds of torque at 2000 RPM, a zero to 60 MPH time of 15.4 seconds in L and D isn't bad but a straight shift would probably be better. Dragging to 70 MPH in 25 seconds using D alone is fast enough for the average Joe but nine seconds for 30 to 60 MPH can be considered a couple too many.

Incorporated with the gearbox, the factory says, is an anti-creep device and hillholder. The latter is a blessing and saves wear and tear on clutch, engine, nerves and brakes. The anti-creeper, on the test car, was inoperative a good part of the time.

Handling in traffic is light and pleasurable once the driver becomes accustomed to the lowness. There is some vision block due to this lack of height but it is not serious. More difficult to get accustomed to is the feeling of greater width than the Starliner 71 inches.

On the highway at cruising speed, re-

sponse to the wheel is fast and little corrective action is needed in crosswinds. The ride is a bit stiffer than other automobiles and road bumps make themselves known—although not sufficiently to affect the steering.

Despite its low center of gravity and racy facade, this is no sport car in the handling department. Body roll has been reduced to a minimum but a weight distribution of 58% front and 42 rear isn't the best in the world. Then, too, with a wheelbase of 120½ inches, the tread of 56½ in front and one inch less in the rear, doesn't provide all the stability one could ask for.

Paradoxically, at wide open throttle, the Starliner feels as if it had taken on weight. At about the midway point of SPEED AGE's high speed course there is a slight hump in the pavement which invariably serves as a take-off point for all four wheels. The Studebaker was no exception but it lit with a difference. There was no bouncing and lunging—the Starliner came down to a perfect four-point landing and resumed its flat, 101 MPH journey to the end of the trap.

These runs also were the quietest the crew has taken in a long time. The body design is so aerodynamicallly clean that there is an almost complete absence of wind roar and it's corollary—the heightening illusion of speed.

But the braking department leaves something to be desired. During acceleration runs, where the Starliner was snubbed down to zero from 30, 40 and 50 MPH, the brakes, anti-creep device and emergency binder wouldn't hold the car with the engine idling, after six such stops.

After this experience—which possibly could be attributed to the fact the linings were very new—the Starliner went back to Dealer Fleigh's for an adjustment. Following this they were more positive, somewhat enduring but not especially endearing from the fade standpoint. Recovery is rapid, however, and the secret is to pump furiously rather than stand on the pedal. Using those tactics the car can be halted in a distance that compares favorably with others in its weight and horse-power bracket.

Part of the trouble may be in a design which has shoes 11 inches in diameter in front and two inches less in the rear. Total area is 160 square inches, less than a number of automobiles of the same weight with less horsepower.

There are a number of bugs in this automobile—as in any new model. Many which were apparent at the beginning of the year have already been eradicated. Those remaining undoubtedly are the focal point of Studebaker engineering.

After 1,500 miles of test driving, the inevitable conclusion is that the design has mass appeal but space restrictions imposed by that design limit its utilitarian aspects.

The true measure of the success of the Studebaker gamble will be reflected when competitors unveil their '54 models. Imitation being flattery, if there are one or two 'radicals' present, the boys from South Bend will have shown the way to the jackpot once again.

Power steering mechanism, bottom center; spring to counteract left turn acceleration, top center; the auto's battery shrouds spark plugs at right.

PERFORMANCE DATA

Engine Specifications

Cylinders 8
Arrangement V
Valve arrangement ....OH
Bore (inches) 3⅜
Stroke (inches) 3¼
Displacement (cubic inches) ...232.6
Compression ratio ....7 to 1
Taxable horsepower 36.4
Brake horsepower 120
Max. torque (foot pounds at
  RPM) ....190 at 2000
Oil capacity (quarts) 6
Fuel capacity (gallons) 18
Water capacity (quarts)
  without heater 17¼
  with heater 18¾

Transmission

Standard
Overdrive
Automatic

RATIOS:

	Automatic	Standard	Overdrive
1st.	Torque	2.57	2.54
2nd.	Converter plus	1.55	1.55
3rd.	1.43 to 1	1.00	1.00
4th.		....	.70
Reverse		3.48	3.48

Interior Specifications

Width of front seat at shoulder
  (inches) 55⅛
Width of rear seat at shoulder (inches) 52½
Depth of front seat (inches) 17¼
Depth of rear seat (inches) 17½
Headroom, front (inches) 36 5/16
Headroom, rear (inches) 35¾
Legroom, front (inches) 44¾
Legroom, rear (inches) 35

Chassis

FRAME:
  Type ....Box Section
  Wheelbase (inches) 120½

TREAD:
  Front (inches) 56½
  Rear (inches) 55½
Shipping weight (pounds) 3,150
  Front 58%
  Rear 42%
Overall length (inches) 201 15/16
Overall width (inches) 71
Overall height (inches) 56 5/16
Road clearance (inches) 8 5/64

SUSPENSION:
  Front ....Coil Spring
  Rear ....Semi-elliptic

REAR AXLE:
  Type ....Semi-floating
  Gearing ....Hypoid
  Ratio 3.54*

TIRES:
  Size 7.10x15**

PRESSURE:
  Front (pounds) 26
  Rear (pounds) 22

BRAKES:
  Drum diameter (inches) 11F,9R
  Effective area (square inches) 160
  Type ....Budd

STEERING:
  Type ....Worm-Roller
  Ratio ....20 to 1

Acceleration
Drive (kickdown)

30-60 MPH ....9.1 seconds

ALL GEARS:	L	D	L and D
0-30 MPH	5.2	6.5	
0-40 MPH	8.8	9.6	
0-50 MPH		13.7	12.5
0-60 MPH		16.5	15.4
0-70 MPH		25.3	23.8

Top speed, average of four runs in opposite
directions over measured mile, timed:
  101.04 MPH

BRAKING:

Complete stop 30 MPH   42 feet, 3 inches
              60 MPH 188 feet, 6 inches

SPEEDOMETER ERROR:

Indicated	Actual
30 MPH	.30
40 MPH	.37
50 MPH	.45
60 MPH	.54
70 MPH	.63
80 MPH	.72

FUEL CONSUMPTION:

30 MPH	21.2 MPG
40 MPH	20.5 MPG
50 MPH	18.5 MPG
60 MPH	17.0 MPG
Traffic	15.0 MPG

STUDEBAKER PRICES

	Factory List Price	Federal Tax & Factory Handling	Preparation	Transportation Charge	Total Delivered at Baltimore, Md.
CHAMPION					
CUSTOM:					
4-Door Sedan	$1,615	$136	$16	$66.90	$1,834.40
2-Door Sedan	$1,585	$134	$16	$66.90	$1,802.02
DELUXE:					
4-Door Sedan	$1,705	$141	$16	$66.90	$1,929.73
2-Door Sedan	$1,675	$139	$16	$66.90	$1,897.48
5-Passenger Coupe	$1,710	$142	$16	$66.90	$1,935.11
REGAL:					
4-Door Sedan	$1,785	$148.17	$16	$66.90	$2,016.07
2-Door Sedan	$1,755	$145.92	$16	$66.90	$1,983.82
5-Passenger Coupe	$1,790	$148.55	$16	$66.90	$2,021.45
Hard-Top Conv. (Starliner)	$1,940	$159.80	$16	$66.90	$2,182.70
COMMANDER					
DELUXE:					
4-Door Sedan	$1,940	$161.40	$19.75	$76.13	$2,197.28
2-Door Sedan	$1,910	$159.15	$19.75	$76.13	$2,165.03
5-Passenger Coupe	$1,945	$161.77	$19.75	$76.13	$2,202.65
REGAL:					
4-Door Sedan	$2,020	$167.79	$19.75	$76.13	$2,283.67
5-Passenger Coupe	$2,025	$168.16	$19.75	$76.13	$2,289.04
Hard Top Conv. (Starliner)	$2,175	$179.41	$19.75	$76.13	$2,450.29
Land Cruiser	$2,120	$175.89	$19.75	$78.17	$2,393.81

Accessory Prices

	Factory List Price	Federal Tax	Total
CHAMPION			
Automatic Drive	$213.28	$17.96	$231.24
Overdrive	$97.66	$7.33	$104.99
Hillholder	$14.03	$1.05	$15.08
Elec. W/S Wiper	$8.97	$.68	$9.65
Oil Bath Air Cleaner	$6.73	$.50	$7.23
Air Foam Rubber Seat Cushion—Per Seat	$12.33	$.92	$13.25
Tinted Glass	$22.21	$1.66	$23.87
5-White-Black Tires—6.40x15—4 Ply	$23.75	$1.13	$24.88
COMMANDER			
Automatic Drive	$224.20	$18.88	$243.08
Overdrive	$109.74	$8.23	$117.97
Power Steering	$150.00	$11.25	$161.25
Oil Bath Air Cleaner	$7.08	$.53	$7.61
Tinted Glass	$22.39	$1.68	$24.07
5-White-Black Tires 7.10x15 4 Ply	$29.20	$1.39	$30.59

* With automatic transmission; 4.09 with standard and 4.55 with overdrive
** Extra cost equipment

Studebaker Joins Wagon Train with 1954-Model Conestoga

By Frank Rowsome Jr.

Better brakes, glossier interiors, and a new entry in the hot station-wagon fight, mark next year's line-up.

STUDEBAKER is back in the wagon business that launched the company more than a hundred years ago. But the wagon they are making now is scarcely calculated to tote pioneers across the plains. This one lugs the kids to school, hauls plywood back from the lumber-yard, and carries the whole family, including the pup, on vacation trips.

This latter-day prairie schooner, the company's bid for the growing market

ers repeat the rear lines that helped make the '53 car such an eye-popper. For the lady of the house who wouldn't mind cutting a wider swath in suburbia, there are some juicy combinations of color and interior details, guaranteed to green the eyes of other matrons whose wagon interiors are finished in utility-gray fiberboard.

Never a company to let the gewgaws crowd out the gears, Studebaker has also built some solid service into its wagon. It is a two-door, two-seat vehicle, able to carry six persons plus some 32 cubic feet of payload. If you want more space, flip-flop the rear seat so it lies flush with the floor, which gives room for three people and 64 cubic feet of enclosed payload space. If you aren't exceptionally tall, you can spread a sleeping bag out on the 69½-inch-long rear floor. (If you're more than five-nine, try it kitty-cornered, or let your feet sleep out on the tail gate.)

Engineering the wagon. When the Conestoga project came up, Studebaker design people figured they might have to beef up their basic chassis. This turned out to be unnecessary (one exception: frame steel on the six-cylinder job is going to be a few thousandths

staked out by the Plymouth Suburban and the Ford Ranch Wagon, is called (more or less inevitably) the Conestoga. On looks, at least, Connie is a comer. Up front, it has the same sloped, downhill lines that made the Loewy-styled 1953 Studebaker such a snaky, "Continental" craft. Beginning at about the door, the lines square out, blending into the same shape that characterizes most current station wagons—that of a miniature and rather sporty hearse. Pert little kickups of rear fend-

thicker). The wagon's dry weight checks out at only 170 pounds more than that of a four-door sedan. The Conestoga does carry, however, these changes:

New rear springs. Standard rear springs, fitted to an experimental Connie, gave a fine ride at moderate loads. When Studebaker engineers piled in a severe overload—some owners will inevitably heave in a passel of cement bags—the Conestoga sat sadly down on its haunches. The answer to that was a special two-stage spring. It has two extra leaves arranged so that they don't come into play until the wagon is heavily loaded. With up to three people aboard,

CONTINUED ON PAGE 70

CONTINUED ON PAGE 70

INSTRUMENT PANEL is redesigned with a single shroud over instruments, and has new flat switch toggles. Interior colors and fabrics are going to be extra-luxurious this year.

VERTICAL FINS on grille are the best recognition feature for '54 jobs. The V-8 hood ornament was put on in mid-1953 after Mercedes squawked about earlier Y-shaped one.

FLOP THE REAR SEAT and there's 88½ inches of floor length with the tail gate down. Tailpipe dumps the exhaust in turbulent air behind wheel to lessen chance of any swirl-in.

COMMANDER STARLINER hardtop convertible highlights the 1954 Studebaker line. The low streamlined styling is set off by new grille design and bumper treatment. Automatic drive and power steering are optional.

New Studebakers Bow

ALL-STEEL STATION WAGON LATEST ADDITION TO LINE

ADDITION of a new all-steel station wagon—bringing the number of body styles to 20—larger brakes, higher compression ratio and redesigned grilles and bumper guards are features of the new 1954 Studebaker models which went on dealer display November 23. All models were designed by Raymond Loewy.

The new pleasure-utility car is named the Conestoga—in memory of the original Conestoga wagon in which the founding brothers of Studebaker traveled to South Bend, Ind. from Ohio more than 100 years ago.

Other types are two- and four-door sedans, hardtop convertibles, coupes and the Land Cruiser. Their design and styling moved executive vice-president K. B. Elliott to declare they "will continue to set the pace for the industry as they have ever since Studebaker's first post-war models were introduced. We believe that the many engineering improvements and colorful new interiors, along with outstandingly original design, will demonstrate even more convincingly the flair and sparkle, performance, riding comfort and economy which our designers and engineers have achieved."

Exterior lines have been enhanced by further refinements. Interior styling is the work of Eleanor Le Maire, decorating expert and color stylist.

Upholstery fabrics are offered in four different basic color motifs that harmonize with exterior hues. Items such as steering wheels, steering wheel columns, instrument panels, moulding, door trim and carpeting likewise harmonize with exterior colors. There are 12 different solid color options and 10 different two-tone combinations.

Other interior features include new instrument clusters, removable center arm rests for the rear seats of hardtop convertibles and coupes, and dome lights which completely light up the interiors.

The Conestoga accommodates six passengers. When used as a utility car, with the rear seat folded down, an area of 64 cubic feet is available for baggage or haulage purposes. The car has a wheelbase of 116½", is 195⅝" in overall length, 69¾" in width, and 62⅜" in height when loaded.

Exterior body changes for '54 models include new grilles with vertical fins; bumper guards which provide increased protection for grilles; new hood ornaments as standard equipment on station wagons and on all sedans with the exception of the custom Champion. Chrome "rub rails" extending on either side of the car from a point near the tail light to the forward edge of the front door are standard on all regal sedans and Land Cruiser models.

Tinted glass, which reduces eye strain by decreasing glare and which cuts heat by filtering out some 65 per cent of the sun's heat rays, is available on all models at slight extra cost. Hydraulic power steering is likewise optional on all models at extra cost.

Stainless steel window mouldings are standard on all '54 Deluxe models. Die cast chrome mouldings are used on all Regal models.

Foremost among the chassis improvements are new and larger brakes for both Champions and Commanders. These, according to intensive engineering tests, provide up to one-third greater braking power for a given effort by the driver and thus adds substantially to driving safety. Front brakes on the Champion have been increased in diameter from 9" to 10". Front brakes on Commanders have been increased in width by a full quarter inch for increased effectiveness and Commander rear brakes boosted in diameter to 10".

The new brakes are self-centering and self-energizing and have, in addition to greater stopping power, increased pedal reserve, heavier drums, more durable brake lining, and labyrinth-type drum seals which keep out dirt and mud. Studebaker engineers say maintenance will be much simpler since only one adjustment per wheel will be required during either periodic or relining adjustments.

Acceleration and performance have been stepped up on both the Champion and the Commander as a result of a 7.5 to 1 compression ratio in the power plants of both cars. Automatic transmissions on Champions now have three power ranges in "Drive" position: automatic low, intermediate, and direct. The automatic low gear start makes possible much greater acceleration at low traffic speeds.

New radiator cores and changes in the design and pitch of the fans assure adequate cooling even under prolonged high temperatures. New clutch linkage on cars equipped with conventional or overdrive transmission make possible lower pedal pressure. Riding qualities of all cars have been further increased by changes in the valving of shock absorbers. ★

EXTERIOR STYLING of the new all-steel station wagon, the Conestoga, follows the lines of Studebaker passenger cars. Named for the old covered wagons, it is available in both Champion and Commander.

REGAL CHAMPION 4-door sedan is one of twenty new Studebaker body styles. 1954 models have larger brakes and compression is increased to 7.5 to 1.

'54 Studebaker Commander:
IMPROVED INTERIOR and

WHEN MOTOR TREND Research tested the revolutionary '53 Studebaker Commander coupe, we pointed out the car's drawbacks and its good features. The new model Studebaker's brakes were average; its carrying capacity was limited. It had good riding qualities and outstanding roadability; its performance was quite acceptable. On most counts, the '53 Studebaker left little to be desired.

When we picked up a '54 Studebaker Commander Regal four-door sedan at the company's Los Angeles plant, we were surprised to find that—aside from the usual alterations to grille and trim—there were several improvements over last year's car.

How is the '54 Studebaker different from the '53? There's not much difference in looks. The Commander Regal has a heavy chrome rub strip along its recessed sides, a waffle-type grille, and slight ornamental changes. Our real surprise began with our first close look: the interior is more colorful and better finished, and the exterior shows a vast improvement (in workmanship) over the early production model we tested last year. Another major change showed up as soon as we drove the car—the brakes were decidedly better than those on the '53.

"Whether or not the radically styled Studebaker (coupes) will meet with public approval is hard to determine," we said last year. Now a Studebaker representative tells us that the company tooled up to make the coupes 25 per cent of their total production for '53. By the

end of the year, they had taken over more than 50 per cent of Studebaker's total sales and production.

Is the new sedan as easy to handle as the '53 coupe? It's not quite as agile, but it's a well-behaved car, one that a new owner can easily adjust to. You'll notice that clutch and brake pedal (the test car had overdrive) are farther to the left than usual. This is a surprise at first, but no problem after a few miles. The car is easy to handle under all conditions; wide, low windows and short overhang help in parking, and well-defined ridges on the steering wheel give positive control. The relation of the steering wheel to the driver's seat means relaxed, proper seating for the driver—a definite asset to driving ease.

Steering was rather stiff; the '53 Commander and Champion had the same peculiarity. We needed an extra tug to turn the front wheels smoothly and easily; in cornering, we had to jerk the wheel slightly to return to a straight-ahead position. The test car had Ross steering (specifying 5¼ turns lock to lock) as do other Western Studebakers. Cars assembled in South Bend come with Saginaw steering (4¼ turns). Studebaker's power steering ($177 extra, 4¼ turns) will ease any steering problem for those who demand effortless driving in close quarters.

How good are the brakes? From all appearances, 1954 should be a banner year in stopping distances, for once again

(see the '54 Nash Rambler test, January MT) we've tested a car that sets an example for others. The pace-setting Commander's stopping ability was excellent at all speeds tested, largely because of new brakes introduced on the '54 models. Stopping the 3380-pound car in 41 feet at 30 mph, 94 feet at 45, and 159 feet at 60 mph, the self-centering, self-energizing brakes showed no fade, had plenty of reserve, and were quick acting at all times. South Bend says they give 30 per cent more braking power than the older type; we say they showed a 37-foot safety margin over last year's brakes at 60 mph —certainly notable progress in what is perhaps the most important phase of performance. The new brakes, the product of a two-corporation effort (Studebaker and Wagner Electric) are slightly larger in diameter than those on the '53.

Does the sedan have the coupe's roadability? Our '53 coupe had a slight edge over the '54 sedan in roadability, but the four-door still gets an excellent rating. In its role as a reasonably roomy and comfortable family car, the sedan has a lack of body roll and an ease of handling at high speeds that make it one of the best in its class (or any other) for roadability. For some years, Studebaker has built comparatively light cars. Yet wind wander was negligible even in a stiff crosswind; the car demanded no correction on normal roads, and streetcar tracks or uneven road shoulders did not affect its stability at all. We feel that the owner of the flat-cor-

THE CAR AT A GLANCE	FAIR	AVERAGE	GOOD	EXCELLENT
ACCELERATION Standing start ¼ mile		X		
30-80 mph			X	
BODYWORK			X	
BRAKES Stopping distance average @ 30, 45, 60 mph and traffic				X
EASE OF HANDLING		X		
FUEL ECONOMY Average @ 30, 45, 60, 75 mph			X	
INTERIOR		X		
RIDE		X		
ROADABILITY			X	

BETTER BRAKES

...ering Commander sedan will gain an ...arly confidence in his car. Should you ...ut the car into a bad turn, the Commander's "stickability," coupled with its ...ager engine, will bring it out of trouble ...ith only an easily corrected drift. Stiff ...uspension and light weight combine to ...nake it bounce on an uneven surface, and ...t has a tendency to lose traction when the ...oing gets rough.

Do flat cornering and "stickability" ...nean a hard ride? No, your passengers ...vill be uncomfortable only when you take ...ough roads at fairly high speeds. At nor...nal speeds, the Commander provides a ...olid but comfortable ride, a ride with a ...oticeable lack of side-to-side body move...nent and roll.

There was no pitching or unusual oscil...ation to the body, even in severe dips; ...ecovery was rapid and the car didn't jar ...he passengers when it settled down again.

Some road shock was transmitted through the body on rough surfaces, and road noise was fairly high (undercoating would help dampen sound and vibration). Engine noise was at a minimum during acceleration and at cruising speeds. Wind noise (with either large windows or windwings open) was bothersome at all but the lowest speeds.

Is the interior comfortable? Wide and comfortable seats give good support to legs, back, and shoulders. Legroom is adequate in front and back, and headroom is low only at the extreme edges of the rear seat. The test sedan had no rear center armrest (there's a folding one in the longer Land Cruiser, and this year all the coupes have one that's removable so a child can stretch out in back). Firm foam-rubber-padded seats proved untiring even after four or five hours behind the comfortably angled steering wheel.

Like the Studebakers tested in '53, the new car's front seat moved slightly when the car stopped or started; unlike previous models, the '54 sedan had an easily adjusted seat that the driver could slide into position without help.

Are interior appointments up to the standard of its class? While the '54 Commander's interior can't be considered plush, it's up there with the others at its price. Workmanship, greatly improved over that in the '53 test car, is on a plane with many higher-priced cars tested in the past.

MT's Commander Regal test car had a pleasant, durable-looking interior. Nylon fabric covered the seats, and the easily cleaned plastic doorpanels seemed scuffproof. The floormats were of average quality, and much better fitted and trimmed than those in the '53 test car.

Rounded steel "bumpers" (one is shown at right of exhaust pipe) protect underbody and pipe if rear end should scrape curb

Washable door panels simplify Studebaker spring cleaning. Foot pedals are placed farther toward the left than in many cars

Wide windshield, low hood combine to give good forward vision. Slanted panel has toggle switches mounted above dials

Studebaker Road Test

Are the Commander's instruments easy to read? Are controls within reach and easy to operate? The new Studebaker's instruments are somewhat low to be read at a glance, but they are clearly marked and well lighted for glareproof night use. The instruments are arranged horizontally in four dials across the panel. This setup, unchanged from last year's model, prompts us to repeat our last year's comment: if the dials were in two rows, they would be easier to read in a hurry. (It's interesting that the lower-priced Studebaker Champion has a more closely grouped, three-dial panel.) The parking brake is handy to the driver, and it's easy to set and release.

MT Research continues to approve of Studebaker's toggle switches. The only suggestion we offer is that the switches could be better marked for "off-on" or "high-low" to simplify things for a driver not familiar with the car. Placed horizontally across the dashboard (just above the hooded instrument panel) the recessed toggles are convenient and safe.

Does the sedan have good all-around vision? Yes, the Commander's wide, one-piece windshield, combined with one of the lowest hoods on any production car, provides an excellent view of the road and both front fenders. Cornerposts are quite thick, but did not rate unfavorable comment from any of MT's testers. The Commander's mirror is wide and allows a broad view of the road behind, yet it is thin enough (vertically) to give unobstructed vision to the right front. This mirror, like those in the '53 Commander and Champion test cars, vibrated badly. At highway speeds it was nearly useless.

How does the Studebaker's heating and ventilating system work? As in last year's car, the Climatizer works well for heating, only fair for cooling. The underseat heater has excellent output without blasting. The fresh air from the side-mounted "doors" isn't adequate for cooling the interior in hot weather, possibly because the intakes are too close to the road surface. A single simple control operates the thermostat. The vent control is under the right side of the dashboard—it's a long reach for the driver.

Does the new Commander have good performance? MT's overdrive-equipped test car turned in performance data very close to those of the '53 Commander with Automatic Drive. Both cars turned 67 mph at the end of the quarter-mile run, and the averages were only 0.5 mph apart; the '54's time was the slower (20.6 seconds). The new Commander's 4.27 to 1 rear axle ratio gave the car a two-second advantage at 70-80 over last year's torque converter-equipped car, but the cars were

nearly equal in other speed ranges. The '54 test car's 93 mph average top speed was slightly less than the '53 car's, which can be explained by the difference in body styles tested. The coupe has a slightly smaller frontal area and slightly better coefficient of wind resistance.

High clutch slippage when going into each gear was experienced during acceleration tests. If the Commander is to be used in a draft-horse capacity like pulling a house trailer, this should be corrected.

Is the '54 Studebaker more economical than last year's car? The new car had better overall economy. The overdrive-equipped '54, using Mobilgas Special, averaged 22.1 miles per gallon for 30, 45, and 60 miles per hour; the '53 averaged 20.5 mpg for the combined speeds. At 75, the '54 averaged 15.1 mpg; the '53, 14.7.

Has the V-8 engine been souped up for '54? No, the Commander's 120-horsepower V-8, considered entirely satisfactory in performance by MT Research, is apparently considered adequate by the Studebaker Corp. also, for they haven't entered their V-8 in the '54 version of America's horsepower race. It's a typical modern short-stroke V-8 in most every way except that it doesn't use hydraulic valve lifters. Compression ratio has gone up 0.5 to 7.5 to 1. The overhead-valve powerplant rates about average for servicing most components; however, the oil dipstick, one of the points most frequently checked, has been buried under the carburetor air cleaner, in a particularly inaccessible spot near the exhaust manifold. No reason not to buy a car, but why burn your hand?

Does the four-door body style make much difference in trunk size? Yes, the added height of the Commander sedan (compared to the coupe) means a more practical, family-type car. (We say that over the protests of those who may scream "Nuts to practicality—we'll take the coupe for appearance and leave the luggage behind!" We like the style of the coupe better ourselves.) A careful packer should be able to load a great deal of luggage into the Commander's trunk.

Is the new Studebaker well built? If our test car is an example of average Studebaker construction, the comment MT made in June 1953 (". . . Later models probably will be built better") has come true. All stainless steel molding was well fitted, and chrome trim was firmly attached; plating was as good as any we've seen since the government lifted restrictions on critical metals. The test car's pastel paint was flawless; workmanship from door jambs to dome lights was good, and all body panels fitted neatly.

Did the car operate well during the test? The car ran smoothly and quietly through- out the 1100-mile road test. There were no squeaks or rattles when it was all over, and the engine started easily and ran cool, even in heavy, slow-moving traffic and on ong mountain grades.

We felt a shudder during low-speed, ow-gear acceleration; it was not clutch hatter, but seemed to come from the Studebaker's two-piece driveshaft. Inspec- ion showed nothing wrong, so the vibra- ion may be simply a result of the double- niversal driveshaft setup.

The Hill Holder (standard on Com- nanders and Land Cruisers) was some- hing we missed when we drove other tandard shift cars after the Stude road test. Through a gravity-actuated sliding ball valve in the brake line, the gadget keeps the car from rolling back when you stop on an upgrade (letting up on the clutch releases the brakes). It doesn't op- erate when you're heading downhill.

Is the '54 Commander sedan a good buy? The Commander did not impress us as being a car suited only to a particular buyer, for it combines many good fea- tures which make it suitable as a family car in general use. It adapts itself to any condition; it's an easy car to drive, it has good performance, and as pointed out earlier, it has top-notch brakes—an item worth considering if you're the type who is as much impressed with stopping ability as you are with lightning acceleration.

The Studebaker's original cost is not prohibitive—it's one of the lowest priced cars in its popular class ($2051 to $2500 list price range). If the resale value of the "independent" cars continues to run true to form, the '54 Commander's value will be reasonably high if you trade it on another Studebaker, not so high on other makes. Its open-market resale value is one of the highest among the independent makes.

The Commander Regal sedan, styled ahead of its time, is a lively car, a pleasure to drive, and because it lacks faults common to many cars, it's a big reason why the medium price class is one of the most competitive of all.

1954 STUDEBAKER COMMANDER (with Overdrive)

THE STORY IN FIGURES

'ERFORMANCE

HASSIS DYNAMOMETER TEST

Checked on Clayton Mfg. Co.'s chassis dynamome- er; all tests are made under full load, which is imilar to climbing a hill at full throttle)

RPM	MPH	ROAD HP
1200	24	33
2000	40	55
2500	50	65
3100	62	75 (maximum obtainable under any conditions)

CCELERATION

n seconds; checked with fifth wheel and electric eedometer)

anding start 1/4-mile (59 mph; 1st, 2nd, 3rd)	20.6
30 mph (32, car speedometer; 1st, 2nd, 3rd)	4.9
60 mph (64, car speedometer; 1st, 2nd, 3rd)	17.2
10-30 mph (2nd gear)	5.0
30-50 mph (3rd)	8.1
50-80 mph (3rd)	18.9

)P SPEED

miles per hour; clocked speeds over surveyed -mile)

Fastest one-way run	94.34
Slowest one-way run	91.18
Average of four runs	93.00

EL CONSUMPTION

miles per gallon; checked with fuel flowmeter, h wheel, and electric speedometer)

	Conventional	Overdrive
Steady 30 mph	20.2	24.4
Steady 45 mph	18.0	22.6
Steady 60 mph		19.3
Steady 75 mph		15.1
imulated traffic over measured course		16.0
tal mileage driven d overall average for entire test		812 miles @ 16.0

AKE STOPPING DISTANCE

the nearest foot; checked with electrically ac- ted detonator)

30 mph	41
45 mph	94
60 mph	159

ENERAL SPECIFICATIONS

GINE

Type	V-8, ohv
Bore & stroke	3 3/8 x 3 1/4
Stroke/bore ratio	0.96:1
Compression ratio	7.5:1
Displacement	233 cu. in.
Advertised bhp	120 @ 4000 rpm
Bhp per cu. in.	.516
Piston travel @ max. bhp	2170 ft. per min.
Maximum torque	190 lbs.-ft. @ 2000 rpm
Maximum bmep	123.2 psi

DRIVE SYSTEM

Standard transmission	Three-speed synchromesh using helical gears
Ratios	1st 2.57, 2nd 1.55, 3rd 1.00, reverse 3.48
Automatic transmission	Studebaker Automatic Drive, torque converter with planetary gears
Ratios	Low 2.31, drive 1.43 and 1.00 (direct drive with converter locked out): reverse 2.00; maximum converter ratio, 2.15 @ 1650 rpm
Overdrive transmission	Planetary type with manual lockout and accelerator downshift
Ratio	0.7:1 (overall 2.98)
Rear axle ratios	Conventional 4.09; Automatic 3.54; Overdrive 4.27 standard, 4.55 optional

DIMENSIONS

Wheelbase	116 1/2 in.
Tread	Front 56 11/16 in, rear 55 11/16 in.
Wheelbase/tread ratio	2.1:1
Overall width	71 in.
Overall length	198 5/8 in.
Overall height	60 in.
Turning diameter	38 1/2 ft.
Turns lock to lock	5 1/4 Ross, 4 1/4 Saginaw
Curb weight	3380 lbs. (factory shipping wt. 3120 lbs.)
Weight/bhp ratio	26.0:1
Weight distribution	Front 57.1%, rear 42.9%
Tire size	7.10 x 15
Tire loading	Front 90.6%, rear 68.5%

DEPRECIATION

Percentage of original value retained by similar previous models at time of publication

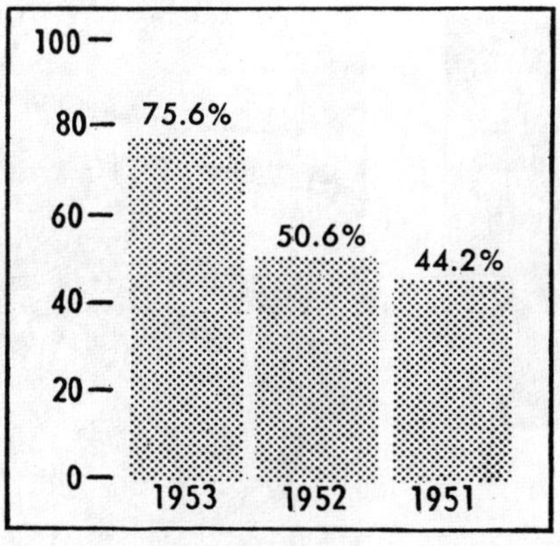

100
80
60
40
20
0
75.6%
50.6%
44.2%
1953
1952
1951

PRICES

(Including retail price at main factory, federal tax, and delivery and handling charges, but not freight)

	Deluxe	Regal	Land Cruiser
Four-door sedan	$2149	$2257	$2408
Two-door sedan	2106		
Club coupe	2203	2311	
Hardtop		2472	
Station wagon	2418	2526	

ACCESSORIES

Automatic Drive	$226
Overdrive	118
Power steering	177
Hill Holder	Standard
Radio 6-tube	76
8-tube	99
Heater	69
Direction signals	27
White sidewall tires (additional cost per set, 7.10 x 15)	30

ESTIMATED COST PER MILE

(The Estimated Cost per Mile is given for comparative purposes and is not intended as a guide to the cost of operating a particular make or car within that make. To provide this comparison, Motor Trend has selected the following maintenance items for each car tested, regardless of whether or not the car would actually require them during the first year of operation)

Cost of year's gasoline (based on overall mileage of test car)	$174.76
Cost of insurance (Includes: $50,000 and $100,000 bodily injury liability, $5000 property damage, $500 medical payments, comprehensive, $50-deductible collision)	141.40
Maintenance: Wheel alignment	6.00
Brake reline (front only)	14.48
Automatic transmission (adjust, change lubricant)	12.95
Major tuneup (Labor only; includes: clean and adjust or renew points and plugs, tighten cylinder head and manifolds, clean and adjust choke and carburetor, clean aircleaner, fuel bowl and adjust valves)	10.80
First year operating cost per mile (based on 10,000-mile annual average)	3.6c

COST OF PARTS AND LABOR

(These are prices for parts and labor required in various repairs and replacements, provided for a comparison of prices for these sample operations in various makes)

	Parts	Labor
Distributor	$ 21.50	$ 2.00
Battery	19.85	
Fuel pump	6.50	1.60
Valve grind	5.40	43.60
One front fender	38.50	22.50
Bumper	49.26	3.50
Two tires	52.46	
TOTALS	$193.47	$73.20

1954 U.S. STUDEBAKER HERE

MAJOR modification to the Studebaker for 1954 is improved braking and braking adjustment. Dominion Motors, the distributors, said that dollar restrictions meant that only one model could be imported, the 6-cylinder, side-valve, 4-door Champion sedan.

Studebaker also make V-8 engined cars.

Models for Australia have overdrive and hill-holder as standard equipment. The hill holder is an automatic brake which prevents the car rolling back when stopped in traffic on a grade.

Styling has been revised. Overall height is only five feet and the overall length is 16 ft. 6 ins. Power plant is a 6-cylinder s.v. unit developing 85 b.h.p. at 4,000 r.p.m., with bore and stroke of 76.2 x 101.6 mm. and capacity at 2,780 c.c. Top gear ratio is 4.1, with steering-column shift. Turning circle is 39', dry weight 25 cwt., and gearing per 1,000 r.p.m. is 18.9 m.p.h. At 2.500 ft./min. the car is doing 71 m.p.h. Brake lining area is good at 121. sq. in.

Above: Interior styling is very tasteful. Luggage space is engulfing (below). At right: The front compartment, with steering-column gearshift.

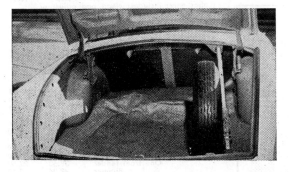

THE CONESTOGA

ADDITION of a new all-steel station wagon—bringing the number of body styles to 20—larger brakes, higher compression ratio and redesigned grilles and bumper guards are features of the new 1954 Studebaker models.

The new pleasure-utility car is named the Conestoga—in memory of the original Conestoga wagon in which the founding brothers of Studebaker traveled to South Bend, Ind. from Ohio more than 100 years ago.

Other types are two- and four-door sedans, hardtop convertibles, coupes and the Land Cruiser.

Exterior lines have been enhanced by further refinements. Interior styling is the work of Eleanor Le Maire, decorating expert and color stylist.

Upholstery fabrics are offered in four different basic color motifs that harmonize with exterior hues. Items such as steering wheels, steering wheel columns, instrument panels, moulding, door trim and carpeting likewise harmonize with exterior colors. There are 12 different solid color options and 10 different two-tone combinations.

Other interior features include new instrument clusters, removable center arm rests for the rear seats of hardtop convertibles and coupes, and dome lights which completely light up the interiors.

The Conestoga accommodates six passengers. When used as a utility car,

with the rear seat folded down, an area of 64 cubic feet is available for baggage or haulage purposes. The car has a wheelbase of 116½", is 195⅝" in overall length, 69¾" in width, and 62⅜" in height when loaded.

Exterior body changes for '54 models include new grilles with vertical fins; bumper guards which provide increased protection for grilles; new hood ornaments as standard equipment on station wagons and on all sedans with the exception of the custom Champion. Chrome "rub rails" extending on either side of the car from a point near the tail light to the forward edge of the front door are standard on all regal sedans and Land Cruiser models.

Tinted glass, which reduces eye strain by decreasing glare and which cuts heat by filtering out some 65 per cent of the sun's heat rays, is available on all models at slight extra cost. Hydraulic power steering is likewise optional on all models at extra cost.

Stainless steel window mouldings are standard on all '54 Deluxe models. Die cast chrome mouldings are used on all Regal models.

Foremost among the chassis improvements are new and larger brakes for both Champions and Commanders. These, according to intensive engineering tests, provide up to one-third greater braking power for a given effort by the driver and thus adds substantially to driving safety. Front brakes on the

Champion have been increased in diameter from 9" to 10". Front brakes on Commanders have been increased in width by a full quarter inch for increased effectiveness and Commander rear brakes boosted in diameter to 10".

The new brakes are self-centering and self-energizing and have, in addition to greater stopping power, increased pedal reserve, heavier drums, more durable brake lining, and labyrinth-type drum seals which keep out dirt and mud. Studebaker engineers say maintenance will be much simpler since only one adjustment per wheel will be required during either periodic or relining adjustments.

Acceleration and performance have been stepped up on both the Champion and the Commander as a result of a 7.5 to 1 compression ratio in the power plants of both cars. Automatic transmissions on Champions now have three power ranges in "Drive" position: automatic low, intermediate, and direct. The automatic low gear start makes possible much greater acceleration at low traffic speeds.

New radiator cores and changes in the design and pitch of the fans assure adequate cooling even under prolonged high temperatures. New clutch linkage on cars equipped with conventional or overdrive transmission make possible lower pedal pressure. Riding qualities of all cars have been further increased by changes in the valving of shock absorbers. ★

*Comparison of coupe body to sedan is shown
by overlay of color outline on photo of sedan*

'54 Studebaker

The "little" Stude that really isn't little at all rates higher in two factors, and lower in a third, than any other U.S. car

By Pete Molson

THE INDUSTRY'S most unusual engine-chassis-body choice was one feature of Studebaker's introduction of its new models last year. There are two basic frames: a 116½-inch wheelbase job that takes all the sedans except the deluxe Land Cruiser, and the 120½-inch base that holds that luxury model and also every Stude coupe, Champion or Commander, fancy or plain. The confusion this has created, with the "little" models being demonstrably bigger than the "big" ones, is something we needn't go into here; but there are some curious corollaries, one of which is that Stude's closest approximation to the perfect 50-50 weight distribution is a Champion coupe, with its light engine. (It is, by the way, a lot closer to this ideal than most cars.) It handles best of all the good-handling Studes.

Where does this leave you if you incline toward South Bend's pride? It means simply that you can have the body style of your choice with whichever engine you want. The chassis are almost identical (the Commander has more brake lining to compensate for its heavier powerplant) and the bodies differ only slightly this year in trim details. So, aside from prestige, performance will be the sole benefit from the $260 premium you'll have to pay for the V8 engine in an otherwise comparable model. The Champion has never pretended to be a hot performer; yet even when you know this, it's hard to step from the eight to the six without a feeling of regret. What was once a suf-

ficiency of power can seem weak in 1954 (and is, for this car's acceleration trails that of all other U.S. makes). The only speeds at which this can objectively be called a serious drawback are the critical highway passing ranges, when the Champion lacks that response that can jump you around another car in a hurry.

There aren't many cars anywhere in the world that are fun to bring to a panic stop from 60 mph. Perhaps it's even stretching a point to say that it's fun in a Stude Champion, but we have never driven a car with such enviable aplomb in this situation of simulated danger. The test car just sat down on its haunches and stopped, in a straight line, and faster than any other U.S. car.

This has been a banner year for brakes. Improvement has been industry-wide, and as the year's testing draws to a close it is a rare car that hasn't beaten the '53 average stopping distance for all cars, let alone its own. As the scores stand now, the two top cars are remarkably close: The Stude showed an average (from 60, 45, and 30 mph) of 91 feet, four inches; the Nash Rambler four-door sedan (it has bigger brakes than the smaller models) lagged only four inches behind.

Brake and clutch pedals on non-automatic-drive Studebakers remain to the left of the steering post. The excellent big right-or-left-foot pedal of the automatic models is due to lend some of its size to the '55 cars with conventional or overdrive transmissions; the change may be

one that owners of '53s and '54s can adapt to their cars without much fuss.

Fuel economy, justifiably a top selling point for Studebakers even when they don't win the Mobilgas Economy Run Sweepstakes, as they did this year, is another top Champion virtue. Last year's test Champion was a duplicate of the model we had this year, in equipment, in rear axle ratio, in transmission, and even in its 7.5 to 1 cylinder head, which was then optional but is now standard. For this reason, MT Research did not run its complete series of fuel checks on the '54 car, since they could have revealed nothing but a change in weather conditions or the existence of an obscure variation in assembly. As regular readers of MT will recall, the Champion was our 1953 economy winner by a margin of nearly three mpg over its nearest competitor, the Henry J Six. Its average in MT's tests was 28.1 mpg, with a fantastic top of 36.2 mpg at 30 mph in overdrive.

MT's testers accumulated such a collection of minor bruises and bumps while working with the test car that we wondered whether Raymond Loewy's famous corps of designers had worked on the interior. Among the awkward arrangements were the long-throw shift lever, which is also too short to let your wrist clear the wheel; the sharp-edged window crank and handbrake lever; and the top rear edge of the front door (when you open it from outside, it takes a swing at your chin or chest, depending on your height). Indus-

TEST CAR AT A GLANCE—'54 STUDEBAKER CHAMPION with Overdrive

REAR WHEEL HORSEPOWER

(Determined on Clayton chassis dynamometer; all tests are made under full load, which is similar to climbing a hill at full throttle. Observed hp figures not corrected to standard atmospheric conditions)
22 road hp @ 1200 rpm and 21 mph
32 road hp @ 2000 rpm and 35 mph
37 road hp @ 2500 rpm and 43 mph
41 road hp (max.) @ 3050 rpm and 53 mph

(In acceleration and fuel economy, the car is rated against the average of cars in its own class. All other items are rated against average of all '53 test cars)

ACCELERATION

(In seconds; checked with fifth wheel and electric speedometer)
Standing start ¼-mile (reached 60.4 mph) 22.7, 0-30 6.3, 0-60 21.7, 10-30 8.6, 30-50 10.0, 50-80 43.7
RATING: FAIR

FUEL CONSUMPTION

(In miles per gallon; checked with fuel flowmeter, fifth wheel, and electric speedometer. Mobilgas Regular used)
Conventional:
30.3 @ steady 30 mph, 24.2 @ steady 45
Overdrive:
36.2 @ steady 30 mph, 31.2 @ steady 45, 24.9 @ steady 60, 19.9 @ steady 75, 20.0 in simulated traffic over measured course
RATING: EXCELLENT

TOP SPEED

(In miles per hour; clocked over surveyed ¼-mile)
Fastest run 86.20, slowest 84.50, average 85.59

SPEEDOMETER ERROR

Car speedometer read 34 @ true 30 mph, 50 @ true 45 mph, 67 @ true 60 mph

STOPPING DISTANCE

(To the nearest foot; checked with electrically actuated detonator)
38 @ 30 mph, 87 @ 45 mph, 150 @ 60
RATING: EXCELLENT

Champion

GENERAL SPECIFICATIONS

ENGINE: L-head, six cylinder. Bore 3 in. Stroke 4 in. Stroke/bore ratio 1 33:1. Compression ratio 7.0 to 1. Displacement 169.6 cu. in. Advertised bhp 85 @ 4000 rpm. Bhp per cu. in. .501. Piston travel @ max. bhp 2666 ft. per min. Max bmep 122.8 psi. Max. torque 138 @ 2400 rpm.

DRIVE SYSTEM: STANDARD transmission is three-speed synchromesh using helical gears. RATIOS: 1st 2.60, 2nd 1.63, 3rd 1.0, reverse 3.53. AUTOMATIC transmission is three-element torque converter with planetary gears. RATIOS: Drive, 2.31 x converter ratio, 1.43 x converter ratio, 1.0 direct drive; Low, 2.31 x converter ratio; Reverse, 2.0 x converter ratio. Converter ratio at stall 2.15 @ 1600 rpm. OVERDRIVE transmission is standard shift with planetary gearset.

REAR AXLE RATIOS: Conventional 4.10, Automatic 4.10, Overdrive 4.56 (Custom series 4.27).

DIMENSIONS: Wheelbase 116½ in. Tread 56½ front, 55½ rear. Wheelbase/tread ratio 2.08:1. Overall width 69.5 in. Overall length 198½ in. Overall height (empty) 60½ in. Turning diameter 41 ft. Turns lock to lock 4. Test car weight 2980 lbs. Test car weight/bhp ratio 35.0. Weight distribution 53.6% front, 46.4% rear. Tire size 6.40 x 15.

PRICES

(Including suggested retail price at main factory, federal tax, and delivery and handling charges, but not freight) CHAMPION CUSTOM, four-door sedan $1801, two-door sedan $1758, CHAMPION DELUXE, four-door sedan $1758, two-door sedan $1875, five-passenger coupe $1972, station wagon $2187. CHAMPION REGAL, four-door sedan $2026, two-door sedan $1983, five-passenger coupe $2080, hardtop $2241, station wagon $2295.

ACCESSORIES: Automatic Drive $216, overdrive $105, power steering $177, six-tube radio $64, eight-tube radio $86, heater $66, white sidewall tires (additional cost per set) 6.40 x 15, $25.

PARTS AND LABOR COSTS

(These are prices for parts and labor required in various repairs and replacements. Your car may require all of them in a short time, or it may require none. However, a comparison of prices for these sample operations in various makes is often of interest to prospective owners. First price is for parts, second for labor.)

Distributor $19.00, $2.00; battery $20.95; fuel pump $5.38, $2.00; valve grind $2.47, $38.00; one front fender $42.00, $18.00; bumper $49.26, $3.50; two tires $44.00; Total parts $183.06, labor $64.20.

ESTIMATED COST PER MILE

(The Estimated Cost per Mile is given for comparative purposes and is intended only as a guide to the cost of operating a particular car. To provide this comparison, Motor Trend has taken into consideration all factors affecting operating costs and ownership costs. All figures given are the average costs nationally. For complete explanation of our method of determining the various figures, see "What It Really Costs to Operate Your Car" in July '54 MT)

OPERATING COSTS:

Gasoline	$109.00
Oil	9.90
Lubrication	16.50
Oil filter	3.60
Wheel alignment and balancing	11.60
Brake relining and adjustment	11.40
Major tune-up	9.60
WHAT IT COSTS PER MILE TO RUN	1.7¢

OWNERSHIP COSTS:

Sales tax and license fees	$ 60.93
Insurance	119.25
Estimated depreciation	678.00
WHAT IT COSTS PER MILE TO OWN	8.6¢
TOTAL PER MILE COSTS IF YOU PAY CASH	10.3¢
Finance charges	99.00
TOTAL PER MILE COSTS IF YOU FINANCE	11.3¢

trial designers, who can turn out such inspired work as this car's exterior with the aid of science, ought to use more of it in perfecting the homely details inside. Barked knuckles and sore arms are a poor sequel to the admiring look you would cast your new Stude before getting in.

In picking the new Stude that will suit you then, remember that very conservative performance accompanies the Champion's clean styling, fine brakes, and unequalled fuel economy. Don't take a Champion unless you're a calm, contented driver, with no aspirations to burn up the road. If you're the careful type, the long-stroke L-head will serve you well.

Further details on the Champion, which has changed little except in the ways described here, are in the September '53 MT

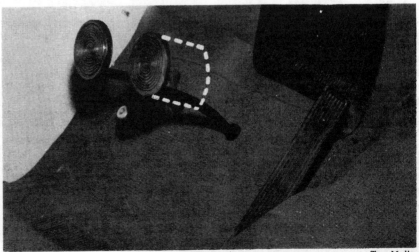

Tom Medley

Awkward pedal positioning will be relieved in '55 by use of larger brake pedal

Testing the 1955 Studebaker Commander

AIR CLEANER · DISTRIBUTOR · COIL · OIL FILLER CAP · OIL DIP STICK · FIBER GLASS HOOD INSULATION

By DON DINWIDDIE

THEY are building more than a car down in South Bend right now. They are reconstructing a few dreams that are not as old-fashioned as some people think—(1) that the smaller guy can keep up with the biggest guy in selling a good product, (2) if the men on the smaller fellow's team are determined to keep that product in competition. Of course, our job is not to tell you how much we admire the courage of both Studebaker's management and employees. Our job is to tell you how well their 1955 Commander is equipped to meet its competition, and the needs and desires of the car-buying public.

Studebaker's big news will be what they hope is a competitively priced car, which at this writing is slated to sell in the same price range as the Ford and Chevrolet—with the Champions priced to attract the low end of this price range, and the Commanders competing directly with Ford and Chevrolet's new V-8s. Specifically, Studebaker hopes that price reductions ranging from $37 to $287 per car

Rounding a curve at 60 mph, this Commander showed good ability to recover after leaving the road or making a sharp turn. For its weight, the car tracked well with a minimum of rear-end swerve even on rough roads.

The 1955 Commander's 140 horsepower power plant rates a real cheer from servicemen, appears to be easier to work on than most V-8 types. Note the oil filling pipe on top of the block, close to the front for easy filling. The air cleaner is turned over the right bank of cylinders uncovering the distributor. The accelerating pump has 3 steps for quick adjustment to climate and altitude variations. No detonation was audible at any speed using regular gas, indicating smooth performance and operating economy.

will put them in the thick of the red-hot battle being waged for the cream of the volume market. You want to keep this price picture in mind if you want to decide how effective a competitor the new Studebaker will be. We can't tell you.

TEST DATA

MAKE OF CAR: Studebaker Regal Deluxe Commander 4-Door Sedan

START OF TESTS: September 7, 1954

GENERAL ROAD CONDITIONS (for gas mileage and acceleration tests): 3 mile black top, curved, oval track with banked turns. Clear sunny days and dry roads with very light winds.

MILEAGE AT START OF TESTS: 10,814

MILES COVERED IN TESTS: 113

GAS USED: Regular Oil USED: 20W

CURB WEIGHT: 3270 lbs. 60% on front wheels, 40% on rear wheels

TIRE PRESSURES: 26 lbs. front; 22 lbs. rear for all tests.

SPARK SETTING: 8° BTC at break

GASOLINE MILEAGE (checked with fuel volume flow meter and 5th wheel. Temperature 78° F. Relative humidity 41. Barometer 29.25 in. Hg. Carried weight 504 lbs. Two runs made in opposite directions on black top, oval proving ground test track, using Drive gear of automatic transmission):

True Speed (5th Wheel)	Odometer Miles per Gallon	Ton Miles per Gallon (true)
20	22.9	23.4
30	21.0	43.1
40	21.5	39.6
50	19.6	36.2
70	15.0 (est.)	15.2 (est.)

OPTIMUM ECONOMY SPEED: 23.1 mpg true at 24 mph

TRAFFIC FUEL CONSUMPTION (simulated traffic pattern of city driving—stops, acceleration, braking. Carried weight 500 lbs.): True mpg 14.3. Odometer mpg 14.65. True ton mpg 27.0.

ACCELERATION (timed with 5th wheel. Carried weight 490 lbs. Temperature 80° F. Relative humidity 41. Barometer 29.25 in. Hg. Spark 8° BTC. Figures are average of two runs in opposite directions):

Gear Range	True MPH	MPH 5th Wheel	Average True Time (sec.)
Lo 0-20	5.3	3.0	
Lo 0-30	5.51		
Lo to 32 mph Then 2nd 0-40	8.60		
Lo to 32 mph Then 2nd 0-50	12.53		
Lo to 32 mph Then 2nd 0-60	17.40		
2nd 20-40			6.85
Downshift to 2nd 20-60			15.50
foot to floor start 20-80			36.0

Minimum time for 0-60 mph (true) over level road with no wind, best spark setting of 8° BTC, premium fuel and driver alone: 14.9 seconds.

ACCELERATION FACTORS (Temperature 80° F. Relative humidity 41. Barometer 22.55 in. Hg. Carried weight 490 lbs. Spark 8° BTC. Figures are average of two runs in opposite directions):

True Speed	Average True Time (sec.)	MPH Per Sec.	Ft. per Sec.
10		6.2	9.2
20		4.7	6.8
30		3.7	5.4
40		2.8	4.1
50		2.3	3.4
60		1.8	2.6
70		1.3	1.9
80		0.9	1.3

HILL CLIMBING (calculated from acceleration readings with allowances made for rotational inertia. Data same as preceding test):

Approx. MPH	Pull in lbs.	Grade in %
15	1190	35
40	530	14

TOP SPEED AND SPEEDOMETER-ODOMETER CORRECTION: Odometer distance 9.21 miles; true distance 9 miles; odometer error at 35 mph .21 (plus) or + 2.4%:

Speedometer Top Speed	True Speed est. 108*	% Error Speedometer	MPH Top Speed	True Speed	% Error Speedometer	Engine RPM	True Speed Speedometer RPM
100	100		50	43.5	11	4300	2000
90	82.3	8	40	35.5	12	3600	1600
80	73.1	9	30	26.7	12	2200	1200
70	63.3	10	20	18	10	900	800

*Top track test at wider minimum speed.

STOPPING ABILITY (Surface, level black top asphalt, clear and dry. Grade level. Surface temperature 75° F. Tires 6.70-15. Firestone 4 ply. Drag factor of road .68. Pedal pressure 100 lbs. on all stops):

SERVICE BRAKE PANIC STOP

ACTUAL SPEED	20	30

Distances: 43.1 · 19.5 · 83 · 33 · 46 (est.)

PANIC BRAKING stops from higher speeds not permitted on proving ground test track due to danger of locked brakes not releasing.

▨	Distance traveled during average driver's reaction time (¾ sec.)
▨	Brake lag: Distance covered between time brake pedal is depressed and wheels grip pavement
■	Brake distance: Distance covered between time wheels grip pavement and car comes to stop. Figure at end of bars indicates total stopping distances in ft. (sum of reaction, brake lag and braking distances)

BRAKE FADE TESTS: As indicated below, number of stops required to double pedal effort was 14.

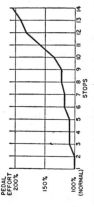

PEDAL EFFORT	STOPS
200%	
150%	
100% (NORMAL)	2 3 4 5 6 7 8 9 10 11 12 13 14

PARKING BRAKE TEST: Brake applied hard and suddenly from 20 mph actual speed.

Braking Distance	54 ft.

PERFORMANCE FACTORS
(Calculated)

HORSEPOWER AT REAR AXLE (values calculated from acceleration data with allowances made for efficiencies and rotational inertia):

MPH True	RPM Engine	Equiv. Engine Torque (lb. ft.)	Axle Horsepower
95	4350	117	92
68	3000	137	78
44	2000	153	58

Per cent of advertised engine horsepower supplied to rear wheels: 66%

MPH (true) at maximum advertised horsepower 104 and torque 63. Engine rpm at 60 mph (also revolutions per mile) 2670 rpm. Average piston speed at 60 mph (also, ft/mile) 1250 ft./min. Cu. ft. per minute of mixture at 60 mph (also, cu. ft./mile) 173. Maximum engine horsepower (adv.) per ton of car (curb weight) 85.6. Reciprocating load per ton of piston area, connecting rod, bore, stroke, connecting rod) 133. Reciprocating load factor at 60 mph .945. Maximum engine horsepower (adv.) per cubic inch displacement 0.625.

speed panic stops are not permitted on proving ground test tracks because of fatal instance in which the brakes have failed to release after the wheels lock), the results of a 19.5-ft. braking distance stop from 20 *mph* and a 46-ft. stop from 30 *mph* are pretty close to the figures registered by all the 1954 cars we tested. They are also well within the limits specified for safe braking distances by National Safety Council tests.

And while we are on the subject of brakes, let's try to straighten out a few misconceptions. You may recall that when we first started these *Science at the Wheel* tests, we reported braking action in terms of percentage efficiency—a measure popular with many British testers. Trouble with this form of an answer is that it implies a greater accuracy than it delivers, based as it is on a standard as fickle as Cassidy's constant, and subject to variables in such a way as to make it meaningless to an engineer. On our '54 tests, we tried a new approach in answering the car buyers' question—how quickly will the car stop? We added together the average driver's reaction time as determined by exhaustive tests (you can beat this, of course, by anticipating braking situations), the brake lag (the interval between the time the driver's foot hits the brake and the car's wheels grip the pavement), and the distance actually covered after the wheels grip the pavement until the car comes to a full stop. Add them all together and theoretically you come up with an answer that will tell the average driver whether or not he can stop his car before he hits that truck suddenly looming up ahead of him.

But, says engineering, the driver's reaction time varies with the driver and his ability to anticipate braking situations. Also the

the peaking speed of the engine.

By now, you may have already spotted the fact that this Commander's bore has been increased from 3⅜ to 3¹¹/₁₆ and its stroke decreased from 3¼ to 2¹³/₁₆—for a net *decrease* in displacement (232.6 to 224 cu. in.). In brief, she's quite a bit oversquare—an ideal design for the stylist who wants to keep down engine height and provide good over-the-hood driver vision Engineering-wise, an oversquare design allows a relatively short stroke with large displacement and thus reduced piston speed—which is a good thing for those who travel at 80 *mph*.

As trends go, Studebaker has been conservative about its horsepower claims and increases. Even with the 20 *hp* increase in 1955, they have still retained the same dual carburetor. It's an odds-on bet that some hot rodders will convert Commanders to 4-barrel carbs for doubly hot performance. Personally, if we were to do any converting, our aching bones and budget would lead us to try a dual range transmission and 3.09 rear axle ratio on this Commander—to secure the last ounce of fuel economy possible with this already economical car.

Speaking of economy, Studebaker has wisely gone to better materials and increased dimensions on their valve lifters, which should cut down the owner's servicing costs and problems. Lifters, as you know, can bring pesky headaches with modern hi-compression engines. Also, that 945 reciprocating load factor at 60 *mph* indicates a relatively low degree of engine wear.

Although we reported on Studebaker's brake improvements last year, we didn't have the opportunity to run an actual performance test on them. This year's test indicates that these changes were effective improvements. On the only two panic stops we could complete (high

1955 STUDEBAKER COMMANDER SPECIFICATIONS

ENGINE: Overhead valve V-8; bore 3¹¹/₁₆; stroke 2¹³/₁₆; advertised maximum brake horsepower rated 140 at 4500 rpm (taxable horsepower 40.6); advertised maximum torque 202 ft. lbs., 136 psi at 2800 rpm, corrected to 60° F. and 29.92 in. Hg.; compression ratio 7.5 to 1 (may offer 8 to 1 on some models); piston displacement 224 cu. in.; fuel specified regular.

TRANSMISSION: Studebaker Automatic Drive (optional) with 3.54 rear axle ratio; (other rear axle ratios: 4.09 conventional; 4.27 overdrive).

STEERING: Turning circle 41 ft, curb to curb. Overall ratio 24-1. Torque to turn 22 ft. lb. static, 3-6 ft. lb. rolling.

EXTERIOR: Wheelbase 116.5 in.; overall length 202½ in.; overall width 69¼ in., overall height 60⅝ in.; curb weight 3270 lbs. (10 gal. fuel, oil and water); minimum road clearance 6⁵/₁₆ in. at extension pipe ahead of muffler.

INTERIOR: Headroom, front seat 36 in., rear seat 35; legroom, front seat 42½ in., rear seat 10¼ in.; hiproom, front seat 59½ in., rear seat 59 in.; total front seat adjustment at floor 4¹/₁₆ in. (5½ incl. second seat position).

VISIBILITY: Windshield area 918 sq. in.; rear window area 944 sq. in.; driver's eye to road over left front fender 24 ft. 8 in., over hood center 32 ft. 5 in., over right front fender 40 ft.

EQUIPMENT: Battery, Willard; 6 volt, 15 plate; 100 amp. hours, located under hood, left front; tires 6.70-15 4 ply; recommended pressure 26 lbs. front, 22 lbs. rear, cold; springing, front coil, rear leaf; frame, box section ladder type—5 cross members.

CAPACITIES: Fuel tank 18 gals.; crankcase 6 qts.; optional oil filter; cooling system 19 qts. with heater; differential 2.5-3 pts.; transmission 19 pts.; luggage comp't. dimensions 52 x 52 x 23 cu. ft. (less tire displ. and tools).

Brake pedal is not as wide as last year's, but it's still located so it can be used by either right or left foot. Gold plating around instrument panel produces softer reflections than chrome, but it's not glareproof, of course. Full circle horn rim may interfere with easy reading of the dials for some drivers, but Studebaker has eliminated the 1954 hoods over the dials and recessed them deeper to cut reflections and make reading easier and more adaptable to all sizes of drivers. The models you see may have a medallion and more chrome than our test car shows on its dashboard. Note new touch of elegance—a two-tone steering wheel.

The fifth wheel tests registered a 2.4% plus error on the odometer and 12% error on the speedometer—slightly higher than last year's average.

how it stacks up against the competition's '55 models, because we haven't been able to test them yet. But, appropriately enough, the test figures show that the Commander could give a licking to the '54 models of the three major cars in 1955—Studebaker expects it to compete with in 1955—on fuel economy, acceleration, hill climbing and top speed. And we've a notion that their fuel economy, for which Studebaker is justly praised, will still stand high when all the '55 figures are in.

With an automatic transmission, the 1955 Studebaker Regal DeLuxe Commander registered its best fuel economy of 23.1 true miles per gallon (23.6 by the odometer) at 24 *mph*, and 14.3 true *mpg* over the city traffic pattern test. This places it well above its size-and-price competition and right near the top when compared with the eleven 1954 cars we have tested (next year's may be a different story, of course).

Nor was this Commander a slouch when it comes to acceleration tests from a standing start. It shaved quite a few seconds off the times registered by other 1954 cars in its size and price range. Of course, it is no match for the giant horsepower luxury wagons on either 'acceleration or top speed, but then it isn't intended to be.

The V-8 engine that produces these performance figures has been upped in horsepower rating from 120 to 140 for 1955, and it is interesting to speculate on just where those 20 extra horses came from. First we find that Studebaker's engine, like others, has gone in for the popular deep breathing exercises—by redesigning and enlarging the inlet and exhaust manifolds and valves, and increasing the exhaust pipe diameter to 2 inches, thereby doing a good job of reducing fluid friction. This allows a greater weight of air to be drawn into the cylinders when the throttle is opened, increasing what the engineers call volumetric efficiency (why don't they call it by a more accurate name—*weight inducted efficiency?*)

These changes in the flow passages' design raise the peaking speed from 4,000 to 4,500 *rpm*, so that if no greater weight of air were inducted than before, you would automatically have a horsepower increase of: 120 (1954's rating)

$$\frac{4500}{4000} = 135 \ hp.$$ Hence the 20 *hp* increase claimed (with no change in valve timing) could be obtained by a 5 *hp* gain from the greater weight of air inducted on the 1955 model (better breathing) and a 15 *hp* gain from the 500 *rpm* increase in

Drivers' Observations

ROADABILITY: Stability and tracking qualities good with little road wander. For its weight, a nice riding car. Whips on and off the road with good recovery and control and handles very well on rough roads. Engine noise and detonation is cut way down for less fatigue on long drives.

DRIVING COMFORT: Driver vision good all around—excellent over hood. Rear view mirror could be a mite deeper. Recessed and unhooded instrument dials easier for tall folks to read. Gold plate on dash panel produces softer reflections than chrome, but still glares at times. Ash tray and lighter have been moved closer to the driver for greater convenience. Nearly vertical backs on the front seats give good back support. Plenty of leg room front and back though knee of tall driver may strike steering column. Window and door handles operate easily, but catch on vent window opening can still trap your finger. Three-spoke steering wheel can be raised or lowered slightly by removable shims.

INSTRUMENTS AND CONTROLS: Ignition key starting. Automatic transmission operates smoothly. Clear, unobstructed view of gear quadrant, and green dot light behind shift positions makes it easy to tell where to shift at night. Full circle horn rim, a tall driver's view of the instruments. All switches on the dash, easily reached from the driver's position on the dash. Extra-wide brake pedal of past models has been narrowed and there is no interference with left foot's operation of dimmer switch.

SPECIAL COMMENTS: For children's safety, back doors can be locked by pushing down button and then closing without holding a release in or down, and you can't open rear door from inside or outside as long as the button is down—a very good feature. On the front door, you must either lock with a key or push down buttons from the inside as usual. Excellent design makes generator, voltage regulator, dipstick, oil filter and filling pipe, coil, air cleaner and distributor very easy to service. See they have a 12 instead of 7 pound pressure cap on this year's radiator. Also production engines will get a paint job—a blue block and aluminium painted valve covers and air cleaners. Cast iron camshaft and hardened lifters. More sound absorbing insulation this year. Stainless steel trim seems to show fingerprint and fingernail marks more than it should.

measurement of brake lag depends on the point during the depressing of the brake pedal at which you start to measure, how you can make that measurement without any loss of time that would be falsely charged against brake lag, and how you determine exactly when the wheels start to grip the road surface, to find out when brake lag ends and car skid begins. Finally, the distance the car will skid before coming to a full stop is determined by that rascal known as the *coefficient of friction* between the car's wheels and the road surface (another variable), and this in turn varies even with such supposedly innocent factors as relative humidity. As for the effect of road surface, here's one example. Tests have shown that it will take a car as much as 20 more feet to stop from 40 *mph* on old, dry concrete than on newly laid dry concrete.

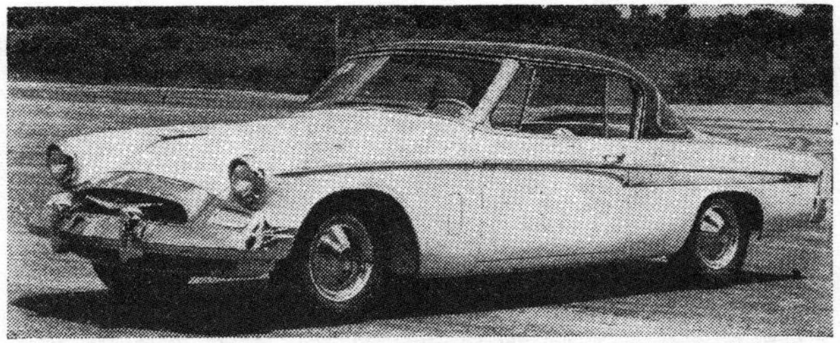

Here is the two-door cousin to the Commander we tested. Lack of fender pants means you'll be able to get at wheels easily, though tubeless tires on all models should reduce roadside tire changing.

Had enough? Now you know why engineers argue with each other over brake testing till the cows come home. For, of all eleven 1954 cars we have tested, the widest variations in stopping distances on the same type road surface ranged from four feet on stops made from 20 *mph* to 17 feet on 50 *mph* stops. As any engineer worth his salt will tell you, the variations imposed by the measuring devices available, plus those created by different weather conditions, make these figures relatively meaningless as a measure of a car's stopping ability.

More to the point and easier to measure accurately is the brake fade test, which gives you a good indication of the ability of the car's brakes to stand up under hard usage. We've added these fade tests to the *Science at the Wheel* chart, and we hope to bring you the same information on all of the 1955 models we test. Under this severe test, the Studebaker Commander showed good brakes. It took 14 successive stops to a little more than double the pedal pressure required, and no serious fading was evident.

The brake loading factor in the 1955 Studie Commander (that is, its pound curb weight per square inch with 195.3 inch brake lining) is an excellent 16.7. Incidentally, they have lowered their high brake pedal to 4 inches from the floor, which should reduce braking reaction time a bit and lessen the chance of catching your foot under it. It also isn't as wide as last year's pedal, which some drivers found a bit awkward. Its location is still somewhat to the left of the steering column, which is fine if you like to do some braking with the left foot (rarely necessary with Studebaker's fine hill-holder transmission feature).

As a purely subjective observation, without rear seat passengers this Commander seemed nose-heavy enough to probably cause some troublesome braking at high speeds. Its 60% front wheel-40% back wheel weight distribution might account for this feeling—but such nose-heavy weight distribution has been more of a trend than an exception on many modern cars.

Our test car rated well on the usual test driver observations—as a good road holder on curves, rough roads, and off-and-on the straightaway shoulders with no rear end swerve. (Sorry we couldn't give it our regular tilt angle test, but the conditions under which we run this could not be duplicated at the proving ground test track). As a hill climber, this car proved to be an eager performer. Vibration and shock seemed a little less noticeable than the average, and the engine, nestling under a fiber glass liner this year, was quiet.

On the theory that it was setting the style with its long, low and sporty look of recent years, Studebaker is showing the courage of its convictions by sticking to the same basic style for 1955, with minor changes in front end grill, rub rail, hood ornaments, and windshield moldings. Note that we didn't call these chrome, because they aren't; they're stainless steel, which won't chip and flake on you. Interiors have been pepped up even more than in 1954 with decorative (and washable) fabrics, and the chrome promoters left the dashboard we inspected pretty much alone. But don't count on that clean, unchromed right hand side of the dash on the models you will look at. The engineers may have to bow to the dealers and add some glare-producing medallions and such, because the dealers believe such gimcrackery is what sells cars.

We prefer to think it's a matter of good performance—and price. Studebaker has had the former for many years and is hoping that—come '55—its price will also be right.—END

Did You Miss a 1954 Test?

If you have missed the 1954 tests covering the Oldsmobile 88 and Super 88, appearing in our October, 1954 issue; the Chevrolet Station Wagon and Cadillac Series 62, appearing in our August, 1954 issue; the Ford V-8, Buick Century, Mercury Monterey and Packard Patrician, appearing in June, 1954; the Plymouth Belvedere and Chrysler New Yorker De Luxe, appearing in April, 1954; or the Nash Rambler, appearing in February, 1954, send 25¢ for each issue you want. Address requests for back issues to SCIENCE AND MECHANICS, 450 East Ohio Street, Chicago 11, Ill.

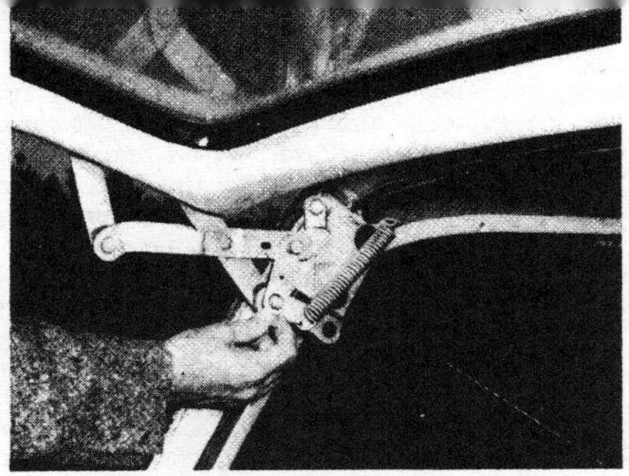

SPRING partly counterbalances weight of rear window. If you want to drive with it up (in hot weather, a wagon is almost as breezy as a convertible), snap this link over a pin to lock it up. But don't forget to unsnap link before closing window or you'll bend bracket.

CONTINUED FROM PAGE 58

the new springs have the same rate as the old ones, and the same easy ride. But when you pile the pounds on the tail gate, she won't squat down like a depressed rabbit.

New shock valving. Having jiggered the springs this way, Studebaker changed the valving on the rear shocks so they'd have a matching damping characteristic. Connie rides well, without that trundling little jowl-shake some wagons have.

Axle and tire options. A Conestoga buyer will have a chance to tailor it to suit his country and his expected service. Depending on the engine he elects (six or V-8), on his transmission (automatic or manual with or without overdrive), and whether or not he lives in a hilly country or wants economy or performance, he may get one of a half-dozen rear-axle ratios. These range from 3.54 to 4.88. If he expects to be lugging heavy loads, larger, extra-ply tires will be fitted.

Other '54 changes. Aside from Connie the rest of the line stays close to '53. There is a new front grille with vertical fins, and bumper guards have been redesigned to overcome an annoying tendency to underride and lock onto other cars. The armrest in the rear of the swanky hard-top coupe has been made removable—not that you can now seat a passenger in the middle, where his tail bone would still clunk inelastically on the drive-shaft tunnel—but a youngster can now stretch out across the rear seat.

Better brakes. The best mechanical news for 1954 is that they've beefed up the brakes. The previous ones got by, but they were hardly distinguished performers. The new ones are bigger, have self-centering brake-shoe pivots, and deliver far better stopping performance.

In the engine department, Studebaker's OHV V-8 has gone from 7.1 compression to 7.5, which was an option last year. This boosts output around two percent, to about 122 or 123 hp. Octane requirements increase slightly, though the engine is still contented with regular gas. (Studebaker doesn't plan to blow any bugles on this power rise.) Other changes under the hood are minor: new linkage to prevent throttle movement on hard turns or panic stops, and a bit more copper in the V-8 radiator.

FACTS ON '54 STUDEBAKER

Model: Commander Regal Station Wagon.

Engine: 90° V-8; 120 hp. at 4,000 r.p.m.; compression ratio, 7.5:1; piston displacement, 232.6 cu. in.; piston travel (in feet per car mile at 20 m.p.h.), 1,637; bore and stroke, 3⅜" by 3¼"; torque, 190 lb.-ft. at 2,000 r.p.m.

Weight: 3,368 lb.; per hp. 28.07 lb.

Transmission: standard, manual shift (overdrive and automatic available); rear-axle ratio, 4.09 with standard transmission, 4.27 with overdrive, 3.54 with automatic.

Steering ratio: 33.8-24-33.8 (over-all); radius of turning circle, left, 19¾'; right, 19¼'.

Effective brake-lining area: 173.4 sq. in.

Springs: front, coil; rear, 6 semi-elliptic leaves, 2½" by 50".

Outside dimensions: height, 62⅜" (loaded); over-all length with bumpers and guards, 195 19/32"; width, 69¾"; wheelbase, 116½"; overhang, front 35 3/16", rear 43 15/16"; tread, front 56½", rear 55½".

Inside dimensions: seat-cushion width, front 59½", rear 59"; leg room, front 42⅞", rear 41½"; headroom, front 38", rear 36"; seat height, front 14¼", rear 14½"; vertical distance, steering wheel to seat cushion, with seat in rear position, 5⅜"; front-seat adjustment, horizontal 5½", vertical 15/16".

Tire size: 7.10 by 15.

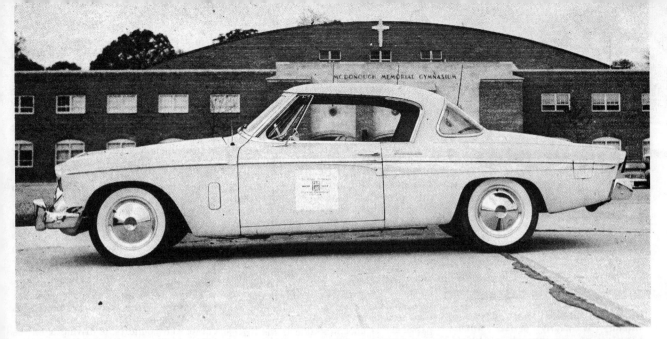

The 'President' looks right for a high performance car, but sports too much chrome on the front end, thereby spoiling, to some degree, its aesthetic lines. But its trim body draws appreciative glances wherever the 1955 model is parked.

Behind the Wheel

It's an axiom that if a high-performance car *looks* all right, its usually *is* all right, and the Studebaker 'President' looks right from the start

By G. M. LIGHTOWLER

AS THE Studebaker-Packard Corporation was the first to introduce its new 1955 cars, we decided to road test one of its products first. For this curtain raiser we selected the latest model, the 'President' V-8 engined, hardtop convertible.

As it was not our intention to test the car from too technical an angle, we did not concentrate on obtaining a mass of accurate performance figures, but rather relied on the impressions of several persons whom we considered could be potential purchasers. We did no more with the car than an owner would do under normal conditions, or what he might have to do in the case of an emergency.

Briefly, we were very favorably impressed, and for those discriminating enough to want a domestically manufactured, sporty sedan with a high performance, the 1955 Studebaker 'President' is the answer to date.

It has always been accepted by authorities on high-performance cars that

The interior is nothing short of luxurious with fine fittings and carefully blended color combinations. The instrument design and placing is not too good, however, and the steering wheel grips lead to wrong hand positioning.

From the driver's seat, all around visibility is nearly perfect without adoption of wraparound windshield.

if a car *looks* right there is every probability that it *is* right, and if it looks wrong it is most probably a dangerous machine.

The 'President' looks right for a high-performance car from the very first glance. It sits on the road in a very purposeful manner, indicating its good road-holding characteristics. Its lines show that it has been very carefully designed with consideration to streamlining and drag reduction. The only aesthetic distraction to the well-proportioned body is the somewhat lavish use of chrome in the front, which looks like a nose bag (an innovation on all the 1955 Studebakers), and the 'butter-knife' trim on the side of most of the latest models. The trim on the top of the fenders could also be dispensed with as it serves neither a utilitarian nor a decorative purpose. If this tendency to add more and more shiny metal continues it is likely to become mandatory for automobile manufacturers to get into the chrome-cleaner business, for it is very difficult to find a cleaner that does a good and lasting job on the gleaming metal.

The car we tested was painted a very attractive lemon-yellow and caught the appreciative eye of many pedestrians at the traffic lights, as well as bringing complimentary remarks from fellow motorists as we drew up beside them. The interior of the car was nothing short of luxurious, with very carefully color-blended seat covers of green vynil and door and side coverings of the same material; the roof was encased in a white washable plastic material of pleasant texture; floor coverings were of light green nylon woven material that should wear very well. A new feature of the '55 State Coupe is the arm rest between the rear seats, which can now be raised or lowered at will. Seating three in the back is now no longer a problem.

The front seat has been raised slightly and the width increased. This has improved a driving position that was already good, and it would be difficult

to find another car that offers the driver a better position from which to control the car—and we would include European cars in this statement. In earlier models, fatigue was experienced on long trips due to the lack of support beneath the knees, but this fault has been eliminated in the '55 'President.'

The back seat, however, is still cramped, particularly if the driver is long limbed and has the front seat pushed well back. We do not consider this a serious fault since the purchaser of one of these cars will not be taking along four passengers too often—this is a car for the discriminating driver and his wife and children, not for the general ferrying of the neighborhood.

It would be nice if Studebaker would make available, at extra cost, optional bucket-type seats with individual adjustments. The front seat is not suitable for three persons due to the hump of the transmission housing; also a long-legged passenger is uncomfortable if the driver is short of stature, the bench-type seat having to be drawn so far forward that the passenger is unable to stretch his (or her) legs. Bucket seats would obviate this condition.

We were not impressed by the new arrangement of the instruments, nor their design. The attempt to make the speedometer look like a rev counter has not come off, and the chromium, jet teardrops hanging in the center of the speedometer and the clustered gauges are distractions. The imitation gold finish surrounding the instrument panel is an addition that cheapens the appearance, and is not a good background for dials that have to be continually studied. The clock, which is positioned well to the right, has a very small face and is quite undecipherable from the driver's seat.

Light switches, climatizer controls, radio knobs and traffic indicator arm are all well positioned and within easy reach of the driver. Although it is bad practice to encourage the driver to smoke, he will nonetheless, and the provision of an ashtray would prevent him from flicking ashes out of the window and spraying the back-seat travelers if they have their windows lowered.

The adoption of the ignition switch-and-starter is good, and a convenient change from the starter button that was beneath the clutch pedal—a system that was good in concept but somewhat poor in operation.

The positioning of the brake pedal is definitely bad. When we returned our test car to the dealer we noticed a considerable number of scuff marks on the lower end of the steering column cover. On practically every occasion when the brake was applied in a hurry, the toe of the right foot came into violent contact with the column. If the pedal was sited a little lower this would be eliminated.

The car we used carried a price tag at the factory of just over $2,600 without extras. This is a lot of money to pay for a car, irrespective of the lavishness of the finish, and one should expect certain standard accessories. But they are virtually all extras with the 'Presi-

dent,' even such necessities as turn-signals, back-up lights, windshield washers, a small light in the trunk, cigarette lighter and the outside mirror. Incidentally, the outside mirror on the car we tested is excellent and in a very convenient position—the driver has only to glace to the left and get a perfect reflection of what is going on in the rear. But when you add such other items, now considered essential, as radio, heater, etc., the price of the 'President' moves closely to the Jaguar sports sedan group.

We noticed recently that a certain contemporary of Studebaker has introduced a steering wheel that induces the driver to hold the wheel in the correct position —'twenty minutes to four.' The Studebaker wheel, with its grip-assisting indentations on the upper half of the wheel, leads the driver to place his hands incorrectly. This should be altered, as the right place for the hands for accurate and comfortable driving is on the lower segment of the wheel.

From the driving seat, all-round visibility is very nearly perfect; in fact, it is doubtful if it can be improved without making many violent changes in body construction—other manufacturers please take note. The interior rear-view mirror would be better if it were on the ledge above the instrument panel instead of being hung from the roof; however hard we tried we could not get a good deep all-round reflection; there was also a tendency for the mirror to vibrate and distort the image.

In earlier models it was difficult sometimes to see in the car with only one small interior light under the instrument panel. In the '55 'President' a very clear light is fitted on one side of the rear compartment, operated as with the light under the dash, when the doors are opened or by a small switch to the right of the parking brake.

The owner of one of these cars has little to criticize on the general interior finish, which is quite the finest we have seen for some time.

We were fortunate enough to experience some bad weather during the time we had the car at our disposal and certain minor defects showed up that would not have been apparent had the sun been shining all the time.

On a longish trip we found the car somewhat draughty, but you must consider that a convertible hardtop is always prone to let the cold air in somewhere. The main draught came from a fairly large aperture that was caused by one of the rear windows refusing to close completely tight. Where there are daughts there are usually holes that let in water, and rain seeped through several spots. None of these annoyances were really serious and a mechanic's spanner and screwdriver would probably eliminate them all.

Before dealing with the performance of the car let us say that the 'President' was one of the most exhilarating vehicles we have had the pleasure to drive for some time.

The take off from a standing start was

positively shattering to most onlookers as it was to us. In low gear (the car we had was equipped with the efficient Studebaker automatic transmission), the acceleration was impressive even to some sports car owners who were testing their Austin-Healeys and Jaguars. This low gear has a quite incredible maximum speed of 56 mph., which was attained without any great effort and in a very short space of time.

In 'normal' drive, the 'President' clearly showed that its 175 bhp. engine was quite capable of taking the car to speeds in excess of 100 mph., and that a cruising speed of around 75 mph. could have held without trouble for hours on end, or so long as the law allows such indulgence.

In the case of emergency there is plenty of power to spare, and a depression of the accelerator to the floor brings into operation the overtake gear, which enables the 'President' to put another car behind it even before the driver of the passed car realizes there is anything there. This sudden surge of power is not confined to the lower speed ranges, but can be physically felt as a strong push in the back when rapid acceleration is demanded at speeds above 65 mph.

Even on a wet, slick-surfaced road the car sat firmly on four wheels and gave no strong indication that its somewhat long back end would break loose. The new Firestone tubeless tires contributed to this feeling of security and however hard the car was cornered there was little or no tire squeal. The suspension, as on all Studebakers, was vastly superior to most cars and although onlookers commented on the amount of roll when cornering, and the nose-diving antics when braking hard, no great sensation was felt from the driving seat.

One serious criticism we have is the utilization of power steering. Power steering leads to oversteer characteristics and this, in such a high-performance vehicle, is definitely bad and highly dangerous. The reason for the development of power steering is to assist in the parking of those cars that have become so big and heavy that it needs an athlete to turn the wheel when the car is traveling at a reasonable speed. It is not logical to assume that the owner of a 'President,' which incidentally has a fine power-weight ratio, is going to spend all his time parking and unparking his car. On the open road the 'President' system becomes superfluous as well as dangerous, as all sympathetic feeling between the driver and the front wheels has been eliminated. No horseman can ride a horse proficiently without being in constant accord with his mount through the medium of reins, and the same applies to driving a car as potent as the 'President.' Power steering on this car is neither necessary nor advisable.

In heavy traffic the 'President' behaved perfectly, and the hill-holder was much appreciated during the two-and-a-half-hour crawl through a football traffic jam. There was a tendency for the car to overheat during this slow progress but

The Studebaker's hood height is slightly above that of the Austin-Healey. We still would like to see such a trim basic body built in a convertible style.

this may have been due to a sticking thermostat.

Starting cold after the car had been outside on a frosty night was no problem and with the automatic choke the engine fired on the first turn of the ignition key.

The layout of the new 175 bhp. engine, and its accessories allows plenty of room for adjustments to be made when necessary.

It is doubtful whether it is a good policy to continue to use the six-volt battery with all the gadgets that now depend on it for power. A 12-volt battery would now seem to be in order. Nowadays, with no starter handle being supplied (and, of course, no aperture being provided for its use), one has to rely implicitly on the battery that is being constantly called upon to supply more and more energy.

Summarizing, we would say that the 1955 Studebaker 'President' is an extremely attractive car that is ideal for the motorist who wants that little bit more, and for the man, or woman, who still appreciates the fact that driving can be a pleasure in a car that is designed to be driven and not just to be sat in. We would, however, be more in favor of the 'President' if it had normal transmission, normal steering and, of course, bucket seats in the front.

With such a fine basis to work on, it seems a pity that the Studebaker people have not used their cars in rally-type competition. It would seem to us that the 'President' has all the attributes of a fire-class rally car and that it could be easily prepared to compete successfully against many of the imported sports sedans.

Specifications

Engine: V-8 type 'Wildcat' with overhead valves; bore, 3-9/16 inches and stroke, 3¼ inches; total capacity, 259 cubic inches (4,244 cc.). Develops 175 bhp. at 4,500 rpm. Compression ratio, 7.5:1. Oil capacity, 6 quarts; cooling system capacity, 17¼ quarts. Rear axle ratio, 7.5:1 or optional, 4.27:1; with overdrive, 4.27:1 or optional, 4.09:1; with automatic transmission, 3.54:1. Tubeless tires, size 7.10x15. Height (loaded), 56.31 inches; width, 71 inches; length, 204-7/16 inches. Wheelbase, 120½ inches. ☆☆

The 175 bhp. power plant packs plenty of punch and is quite capable of pushing the 'President' up around the 100 mph. mark with power to spare in the pinch.

Photos by Bob D'Olivo

'55 Studebaker President State Sedan

**MT's full-scale test program gets off to a good start with the lively
performance and exceptional roadability of the Studebaker President**

By Jim Potter

WE'VE JUST COMPLETED our first full-scale road test for the 1955 model year, and the car, a Studebaker President State four-door sedan equipped with automatic transmission, power steering, and power brakes, gave the testing crew many pleasant surprises.

"If the Studebaker President is a good sample of what's in store for us when we begin testing other 1955 cars," commented Fred Bodley, our Technical Editor, "we've got some mighty pleasant duties ahead of us this time."

He was referring, of course, to the increased power under the hood of our road test car and its highly competent roadability. Current and former owners of Studebakers who complain about low power may look forward to turning in their car on a '55 President, for its 175-horsepower engine (that's 55 more than the '54 Commander) lets it accelerate as well as, and in some cases, better than its nearest competitors among '54 cars.

Last month we gave you a preliminary rundown on this car in both "Spotlight" and "Driving Around." You'll be interested to know that our official test results were even more favorable than the informal checks of the car at South Bend made by Detroit Editor Don MacDonald; and, if you're really interested in improved

performance, a comparison of the President's test figures with those of last year's lower-powered Commander (which, incidentally, was equipped with overdrive) is really astounding.

For instance, an even five seconds was lopped off the time of the 0 to 60 mph runs, and an improvement of four seconds was indicated in the 50 to 80 mph runs. All other acceleration times were bettered, too; but the most surprising comparison is yet to come (we double-checked our figures twice before we convinced ourselves)—the '55 Studebaker President out-accelerated every '54 car in its price class in the 10 to 30 and 50 to 80 mph categories, and every '54 car in *any* price class from 0 to 30!

Now here's where we're going to save you some time. Put away that letter paper and pen! We'll explain how Studebaker is able to accomplish this remarkable acceleration with "only" 175 horsepower. You've heard us speak often of weight-power ratio. With the increase in horsepower from 120 to 175, the weight-power ratio has been lowered from 26 to 1 to 20.7 to 1; this, despite a test car weight increase from 3380 to 3620 pounds! This, plus the increased torque (60 more in '55) gives it that added jump.

Another factor that improves accelera-

tion is the low-gear-start feature of the automatic transmission. It's the same whether you have the select lever in DRIVE or LOW: 2.31 times the converter ratio. This makes it unnecessary for you to use the selector lever to get better acceleration. Formerly available only in Champion models, this drive next utilizes an intermediate (1.43) range, also with the converter, then shifts smoothly to direct drive. The new power of the Studebaker President gives it that desirable nimbleness in traffic. To us, it spells safety, because you can get out of the way of the other fellow in case of an emergency, not a bad ace in the hole for today's congested traffic.

While we're speaking of performance, how does the increased horsepower affect fuel economy? Before the '55s, the name Studebaker was legend as a car with stingy appetite; it's been a consistent winner of the famed AAA-supervised Mobilgas Economy Runs. We're happy to report it will probably stay right up there holding onto its grand sweepstakes position, although our test results indicated slightly higher fuel consumption than last year's car (with overdrive) in each category. To make our comparison complete, here are the figures for your own amazement testing the car at steady speeds of 30, 45, 60, and 75 mph gave an average fuel consumption figure of 18.8 mpg for the '55 President; the 120-hp '54 Commander average was 20.3 mpg.

When it comes to brakes, it's a slightly different story; last year the Commander's brakes stopped our test car in a shorter distance than the average car in its class. This year the footage was lengthened by an overall average of 10 feet; the brakes are the same, but the car is heavier and the coasting effect of the automatic transmission had to be overcome. With the engine off and gear selector lever in NEUTRAL, the power brakes held remarkably well, even after *all* the vacuum had been expended. The brakes were then no harder to apply than nonpower brakes. And there's still that exclusive Studebaker feature which prevents automatic-drive creep when you're sitting at a stoplight: that's its hill holder, standard equipment on President and Commander models and available at extra cost on Champions.

We've commented favorably on the excellent roadability of the Studebaker cars that we've tested since they introduced their popular hardtop coupe model in '53. If anything, this year's test sedan was even better in this regard, due presumably to stiffer shock absorbers.

Associate Editor Jim Lodge had this to say: "It's one car I've really enjoyed from a roadability angle. The Stude could be thrown brutally into a deliberate slide

that would wash out another car, yet in throwing it into a hard corner, you knew exactly how far it was going, how you could pull it out, and where it would come out. It was unnecessary to utilize its available power in cornering (most of the time) because of the confident way it went into and negotiated turns (handled by the steering alone). The driver is the master." Basically, other testers agreed with these remarks with the additional comment that when they took the Stude over rather bad dips, pitch was absent, a characteristic which has not been licked by some manufacturers.

"The ride is in no sense uncomfortable," comments Pete Molson, MT's Assistant Managing Editor, "but neither is it particularly luxurious; it is certainly not quiet. The noise of road strips still comes right into the car." Perhaps if they would install Fiberglas pads under the floor mats as they have in the roof panel, it would help to eliminate road noises.

The '55 hoods are wider, and slightly higher, but this change doesn't hurt the unusually good vision that you get through the windshield. Studebaker hasn't gone to the wrap-around yet, and actually, we felt no need for that design with this car. Vision is excellent without it.

The instruments are deeply set in two large circular dials, which are difficult to read at a glance as there is considerable

reflection. The speedometer needle is too slim for easy reading. The aircraft-type toggle switches for the lights, heater, etc., have larger shafts and are arranged handily for the driver.

The seats are firm but fairly well-padded, and the front seat can be easily adjusted, something new for Studebakers. On quick stops, the seat still moves forward on its own volition. The upholstery fabric is attractive enough but not too practical if you use a car hard.

It's always hard to evaluate the first car of a new year, and when that car is actually a new series in the maker's line, the task approaches the impossible. Assuming that prices remain the same in other lines, Stude has one of the most compelling sales arguments in its favor, for the reborn President sells for $193 less than the '54 Commander Land Cruiser, its closest comparable model. This brings it into a price spot where it can attract the interest of potential buyers of the Buick Special, Mercury, Dodge Royal, or Oldsmobile 88. The low-priced field will offer some new choices, too; not only has the Champion reduced its prices, but the Commander V8, with reductions of as much as $287, is now well within that field. If these low-medium price field buyers want an eager car that it's almost impossible to embarrass, they'll be wise to try out the new President.

Sun visor has little function, rattled when buffeted by wind. Non-wrap-around windshield affords excellent visibility

'55 Studebaker Road Test

GENERAL SPECIFICATIONS

ENGINE: Ohv V8. Bore 3¹¹⁄₁₆ in. Stroke 3¹⁄₄ in. Stroke/bore ratio .912:1. Compression ratio 7.5:1. Displacement 259.2 cu. in. Advertised bhp 175 @ 4500 rpm. Bhp per cu. in. .675. Piston travel @ max. bhp 2437 ft. per min. Max. bmep 145.4 psi. Max. torque 250 lb. ft. @ 3000 rpm.

DRIVE SYSTEM: STANDARD transmission is three-speed synchromesh using helical gears. RATIOS: 1st 2.57, 2nd 1.55, 3rd 1.00, reverse 3.48. AUTOMATIC transmission is Studebaker Automatic Drive, torque converter with planetary gears. Maximum converter ratio at stall 2.15. RATIOS: Drive, 2.31 x converter ratio, 1.43 x converter ratio, 1.00 direct drive; Low, 2.31 x converter ratio; Reverse, 2.00 x converter ratio. OVERDRIVE transmission is standard shift with planetary gear set.

REAR AXLE RATIOS: Standard 3.92, Automatic 3.54, Overdrive 4.27.

DIMENSIONS: Wheelbase 120½ in. Tread 56¹¹⁄₁₆ front, 55¹¹⁄₁₆ rear. Wheelbase/tread ratio 2.14:1. Overall width 70⁷⁄₁₆ in. Overall length 206¼ in. Overall height (empty) 60 in. Turning diameter 40 ft. Turns lock to lock 4⅔. Test car weight 3620 lbs. Test car weight/bhp ratio 20.7:1. Weight distribution 58.3% front, 41.7% rear. Tire size 7:10 x 15 tubeless.

PRICES: (Including suggested retail price at main factory, federal tax, and delivery and handling charges, but not freight.) PRESIDENT DELUXE, four-door sedan $2245; PRESIDENT STATE, four-door sedan $2315, five-passenger coupe $2240, hardtop coupe $2390.

ACCESSORIES: Automatic Drive $226, overdrive $118, power steering $134, power brakes $35, radios $59 and $91 (including internally controlled antenna), heater $56.75, white sidewall tubeless tires standard. (Radio and heater prices do not include installation cost.)

PARTS AND LABOR COSTS and **ESTIMATED COST PER MILE** for the Studebaker President will appear in an early issue.

TEST CAR AT A GLANCE
'55 Studebaker President State with Automatic Drive

REAR WHEEL HORSEPOWER
Determined on Clayton chassis dynamometer. All tests are made under full load, which is similar to climbing a hill at full throttle. Observed hp figures not corrected to standard atmospheric conditions.)

46 road hp @ 1500 rpm and 36 mph
60 road hp @ 2000 rpm and 49 mph
73 road hp @ 2500 rpm and 60 mph
Max. 82 road hp @ 3200 rpm and 80 mph

TOP SPEED
(In miles per hour over surveyed ¼-mile.)
Fastest one-way run 107.1
Slowest one-way run 102.7
Average of four runs 104.8

ACCELERATION
(In seconds; checked with fifth wheel and electric speedometer.)
Standing start ¼-mile (66 mph) 19.4
0-30 mph 3.0
0-60 mph 13.2
10-30 mph 3.2
30-50 mph 6.2
50-80 mph 14.9

SPEEDOMETER ERROR
(Checked with fifth wheel and electric speedometer.)
Car speedometer read 33 @ true 30 mph
50 @ true 45 mph
66 @ true 60 mph
81 @ true 75 mph
109 @ top speed

FUEL CONSUMPTION
(In miles per gallon; checked with fuel flowmeter, fifth wheel, and electric speedometer. Mobilgas Special used.)
Steady 30 mph 22.6
Steady 45 mph 22.1
Steady 60 mph 18.5
Steady 75 mph 14.1
Simulated traffic over measured course 15.9
Tank average for 1021 miles 15.1

STOPPING DISTANCE
(To the nearest foot; checked with electrically actuated detonator.)
30 mph 44
45 mph 101
60 mph 174

Basically unchanged from 1954, the Studebaker hard-top convertible is still the sportiest, most foreign-looking car in America.

This low-medium priced V-8, with 1

YOU SAY you're not satisfied? You say you want more for your money? Studebaker may have the answer to your prayers this year with a line of the fastest, slickest cars they have ever produced—at greatly reduced prices.

The model chosen for the test was the medium-priced Commander hard-top convertible, one step below the big new President but more expensive than the Champion. Its price has been reduced about $220 from the comparable model of last year, which puts it in the $2,300 bracket—at the factory.

But you don't realize what a good buy the new Stude is until you drive it. This is a real car! I purposely picked the Commander instead of the more powerful President because I didn't want my impressions to be based solely on speed and acceleration. Besides, it is likely that there is more market for the Commander, considering its price.

I did make one mistake, though. I borrowed a car without power steering. This seemed to be a good idea at first because I am still not a real power steering fan, but after five minutes behind the wheel I was extremely sorry. Without the power unit, the steering wheel goes six turns from lock to lock, and what's more, it seems to have almost no correction control at low speeds. Besides, when it comes to parking this buggy you have to have the arms of a gorilla or you just won't get the wheel around. I didn't mind the steering at ordinary cruising speeds on the highway, but I still wish I had chosen a Stude equipped with a power gizmo. My poor shoulders!

But criticisms stop there. The Commander is a thoroughly delightful machine to drive, with plenty of acceleration, fine brakes and a suspension set-up that gives comfort without mushiness and stability without Continued on next page

This powerful V-8 engine displaces 224 cu. in. or about three-and-a-half liters. A dual-throated downdraft carb is employed.

In profile the car is at its best. That long, wide chrome strip along the side is new this year, seems to detract, if anything, from Stude's beauty.

STUDEBAKER'S "55 Commander

horsepower, is a right smart wagon.

Studebaker's suspension affords a happy medium between comfortable riding and good handling. In tight cornering, as shown, there is very little lean.

Trunk space, while not tremendous, is adequate for most trips. Only problem is the spare tire which lies on its side, breaking usable space in two. ▶

Studebaker's 1955 Commander

harshness. I'd say the ride compared favorably with any of the low-priced American cars with much better handling than average. The driving position in particular impressed me and this contributed greatly to the over-all feel of the car in turns. You sit *in* the Studebaker, not on it, and the angle of the steering wheel and the brake and gas pedals is highly conducive to fast and yet relaxed driving. In this respect I was reminded of some of the currently-popular European sports cars.

In general handling and cornering tests I was delighted to learn that the Studebaker is just about as tough to turn over as most sports cars, too. Fortunately it never even came close. In fact, I found that the car hardly leaned at all on ordinary turns and very little more when the going got rough. I managed to break the rear end loose only once—during a driving rain—and then I got right back on course with a minimum of correction and nary a missed heartbeat.

I had picked up the test car on a Friday afternoon and my first destination was a neighborhood Amoco station. With the tank filled and the mileage checked, I pumped a few extra pounds of air into the tires, ending up with 25 psi in front and 28 in the rear. All 1955 Studebakers feature tubeless tires as standard equipment.

With all minor details—like gas and oil checked, I headed for the hills. The car was still too new to even consider any timed acceleration runs and this gave me a perfect opportunity to get used to its driving subtleties while putting on some mileage. The more I drove it the more I liked it. With the "over-inflated" tires I noticed that squeal on hard turns was reduced almost to the point of being non-existent. I mention this only because there has been so much comment on tire squeal these days. The truth of the matter is that such noise is not directly related to car stability. There are cars that will scream like banshees at the slightest bend in the road and yet hang on like champions when the chips are down. On the other hand some cars will break loose completely without a sound. But I suppose if you've got to go you may as well do it quietly.

Coming around one particularly sharp downhill turn I noticed one handling characteristic that was, to me, very comforting. The car will drift if it is purposely broken loose before the rear end has a chance to come around by itself. By "drifting" I mean that the whole car can be thrown into a broadside slide to position you for the next turn. This process is not recommended on narrow roads or ones with cliffs or stone walls on the far side because the Commander weighs over 3,200 lbs. and it has a

tendency to keep sliding. The only thing that can bring you out of it is fast steering correction, which this particular car sure didn't have. But I brought it on myself so I have no complaints. I got through the turn anyway, and the reason I say that the car's tendency to drift was comforting is because drifting acts as a sort of safety valve, releasing energy that might otherwise be used to flip the car. If you would rather turn over than spin out you will never like a really stable car. But that's your privilege.

When I had driven several hundred fairly hard miles, and made numerous brake checks which failed to bring on any degree of fade, I got out my trusty stop watch and headed for a favorite stretch of straight road. By this time I had gotten the impression that the car was quite fast in low range (automatic drive), somewhat disappointing in intermediate gear and very good in high. Corrected acceleration runs seemed to bear this out, especially when compared with Studebaker's own figures for the 175-hp President model. The Commander, for instance, averaged 5.1 seconds for the zero to 30 run; exact time for the President came to 5.12 seconds. The Commander picked up even more time from zero to 40, averaging 7.2 seconds as compared to 7.54 for its big brother. (That's what Studebaker said!)

But from a standing start to 60 mph, a large part of which is run in intermediate gear, the Commander pooped. The best I could get out of it was 14.2 seconds while the President's time was 13.27, almost a full second better. This is as it should be, but what I want to know is, what happened to the President up to 40 mph? The only thing I can think of is that the Commander hits its maximum torque at a lower speed; gear ratios are exactly the same on the two cars.

My top speed runs weren't terribly conclusive. There was a strong crosswind and the road was still wet from a recent downpour. Consequently I got several distinctly different readings, all over 100 mph. I feel that this car will do an honest 100 or maybe a little better if you give it a chance to wind out. Standard transmission with overdrive would help.

There are a few other things that I feel should be mentioned. Wind noise seemed to me—and several friends—to be above average, even with the windows shut tight. Perhaps that extra chromium stripping this year sets up a turbulance or two. The Commander was, however, quite stable even in relatively high crosswinds. Front seats are comfortable with lots of leg room but it was a little cramped in the rear. Head room all around has been cut to a bare minimum and you might do well to wear a soft hat on a really bad road if you are anything over average height from the waist up. Upholstery is of a bright and colorful plastic that should wear well and the arm rest in the rear seat folds flat in case the two adults back there should want to seat a small child between them. The heater, by the way, is a very good one with a wide range of adjustment.

Would I recommend the 1955 Commander? The answer is a resounding "yes." It's an economical car—I got better than 20 mpg—and it's still about the best looking thing around. The handling is good and it's got lots of pep. The hard-top isn't what you'd call a big family-type car but Studebaker make a four-door six-passenger sedan for that purpose. What more could you ask?

SPECIFICATIONS

ENGINE: V-8, overhead valves; bore, 3.65 in.; stroke, 2.81; total displacement, 224.3 cu. in.; developed hp, 140 at 4,500 rpm; maximum torque, 202 ft./lbs. at 2,800 rpm; compression ratio, 7.5 to 1; dual-throat, downdraft carburetor; ignition, 6 volt.

TRANSMISSION: torque converter with three forward gears and reverse; standard three-speed manual also available, with or without overdrive.

REAR AXLE RATIO: 3.54 to 1 standard; 4.10 to 1 optional.

SUSPENSION: front, independent by coil springs with rubber-bushed support arms; rear, semi-elliptic leaf springs; double-acting piston-type hydraulic shock absorbers.

BRAKES: four-wheel hydraulic, self-energizing; vacuum power booster optional.

DIMENSIONS: wheelbase, 120½ in.; tread, (front and rear) 56.69 in.; width, 70.44 in.; height, 56.31 in.; over-all length, 204.44 in.; turning circle, 40 ft., six in.; weight, 3,220 lbs. (approx.); 6.70 x 15 tubeless.

PERFORMANCE

ACCELERATION:

Zero to 30 mph: 5.1 seconds
Zero to 40 mph: 7.2 seconds
Zero to 60 mph: 14.2 seconds

TOP SPEED:

100 mph plus.

AUTO REVIEW

Studebaker's new 1955 models are accentuating the long and low distinctive styling of the popular hard-top convertible.

Presenting—

The 1955 Studebaker

The 'President' series, a popular South Bend product before World War II, supplants the 'Land Cruiser'

IN PRESENTING the first of the 1955 models to be announced, CAR LIFE offers the Studebaker and Chevrolet.

Following an earlier announcement that the new Studebaker would be a higher-powered, lower-priced car, the recently consolidated Studebaker-Packard Corporation appears determined to get into the rough competition ahead for 1955. The new line features twenty-four different body styles and a return to the old 'President' series, popular Studebaker model of the 1920s and 30s, supplanting the big Land Cruiser.

The Champion and Commander series features sedans, coupes and station wagons, with the Champion powered by a new 'Victory 6' now rated at 101 horsepower. The Commander V-8 also offers increased engine performance with a 'Pacesetter' V-8 developing 140 horse-

power. In keeping with the race for more power under the hood the 'President' line has a 175-horsepower 'Wildcat' V-8.

While general body lines of the new Studebaker conforms very closely to those of the 1954 series, the cars have been dressed up with heavy chrome, grille guards and bumpers and a flashier appearance around the rear end. The new models may be had in eight solid colors and eight two-tone combinations.

Oddly, the tremendous popularity of the 1954 wraparound windshield intro-

duced by General Motors apparently had no influence on Studebaker's plans for 1955.

Low gear start is in all Automatic Drive units, thus assuring a fast, smooth acceleration. Gears shift automatically through the two low ranges and then lock into economical direct drive. An automatic kickdown at speeds up to 70 miles an hour shifts the Automatic Drive to the intermediate gear range when an additional surge of power is needed.

Car and background are a blur as Fermoyle whee's down long straightaway with throttle punched hard against Speedster's floor.

DRIVER'S REPORT

STUDEBAKER'S

LIVELY is the word for the Studebaker Speedster—both in appearance and performance. For the past few years many automobile fanciers have wondered why Studebaker didn't supply a little more urge in the engine compartment to go with the beautiful and distinctive styling of its cars. Those who felt this way should be very happy with the new Speedster.

"Designed to appeal particularly to owners who desire special sports car styling and performance with traditional American car comfort," Studebaker says of this model. And that pretty well tells the story. Originally planned as a show car for exhibition purposes only, the Speedster aroused so much popular in-

terest it was put into limited production.

Since interest in this new car is high, it was arranged for me to drive one for several days and pass along my findings.

I was introduced to the Speedster by Jerry McLeod, Studebaker dealer in Royal Oak, a Detroit suburb. The car I drove was one he had been using personally. "My pet," he called it with a good deal of pride. My first impression was that the car's looks are striking. A two-tone "tri-level" paint treatment combined with the now-familiar low, sleek Stude lines make the Speedster a car you'll look at twice. This one had a Hialeah metallic green top and lower section with yellow center section, deck and hood.

The interior is finished in diamond stitched top grain leather. The one drove had yellow upholstery to match the exterior colors.

"So much for show," I thought; "how will it go?" McLeod took me for a shor spin to explain the various controls, the turned the car over to me. As I slid be hind the wheel and glanced at the instru ment panel, I noticed that all the gage and instruments were large, easy to rea and grouped in front of the driver fo best possible visibility. The more I drov the car, the better I liked this setup and in my opinion, this is one of the best in strument panel designs I've ever seen There is a large, circular tachometer a right balanced by a speedometer at lef In between are smaller gas, oil, ammete and temperature gages. The panel itself i stainless steel, is hooded to reduce glare

To check on the "go," I headed out fo one of the few spots near Detroit wher you can really wind a car up.

First 0-60 runs timed out at about 11½ seconds in drive only (the car ha automatic drive). Winding up to 5,00 rpm in lo and shifting to second choppe a full second off. In 50-80 mph checks, got an average of 12.6 seconds for sev eral tries. The 259-inch engine needs little time to wind up to deliver its max imum at the top end. I had it up to a indicated 110 at one point and it was sti climbing when I had to back off as I ra out of the straightaway.

The Speedster, according to Studebaker, originally was intended to be only a show car, with some 20 models built. But interest caused the car to be put into production.

80

MOTOR *Life's Detroit Editor*
put a stop watch on
the pride of South Bend—
this is how he found it goes

NEW SPEEDSTER

BY KEN FERMOYLE

(The speedometer on this car seemed amazingly accurate, incidentally. I checked it by timing the car thru a measured strip, by comparing it against the [speed]ometer using a stop watch and by comparing indicated speed against the rpm figure on the tach—Studebaker 24.53 mph per 1,000 rpm in drive—and found that the indicated error was so slight it was hardly measurable.)

These figures might be a shade off because I was using a hand-held stop watch. However, I tried to make enough runs in each case to arrive at a reasonably true average. Using an electric 5th wheel and Weston speedo, as our road test crew does for full-scale tests, might

make a difference of a few tenths of a second here and there.

Acceleration-wise the car was sneaky. It doesn't feel like it's getting up to speed as fast as it does. In fact, I was amazed with the times. Jerry McLeod later said he had that feeling when he first drove the car too. He also said he thought he could improve on my 0-60 times—and did! I clocked several runs with him driving and he was able to get up there in just about 10 seconds. He made it in 10 seconds flat twice, took about 10.2 several other times. That shows it helps to be familiar with your automobile.

As for handling, you can find very few

faults with the Speedster. It lays right on the road and gives you a nice secure feeling at any speed. My only complaint was with the slow steering—almost 4½ turns lock to lock. This doesn't seem necessary with power steering—standard equipment on this model.

The power brakes added to the feeling of security. They aren't overly sensitive unless you really stand on them hard and give you that nice safe impression that you can stop right now, or any time it's necessary. There wasn't even a suggestion of fade. They have a husky brake lining area of 195.25 square inches.

The Speedster's ride is comfortable
(*Continued on page* 108)

[Fe]rmoyle checks duals and running gear [be]fore starting test. Several 0-60 mph [ru]ns produced times at 10-second mark.

Engine compartment has little space to spare. Car turned 110 mph, had not peaked before driver ran out of road.

Instrument panel with sports car flavor. Tach, at the right, showed engine produced 24.53 mph per 1000 rpm in drive.

STUDEBAKER PRESIDENT

A great old name returns, and the new car behind it is no disappointment

From 1927 until 1942, the Studebaker President was considered one of this country's five finest cars. Limousines, seven-passenger sedans and even seven-passenger touring cars once bore this famed label, competing with Cadillac, Lincoln, Pierce-Arrow (absorbed by Studebaker) and Packard, now Study's ally in new ventures.

Now the President has re-appeared as a successor to the discontinued Landcruiser. The styling is basically unchanged but chrome has been liberally added in side spears and up front the former uncluttered, functional (and economical to repair) styl-

ing has given way to the understandable whims of the sales department to the extent that probably 50 pounds of dead weight grille structure now breaks the former lines. This is probably responsible for a slight tendency toward noseheaviness that was not noticeable on the '54 Landcruiser.

The interior of the new President should set something of a luxury standard in the low-medium priced range. Gold-plated hardware adds richness to the State series which is not present on the slightly cheaper Deluxe line. Even the State's rear seat ashtray is gold-plated as is the radio grille and

CHASSIS & BODY

Wheelbase 120-½
Tread ....56-11/16 front, 55-11/16 rear
Length overall ....206-¼ (204-7/16 coupes and hardtops)
Width overall 70-7/16
Height overall ....60 (56-5/16 coupes and hardtops)
Ground clearance ....7-5/16 (6-15/32 coupes and hardtops)
Turning circle diameter ....41 feet
Steering wheel lock-to-lock ....4-¼ turns (mechanical & power)
Tire size ....7.10 x 15
Weight, shipping ....3230 lbs. approximately
Overhang ....37-¾ front, 48-¾ rear (coupes and hardtops)
                                35-¾ front, 48-9/16 rear)
Brake lining area ....195-3/10 sq. inches
Weight to brake area ratio ....16.53 lbs. per sq. inch
Weight to power ratio ....18.5 lbs. per BHP

ENGINE and contributing equipment

Cylinders, block, valves ....8, 90-degree V, Overhead
Bore and stroke ....3-9/16 x 3-¼
Displacement ....259.2 cu. in.
Compression ratio 7.5:1
Brake horsepower (maximum) ...175 @ 4500 RPM
Torque ....250 ft. lbs. @ 3000 RPM
Carburetor ....Four-barrel, downdraft
Choke ....Automatic
Fuel pump ....Mechanical
Fuel recommended ....Regular
Fuel tank capacity ....18 gallons
Exhaust system ....Single with crossover, reverse-flow
Crankcase capacity ....6 qts. (add 1 for filter)
Drive shaft type ....Exposed
Rear axle type ....Hypoid
Rear axle ratio ....Manual 3.92:1
                              Overdrive 4.27:1
                              Automatic 3.54:1
Available transmissions ....Manual (3-speed), overdrive, automatic
Piston speed @ maximum RPM ....2437.5 feet per minute
Electrical system ....6 volts
Cooling system capacity ....18.75 qts. (with heater)

Acceleration (from standing start
in DR-4 with low gear start) ....to 30 MPH true speed: 4.40 seconds
                                        to 45 MPH true speed: 8.53 seconds
                                        to 60 MPH true speed: 13.67 seconds

Highway acceleration (with kickdown
to 60 MPH) from 50 to 80 MPH ....: 13.80 seconds
NOTE: tests were with automatic transmission; faster times can be expected
with manual shift car.

Fuel consumption ....17 with automatic transmission
Maximum speed ....over 103 MPH
Weather during tests ....Cloudy, humid, dry roads

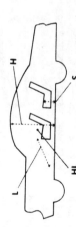

INTERIOR DIMENSIONS Measurements in inches on all body types

Hi Hiproom ....59-½ front, 59 rear (58 rear coupes & hardtops)
H Headroom ..36 front, 35 rear (34-⅞ front, 32-⅞ rear coupes & hardtops)
S Seat Height 13-½ front, 12-½ rear (10-¾ front, 12 rear coupes and hard-
tops)
L Legroom ....42-½ front, 41 rear (43-¾ front, 36 rear coupes and hardtops)

— 15 ft. 3 in. —
VISION forward over Hood (driver 5'10") ......15 ft. 3 in. forward of bumper

This photo, taken after water bath, shows Stude's center-point steering, an excellent feature

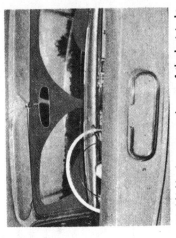

Windshield wiper pattern is one of the best to be found, with comparatively small blind spots

Studebaker Proving Ground at South Bend is old, but a wonderfully abusive place for car testing

■ STUDEBAKER PRESIDENT

the bottom edge of the instrument panel. Well done details make a good impression on a critical car enthusiast: things like the large and well-lighted dual instrument dials which cause less windshield and driver's window reflection than is encountered on the majority of cars, handy toggles that are not ridiculously large for auxiliary controls, armrests that actually allow the driver's left arm to rest comfortably while driving, etc.

On the debit side is the foot brake pedal on the automatic transmission equipped models; it's a bit too small for convenient left foot action. The too narrow rear-view mirror doesn't take in the excellent rear view accorded by the large rear window (a fault shared by all stock cars this year). The far right glove case could easily be relocated within easy reach of the driver (again a fault shared with some other cars).

Roadability and handling ease of the President are above average. This car can be flung around to a degree that will delight those who go for sports car handling, and its ease of maneuverability and good acceleration in traffic will delight any person who fancies himself a good driver and who likes to stay out of the other guy's way. Hard cornering lean, while present, is not too much, and this heaviest of all Studebakers gives very fair warning before the rear end breaks away. This break-away, common in varying degrees in all passenger cars, is not to be considered bad, and the President has the necessary "pop" to enable one quickly to bring the rear end back in line by throttle action.

Brakes are improved this year (on the entire line) and a newly designed drum and backing plate does wonders to keep water off the lining. After a dozen or so repeated dashes through the water tank, the brakes had so little tendency to grab that I asked, feeling foolish as I did, if the engineers had discovered some way to waterproof the lining and thus prevent soaking. However,

even a non-power equipped car is easy.

Superior, I believe, is a truthful way of describing the entire Studebaker line's handling and roadability. Shock absorbers up front are inside the coil springs and seem a bit stiffer than previously—not enough to impair good riding qualities, but sufficient to prevent bottoming on all but the hardest bumps and dips. Such placing of the front shocks allows them to be spaced farther apart providing what the designers call "sea legs." Aft, the rear springs are mounted slightly diagonally with relation to the longitudinal frame members and the shocks slant outward. Personally I would prefer much faster steering—with or without power the steering is slow (though to be fair it's on a par with the competition and faster than some). Since all Studebakers have center-point steering—linkage is centered and tie-rods are of equal length—steering

it's just good drum design.

abrupt down grades is done at any speed up to 62 mph (compared to 60 on the Champion and Commander described elsewhere), and idling creeping was much decreased over last year's Stude's.

Green light "go" artists will like the average of 13.67 seconds from dead still to a true 60 mph, achieved on runs in both directions. Those who have never experienced Studebaker's exclusive Hill Holder, used successfully for many years, should get briefed on this handy gadget and try it.

Throw away the hood ornament (on any car for that matter) and the new Studebaker still has the lines of a sports tourer with all the interior roominess and comfort that one could desire. Seeing both front fenders without stretching, and the road ahead just 15 feet 3 inches forward of the bumper, is still unusual enough to merit attention.

For several years this famous name's best line has been relatively underpowered. The new 175-horse engine has corrected this, and there's real good dig on this President, enough for even those accustomed to far more than 200 pony-power. Cruising on the highway in high ratio on the automatic transmission test car, I was able consistently to "scat" from a steady 50 mph to 80 mph (true speed—not speedometer) in an overall average of 13.8 seconds, which compares very favorably with several much more powerful and costlier cars. The new Studebaker automatic transmission combines a torque converter with gears and allows a low gear start in drive by full throttling the pedal, making it unnecessary to start in low and shift up by hand for fast starts. Downshift for engine braking on corners and

The Champion has moderate performance, but good economy

Joe Wherry stops before entering the oval, where this Commander hit speeds of 94-97 mph

STUDEBAKER CHAMPION and COMMANDER

This pair still trails in horsepower, but makes up for it in many ways

The 1955 Studebaker Champion six-cylinder job, with power increased to 101 horses, will remain one of the best buys for those interested in a combination of reasonable performance with downright gas-saving. Its brother, the Commander V-8 (the engine is about the only difference), with the shortest stroke pistons in the entire domestic industry, has overcome its former power shortage and come up with a decent 140 horsepower.

A full line running from the low-priced Custom up through the Deluxe and Regal series includes station wagons in both the Champion and Commander. The two go together as worthy competitors in the low-priced field. Driving either is much the same as tooling the President, but they both handle a bit better because they are slightly lighter up front. They have lighter engines and, therefore, a shade better longitudinal weight distribution. Studes are above the average in handling, anyway. In my opinion, the Champion is the handling star of the

lot, but by no more than a hair. That little flathead "Victory 6" engine will not give you breathtaking performance, but it's light, and a Champ will slither around hard corners with greater ease and a little less roll.

I tested the mechanical shift version, equipped with overdrive, which gives perhaps 5-10 per cent better acceleration than the optionally fitted automatic transmission. In spite of a better weight to power ratio than the Rambler, the Champ's 11 more brake horsepower, higher ratio rear axle, and faster manual transmission fail to give the expected better acceleration times. Of course many different factors, other than brute horsepower, affect velocity performance. The Rambler's almost equal dig to 60 mph is due, briefly, to its having approximately the same torque at 200 fewer rpm's and a lower ratio rear axle. On the other hand, the Champion will usually prove to be the most miserly gas consumer of the two. These two cars are often compared on a value-for-value basis; in my book, they're about equal with the Rambler having a slight edge in top speed, tighter cornering because of its shorter wheelbase, and a theoretical claim to slightly longer engine life span due to a lower piston speed at full gun. Actually the two cars are so close in price and other considerations that size and styling would seem sufficient basis for the

layman to judge between them

The Commander is a different story. Upped to 140 horsepower, this car now has a little more dig than the '54 model in low speed ranges but a lot more pop at highway passing speeds. Whereas the Champion engine received a boost over last year's four-inch stroke with an accompanying raise in displacement (and torque) to achieve its power and low speed acceleration gain, the engineers went the other way with the Commander by increasing the bore and decreasing the stroke and improving the fuel intake manifold; consequently the displacement is about eight cubic inches less. Torque on the Commander, therefore, got a 12 foot-lbs. maximum increase but at an accompanying increase of 800 rpm's to develop that torque. The oversquare engine with a more or less conventional combustion chamber will be much more durable than its worthy forebears, but even though the low speed acceleration is not a great deal more, you'll be able to pull out around that 50-mph truck, get past him, and back on your own side in less time. Top speed is better by about four-five mph than in the '54 Commander; fuel mileage will, or should, be increased, and that sluggish feeling at 50 to 60 mph will be all but gone.

The Champion should suit any person who is not interested in more than moderate

PERFORMANCE

Measured by actual tests on both models

Acceleration (from standing start)	CHAMPION	COMMANDER
to 30 MPH	5.8 seconds	5.4 seconds
to 45 MPH	10.64 seconds	9.9 seconds
to 60 MPH	19.92 seconds	16.7 seconds
Highway acceleration (with step-down) from steady 50 to 80 MPH	29-34 (estimated)	17.2 (test)

NOTE: Test Champion equipped with manual transmission and overdrive; slower times to be expected with automatic. Test Commander equipped with automatic; faster times likely with manual shift.

	Champion	Commander
Maximum speed (during tests)	84 MPH	95 MPH
Weather (during tests)	cloudy, humid, roads dry	

INTERIOR DIMENSIONS

In inches

Hiproom ....59-½ front *all* models (59 rear sedans, 58 coupes, 56-½ station wagons)

Headroom ....36 front sedans, 34-⅝ coupes, 37-⅝ station wagons (35 rear sedans, 32-⅞ coupes, 36 station wagons)

Seat Height ....13-½ front (10-¾ coupes); 12 rear (12-½ coupes, 14-½ station wagons)

Legroom ....42-½ front (43-¾ coupes); 39 rear (36 coupes, 41-½ station wagons)

VISION forward over hood (driver 5' 10") ....15 ft. 3 in. ahead of bumper

SPECIFICATIONS

In inches unless otherwise noted

CHASSIS & BODY

Wheelbase ....116-½ (coupes 120-½)

Tread ....56-11/16 front, 55-11/16 rear

Length overall ....202-¼ (204-7/16 coupes, 197-¾ stn. wag.)

Width overall ....70-7/16 (70-11/16 station wagons)

Height overall ....Champ 59-¾ (61-⅝ station wagons), Comm 60 (61-⅞ station wagon), all coupes 56-5/16

Ground clearance (minimum) ....Champ 6-½ (6-⅞ station wagons) Comm 7-5/16 (7-⅛ station wagons)

Turning circle diameter ....39-½ feet (coupes 41)

Steering wheel lock-to-lock ....4-¼ turns (5-¼ Comm mechanical)

Tire size ....6.70 x 15 all except Champ 6.40 x 15

Weight, shipping ....Champ 2780; Comm 3120 pounds

Overhang ....37-⅜ front (35-⅜ coupes); 48-⅜ rear (48-9/16 coupes; 43-⅞ station wagons)

Brake lining area ....Champ 166; Comm 195.3 square inches

Weight to brake area ratio ....Champ 16.74; Comm 15.98 lb. per sq. in.

Weight to power ratio ....Champ 28.4; Comm 22.3 pounds per BHP

ENGINE and contributing equipment

	CHAMPION	COMMANDER
Cylinders, block, valves	6, inline, L-head	8, 90-degree V, OHV
Bore and stroke	3 x 4-⅜	3-9/16 x 2-13/16
Displacement	185.6 cu. in.	224.3 cubic inches
Compression ratio	7.5:1	7.5:1
Brake horsepower (maximum)	101 @ 4000 RPM	140 @ 4500 RPM
Torque	152 ft. lbs. @ 1800 RPM	202 ft. lbs. @ 2800 RPM
Carburetor	Single, 1-barrel	Single, 2-barrel
Choke	Automatic	Automatic
Fuel pump	Mechanical	Mechanical
Fuel recommended	Regular	Regular
Fuel tank capacity	18 gallons	18 gallons
Exhaust system	Single, Reverse-flow	Single, Reverse-flow
Crankcase capacity	5 (add 1 for filter)	6 qts. (add 1 for filter)
Drive shaft type	Exposed	Exposed
Rear axle type	Hypoid	Hypoid
Rear axle ratio (and available transmissions)	Manual 4.10:1	4.10:1 (station wagon 4.09:1)
	Overdrive 4.56:1	4.27:1 (station wagon 4.55:1)
	Automatic 3.54:1	3.54:1
Piston speed @ maximum RPM	2916.7	2109.4 ft. per min.
Electrical system	6 volts	6 volts
Cooling system capacity	11.5 quarts	18.75 qts. (with heater)

New '55 Studebaker! Sports car styling at its best!

The 1955 President State V-8—one of a thrilling trio of Studebaker hard-tops that includes style-setting Commander V-8 and Champion team-mates

■ STUDEBAKER CHAMPION AND COMMANDER

acceleration and speed. Personally I would recommend the manual shift transmission plus overdrive, but Studebaker's excellent automatic is available; the former gives the best performance and mileage.

The steering, too slow for me, will be what the average driver would expect, and these cars are exceptionally easily maneuvered. It still strikes me. oddly that the coupes should be longer overall and in wheelbase than the sedans and station wagons, but here again is an engineering concession to the public's desire for greater length. Wisely the designers of the interior have changed the former stationary center armrest in the coupe's rear seat (where it prevented a third passenger's occupancy) to a neat retractable unit that folds down flush with the cushion. Unwisely the top edge of the front doors on the sedans is sharp, and one is cautioned to stand well back when opening the door or risk losing some chin skin. Otherwise, dash controls are well placed, the rear view mirror is no more inadequate than in any other make, the visibility all-around is excellent, and the driver can see both front fenders with ease.

What about wrap-around windshields? Are you gypped because Stude does not have them? You are losing nothing sticking to the "old" windshield except in the matter of fashion. The Studebaker's excellent windshield visibility in rain, sleet, etc., is rivalled only by the Willys. Studebakers (all models) have an excellent wiper pattern which tops others in omitting corner blind spots; there is a very narrow space in the center where the wipers come close to each other.

Quality-wise Stude's craftsmen are upholding a great tradition; I believe buyers should consider this car's many merits.

NO WONDER STUDEBAKER IS THE LARGEST BUILDER OF SPORTS CARS IN AMERICA

THE LOW SILHOUETTE that made Studebaker the automobile style leader has won 30 outstanding awards. But now, pace-setting Studebaker has moved more commandingly out ahead. We picture here, one of the most exciting 1955 Studebaker sports models.

Look at the low-swung lines of this unusual new hard-top! Look at the racy length of it! This is a car you want to drive on sight—and how it thrills you when you do! Underneath this Stude-

baker's hood is the brilliant new "Passmaster" V-8 engine—unsurpassed for spine-tingling getaway and take-command go!

Brand-new for '55 are Studebaker's low-level competitive prices, too—assuring you the delights of sports car ownership without the customary big investment. What's more, a Studebaker is a sports car you can share with your family. It's a full-bodied, fully-weather-protected 5-passenger automobile.

See Studebaker-Packard's TV Reader's Digest — a weekly feature on ABC television network

Studebaker Division of the Studebaker-Packard Corporation..... world's 4th largest full-line producer of cars and trucks

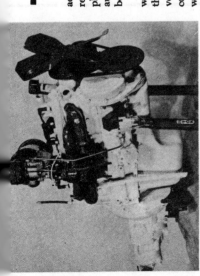

Commander's Pacesetter V-8 is easy to work on, requires no special plug wrenches, etc.

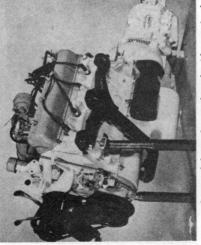

Increased bore, decreased stroke (shortest in the industry) boost engine's efficiency

Wide choice of upholstery materials is available; brake pedal is small

President series four-door sedan shows extent to which Studebaker was able to revise the body shell by modifications. The result is the best-looking four door the firm has had in several years. The wide yet simple grille seems Cadillacish.

THE 1957 STUDEBAKER

STYLING—Major facelift makes Stude look better than it has for years.

PERFORMANCE—Slight improvement in acceleration.

ENGINEERING—Big changes in springing, differential and steering

BODY TYPES—Further breakaway in Hawk line (see separate report).

STUDEBAKER obviously couldn't make a complete model changeover for 1957 in view of the financial crisis which prompted the arrangement between Studebaker-Packard and Curtiss-Wright this summer. It probably wouldn't have done so anyhow. The company ran a series of surveys to get public reaction to its '56 styling. The majority found it very acceptable. So, logically enough, Studebaker has merely refined those designs to increase their appeal for '57.

Grilles, for example, are similar in texture and design, but they have been extended across the entire front of the cars and wrapped around the sides of front fenders. Front bumpers now have a "gull-wing" appearance. A wide center section was dropped to accent the cars' lowness.

Side body trim has been changed—for the better, it would seem. The rather garish and meaningless multiple spears on President models have been dropped in favor of a more restrained effect which lends itself to more attractive two-toning. A single molding which follows the pattern of the belt line is used on lower-priced models. It serves as a natural dividing point for two-tone treatment.

Rear fenders have been changed to give the cars a longer look. They end in shallow vertical Vees which enclose tail lights, backup and turn signal lights. This whole rear light assembly looks like a big arrowhead pointing toward the front of the car when viewed from the side, with the taillight in the center of the V.

Interiors have been dressed up considerably. This goes not only for the higher-priced President models, but for Commanders and Champions too. In fact, the interiors of these smaller cars are as luxurious in appearance as many more costly cars.

Instrument clusters have been redesigned quite tastefully. Ammeter, temperature, oil pressure and fuel gages are mounted in simple round housings on a textured background surrounded by a rounded, rectangular chrome frame. Above this is the safety-eye speedometer introduced last year; its housing, however, has been enlarged and restyled.

Below the instrument cluster is the ignition key/starter switch and toggle switches controlling lights, etc. The overall instrument panel layout is clean, simple, attractive—a rather refreshing change from the over-gimmicked arrangements seen so often today.

STUDE BODY TYPES

PRESIDENT SERIES
Two-door sedan
Four-door sedan
Classic four-door sedan
Four-door station wagon

COMMANDER SERIES
Two-door sedan
Four-door sedan
Two-door station wagon
Four-door station wagon

CHAMPION SERIES
Two-door sedan
Four-door sedan
Two-door station wagon

Note—Hawk series of Studebakers is reported upon in a separate story in this issue.

STUDE SPECIFICATIONS

Wheelbase: 116.5 inches
Length: 200 to 203 inches
Width: 71 inches
Height: 60 inches

Transmissions:
Conventional
Overdrive
Automatic

289-cubic-inch engine:
Compression Ratio: 8.3
Horsepower: 225

259-cubic-inch engine:
Compression Ratio: 8.3
Horsepower: 195

Note—President Classic wheelbase is 120 inches. Compression ratio in 101-hp 185-cubic-inch six is 7.8.

New standard Stude dash is neat. The Hawk series, breaking further away, retains own styling and interior features.

Studebaker is moving more and more into the station wagon market and this is its top effort for '57, the President four-door wagon. A full array of two- and four-door versions is now available. License plate drops into view when tail gate is lowered.

STUDEBAKER ENGINEERING

STUDEBAKER traditionally has offered well-engineered cars. The same will be true in 1957. In addition it will pioneer two engineering innovations in the low-priced field. One, a limited-slip or power-dividing differential, was introduced by Packard last year and is now offered on Lincolns. The other, variable rate front coil springs, is not offered by any other car manufacturer.

Studebaker also has boosted the power of its V-8 engines so they are now the most powerful in Studebaker history. Two V-8's are again offered. Their displacements are the same as last year—259 and 289 inches—but their compression ratios are up from 7.8 to 8.3-to-1.

(The familiar Champion six with a well-deserved reputation for economy is continued unchanged. The little 185.6 L-head is rated at 101 hp and has a 7.8-to-1 compression ratio. Torque is 152 lbs./ft. at 1800 rpm.)

Despite the higher compression ratios, all '57 engines can be operated on regular gas. In fact, they have been designed to do just that, in keeping with Studebaker's tradition of offering cars which are economical to operate.

This tradition goes deeper than mere fuel economy, too. Studebaker engines are plenty rugged and have been designed with lots of safety margin to insure long life with a minimum of repair bills.

One of Studebaker's weak points in recent years has been relatively poor steering and handling in general has suffered as a result. This has been changed for the better by a steering gear change on all V-8's. A roller-mounted single stud is now used in place of twin fixed studs. This reduces steering effort and has permitted a reduction in steering wheel turns lock-to-lock from 5.75 to 4.5 which providing a more positive steering response.

The variable-rate front springs add to riding comfort and general roadability.

They get progressively stiffer as road conditions, speed and load require—providing almost constant spring frequency at all times. This means you get a stiff, firm spring action for a smooth ride over rough surfaces and at high speed without sacrificing the comfort of soft springing over normal roads. The spring rate actually changes four times from normal conditions to full jounce—when it is almost four times higher than normal.

Studebaker's "twin-traction" differential is similar to the unit used on '56 Packards. Briefly, it divides engine power automatically under poor traction conditions, sending as much as 80 per cent to the wheel with the best "bite." A conventional axle differential, of course, follows the line of least resistance. Power goes to the wheel with least traction, which then spins fruitlessly.

These are the major engineering changes for 1957. There are a few others —higher capacity fuel pump, improved shock mountings, etc.—but those are the high spots.

Driver's Report—

By George Knight

SINCE there were no major changes made in Studebaker for 1957, we didn't expect it to be much different to drive. Though you can't say it feels like an entirely new and different automobile, there are noticeable improvements.

The most important doesn't take long to discover. The new steering setup with only 4.5 turns required lock-to-lock (vs. 5.75 last year) is it! Studebaker's slow steering was often criticized—and justly —in the past. While the new gear ratio certainly doesn't result in sports car style steering, it puts Studebaker at least on a par with other makes—and ahead of many. Nice thing about it is that it doesn't increase steering effort noticeably.

This one change alone has made a big difference in overall handling. Corners can be taken with much greater ease and security, helped by variable rate springs.

Studebaker's South Bend proving grounds has a road course with an amazing variety of bumps, dips, corners of varying radii and sundry other hazards designed to give a car a thorough—and literal—shake-down. Charging through this automotive obstacle course demonstrated that those springs with their unequally spaced coils really work. The way they adapted to conditions underfoot (or tire, actually) was eye-opening.

The surprising thing about these variable rate springs is that they haven't been used long ago. It seems like such a simple, obvious idea. Mike DeBlumenthal, Studebaker's chief research engineer, told us that developing them was not as easy as it might appear, however. The problem was to get them wound just right to achieve the desired effect. Now that it's been done, it wouldn't be surprising to see them used more widely.

As far as performance is concerned, there didn't seem to be a tremendous amount of difference from last year. Low-end and mid-range acceleration is a shade better, perhaps, but not markedly so. Unfortunately, we didn't get a crack at a President with the bigger engine.

Driving Stude's new Golden Hawk

BY KEN FERMOYLE

South Bend comes up with a new combination of power and styling. From behind the wheel, it feels like a car that will go places

WATCHING Bill Holland drive Studebaker's new Golden Hawk around the 2½-mile Packard test track at average speeds of more than 120 mph during the Studebaker-Packard press preview convinced me that here was a car the public would want to hear about—in detail—at first opportunity!

What is the Golden Hawk? Actually it's the successor to last year's Speedster hardtop coupe, but it's been drastically restyled—and uses the big 352-cubic-inch engine which powered the 1955 Packard. This engine develops 275 hp and puts out 380 foot-pounds of torque at 2800 rpm. This is a combination you would expect to go, and it does!

After spending some time driving it at Studebaker's South Bend proving ground I'm sure this will certainly be one of the top performing cars of 1956. The Golden Hawk I drove turned in 0 to 60 mph times of between 9.2 and 9.6 seconds; 50 to 80 mph averaged about 9.5 seconds, and the car jumped from a dead stop to 30 mph in 3.5 seconds. From 30 to 60 mph takes about six seconds.

As for top speed, few 1956 cars will be able to match it. I already mentioned Holland *averaging* over 120 mph on the Packard track. I had it up over 115 (indicated) on the eight-tenths of a mile straights on the Studebaker track; with more room to wind up it will probably nudge 125 mph.

The car I drove was a pre-production model, practically a hand-made prototype, and weighed about 3600 pounds. Production models will probably run some 150-200 pounds lighter, which should make performance even better. Another thing about the excess weight is that much of it was concentrated at the front of the car—the hand-made hood was so heavy it took a real effort to raise it. This undoubtedly hurt handling slightly.

In fact, the Golden Hawk's handling characteristics were among the things I was most interested in checking. I wondered if the heavier Packard V-8 would have much effect, although I knew the weight difference would not be too great since the Studebaker V-8 at 685 pounds is no lightweight.

Briefly, here's what I found. Although it is definitely nose-heavy, the car doesn't handle too badly. After a few runs to familiarize myself with the car and the track, I was able to get around the not-too-steeply banked corners at close to an indicated 90 mph. The car felt solid at those speeds, gave no indication that it was near the point of breaking loose.

Over the various paved road courses at the proving ground, the Golden Hawk maintained it's footing quite well, although we didn't attempt any really drastic cornering maneuvers. The ride was comfortable at all times.

The car has obviously been set up with riding comfort foremost and Studebaker has not attempted to give it real sports

car handling characteristics. In fact, they call the Hawks "sports-type cars" and let it go at that. Future Hawk owners who are willing to sacrifice a little comfort for a flatter ride will probably be able to do so by installing Air-Lifts, stiffer springs or by making similar modifications to the stock suspension.

While driving the car, I wondered what the future possibilities of adding Packard's torsion bar setup to it might be. Both Studebaker and Packard officials are very non-committal on this point, but it's not hard to foresee such a move being made in the future. That would make an extremely interesting combination!

The Golden Hawk has the new cast iron finned brake drums and they really do the job. These new brakes reduce fade to the point where it should be practically non-existent, even under severe braking conditions. My one complaint is that there is an awful lot of front end "dive" in anything but very moderate stops. Incorporation of an anti-dive arrangement similar to that used by Chevrolet would be a big improvement.

Another minor complaint I had was that the brake pedal (there was no clutch pedal since this car had the Twin-Ultramatic transmission) was in a rather awkward position. My toe repeatedly hit the steering column when I hit the brakes. A larger brake pedal which could be operated by either foot would cure this.

As I said, the Hawk I drove had an

Golden Hawk, successor to the 1955 Speedster and top car in a new sports-type series, shows modern classic style influence. Fins and deck lid are fiberglass.

Instrument panel is exceptional, even includes a built-in vacuum gage, alongside large easy-to-read tach and speedometer.

automatic transmission, but overdrive is available (no standard three-speed transmission is being offered, however). With automatic, a 3.07-to-1 rear axle ratio is used. With overdrive the ratio is 3.92-to-1, which should make the car even faster on acceleration.

The Golden Hawk is the top car in Studebaker's new Hawk series of low-slung hardtop and five-passenger coupes. The other models are the Sky Hawk, Power Hawk and Flight Hawk. The Sky Hawk is a hardtop, has a 289-cubic-inch V-8 rated at 210 hp. The Power and Flight Hawks are five-passenger coupes. The Power Hawk 259-cubic-inch V-8 delivers 170 hp, 185 with a four-barrel optional carburetor. Flight Hawk 185.6-cubic-inch Champ six is rated at 101 hp.

Compression ratio on the Golden Hawk is 9.5-to-1. A ratio of 7.8-to-1 is standard on other Hawk models but optional heads giving 8.3-to-1 can be had on the Sky and Power Hawks. •

Studebaker Engineer Ed Reynolds gives Fermoyle a briefing on the 352-cubic-inch engine. Note the novel hood-grille combination on this pre-production car.

Fermoyle bends the Golden Hawk through a tight corner. Although the suspension has been set up with comfortable ride in mind, the new sports-type of car handles well in most hard turns.

PETER CLARK with his controversial Studebaker.

STUDEBAKER COMMANDER
By Peter Clark

[*There was some leg-pulling in motoring circles last February when Peter Clark, well known as a vintage and Edwardian enthusiast pre-war and as a driver of H.R.G.s and Aston Martins for many years, bought a Studebaker. Some of our readers may indeed have noticed this striking " custard and blue " machine, with B.R.D.C. and V.S.C.C. badges looking mildly incongruous upon it, at Silverstone and elsewhere. Having known Peter throughout our respective careers, we had no hesitation in demanding " reasons in writing."—ED.*]

I DON'T think the Editor really believes that I own a Studebaker because I like it, but that is indeed the truth. At the end of 1953 I decided to give up active motor-racing, having reached the stage at which, in an era of intense competition and progress, I was spending more and more money for less and less return, and with my moderate abilities as a driver proving less and less capable of doing justice to the machine. I also decided to sell my much-developed Aston Martin DB2, in order to " put temptation out of my way."

At this moment, on a business visit to Holland, I made my first acquaintance in the flesh with the " new look " Studebaker with Italianate two-door coupé body designed by Raymond Loewy. I don't think even the most prejudiced Americano-phobe can deny that the car is beautiful to look at. What surprised me was to find that it was also a delight to drive, and seemed to possess a marked sort of personality. I think I was " sold " there and then.

Rather more than a year later came an opportunity to put these ideas to the test, when Henlys offered me a January, 1954, " Commander " with Borg-Warner automatic transmission and power steering at a not-too-ridiculous price. I had previously rejected one or two specimens either on price or for not having all of the desirable optional equipment. The American industry seems to operate in precisely the opposite manner from ours : here, a new car invariably seems to be tendered for delivery complete with radio, heater and every possible accessory including the kitchen stove ; with an American car, even the wheels and tyres are, if you will pardon the exaggeration and see what I mean, optional extras.

Anyway ; I duly bought OLF 580, and whilst waiting for it to be checked over and treated with Underseal, I telephoned my friend in Holland to ask what spares he had needed in 15 months of pretty hard use. His reply—" two fan belts "—was pretty encouraging.

I have appended a " data panel " to these notes, and no doubt the Editor will publish it if he considers it to be of sufficient general interest. Briefly, a 3,811-c.c. overhead-valve V8 engine drives through a Borg-Warner gearbox and an articulated two-part prop.-shaft to an orthodox hypoid rear axle. Front suspension is by dual wishbones with helical springs and telescopic dampers ; the rear end by very wide, very thin leaf-springs with dual telescopic dampers.

If I remember rightly, the weekly motoring journals gave a maximum speed of just over 100 m.p.h. for the car when road-tested, and this seems to be in line with mine. So also does the fuel consumption of around 20 m.p.g. under normal touring conditions.

Turning now to my particular reasons for liking the car, I would say that I like :

(1) The most comfortable driving position, with the best all-round visibility, I have ever known.

(2) The way in which, without having any apparent performance at all, the car innocently out-performs most others encountered on the road.

(3) The Borg-Warner automatic transmission which, if one is driving well, can be made to do exactly what one wants when one wants, but which, if one is driving like a clot, behaves like a double clot. Who then is laughing at whom ? Incidentally, although a great deal of the power developed by the engine gets lost along the transmission line a great deal of road performance is regained by those instantaneous gear-changes under full power.

(4) The steering and roadholding, which, once one has ceased to be alarmed by a good deal of " thumping and punching " from the suspension, are of a very high order. Indeed, I know of few cars

which can be put over the broken-up edges of a heavily cambered Continental secondary road at high speeds with greater equanimity. But the noises from the suspension system when one does so are, until one realises that they don't mean a thing, quite terrifying.

There are, of course, features on the debit side which have led to the car not being an outstanding commercial success and to its subsequent modification. First and foremost, for a car which although small by American standards is large in our eyes, there is surprisingly little room in it. Owing to the low bonnet line, the untidy-shaped V8 engine has to be set unusually far back, with the result that a third passenger on the front seat has either to be legless or a contortionist capable of folding his or her feet into his or her pockets—the central part of the front compartment being full of gearbox. Similarly, rear-seat passengers must not exceed 5 ft. 0 in. in height, otherwise they find an inadequacy of both headroom and legroom. The boot, so spectacular from outside, is rather a snare and delusion, too, for it is very shallow and irregular in shape. Thus although it will carry a vast number of squashy zip-bags which can be manoeuvred into odd shapes, it is defeated even by a single Revelation Rev-robe.

Mechanically, the brakes are the weakest feature, and a hurried journey on second-class winding roads—or a number of applications from 90 m.p.h. or so, as for a series of roundabouts—can produce appreciable fade. But, curiously enough, under true mountain conditions they were not nearly as bad as I had feared they were going to be, in fact they behaved very much better than those on the car I used on holiday last year, whose brakes under normal road conditions have always been excellent. This is perhaps not so illogical as might at first sight appear, as the Studebaker has such a vastly greater performance on the normal road.

Tyre wear is also a bit of a problem, in fact one's use of the car's full performance on the Continent tends to be moderated if one observes tyre temperatures after a couple of hours' high-speed run. This is by no means peculiar to the Studebaker, needless to say.

In the near future I hope to fit a four-choke carburetter conversion and have every intention of keeping this lovable car for at least a couple of years.

THE 1954 STUDEBAKER COMMANDER COUPE

Engine : Eight-cylinder, 85.73 by 82.55 mm., 3,812 c.c.; o.h.v. (pushrods); 7.5 to 1 compression ratio; twin-choke Stromberg carburetter; 120 b.h.p. at 4,000 r.p.m.

Rear axle : Salisbury hypoid, ratio 3.54 to 1.

Gearbox : Borg-Warner Automatic, with fluid coupling.

Brakes : Wagner Lockheed hydraulic; 173.4 sq. in. total area.

Tyres : 7.10 by 15.0 Firestone Whitewall, on bolt-on disc wheels.

Weight : 31 cwt. (less occupants, but ready for the road with nominally one gallon petrol).

Steering ratio : 4½ turns, lock-to-lock. Power-assisted.

Fuel capacity : 15 Imperial gallons, range approx. 300 miles. 20 m.p.g. at steady 60 m.p.h.

Wheelbase : 10 ft. 0½ in.

Track : 4 ft. 9 in. front, 4 ft. 8 in. rear.

Suspension : Front coil-springs and wishbones, telescopic dampers, torsional anti-roll bar. Rear semi-elliptic leaf-springs, twin telescopic dampers.

Overall dimensions : 17 ft. 0 in. by 5 ft. 0½ in. (high) by 5 ft. 11 in. (wide).

Makers : The Studebaker Corporation, South Bend 27, Indiana, U.S.A. (Studebaker Distributors Ltd., London, N.W.1).

1956

STUDEBAKER'S STATION WAGON offering for 1956 is one basic body shell, a two-door, six-passenger job on a basic 116½" wheelbase chassis, with three different engines and considerable variation in trim details.

Studebaker wagons are designed with passenger comfort as first consideration. The divided front seat is wide and comfortable, while the rear seat, equally accessible from left or right doors via the tilted seat backs, is very roomy considering the wagon's short wheelbase. Headroom, too, is adequate for both front and rear passengers.

Top of the line is the Pinehurst model powered by Studebaker's 289-cu. in. engine developing 195 bhp. (Optional 4-barrel carburetor increases horsepower to 210.) The Parkview wagon is powered with the smaller, 259-cu. in. engine developing 170 bhp. (An optional 4-barrel power pack boosts this wagon's bhp to 185.) The lowest priced wagon is the Pelham, powered by the 101 bhp Champion 6-cylinder engine.

The 6-cylinder Pelham wagon, although it shares the basic body and chassis with the V8s, differs in several respects. Biggest difference, of course, is performance. The 101-bhp Champion engine falls considerably below the performance standards that have come to be accepted as normal for smaller low-priced cars.

A full six passengers and baggage will put quite a load on the engine and limit performance considerably, particularly in hill climbing. Overdrive transmission is by far the best bet on the Pelham; it provides a very necessary extra gear ratio for acceleration and hill climbing without actual gear shifting on the driver's part. It is strongly recommended that prospective buyers choose one of the V8-powered wagons if they intend hauling any loads or want brisk acceleration.

Summing up: A graceful, compact and well-built group of two-door, six-passenger wagons designed for passenger comfort and convenience as well as cargo hauling potential. A wide selection of five separate engine horsepowers available permits choice in performance from barely adequate to excellent. Handling and roadability of V8 wagons are a bit below average, comfort a bit above. ●

☑☑☑☑ MEANS TOP RATING	**studebaker**
PERFORMANCE ☑☑☑☐	Ranges from excellent on 195-bhp, V8 Pinehurst model through good on 170-bhp Parkview to very mediocre on 101-bhp Pelham 6-cylinder wagon.
STYLING ☑☑☑☐	Generally pleasing and definitely a well-integrated wagon design, with emphasis on a total "passenger car look."
RIDING COMFORT ☑☑☑☐	Riding qualities are on the firm, well-controlled side, with a minimum of pitching or swaying.
INTERIOR DESIGN ☑☑☑☑	Excellent throughout, with a wide and fairly roomy second seat that's easy to reach via either half of divided front seat. Studebaker wagons emphasize passenger convenience and comfort above sheer cargo-carrying capacity. Cargo area is shorter than other wagons, although just as wide.
ROADABILITY ☑☑☑☐	About average for wagons of this wheelbase and weight. Soft springing and somewhat slow, sluggish steering proves difficult in sharp curves.
EASE OF CONTROL ☑☑☑☐	Good on 6-cylinder Pelham wagon. Heavier engines and corresponding higher steering ratio cuts down road sense and steering ease of other models, on which power steering is recommended.
ECONOMY ☑☑☑☑	Good on all models using manual transmission with overdrive. The 6-cylinder Pelham wagon with this combination offers gasoline mileage superior to all but similarly equipped Rambler.
SERVICEABILITY ☑☑☑☐	With new styling this year adding more room under the hood, the accessibility of engine parts is satisfactory.
WORKMANSHIP ☑☑☑☐	Better design of body parts has come with this year's major face lift; all traces of past flimsiness have disappeared.
DURABILITY ☑☑☑☐	Although not primarily intended for heavy commercial hauling, the Studebaker wagons give every indication of holding up well under years of use at the hands of an average private owner.
OPERATION OF DETAILS ☑☑☑☐	Back seat converts easily into a firm and rattle-free load platform. Tailgate and transom are solid and operate smoothly.
VALUE PER DOLLAR ☑☑☐☐	Studebaker has been plagued with low resale value in recent years. In addition the wagons have less physical load space behind the front seat than other low-priced wagons. Good performance and a well-designed body and chassis make Studebaker well worth considering for long-term ownership.

FACTS FOR THE BUYER

Wheelbase	116½"
Overall Length	198"
Width	71"
Rear Opening	
Width	40"
Height	30½"
Length of Load Space	
Seats in place, tailgate shut	25"
Seats folded, tailgate closed	73"
Back of front seat to end of open tailgate	92"
Width of Load Space	
Widest Point	58½"
Wheel Housings	42"
Height of Load Compartment	37"
Factory Delivered Price	
Pelham	$2229
Parkview	2350
Pinehurst	2525

PARKVIEW

PINEHURST

PELHAM

1956 STUDEBAKER

STUDEBAKER claims to be 80 per cent new for 1956. The Loewy-inspired body of 1953-55 did not go over too well with the general public, although purists approved. The low, sleek lines and unexcelled over-hood vision turned out to be a costly experiment.

Now Studebaker has an almost entirely new body, a longer and higher hood, and of all things, an egg crate grille.

The regular line of passenger cars, two and four-door sedans, are only slightly changed inside. The acoustical headliner, "Safety-Eye" speedometer that stands out boldly and efficiently from the top of the dash immediately in front of the driver and somewhat resembles a compass, and a wider selection of color tones account for interior changes.

Safety features include optional seat belts that are uniquely attached: the outside straps are secured to the doors. Brought across the body, these straps buckle to the inside straps which are attached in the conventional manner through the floor to the frame. Safety door latches are standard equipment.

Carrying the safety advances down below to the undercarriage, Studebaker has laterally finned brake drums, and effective brake lining area is increased. The past several years Studebaker brakes have been right at the top as far as efficiency is concerned; this year's brakes bring these very roadable cars to a quick stop in a straight line with only slight nose dipping.

Roomy enough for comfortable long distance traveling for 5 to 6 adults, there are four sedan models: Champion (with the economy-winning 6-in-line engine that delivers 101 horsepower), Commander V8 (with power upped to around 185), President State (with a more elegant interior that includes gold plated hardware and a variety of expensive upholstery and leather), and President Classic (with a new 289 cu. in. V8 engine that

delivers more than 200 horsepower). All sedans except the plush President Classic are on the 116½ inch wheelbase, the P. C. utilizing an adoption of the 120½ inch chassis common to the several sports type coupes covered elsewhere in this issue.

Studebaker continues to be a driver's car in that instrumentation is extremely easy to read. Unique black lighting causes no windshield glare. The best speedometer advance in years, the new unit is treated with luminous material, shows green to 35 mph, yellow to 60, and from there on up to the end a bright orange-red.

Manual transmission with or without overdrive is available, as is Studebaker's automatic unit which operates conventionally and indicates within the usual quadrant atop the steering column. You always get a Low ratio start in this automatic box as long as you floorboard the throttle.

Starting from a stop, and with the throttle pedal on the floor, the President Classic's big 289 cu. in. engine snapped to a calibrated speed of 60 mph in exactly 11 seconds. This sedan weighs about 3400 pounds ready for the road, giving a weight to power ratio of approximately 17 pounds per bhp. This most powerful Studebaker family car will flash to 80 mph from a cruising speed of 50 mph in a shade over 9½ seconds—very respectable performance for a car that has never laid claims to being a dragster.

The new series will continue to be economical with mileage going all the way to around 28 miles per gallon in the Champion and averaging out to about 17-19 in the 200-plus horsepower President Classic.

Roadability is improved over last year's car, probably due mostly to reworked rear shock absorbers and changed spring rates. Lapping the track full bore pushed the needle to over 100 mph. This is a fine-handling car that sticks to the road like a thoroughbred. ●

YOUR CHECK LIST
☑ ☑ ☑ ☑ ☑ means top rating

PERFORMANCE ☑ ☑ ☑ ☑ ☑
More dig and top speed than the average family man is likely to need is what the top car of the line, the President Classic offers. Other models are also right up with the pack in their class.

STYLING ☑ ☑ ☑ ☑ ☐
In spite of arguments that are bound to develop, the '56 has had a functional restyling job both inside and out. Rear luggage capacity has been increased, the hood is broader and has a slightly raised line, and low overall height has been retained without sacrificing any interior space. Many new color tones are available.

RIDING COMFORT ☑ ☑ ☑ ☑ ☐
Firmness that resists excessive roll-over and yet allows one to keep his seat position without undue tossing around the inside of the car is a Studebaker strong point. One of the lowest centers of gravity in the industry make this a fine small-medium sized car on any kind of terrain.

INTERIOR DESIGN ☑ ☑ ☑ ☑ ☑
Many of the upholstery materials are such rich looking fabrics and plastics throughout the 4 series that they look like higher-priced cars rather than a line that starts down low and goes into the medium-priced range.

ROADABILITY ☑ ☑ ☑ ☐ ☐
Although not the best due to comparatively soft springing and too slow steering, this car remains remarkably stable on all but the tightest curves.

EASE OF CONTROL ☑ ☑ ☑ ☑ ☐
Easily handled on the open road, this fairly light car is *not* a wind wanderer. Handling would be just about what the traveling family's doctor ordered with faster steering, because even without power, the center point steering (equal length tie rods) gives this car the easiest steering in its low-medium price class.

ECONOMY ☑ ☑ ☑ ☑ ☑
From Champions through the Commander V8 and on into the new President line, the new model will probably prove to be one of the most economical cars to operate. The Commander engine, especially, offers sprightly performance with economy up to 19 miles per gallon when traveling at from 50 to 60 all day long on the open road.

SERVICEABILITY ☑ ☑ ☑ ☑ ☐
Considering the ease of servicing the Champion 6 engine, and now becoming accustomed to the two sizes of V8 engines, mechanics will have little trouble on this score.

WORKMANSHIP ☑ ☑ ☑ ☑ ☐
The new model shows a decided improvement over the last three years when the workmanship, at times, was not up to snuff. Now, however, we noted new attention to die work and consequently a high quality of workmanship on the interior.

DURABILITY ☑ ☑ ☑ ☑ ☐
Class for class, Studebaker has kept the faith with those who demand economy along with durability. This is a relatively uncomplicated car and is therefore likely to exhibit durability traits that other cars may have passed up in their race to attain speeds and acceleration figures that are not practical in everyday use.

VALUE PER DOLLAR ☑ ☑ ☑ ☐ ☐
In most sections of the country Studebaker's resale value has risen in the past year. The lines of this new model and many of the new features will result in a gradual rise in the resale value.

THE STUDEBAKER IS THE CAR FOR YOU

If . . . you want a car that's freshly designed for 1956 with many practical improvements such as the "Safety Eye" speedometer.

If . . . you want a car that has plenty of go and yet will give economical performance. at all speeds.

If . . . you want a light car that handles well at turnpike speeds and is especially easy to steer.

If . . . you want a car that has been a consistent style leader since the end of the second world war and will probably continue to be one.

If . . . you want a car that carries all the latest safety devices—and has the brakes that make it one of the safest to stop in emergencies.

STUDEBAKER

PACKARD IS DEPENDING on Studebaker for volume in their merged business, but the results have been disappointing. Registrations as of last October (latest conclusive figure available as we went to press) show about 80,000 '55 model Studebakers sold. This was slightly better than the year before, but compares badly with the 1950 heyday when 230,000 units were in the hands of owners on an equivalent date.

Studebaker-Packard President James Nance has frankly and often stated his opinion as to the why of the slump. In effect, he feels that controversial (European) design does not appeal to the average American. 1956 is the 1st chance he has had to apply corrective measures; the new sedan models combine beauty with orthodoxy tho the Hawk series (see page 20) is more continental than ever.

Test car: President Classic 4-door sedan with Flightomatic (Borg-Warner type) automatic transmission, 3.31 to 1 rear axle ratio. Car was not equipped with either power steering or power brakes, but had many luxury items such as power windows and front seat, padded dash, radio, thermo-

statically controlled heater, and windshield washers. Essentially, it is a newly named version of last year's top-line President State sedan.

Engine: The Classic's ohv V8 is a power-pack on top of the 289-cubic-inch engine used in lesser Presidents. Developing 210 horsepower at 4500 rpm, it boasts a 4-barrel carburetor and dual exhausts as standard equipment. Acceleration, both from a standing start and in the passing ranges, really surprised us, perhaps because of the modest (compared to competitive makes) torque claim of 292 pounds-feet at 2800 rpm.

Other options: Three-speed or overdrive transmissions can be had, both equipped with hill holder. Power brakes and steering are not very necessary (see below) extra-cost options. Electric windows are optional in either the front or both sets of doors and air-conditioning is available for the first time this year.

WHAT THE CAR IS LIKE TO DRIVE

Exit and entry: Altho the doors seem less

wide than other cars at 1st glance, drive and passengers find it easy to get in or ou There is enough height between sill an rain gutter to maneuver without knockin your hat off, but you should guard again hurting yourself on the sharp top corne of the front doors. Operation of the do check was not positive, at least on the te car, but the new outside handles are ea to use even after the car has stood out a night in an ice storm. Inside handles a placed too far forward to gain levera when opening the door, requiring a com bination of pull and body block to get ou

Driving position: The Classic offers a unusual amount of elbow room for t driver, as the steering column seems move over from the left door more than other cars. The wheel itself felt a little t upright at first, but we soon became us to it. Most novel instrument is the ne "Cyclops-Eye" speedometer, reminiscent the old magnifying type used on Model Fords and very readable. It changes colo from green through orange to red as ye go up thru the speed range. Other gaug are arranged in a line below and cou well be slanted upward at the driver

These Studebakers have gone American—in looks, power, new accessories—and at a price to please the hunter for a bountiful bargain

PRESIDENT ROAD TEST

AN MT RESEARCH REPORT

better readability. Readings are approximations at best on the gas and temperature dials, as there is nothing to guide you but the relative areas of green and red showing. Oil pressure gauge and ammeter at opposite ends of the cluster are elaborations on the usual warning light, reading "low oil pressure" or "no charge" when applicable, dormant otherwise. Foot controls are conveniently placed, especially the brake for left-foot addicts.

Vision: Studebaker's windshields are moderately wrapped (on sedan models only), being more akin to Chrysler than to GM or Ford products. Forward vision is still excellent despite this year's much higher hood line, except in bad weather when the extra glass area is wasted by the inadequate sweep of the wiper blades. "Camomatic" or equivalent action could at least be sold as an accessory. All fenders can readily be seen by the driver, and rearward vision is exceptional—you can see almost as much in the mirror as you can by turning around.

Operation of accessories: The unlighted switches are all of the push-pull type except one of the heater controls which must be turned. We'll wager every new owner will pull the handle off at least once on this. A simple solution would be to etch an arrow as a guide to unwary novices in the car. We grant that mysteries in the operation of controls are soon solved by an owner (or you can check out with the instruction book), but we feel justified in carping on a small item like this because oftentimes other people, such as parking lot attendants and maiden aunts, get behind the wheel and they can't be expected to figure things out immediately. Another Classic classic in inconvenience is the well-hidden control for the power seat, the location of which (roughly under the cushion between the driver's legs) our test crew never did get used to. Other units are admirably thought out. The radio is as close to the driver as any on the market, as is the well-lighted glove compartment. Power window controls are at the fingertips of your left hand. We liked the right-hand operation of the easy-sliding T-handled emergency brake.

Ease of handling: For a fairly big (nearly 205 inches overall) car not equipped in test form with power steering, the Classic handled with delightful ease. Even without ideal weight distribution, maneuvering at parking speeds could be hard for no-one. The rather high steering ratio (5¼ turns from lock to lock) helps here but still feels good at high speeds on winding roads. We have never driven an American-made car without power steering that was so little bothered by car tracks and similar types of obstructions.

Acceleration: The Classic offers dramatic improvement in this department (see table for comparison). It's right on a par with such dragsters as the '55 Oldsmobile Super 88. Some years ago we used to complain that even V8 Studebakers were lacking in that extra margin of high-speed passing ability that sometimes can spell the difference between an accident and a close squeeze. From 50 to 80 mph in DRIVE range, the Classic was exceeded by only 5 of last year's test cars, and 3 of these were in the highest price field. *(Continued)*

photos by Jim Lodge

New higher hood line, as well as imparting American look, improves servicing by making all equipment easier to reach. Hood is not counterbalanced, tho

Similar improvement occurs at rear, for the higher decklid gives the President Classic and all Studebaker sedans much more room for luggage (or equipment)

The Flightomatic selector handle was reasonably positive in operation with the quadrant well lighted for night operation. This type of transmission, while not the smoothest nowadays, is still a good compromise. There is no advantage to manual selection of ranges for greater performance.

Braking: Studebaker brakes have lately been noted for their fine performance, and those on the Classic were no exception. They have finned drums for better cooling, which is perhaps one of the reasons the car passed our severe fade test (12 consecutive stops from 60 mph at a deceleration rate of 15 feet per second per second) without a trace of tiredness. Stopping distance hasn't been materially improved over last year's excellent 174 feet from 60 mph. The wide pedal is easy to reach, especially with the left foot, so reaction time is cut to a minimum.

seems a little less stiff than some other makes of cars.

WHAT THE CAR IS LIKE TO LIVE WITH

Riding in the front seat: Legroom is exceptional without having the seat in full back position. Armrests are well-positioned for the average driver. Even tho equipped at the factory with foam cushions, seat is firm enough for long trip comfort.

Riding in the rear seat: Fair space for 3 overcoated adults. Tunnel is not bothersome, due to 2-piece construction of driveshaft. Ideal loading is 2 people, as a folding center armrest is standard.

ECONOMY AND EASE OF MAINTENANCE

Fuel economy: More power and the tendency to use it will have an adverse effect

test mileage (450 miles) failed to produce any sign of abnormal wear. Our general impression is that Studebakers are husky cars that are capable of coping with most any driving condition.

Servicing: Garagemen will appreciate the greatly improved engine accessibility in this year's car. Even with power accessories (our test car had none) there is plenty of room to work. We don't particularly favor a non-counterbalanced hood, especially a heavy one; once the support is in place, you feel reasonably secure. Yet there is the possibility of knocking against it and having the hood slam down on you.

SUMMING UP

The Classic is Studebaker's luxury automobile, and unless you go wild with the accessory list, it can be gotten at a price well within the low-medium price field.

Ford Model A type magnified speedometer is good-looking, supremely readable. Other gauges are too low and tipped at wrong angle to make most of the design

Glove compartment is in safest location, not overly roomy. Why-did-they-do-it note: ashtray is too far from driver, collides with compartment door when open

Roadability: The Classic is a good road car, even when compared to its very agile Hawk brothers. Lean during hard cornering is not disturbing to driver or passengers and there is plenty of power to correct any tendency to slide. It hugs the road at high speeds, not being too much disturbed by crosswinds or crowned surfaces. Vibration from the 2-piece driveshaft, a chronic complaint against past Studebakers, has all but been eliminated.

Ride: Road noise is apparent at certain low speeds but paradoxically, not in higher ranges. Springs are firm and will allow the front end to bottom only on severe potholes. This would be one wheel or the other; we didn't encounter any condition that would bottom front or rear sets of wheels. Judging from mild body creaks on rough roads at slow speeds, the frame

on your fuel bill. Economy is still good for a full-sized, high-powered car. Our tank average on this particular test is artificially low as much of our driving (with the exception of performance checks) was limited by bad weather to city streets.

Is the car well put together? Our test Classic was one of the 1st cars to come off the South Bend production line at the start of the '56 model run. Despite this handicap, everything fit well. We particularly liked the rigid trunk lid with just the right degree of counterbalancing. Upholstery was nicely tailored but the interior in general lacked the degree of richness one might expect from a top-of-the-line car. Paint and chrome showed no flaws. The heater switch needs to be sturdier.

How did it hold up? Lower than usual

We think the new styling is outstanding and the car performs as well as it looks. There isn't much more you can ask for in a new family car.

OTHER STUDEBAKERS

Unusually broad coverage of automotive buyers' likes and dislikes results from the new Studebaker-Packard policy. Unlikely to attract too much attention this year is the relatively simple, ultra-economical Champion, which is mechanically much like MT's '55 test car (tested in Sept. '55). Otherwise, it shares many of the President's features in less glamorous form. The compact Commander V8 attempts with considerable success, to give its owner some of the advantages of both Champion and President. It has excellent economy (tho not up to the Champion's), good performance, quality trim.   **—Don MacDonald**

'56   '55

	'56 (210-bhp engine)	**'55** (175-bhp engine)
ACCELERATION	From Standing Start 0-30 mph 4.0 0-60 mph 11.1 Quarter-mile 18.3 and 77 mph	From Standing Start 0-30 mph 3.0 0-60 mph 13.2 Quarter-mile 19.4 and 66 mph
	Passing Speeds 30-50 mph 5.1 50-80 mph 12.6	Passing Speeds 30-50 mph 6.2 50-80 mph 14.9
TOP SPEED	Fastest run 104.7 Slowest 95.2 Average of 4 runs 101.2	Fastest run 107.1 Slowest 102.7 Average of 4 runs 104.8
FUEL CONSUMPTION	Used Mobilgas Regular Steady Speeds 20.8 mpg @ 30 19.8 mpg @ 45 16.6 mpg @ 60 13.3 mpg @ 75	Used Mobilgas Special Steady Speeds 22.6 mpg @ 30 22.1 mpg @ 45 18.5 mpg @ 60 14.1 mpg @ 75
	Stop-and-Go Driving 13.2 mpg over measured course 13.5 mpg tank average for 447 miles	Stop-and-Go Driving 15.9 mpg over measured course 15.1 mpg tank average for 968 miles
STOPPING DISTANCE	171 feet from 60 mph	174 feet from 60 mph
SPEEDOMETER ERROR	Read 33 at true 30, 48 at 45, 65 at 60, and 80 at 75	Read 33 at true 30, 50 at 45, 66 at 60, and 81 at 75
REAR-WHEEL HORSEPOWER	Clayton chassis dynamometer showed: 64 road hp @ 2000 rpm and 39 mph 78 road hp @ 2500 rpm and 64 mph 87.5 road hp @ 3000 rpm and 80 mph 89 road hp (max.) @ 3200 rpm, 84 mph	Clayton chassis dynamometer showed: 46 road hp @ 1500 rpm and 36 mph 60 road hp @ 2000 rpm and 49 mph 73 road hp @ 2500 rpm and 60 mph 82 road hp (max.) @ 3200 rpm, 80 mph

'56 STUDEBAKER
President Classic
4-door sedan
with Flightomatic

S P E C I F I C A T I O N S

ENGINE: Ohv V8. Bore 3.56 in. Stroke 3.63 in. Stroke/bore ratio 1.02:1. Compression ratio 8.3:1. Displacement 289 cu. in. Advertised bhp 210 @ 4500 rpm. Bhp per cu. in. 0.727. Piston travel @ max. bhp 2726 ft. per min. Max. bmep 152.4 psi. Max. torque 292 lbs.-ft. @ 2800 rpm.

TRANSMISSION. Standard transmission is 3-speed synchromesh with helical gears. Automatic transmission is Flightomatic, 3-element torque converter with planetary gearset. Overdrive transmission is standard shift with planetary gearset.

RATIOS: Drive 1st 2.40 x converter ratio, 2nd 1.47 x converter ratio, 3rd 1.00 x converter ratio; Low 2.40 x converter ratio; Reverse 2.0 x converter ratio. Maximum converter ratio at stall 2.15 @ 1800 rpm.

REAR-AXLE RATIOS: Conventional 3.54, Flightomatic 3.31, Overdrive 4.09.

STEERING: Turning diameter 41 ft. Number of turns lock to lock 5.25. Overall ratio: mechanical 24 to 1, power 20 to 1. TYPE: Mechanical, Cam and twin lever. Power, Saginaw integral.

WEIGHT: Test car weight (with gas, oil, and water) 3750 lbs. Test car weight/bhp ratio 17.9:1.

TIRES: 7.10 x 15 tubeless.

PRICES: (Including suggested retail price at main factory, federal tax, and delivery handling charges but not freight.) 2-door sedan $2184, 4-door sedan $2231, Classic 4-door sedan $2485, 2-door station wagon $2525.

ACCESSORIES: Flightomatic $189, overdrive $118, power brakes $38, power steering $108, power windows (4) $103, (2) $54, power seat $45, radio $74 and $97, heater $68, air conditioning $459.

DIMENSIONS

A	FRONT OVERHANG **36.4**		H	FRONT HEADROOM **36.5**
B	WHEELBASE **120.5**		I	REAR HEADROOM **35.5**
C	REAR OVERHANG **47.9**		J	OVERALL LENGTH **204.8**
D	OVERALL HEIGHT **60**		K	OVERALL WIDTH **71.3**
E	MINIMUM GROUND CLEARANCE **7.3**		L	FRONT SHOULDER ROOM **55.5**
F	FRONT LEGROOM **42.5**		M	REAR SHOULDER ROOM **54.5**
G	REAR LEGROOM **41**			

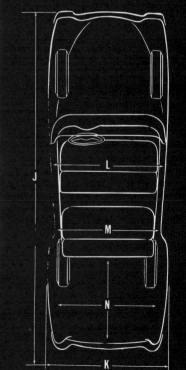

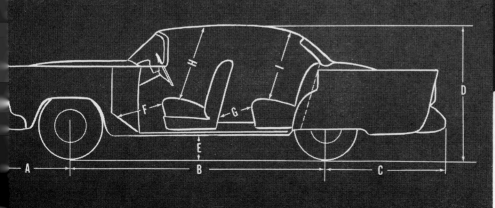

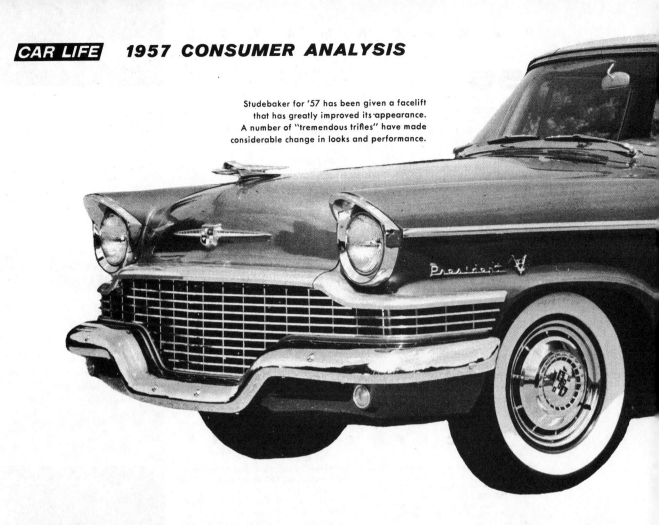

Studebaker for '57 has been given a facelift
that has greatly improved its appearance.
A number of "tremendous trifles" have made
considerable change in looks and performance.

STUDEBAKER

By JAMES WHIPPLE

STUDEBAKER is one of the three low-priced cars that do not have completely new chassis and bodies for 1957 (the others are Chevy and Rambler). Studebaker went through a major re-design in '56. Even a major auto-maker can't afford a complete change every year; for an independent like Studebaker it would spell immediate bankruptcy.

Stude has been given a styling facelift that has, we feel, considerably improved the car's overall appearance. The changes involve grille, front bumper, tail-lights and side trim strips which define the two-toning.

The whole front end of the car has been "cleaned up", with one grille made up of thin horizontal strips "wrapped around" the fenders instead of last year's somewhat oddly shaped combination of egg-crate central grille and two flanking air intakes.

Appearance is important to the owner of a car, as Studebaker Corporation learned to its sorrow back in 1950 and '51 when a shark-like torpedo nose was tacked onto the crisp, squarish Loewy-designed body. The lines of a car are even more vital to public acceptance than the horsepower, as witnessed by the healthy minority who order less powerful engines under sleek hoods.

This year Studebaker has completed the job of smartening up the basic two and four door sedans and wagons that started with last year's model. The cars stand out as a variation on the general Detroit theme, yet do not appear odd or awkward as they have in years past.

Although Studebaker advertising can boast of no world-shaking engineering advances this year, we found that a number of "tremendous trifle" changes have improved the car very considerably.

After putting the '57 Commander through a thorough workout on Studebaker's own proving ground I came to the conclusion that the Studebaker-Packard Corporation's financial difficulties have had no ill effects on Studebaker engineering or production. The automobile is rock-solid with a high level of quality control evident throughout. In fact, the fit and finish of paint, trim and upholstery were superior to that of some competitive cars produced by the billion-dollar automotive goliaths.

The two most important engineering changes for '57 affect the Stude's ride and handling, and among other things prove that definite improvements can be made in steering and springing without a complete re-design of chassis and suspension components.

Possibly the most interesting improvement is the variable rate front suspension. This consists of a unique type of coil spring used in the Studebaker parallel control arm independent suspension set-up which is otherwise unchanged. This special spring has unequally spaced coils, set close together near each end and further apart in the mid-section.

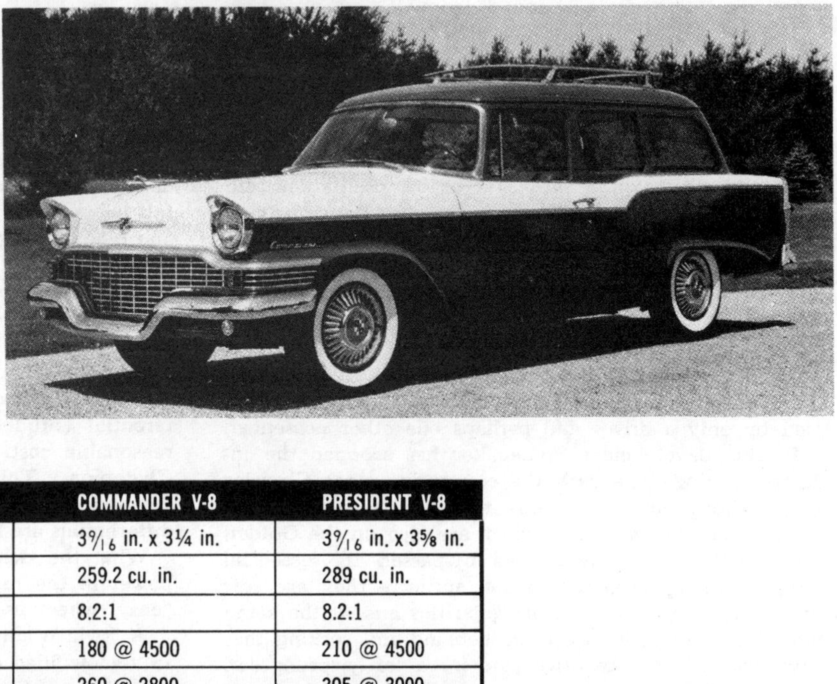

A revamped suspension system, utilizing a "helper" spring, supplies a firmer support to Stude station wagon bodies when they're loaded with cargo. Wagons seat six.

ENGINES	SIX	COMMANDER V-8	PRESIDENT V-8
Bore and stroke	3 in. x 4⅜ in.	3⁹⁄₁₆ in. x 3¼ in.	3⁹⁄₁₆ in. x 3⅝ in.
Displacement	185.6 cu. in.	259.2 cu. in.	289 cu. in.
Compression ratio	7.8:1	8.2:1	8.2:1
Max. brake horsepower	101 @ 4000	180 @ 4500	210 @ 4500
Max. torque	152 @ 1800	260 @ 2800	305 @ 3000
DIMENSIONS		(President Classic)	
Wheelbase	116½ in.	120½ in.	
Overall length	202⅜ in.	206½ in.	
Overall width	67¾ in.	67¾ in.	
Overall height	60 in.	60 in.	
TRANSMISSIONS	Standard synchromesh Overdrive, Flightomatic		
PRICE RANGE	(Factory List Price) $1,823 (Six) to $2,314 (V-8)		

New tail-lights give an impression
of greater styling change than actually
exists. Stude has completed a process
of "smartening up" that began last year.

The theory behind it is ingeniously simple; on moderate irregularities such as brick, cobblestones or broken concrete, the entire spring flexes at a low oscillation rate giving a soft, "boulevard" type of ride; when the going gets rougher and you're on a bumpy, high-crowned stretch of macadam, the closely-spaced coils come in contact with each other and act to stiffen up the spring, increase the oscillation rate and prevent the car from pitching, "plowing" and bottoming.

These springs also act to level out the differences in riding qualities between a fully loaded car and one occupied by only a driver and perhaps one other passenger.

In this development Studebaker has scooped the industry, having done with the coil spring what Chrysler and Packard have been able to do with torsion bars. Stude's variable rate coils, which are also on the Golden Hawk and Silver Hawk, have by-passed the essential compromise of conventional coil springs — they are soft enough to blot up surface irregularities and at the same time firm enough to resist the bobbing and rocking that have always been the price paid for a softly-sprung car.

You will find when you try a new Studebaker that it is one of the better riding cars on the market, whereas previously it was a car of indifferent riding qualities.

An important change in steering action has combined with the firmer suspension control to make a substantial improvement in Studebaker handling.

A roller-bearing mounted single stud has replaced the solid twin-stud set-up in the steering gear and it cuts operating friction up to 60 per cent. This has enabled Studebaker engineers to reduce the number of steering wheel turns from left to right lock from 5¾ to 4½ turns. Although the reduction doesn't sound very impressive, this "quicker" steering has made handling much more positive.

Studebaker continues the variable ratio steering worm gear which provides more mechanical advantage (i.e. more turns of the steering wheel per degree of pivoting of the front wheels) as the wheels are turned more to the right or left. The theory is that these sharp turns which call for full swing of the front wheels will be taken at a slow speed and require greater effort on the part of the driver, such as cutting the wheels sharply in parking maneuvers, etc.

As a result of this steering set-up we don't believe that most buyers of '57 Champions or Commanders will need the optional power steering.

Another bit of pioneering done by Studebaker this year is the option of a factory installed limited-slip differential (Studebaker calls it "twin traction") at a very reasonable cost. (Twin traction is not available on the Champion.) This is an exclusive for Studebaker in the low-priced field. The only other cars to offer limited-slip differentials are Lincoln and Packard.

What the twin traction differential does is to provide power to the rear wheel with traction as well as to the "easy" wheel, as in the case of a conventional differential.

A "twin traction" equipped Studebaker with one wheel in a snow-filled ditch and the other on dry pavement will be able to pull out with ease, whereas a car with conventional differential will be hopelessly stuck. The cost of the limited-slip differential will be paid for in the savings of a few tow charges and a set of chains during the first winter of ownership.

Interior styling is excellent this year. Studebaker styling is bright and attractive without the gaudy or "jazzy" look of so many Super DeLuxe models where violent colored bits of cloth, metal, striping and plastic are tossed around indiscriminately to create a "juke box" effect.

SUMMING UP: The Studebaker is a well styled, attractive car with a very satisfactory degree of quality workmanship that offers superior riding comfort, a durable V8 engine of good performance and a smoothly operating automatic transmission. ●

Studebaker has changed the instrument panel and radio grille for '57. Iluminated toggle switches designate the various controls.

STUDEBAKER
is the car
for you

If . . . You want a well-designed car that's roomy yet not too bulky or overly long.

If . . . You want fresh, well-balanced, modern styling done up in pleasing colors that avoid the "rocket-ship" look.

If . . . You want one of the most comfortable riding, easy handling cars in the low and medium-priced class.

If . . . You are willing to accept a higher rate of depreciation and plan on long and loyal ownership of a soundly engineered, well built car.

Category	Description	Rating
PERFORMANCE	The 195 bhp V8 of 259 cubic inches provides excellent acceleration and effortless cruising speed for the Commanders and Station Wagons. The Champion, although fairly light in weight, needs more power than the 101 bhp provided by the familiar flathead six of 185 cubic inches. The President's 289 cubic inch engine rated at 225 provides adequate but unsensational performance somewhat below that of the other '57's in its price class.	✓✓✓☐☐
STYLING	Although not startlingly low or screamingly outstanding the '57 Studebakers are very well balanced and good-looking cars, by far the most handsome cars the firm has turned out in some years. We found that the more time we spent with the car the more we came to like its new grille and trim lines.	✓✓✓✓☐
RIDING COMFORT	Studebaker's new variable rate coil springs front suspension plus remounted shock absorbers have given it one of the best all around rides in the indutry — soft enough for vibration absorption, firm enough for stability.	✓✓✓✓☐
INTERIOR DESIGN	Although not quite as wide as some of the competition, Studebakers have plenty of legroom for both front and back seat passengers, as well as comfortable seating position and adequate headroom. Wrap around windshield does not jut into front door opening. All-around vision is very good.	✓✓✓☐☐
ROADABILITY	New springing has improved the stability of all models, cutting down roll and "plowing" during negotiation of sharp curves. However, there is some tendency for the rear end of the V8 to break loose when car is lightly loaded and is being cornered on rough pavement or dirt and gravel.	✓✓✓✓☐
EASE OF CONTROL	The re-designed steering gear has brought Studebaker handling up to the level of its competition. Combined with the new stability of suspension, the "quicker" steering (without power assist) makes Studebakers easy to handle on indifferent roads.	✓✓✓✓☐
ECONOMY	Studebaker Champion with overdrive is probably the most thrifty car in the ranks of full-sized U. S. autos. The V8 Studebakers will match their competition in economy, but are not outstanding.	✓✓✓✓☐
SERVICEABILITY	Simple, soundly-engineered components of Studebakers and relatively uncluttered engine compartments make them as easy to service as any of the modern V8's.	✓✓✓☐☐
WORKMANSHIP	The few cars we've observed of the model '57 run were very well assembled and showed no rough edges. The quality of interior trim and upholstery was outstanding.	✓✓✓✓☐
VALUE PER DOLLAR	As an outright transportation buy Studebakers are equal to most of their competition. However, a higher-than-average rate of depreciation makes them a good investment only on the basis of subsequent trade in on newer Studebakers or careful maintenance and long term ownership.	✓✓✓☐☐

STUDEBAKER OVERALL RATING . . . 3.6 CHECKS

Studebaker

What's New?

McCulloch supercharged, Studebaker-powered Golden Hawk . . . Moderate face-lift on Hawk series, more major on sedans and wagons . . . Newly available four-door station wagons . . . Variable-rate coils in front suspension . . . Optional limited-slip, balanced traction differential.

Your Choice

The Hawk series, still based fundamentally on the original Loewy design of 1953, is as close to a sports car as you can get at a reasonable price and still carry the whole family in closed comfort. A McCulloch supercharger is standard equipment on the Golden Hawk hardtop. Silver Hawk V8s and sixes come in coupe form, use unsupercharged engines. Pricewise, the Hawks embrace competition from the low to upper middle field. However, since there is nothing else quite like them, they are not usually compared with other cars. They are bought by people who have driving fun with the family in mind.

The six-cylinder Champions, V8 Commanders and Presidents have some of the Hawk's styling flair, but are higher, more conservative. Following the trend set last year, grilles are entirely different. The sedans and wagons have been Americanized, the Hawks made even more European in flavor.

The only hardtop available is the Golden Hawk. There are no four-door hardtops. The President Classic sedan is mounted on the longer (120.5 inch) Hawk wheelbase while all other Studebaker sedans and wagons use a short and maneuverable 116.5 inch chassis. Two-door sedans can be either President, Commander, or Champion; two-door station wagons the latter two, and four-door wagons the first two. Some sort of Studebaker should be priced and inspected if you are buying in the low or medium price field. If you can pay a little more, check the new Packard (see page 56) Clipper which is still basically Studebaker but fancier.

Studebaker Power

Big news is the McCulloch blower, last used on an American production car by Kaiser in 1955. Studebaker doesn't have to try and make gold out of bricks though. The 289-cubic-inch, Studebaker-built V8 responds beautifully to the boost. Although the 65 added horsepower claimed (to 275 from 210) seems extravagant, the performance belies our doubts. Our check (MT, Dec. '56) shows the supercharged Hawk to perform almost exactly on a par with last year's Packard-powered model; further testing may prove it's better!

Presidents use the same engine unsupercharged. With a four-barrel carburetor, it is rated at 225 horsepower and drops 15 units when equipped with the standard two-barrel. The smaller, 259-cubic-inch Commander V8 puts out 195 and 180 horsepower with corresponding equipment. Silver Hawks use the President engine, or Champion sixes which are strictly for the economy-minded.

Three transmissions are optional on all but the Golden Hawk, with, of course, synchromesh being standard for the lesser cars. Studebaker's Flightomatic is of basic Borg-Warner design and quite similar to the automatics used by Ford and Mercury, namely a torque converter coupled to a two-speed planetary gear box. A throttle kickdown for fast takeoffs or passing is a useful feature. So is the automatic hill-holder on cars equipped with three-speed or overdrive. It has saved many a clutch in its long history.

Studebaker on the Road

Last year's Golden Hawk had the weight distribution of a blackjack. The heavy Packard engine mounted well forward in the otherwise light car caused the rear wheels to have at most times only the loosest kind of a relationship to the highway. Studebaker-powered Hawks, on the other hand, handled beautifully. This year, the light engine with a supercharger (that only weighs about 40 pounds installed) proves to be an ideal combination for both performance and handling, though reliability may suffer.

Sedan and wagon models feature variable rate front coil springs in an effort to equalize action under all load and surface conditions. Unevenly spaced coils are eliminated individually from the springing action as they progressively nest against adjoining coils. The optional limited slip differential is a real boon for an owner who drives much on icy or muddy roads. Tractive effort can be directed through one wheel when the other can't get a bite.

Inside Your Studebaker

The enthusiastic driver-owner of a Golden Hawk will delight in the machine-turned panel containing a complete set of Stewart-Warner instruments, including tachometer and vacuum gauges. Lesser Hawks have everything but the latter two. Sedan and wagon models feature the "Cyclops Eye" speedometer, reminiscent of the Model A's rheumy gas gauge, and interesting lesser gauges that overlap red on green or vice-versa, depending on the state of your fuel, oil, generator, or water in the radiator.

Seating position in sedans is normal chair height and quite comfortable. Visibility over the slope-down hood cannot be equaled. Hawk seating position is a little too close to the floor for long-distance comfort. It is similar to a rowing machine and we found that our thigh muscles tired after several hours behind the wheel. The Hawk rear seat is adequate for two adults on short trips, excellent for children on any length trip.

Why Buy?

If you want an American-built sports-type car and your family insists on coming along, a Hawk is your *only* choice . . . Supercharged power is not only practical but a fine conversation piece . . . Studebaker workmen, ever since 1953 complaints, have been quality-conscious to an extreme . . . Car is consistently rated by independent authorities as giving most value for the money.

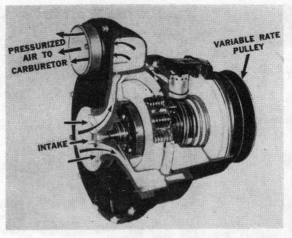

MC CULLOCH supercharger on Golden Hawks is a five-pound boost, full-pressure system, makes '57 version as hot as big Packard-engined '56 Golden Hawk.

BETTER RESISTANCE to fade on Studebakers results from use of 11-inch, finned drums.

Labels on image 1: PRESSURIZED AIR TO CARBURETOR; VARIABLE RATE PULLEY; INTAKE

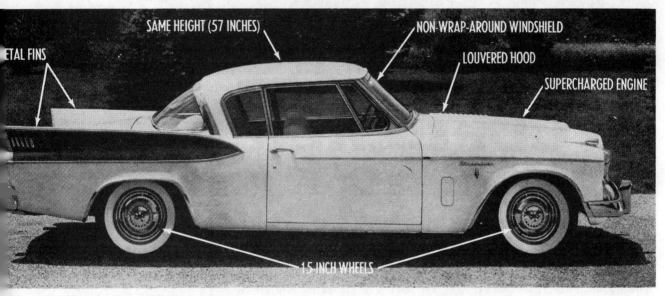

ETAL FINS · SAME HEIGHT (57 INCHES) · NON-WRAP-AROUND WINDSHIELD · LOUVERED HOOD · SUPERCHARGED ENGINE · 15-INCH WHEELS

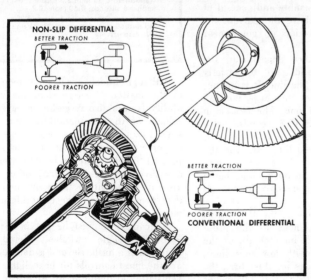

NON-SLIP DIFFERENTIAL
BETTER TRACTION
POORER TRACTION

BETTER TRACTION
POORER TRACTION
CONVENTIONAL DIFFERENTIAL

OPTIONAL on all Studebakers is limited-slip differential that allows up to 80 per cent of engine power to go to wheel with the best traction.

1956 CONVENTIONAL FRONT COIL SPRING

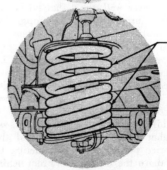

NEW 1957 FRONT COIL SPRING COMPRESSES AT AN UNEQUAL RATE, COIL BY COIL

SPECIAL 1957 SHOW ISSUE !

STUDEBAKER, WITH ITS '57 MODELS, FINALLY HAS ACHIEVED A LATE BUT QUITE SATISFACTORY STYLING FOR ITS LINE OF FOUR-DOOR SEDANS.

STUDEBAKER
ROAD TEST

ONE OF Studebaker's greatest handicaps with its products during the past four years, indeed ever since the introduction of the "Loewy" look, has been a successful four-door sedan.

While the coupes won considerable popularity, the distinctive styling, it seemed, just couldn't be made to fit the vehicles of larger passenger capacity.

In the past year or so, however, and especially for 1957, Studebaker has made substantial progress in this direction. At this point, it must be conceded that the South Bend artists have done their best job since the first postwar designs were replaced. But other auto makers, meanwhile, also advanced. So while it appears that Studebaker has done very well, the question is whether the formula was found soon enough.

What has happened, in brief, is Americanization of the European-type styling. The hood is now high over a Cadillac*ish* grille and the squared deck is now flanked by rakish fins and fishtail taillights. All fairly up to date.

The car used for this test was the Classic model in the higher priced President series. Its base price puts it into the class just a little above the deluxe Fords and Chevrolets, and just below the costlier Pontiacs and Dodges. When compared with its competition, it has as much to offer as most, plus a few unique features of its own.

It has been determined, for instance, that Studebaker is in the forefront of the quality race. This is particularly apparent when a group of its cars are examined. Care in assembly and general fit are substantially above the current average. Surface materials do not appear to be exceptional.

In the performance department, the test Studebaker adds up to strictly average right down the line. It is neither a hot car, by present standards, nor can it be called a slow one. The 0-60 mph time, for instance, is 10.7 seconds, just a few tenths more than the average of all 1957 cars road tested thus far. And the overall gas mileage is another figure that lands squarely in the middle, being 14.6 mpg, almost the standard for today's V-8 sedans.

Getting in and out of the President's front seat involves none of the problems found in some, but not all, of the new body designs with low roof lines. There are two reasons for this: first, the Studebaker is a good, full 60 inches high; and, second, there is no abnormal jutting of the forward windshield post obstructing the door area.

From behind the wheel, there is a good view of the road from a comfortable seat. The general feeling is one of sitting in a car of somewhat earlier design; there's nothing to develop a sense in the driver of occupying a low-slung, squatty machine.

Although Studebaker has not stood still in the matter of suspension, the roadability factors also resemble the average vehicle of the pre-torsion-bar and pre-spread-frame era. Thus, while the ride is commendably good, it still does not present the best qualities in flat cornering and dive-free braking. Many other cars also are deficient in these matters, but they nonetheless are the desirable maximum.

A good word must be put in for the excellent toggle switches offered on Studebaker's dash. Beyond a doubt, they are the finest controls for heat, lights and ventilation available in an American car. The instrument panel gauges have some eye appeal, but are less functional, particularly the odd compass-like speedometer.

Judged by the President test car, Studebaker has its best sedan in years. If this would have been produced in 1954, or even '55, they might not have been able to make enough of them. ●

STYLING OF THE STUDE HAWK SERIES IS GENERALLY ACCEPTED TO BE EXCEPTIONALLY GOOD FOR THE FAST-TOURING TYPE OF CAR IT IS.

GOLDEN HAWK ROAD TEST

THE STUDEBAKER Golden Hawk is one of the most distinctive cars of 1957 in many ways.

One facet of its individuality is its styling. It is almost impossible to confuse a Hawk with any other car on the road.

Its engineering adds to the car's distinctiveness. It is one of the two makes featuring a supercharger as standard equipment. It has several unique features in its suspension and steering systems.

Even the market direction of the Hawk is different. It is not a sports car and is not aimed at purists who demand a full dose of sports car characteristics in their automobiles.

It *does* offer enough of the sports car flavor, in styling and performance particularly, to warrant the attention of those who want some of that kind of touch in their cars.

Studebaker calls its Hawk models "family sports cars," and that is probably as good a description as any. A closer look will show why:

The sporty flair of Hawk styling can't

be denied. Based fundamentally on the 1953-55 Studebaker coupe designs, ingenious styling changes since then have definitely kept the Hawks from appearing old hat.

The canted, flaring fins are right in style. The unusual hood and grille design together with long, low lines add to the sports car illusion.

A Hawk is definitely an attention-getter—as was evident from the groups of curious onlookers who gathered around the test car every time it was parked.

The car's performance adds to the sports car flavor. The Hawk tested was not the hottest model checked this year, but it was far from the slowest.

Acceleration times were more than adequate, as shown by times quoted in the test data table. They would have been even more impressive had the car been equipped with standard shift rather than the optional automatic transmission.

(Judging from past performances and checks made in overdrive cars driven briefly, but not fully road tested, 0-60 mph times would have been down around 8.5 seconds with stick shift.)

SUCCESS of the Hawk's rear-end treatment can be judged by the fact that something resembling it is scheduled to appear on a volume make with its 1958 introduction.

LOADED engine compartment, topped by the supercharger, is not situated for easy accessibility. One of the handicaps is the attachment of the grille to the hood.

Nor was good performance restricted to the low end. Plenty of power was available for highway passing well up into the speed range. It wasn't until the speedometer hit 90 mph that any flat spot was experienced. From there on up, the gain was slower. Top speed is more than ample, however, since almost any Golden Hawk will turn 115 mph. Properly tuned, the maximum would be even higher.

Where the similarity to a sports car falls down is in handling. Although it rates as excellent in comparison to most U.S. passenger cars, it doesn't have the extra bit of nimbleness we associate with sports models.

Steering, though greatly improved over 1956, is still too slow for maximum maneuverability. In addition, the steering wheel is so positioned that the driver's hands strike his thighs in corners which require much wheel movement.

Counter-balancing its slight deficiencies in handling, however, is the fact that a Golden Hawk offers a much smoother ride than does a typical sports car.

This is typical of the "compromise car" nature of the Golden Hawk. Its designers have attempted to blend the good qualities of the foreign sports model and the typical U.S. family sedan. Further examples:

The rear seat offers added seating capacity in comparison with two-seater sports cars. Foot room is rather cramped, however, by comparison with current U.S. models. Two adults will not be very comfortable back there on long trips, but the space is more than ample for two or three children.

Trunk space is huge by sports car standards, just average when compared with most other 1957 models. Luggage area should be plenty adequate for most families, however.

One of the features which has been widely—and deservedly—admired in Hawks is the instrument layout. The dash of this car is near-classic in design. It includes a tachometer, vacuum gauge, speedometer and full complement of other necessary instruments. No blinking warning lights here! All are sensibly placed and easy to read. There is none of the cluttered effect seen so often today. All control switches are the toggle-type, positive and simple to operate.

Less commendable is the ashtray situation. There is no ashtray on the dash; driver and front seat passengers must use door-mounted receptacles. This is inconvenient, except, maybe, for left-handers—and could be a safety hazard for the driver.

Interiors are attractive, with leather being used extensively.

Lack of a wraparound windshield is scarcely noticed and visibility suffers little. Rear roof pillars are no thicker than on many of the Hawk's contemporaries.

Things are pretty crowded under the hood of a Hawk, particularly on those equipped with power steering and power brakes. This is an almost universal fault in these gadget-happy days, however, and the supercharged Hawk is no worse than most in this respect.

The same is true of fuel consumption. If the car's performance is used, gas mileage drops. Driven with economy in mind, the Golden Hawk is capable of delivering more miles per gallon than most of the bigger-engined '57s.

The 14 mpg average quoted in the data table was compiled largely in city driving under light to medium traffic conditions.

It bettered that figure by about two miles per gallon on the highway cruising at 60-65 mph. If more of this type of driving could have been included in tank-average mileage checks, the overall average would probably have been about 15 mpg.

Taking everything into consideration, it seems obvious that the Golden Hawk will not suit the purposes of all drivers. For those who want a sporty looking car with performance to match, handling qualities that are better than all but the most outstanding current models along with a comfortable, controlled ride, the story is different.

It definitely seems to be the type of car best suited to the enthusiast-type car buyer—particularly if he has two or three children to consider. For approximately the same price as a Corvette, T-Bird or Jag, a Golden Hawk offers him many of the same advantages of those cars without the drawbacks of space and general utility that they have. •

GOLDEN HAWK TEST DATA

Test Car: 1957 Golden Hawk hardtop coupe.
Basic Price: $3181.82.
Engine: Supercharged 289-cubic-inch ohv V-8.
Compression ratio: 7.5-to-1.
Horsepower: 275 @ 4800.
Torque: 333 @ 3200.
Dimensions: Length 204 inches, width 71.3, height 55, tread 59, wheelbase 120.5.
Shipping Weight: 3400 lbs.
Transmission: Three-speed torque converter.
Carburetion: Single two-barrel (with supercharger).
Acceleration: 0-30 mph 3.5 seconds, 0-45 mph 6.1, 0-60 9.1.
Gas Mileage: 14 mpg average.
Speedometer Corrections: Indicated 30, 45 and 60 mph are actual 29, 43 and 57 mph, respectively.

STUDEBAKER'S SPEEDSTER

(Continued from page 81)

without being feather-beddish. The second day I had the car I drove it about 150 miles over all types of roads—including some eight miles of brutal gravel. I wound it thru all types of curves, gaining confidence in its ability to handle them with every mile. The low center of gravity gives it a firm, tight, all-of-a-piece feeling that makes it hard not to drive it hard. There isn't enough heel-over to bother either driver or passengers and it tends to slide rather than spin out if you hit a turn a bit too optimistically. I wouldn't say that it handles like a true competition sports car, but then that isn't what it's meant to be. I would say that it behaves itself perfectly for the purpose Studebaker designed it—a sporty type car that's a lot of fun to drive and is ideally suited for fast cruising on almost any type of road or highway.

To get back to performance: The morning I had decided to make a second attempt at top speed runs dawned grey and foggy. I did make a couple of standing start quarter-mile runs, however. By starting in lo—with the engine revving up, as was done in most of the acceleration checks—and shifting to drive at just over 5,000 rpm, I got times averaging out at about 20 seconds. The car was turning just over 80 mph at the end of the quarter mile in all cases. In 0-30 runs, the Speedster consistently ticked off from 3.5 to 3.8 seconds by the clock.

The Speedster is basically a President hardtop coupe with trim and instrument modifications already noted. (It also has dual exhaust.) As to the engine, it's the same overhead V-8 that's in the President. An official specification sheet I got from the factory gave the horsepower as 185 at 4500 rpm. Like the President, it has a four-barrel carburetor, 259.2 cubic inches displacement and a 3.54 rear axle ratio (with automatic drive). Peak torque is 258 ft. lbs. at 2800 rpm. President valve timing is already hot, so any changes there to improve horsepower at high rpm would probably have shown up in acceleration checks—although as has been noted, best times were achieved by holding it in lo range up to 5,000 rpm. I feel times quoted here could be bettered with overdrive transmission, available as an alternative to the automatic.

To sum up, I liked the car. I hated to return it to McLeod after driving it some 300 miles. It's fun to drive, both from a performance and handling standpoint. It should make an ideal automobile for anyone who wants a car with semi-sports car characteristics and a "different" appearance, but who needs room for four or five people. The many custom touches and "extras" which are ordinarily added cost items—power steering, power brakes, special paint job, tach, leather upholstery—combine to make it a high performer ideal for family driving! •

First Feel Behind the Wheel

STUDEBAKER-PACKARD is entering the 1958 car season with reassured hopes that the recent slump—the worst in its 105-year history—is nearing an end.

In 1956, after the merger with Packard, the company hit an all-time low. To the rescue came Roy T. Hurley at the head of the Curtiss-Wright Corp. Excess production facilities were disposed of by S-P, and a blood transfusion in the form of hard cash shot new life into the ailing organization. To the helm as president went Harold Churchill, who had been chief engineer and who, with Mike De Blumenthahl, presently chief research engineer, has been largely responsible for many notable automotive developments—free wheeling, overdrive, hill-holder, etc.

A pruning of the brass took place; an economy model, the Scotsman, was successfully launched amid fancied obituaries suggested by a few well-meaning pessimists; and finally the announcement came as this was being written that current losses,

studebaker

SMOOTH HOODS of Champion (top) and Commander wagon carry block letters only. Dual lights are option on Champion, standard on Commander and President.

while still too great, have been cut to one-fifth of their former size and that, if all continues as indications now suggest, the struggling firm could very well finish the year with a switch in bookkeeping ink—from red to black.

Generally speaking, the current models will be continued with little change, and at least two new body models will be announced some time after initial on-sale dates for the Studebaker Scotsman, Champion, Commander and President. Packard will be in showrooms with some traditional lines early in November also. In our December issue we'll have more new Studebaker models to show and to discuss, but as things now stand, here are the new features for '58.

Starting at the ground and working up, we find that 14-inch wheels are standard on all Commander, President and V8 station wagon models. Due mainly to completely new floor pan and roof stampings, the overall height is now two inches lower in the sedans, about one inch lower in the already very low Hawk coupe models, and a shade lower in the wagons.

This lowering has been accomplished without any sacrifice in interior space—even in headroom—for a new one-piece driveshaft has permitted a lower transmission tunnel. The gearbox has an extended shaft, too, and for the first time in years only two U-joints are to be required on Studebaker cars.

Only the Scotsman continues to ride on the 15-inch wheels—the car has found favor in many rural areas—and the Champion, while being listed with the large wheels as standard equipment, will offer 14-inch wheels optionally.

With the exception of the roof and floor stampings, '58 Studebakers will use the same basic body structure as in recent years. New external sheet metal, however, will impart a modernized appearance although no radical changes have been made.

Dual headlights and tail fins—the latter patterned somewhat after those of the Hawk—are now featured across the board on all models, wagons as well as sedans, with the exception of the Scotsman and the Hawks. The Scotsman will be little changed

"Studebaker-Packard improvements for '58 are not in vain...their cars show greater promise than at any time in past three years."

continued

according to this writer's conversations with Duncan MacCrea, chief stylist, and others in South Bend. In the belief that a fairly substantial market exists for basic, though full-sized, family cars, the Scotsman will be cleaned up here and there in minor details while its identity will be even more pronounced from the rest of the line.

The Champion will have dual headlights as a factory-installed option—the prototype we drove at the proving ground had conventional single lights. When we asked why this exception to duals as standard equipment, we were reminded that S-P enjoys an unusually good export market; it seems that many of these overseas customers prefer the single lights. A few dollars are saved in this way for those who are price-conscious.

Other principal styling changes are confined to details: all sedan and wagon hoods are now smooth and lack the customary ornament—instead, chromed letters spell out the name across the hood just above the grille. The latter is of the same shape as in '57—only the vertical spacers

have been changed in number.

The Champion and Commander models have new, thin, full-length stainless steel strips; the larger President (the prototype was unavailable during our visit) will have different trim. The tail fins have a pronounced flair; they are longer and thicker than those of the Hawks and tail lights are distinctive from the coupes'.

Little change has been made in any of the S-P engines from the L-head Champion unit shared with the Scotsman to the largest 289-inch ohv V8 unit which, combined with the "Jet Stream" McCulloch-made supercharger, powers the Golden Hawk Stude and the Packard running mate. Compression ratios have, in the V8s, been raised about one point. At this writing little else can be said other than that '58 will probably see the blower confined to the Studebaker and Packard high-performance Hawks.

Automatic transmissions will out-number mechanically shifted units. The dual ratio lever-operated Borg-Warner gearbox or the three-speed synchromesh stick-shifted box, with or without overdrive,

will be available on all models except for the low-priced Scotsman, in which automatic is not available, and on the Hawks, where choice is overdrive or automatic.

Studebakers have always been good road cars but in recent years, in all frankness, they have not quite met the competition insofar as off-the-beaten-path roadability and preciseness of handling are concerned. Finned-type brake drums of about 195 square inches gave recent Golden Hawks exceptionally good braking with less than normal fade; in '58 the large President sedans will share this advantage. The Commander V8 and lesser six-cylinder models as well as most wagons will have conventional smooth drums.

The lower overall height has helped handling to some extent, but in the driveable Silver Hawk V8 (259.2-cubic-inch engine), in the Commander and the Champion, a better feel was evident. A look underneath the front end partially explained the improvement—a new anti-sway bar fitted between the lower control arms assists stability when cornering smartly. Nose-diving on fast stops seemed to be less, too, and there was not quite as much rear end squat when digging out from a standstill. The front end geometry and the steering are unchanged, but the variable rate front springs have been im-

BASICALLY ALIKE are chassis of 116.5-in. wheelbase sedans. Here, with Commander V8 engine, are new one-piece propeller shaft, longer transmission shaft housing which lowers front compartment tunnel, new anti-sway bar, small wheels.

110

proved with new rate calculations and the shock absorber valves have been altered to some extent.

The rear suspension has been considerably changed, though this will not readily be apparent at first glance beneath. New semi-elliptic leaf springs aft are asymmetrical throughout the line. The rear axle—still a rigid type despite many rumors stemming from the Mercedes-Benz link—is U-bolted to the springs in the usual manner, but the rear portion of the spring is approximately one-third

These claims are justified—to how large an extent it is impossible to say at this writing, for the cars driven were prototypes and maximum performance and roadability tests were impossible due to the cars being scheduled for advertising photography, dealer appraisal, and the like. Certainly the cars rode better, cornered better, and were generally improved on all counts, so far as roadability and handling ease are concerned.

Performance tests, as regards acceleration and fuel consumption, were out of

cars show greater promise than previously.

Inside there are new instrument groupings in all sedan models. The Cyclops-Eye speedometer is retained—it should be —but it is now incorporated within the main instrument panel, requiring a downward glance. Toggle switches continue to be used for auxiliary controls; windshield wipers and air ventilation and heat controls are still operated by horizontally moved levers. The condition of the generating and oil pressure systems is indicated by warning lights. The foot controls have

STUDEBAKER Golden Hawk retains sportive flavor; has new side grille mesh, center medallion.

longer than that forward of the axle. This has resulted in frame modifications and new and stronger trunion mountings for the springs. Greater rear end stability, less tendency to sway or to break away under extreme handling circumstances, decreased tail end dipping on acceleration or rising on severe braking are some of the advantages claimed for the car.

the question. Several fairly fast laps of the proving ground high-speed oval were made in the Silver Hawk V8, however, and speeds over 90 mph (true) were accomplished without strain. On the back road we were able to snake through the handling and ride patterns with enough dispatch to feel assured that the '58 improvements have not been in vain—these

been slightly repositioned—the optional power brake pedal now sits lower, allowing much quicker shifting of the foot from accelerator to brake.

The Hawk models are the least changed in the entire line as far as styling is concerned. "Why change drastically when Hawk acceptance has proven we're on the right track for those who want a jaunty
continued

STUDEBAKER SPECIFICATIONS

ENGINE:	Champion*	Commander	President
Type	L-head 6	Ohv V8	Ohv V8
Bore and Stroke	3.00 x 4.38	3.56 x 3.25	3.65 x 3.62
Displacement	185.6	259.2	289
Advertised bhp	101	180 or 195	225
Compression ratio	7.8:1	8.3:1	8.3:1
Torque	152 lbs.-ft.	260 lbs.-ft.	305 lbs.-ft.
@ max. rpm	@ 1800 rpm	@ 2800 rpm	@ 3000 rpm
DIMENSIONS:			
Wheelbase	116.5	116.5	120.5
Length	202.4	202.4	206.2
Width	75.8	75.8	75.8
Height	58.0	57.8	57.5
REAR AXLE:			
3-speed Synchromesh	4.10	3.54	3.54
Overdrive	4.56	3.73	4.09
Automatic	3.54	3.31	3.31

*All specifications for Scotsman are same as for Champion except overdrive axle ratio is 3.54, and no automatic transmission is available.

INTERIOR of Golden Hawk offers power window lifts, keeps full instrument panel; no leather upholstery.

"Studebaker-Packard chassis modifications offer improved roadability, handling, comfort."

continued

sports-like family car?" is the way De Blumenthahl countered our query as to the reasons behind no important styling changes.

That is a pretty good answer, it seems, since Hawk sales have been one of the main bright spots in the recent S-P picture. Most reports indicate that the average Hawk owner is a youngish family man with two or three youngsters—he can afford but one car, wants it to be something of a sports type with spirited performance as well.

In '58 the chief Hawk change is in the rear seat. The collapsible center armrest has been omitted so that three persons can now be accommodated where only two were carried formerly. Leather upholstery is no longer an option; in the sedans there's a wide range of long-wearing fabrics featuring metallic thread as well as attractive plastics. Foam rubber is used over the coil seat springs, of course, as it is in sedans and wagons.

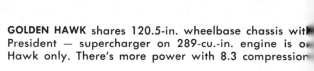

GOLDEN HAWK shares 120.5-in. wheelbase chassis with President — supercharger on 289-cu.-in. engine is on Hawk only. There's more power with 8.3 compression.

NEW ANTI-SWAY BAR with improved coil spring rate build-up improves Golden Hawk handling. Rear-swept control arms give some trailing link effect. Lack of frame crosspiece underneath crankcase facilitates servicing.

ASYMMETRICAL SPRING, shared with all other models is principal rear suspension change on Golden Hawk. Big finned brake drums, for reduced fade, are standard on Golden Hawk, President, and new Packard Hawk.

'58

and **packard**

by *Joe H. Wherry* Detroit Editor

THINNER ROOF (see Champion, top) and smaller wheels lower all models without cramping interiors. Luggage space is large. Commander has chromed tail lights.

EASILY READ Cyclops Eye speedometer is incorporated in new instrument grouping; telltale lights are for ammeter and oil pressure. Dash is efficient, simple.

STUDEBAKER

THE COMMANDER V-8 is the middle car of the Studebaker line, and at a factory list price of $2387 for the four-door sedan, it lands smack in the middle of the low-price field. Its competition is Chevy's Biscayne, Plymouth's Savoy, Ford's Custom 300 and the Rambler Rebel, all V-8s.

With a wheelbase of 116.5, the Commander is as compact and maneuverable as any of the others except the 108-inch wheelbase Rambler. Although the Commander's body is comparatively narrow, its interior dimensions are just about as roomy. Front and rear seat widths of 56 inches compare favorably (about three inches less) with the other four cars.

The Commander is a couple of hundred pounds lighter than the others (150 less than Rambler V-8) and thus its smaller engine can provide nearly as brisk performance as its competitors. The 259 cu.in. V-8 powering the Commander comes with a two barrel carb as standard equipment. (An optional power pack with single four barrel carb and dual exhaust system raises output to 195 bhp.)

This engine compares favorably with the 283 cu.in. Chevy V-8 which develops 185 bhp. and 275 lbs. ft. of torque compared to Commander's 180 bhp. and 260 torque. The Plymouth Savoy has considerably more power, with a 318 cu.in. engine developing 225 bhp. and 330 lbs. of torque. Ford's 292 cu.in. V-8 fits somewhere in the middle with 205 bhp. and 295 lbs. of torque. Rambler Rebel V-8 is rated considerably higher than the Commander with 215 bhp. for a smaller engine of 250 cu.in. displacement, but its torque output (and thus potential acceleration) is the same—260 lbs. ft.

With the lowest compression ratio of the group (8.3), the Commander's engine operates without fuss on today's "regular" (90-92 octane) gasoline.

Commander's transmission options come with a selection of rear axle ratios favorable to fuel economy. With standard synchromesh the ratio is 3.54 to 1, with overdrive 3.73 to 1, and with the Flightomatic three-speed and torque converter automatic transmission, 3.31 to 1.

Of course, when you compare the Commander's engine with the "big" engines of its competition (except Rambler which doesn't have an option), it isn't hard to see that the 300-horsepower super engines of Ford, Chevy and Plymouth will outpull it.

However, Studebaker didn't design the Commander for the all-out performance fans, but for those who want a "cake-and-eat-it-too" compromise of more than enough performance for all driving needs plus gasoline mileage that the others can't touch even with their so-called standard engines.

With the current return of interest in economy of operation plus reasonable first cost, Studebaker is happily

Champion two-door sedan for '58 has an all-new suspension and one piece driveshaft. It is powered by Studebaker's Sweepstakes Six L-head engine. Champion options include Flightomatic and Twin Traction differential. Overall length of Champion sedan is 202.4 inches.

STUDEBAKER
is the car
for you

f... You want something "different" in a pleasingly styled car.

f... You've been looking for a good combination of economy for city driving and performance for the open highway.

f... Somewhat higher depreciation doesn't deter you from investing in longer-than-average ownership of a well-built, well-balanced car.

STUDEBAKER SPECIFICATIONS

ENGINES	PRESIDENT V-8	COMMANDER V-8	CHAMPION SIX
Bore and stroke	3-9/16 in. x 3⅝ in.	3-9/16 in. x 3¼ in.	3 in. x 4⅜ in.
Displacement	289 cu. in.	259.2 cu. in.	185.6 cu. in.
Compression ratio	8.3:1	8.3:1	7.8:1
Max. brake horsepower	225 @ 4500 rpm	180 @ 4500 rpm	101 @ 4000 rpm
Max. torque	305 @ 3000 rpm	260 @ 2800 rpm	152 @ 1800 rpm

DIMENSIONS	PRESIDENT	CHAMPION, COMMANDER	
Wheelbase	120.5 in.	116.5 in.	
Overall length	206.4 in.	202.4 in.	
Overall width	75.8 in.	75.8 in.	
Overall height	57.7 in.	58 in.	

TRANSMISSIONS   Standard synchromesh, overdrive, Flightomatic

Studebaker Champion's Sweepstakes Six L-head engine has a 185.6 cu. in. displacement and produces 101 horsepower. Rugged, gas-saving Sweepstakes is Studebaker's bid for the economy-minded.

President is Studebaker's top-of-the-line series. Like Champion and Commander, it has inherited some Hawk lines, noticeably in the fins.

out of the horsepower race with the only V-8 that can provide 20-miles-to-the-gallon fuel economy under average driving conditions.

The Commander's engine does its work quietly most of the time, making noticeably more noise only under "full-throttle" acceleration in overdrive "kick down", or intermediate gear of Flightomatic.

Studebaker has restyled the Commander for '58 with a set of outwardly canted fins that were "added" to the basic body structure yet manage to look like an integrated part of the design. On the front end the chief difference noted will be the addition of 5¾-inch headlamps. The pressed steel housing used to adapt the wider span of the dual lamps to fenders that are basically unchanged is the only really inharmonious styling on the car.

The roofline of the sedan has been lowered, as on other Studebakers, by some clever engineering. A new one-piece drive shaft has permitted lowering of the floor pan and reduction of the shaft tunnel. The gain in floor to roof measure that this permitted was utilized to lower the overall height of the car by means of a shallower roof pan and a headliner placed closer to the roof itself.

Coupled with smaller 14-inch tires, this lowering has given the Commander a noticeably sleeker appearance which, added to the new rear fender fins, makes the car appear longer.

A two-door hardtop, a model brand new to the Studebaker line (Golden Hawk sports model excepted) has been added.

From the standpoint of riding qualities, handling and roadability, the Commander has been improved in '58 by several changes. First of all, a softening of spring rates and shock absorber action has cut down on transmission of harsh surface vibrations and slowed jounce frequency on wavy blacktop roads.

Behavior in cornering has been improved by the lower center of gravity and a new link-type anti-roll bar. We noticed a definite reduction in sway after trying out '57 and '58 Commanders on the Studebaker track.

Handling has also been improved, too, by the new assymetrically-mounted rear springs in which approximately two-thirds of the springs' length is set to the rear of the axle. The short one-third at the front acts very much like a trailing link torque arm and goes a long way toward pre-

venting brake dip and the "torque wrap" squat of full throttle take-off.

In addition, these springs hold the rear axle more precisely in alignment with the frame on rough going (e.g. washboard roads) which does a lot to prevent the rear end from skittering out on a curve.

Of course, like all Studebakers, the Commander has the variable-rate front springs introduced last year. The principle of these springs is simple and has made a definite improvement in the ride. Some of the coils of these springs are spaced more closely than others so that when a fairly major bump is encountered they come into contact and "stiffen up" the spring while on lesser bumps all the coils are in action. This permits a basically softer action on smaller surface bumps.

Studebaker steering is paradoxical. There are times when we appreciated its variable ratio as in parking on dry pavement. At other times, on a winding back country road we felt annoyed as the ratio "slowed down" as we cut deeper into curves. Here's what happens. As the wheels are turned to the left or right the gear ratio gradually changes from 24.5 to 1 overall to 27.5 to 1 overall as you turn. This makes it easier to turn the wheel but means that

Commander four-door sedan, powered by Sweepstakes V-8, shows off low, wide, conservative styling, with strong fin treatment. Hood is clean, massive grille emphasizes width.

Sweepstakes 259 cu. in. V-8 has 180 horsepower; with 4-barrel carb, 195 horses.

you must turn it more to get a given change of direction of the car. This device goes a long way toward replacing the need for power steering in the Commander but we don't feel that it is as good a solution as the low-friction recirculating ball gear.

Summing up. The Commander is a pleasant, well-built car with a very good compromise between gasoline economy and performance. Its ride and handling has been improved so that it is in line with most of its competition. It has a smooth automatic transmission, satisfactory brakes and a low noise level. The four-door station wagon is accessible but has somewhat less cargo space than its competition.

CAR LIFE'S overall rating for the '57 Studebaker was 3.6 checks. The following cars in Studebaker's price range have already been tested by CAR LIFE. The issues in which they appeared may be obtained by sending 35¢ for each issue to CAR LIFE, 41 East 42 Street, New York 17, N. Y.: Chevrolet, January, 1958; Ford, Plymouth, Rambler, February, 1958.

STUDEBAKER CHECK LIST

5 CHECKS MEAN TOP RATING IN ITS PRICE CLASS

Category	Description	Rating
PERFORMANCE	Compared with the powerful, large-displacement engines of its competition, the 180 (195 optional) Commander V-8 might seem underpowered. However, with automatic transmission, the performance is entirely up to all normal driving requirements and there is the bonus of fuel economy.	✔ ✔ / ✔ ✔
STYLING	Generally pleasing with the possible exception of bulging headlight "pod" and extremely flat roof pan. It has one of the better treatments of rear fender fins. Hardtop coupe is a very handsome car.	✔ ✔ / ✔ ✔
RIDING COMFORT	Although good engineering has brought the Commander's riding comfort up to the average level of the low-priced field, Plymouth and Chevy are still noticeably better.	✔ ✔ / ✔ ✔
INTERIOR DESIGN	The Commander lacks about three inches of its competition's seat width but this is the only dimension that suffers in comparison with many larger cars. Vision is excellent with a minimum of "wraparound distortion."	✔ ✔ / ✔ ✔
ROADABILITY	Lower center of gravity and suspension improvements have brought Studebaker in line with most of its competition although the slightly numb variable steering detracts from positive control in handling.	✔ ✔ / ✔
EASE OF CONTROL	Smooth-acting brakes and a well-designed automatic transmission plus the variable-ratio steering make the Commander easy to maneuver in traffic, but steering action is a handicap on winding roads.	✔ ✔ / ✔ ✔
ECONOMY	The Commander shines as one of the top economy cars among all U.S. V-8's, offering a hard-to-equal combination of good performance and gasoline mileage.	✔ ✔ / ✔ ✔
SERVICEABILITY	Studebaker's relatively uncluttered engine compartment and its common-sense engineering make it a better than average service proposition.	✔ ✔ / ✔ ✔
WORKMANSHIP	Although they're not the most expensively designed cars available, the Commanders give evidence of careful manufacture, too seldom seen in the low-price class.	✔ ✔ / ✔ ✔
VALUE PER DOLLAR	A higher-than-average rate of depreciation handicaps the investor in what is otherwise a well-built and honest value. Hawk models have much more favorable depreciation.	✔ ✔ / ✔

STUDEBAKER OVERALL RATING... 3.9 CHECKS

STUDEBAKER ROAD TEST

The Commander, Studebaker's middle-priced and middle-powered V-8, displays quiet but strong qualities

CLEAN COMMANDER LINES CARRY QUIET FINS IN A BOW TO PRESENT STYLE TRENDS.

THE 200 and some miles distance from Detroit to South Bend seems to have separated the Studebaker-Packard corporation by more than roads from many of the trends of the rest of the automotive industry. The first impression from behind the wheel of Studebaker's middle-priced Commander is the thought that here is a product of a design philosophy quite different from the one practiced in the Motor City. Granted, the car is loaded with concessions to the fin, dual headlamps and the like, but the Commander's basic austerity is in direct contrast to the chromed and gimmicked entries of the bigger manufacturers. It's a contrast from which S-P's ideas do not always suffer.

The most common comment of testers is to marvel at the ingenuity of Studebaker engineers in making use of the equipment on hand to keep their product up to date. The front suspension dates back to the pre-ball-joint days and, yet, clever concepts elsewhere give good handling and stability. The body shell is not new but it has been lowered and decorated with most of the recent improvements.

This lower silhouette has been brought about this year by a change to a one-piece driveshaft and 14-inch wheels. Other new engineering features noted are an improved rear spring design, different spring and shock rates and a more flexible link-type stabilizer bar.

The leaf-springs on the rear have grown four inches so that the rear axle may now be mounted ahead of the springs' center point. This set-up, which was proven successful on some other makes last year, tends to minimize spring

wind-up, nose dipping on braking and rear end squatting with heavy acceleration.

Up on a hoist the underside presents a view of some very unconventional frame rails. Instead of being straight box sections extending fore and aft, the rails actually wiggle back and forth in the shape of a series of elongated z's. Evidently this configuration is used to obtain greater rigidity since there are very few frame cross members. There were numerous body attachment brackets fastened to the outside of the frame rails which possibly add to the overall strength of the automobile.

Found between each spring leaf was a

AUSTERE INTERIOR sees very little styling foolishness. Instruments are behind wheel with aircraft-type switches for the controls.

STANDARD two-barrel carburetor sits on the Commander's 259-cubic inch, 180 hp V-8. The President's engine has 289 cubic inches.

UNCONVENTIONAL frame rails wiggle to the rear in an effort to gain greater frame rigidity. Note the many attachment brackets.

strip of rubber which extended the full length of the spring. These rubber sections have a bead on each side which centers them between the spring leaves. This novel arrangement somewhat reduces the friction among the leaves and eliminates the possibilities of metal to metal squeaks.

Two engineering improvements, born in the Studebaker plant in 1956, are maintained in 1958. They are the laterally finned brake, which the tests showed highly efficient, and the Twin Traction limited-slip differential. Modifications of this latter S-P offspring are now offered as optional equipment for all U.S. auto makes today.

The power source for the Commander, which is the medium priced contender of the Studebaker line, is a 259-cubic-inch V-8 with a rated horsepower of 180. This is the junior V-8 in the S-P stable and its acceleration, while not outstanding, is quite acceptable. Its single two-throat carburetor breathed through times of 0-30 mph in 4.5 seconds, 0-45 mph in 8 seconds and 0-60 mph in 13.5 seconds.

Out on the road the test car demonstrated quite remarkable steering ability. Its lack of power assistance was never noticed and was, in fact, thought to be there by a few drivers. The ride was adequate for a light car (Its 3470 lbs. make it quite low in bulk for a modern full-size automobile), except for noticeable road vibration, which can be traced, no doubt, to the stiffer suspension.

The mileage figures of 13.78 miles per gallon were obtained through city driving and could be improved substantially on the road. A big feature in this department is the fact that the Studebaker engines can live easily on a diet of regular gas.

The interior of the Commander brings home once again the thought of austerity. From its simple controls and instruments to the unornamented upholstery, it implies that many other American cars are overly luxurious in decoration in the eyes of the Indianians. Even the seats, in their sit-up-straight design, say that there will be no foolishness here.

The speedometer is reminiscent of the drum-styled instruments of some time ago. Speed ranges are on a floating dial similar to a magnetic compass. The color of the figures changes as the speed increases.

Most of the controls on the dash panel are actuated by two-position toggle switches similar to those found in aircraft cockpits. This is a feature traditional and popular with Studebaker.

One very interesting feature this year is a pedal-operated windshield washer. A touch of the pedal squirts a stream of water on the windshield and engages the wipers. The latter under the control of a time-delay switch sweep over the sur-

FACIAL EXPRESSION SEEMS A BIT OVERLOADED BY THE PODS FOR DUAL HEADLIGHTS.

face for a few strokes. A definite improvement could be effected in this accessory by extending the time delay to offer more strokes for more complete washing.

Ventilation of the Commander seems adequate. It is one of the few cars to retain an under-seat heater. Arguments on the wisdom of this feature are good on

Test Data

Test Car: 1958 Studebaker Commander
Body Type: four-door sedan
Basic Price: $2378
Engine: ohv V-8
Carburetion: single two-barrel
Displacement: 259 cubic inches
Bore & Stroke: 3⁹/₁₆ x 3¼
Compression Ratio: 8.3-to-1
Horsepower: 180 @ 4500 rpm
Horsepower per cubic inch: .69
Torque: 260 lb.-ft. @ 2800 rpm
Test Weight: 3470 lbs. without driver
Weight Distribution: 57% of weight on front wheels
Power-Weight Ratio: 19.28 lbs. per horsepower
Transmission: Flightomatic
Rear Axle Ratio: 3.31
Steering: 4.5 turns lock-to-lock
Dimensions: overall length 202¾ inches, width 75²⁷/₃₂, height 57¾, wheelbase 116½, tread 57⁷/₁₆ front, 56⁵/₁₆ rear
Springs: coil front, leaf rear
Tires: 750 x 14
Gas Mileage: 13.78 mpg average (city)
Speedometer Error: Indicated 30, 45 and 60 mph are actual 29½, 44 and 57½ mph respectively
Acceleration: 0-30 mph in 4.5 seconds, 0-45 mph in 8.0 and 0-60 mph in 13.5 seconds

both sides so that no conclusions will be made here.

Two minor features that point out a prior statement on the ingenious use of existing equipment are the oil fill pipe and filter. At one time Studebaker mounted a fuel pump on the oil fill pipe. Instead of discarding this type of cast iron pipe, S-P engineers revamped the casting to close the hole previously occupied by the pump. The outline of this flange still appears, although the pump itself is mounted on the block.

The oil filter is not of the full-flow type. It is a member of the older by-pass family which filters a small quantity of oil tapped from the oiling system. With this system, the oil does not flow through the filter before reaching the bearings. One modern feature that it does possess is easy replacement by unscrewing.

Revamping in the styling department appears on the whole to be quite acceptable. The new fins blend well with the fenders and do not seem to be an addition. The most sour point is the podded dual headlight addition. This rather awkward attachment has all the earmarks of a do-it-yourself kit. But if the dual lights were commanded, and they seem to be the cry of '58 styling, we must again bow to the crafty renovators of S-P.

A number of little points such as the above can be used to show that the Studebaker does not wear all the polished buttons of the rich offspring of the Big Three. But basically it is a sound and conservative car which bases its sales appeal upon a search for quality and a long tradition of craftsmanship. There will always be room for a soft-spoken representative in the American car market. •

Studebaker Banks on 'Common Sense' Lark Car

LARK by Studebaker, a completely new series of smaller, more economical, more maneuverable, "common sense" cars go on display November 14 in Studebaker dealer showrooms throughout the country.

Establishing a revolutionary new concept of automotive transportation, the brand new 1959 Studebaker Larks were newly designed from tires to roof-top to meet the specific demands of today's driving needs.

The new Larks are smaller in overall size, yet actually are roomier inside than previous models. This was accomplished primarily by reducing front and rear "overhang" to a minimum, while at the same time maintaining a "big car" passenger compartment to enable six adults to ride in comfort.

The wheelbase of sedan and hardtop models is 108½ inches, while over-all length is only 175 inches—shorter than previous models by more than two feet. Yet, front leg room is equal to last year's Studebaker, and rear leg room is actually greater. (The new station wagons measure 113 inches in wheelbase, 184½ inches in over-all length.)

Although slightly lower-over-all, the new Studebaker Larks provide headroom that is unexcelled in the low-price field. Shoulder and hip room are similar to last year's models.

Available in Deluxe and Regal versions, the 1959 Larks by Studebaker are richly and tastefully appointed both inside and out to appeal to the public's desire for luxurious transportation. Yet, despite this luxury concept, the new models are priced below other cars in the low-price field.

In describing the new models, Studebaker-Packard President Harold E. Churchill explained that "the completely new 1959 Studebaker Lark is the car the motoring public has told us it wants —and has urged us to build. It is a car of modest price, yet featuring the high quality, sound engineering and distinctive styling that is traditional with Studebaker. It is a functional, comfortable, family-size car that is economical to buy, economical to own, and economical to operate. And it establishes a wholly new concept of handling and parking ease among American cars."

Studebaker's reputation for style leadership is further advanced by the distinctive, modern design of its 1959 Larks. The basic design theme reflects elegance, tasteful simplicity and functional purpose.

Duncan McRae, Studebaker-Packard's director of styling, pointed out that "because the 1959 Lark by Studebaker is based on sound engineering principles, rather than on exaggerated styling cliches, the new car achieves a permanence of design that will result in higher resale value. The new models were designed deliberately to stay in style indefinitely, for we feel strongly that most buyers resent their new car being obsoleted by each ensuing year's model."

The instrument panel of Studebaker's new Lark series for 1959 features large, easy-to-read dials located directly in front of the driver. Safety padding—both at the top and bottom of the panel—is standard on Regal models, optional on Deluxe models. The glove compartment is conveniently located in the center, within easy reach of either driver or passenger.

The new smaller Lark is available in two- and four-door sedans, two-door hardtop and station wagon models.

Also offered for 1959 are Studebaker's popular Hawk Six and V-8 five-passenger coupes. The new Hawk retains its sleek, classic styling with minor modifications and refinements. Among these are new combination parking-directional lights, new rear fender styling and an all-new, more luxurious interior.

The dominant design theme of the new Lark by Studebaker is its distinctive grille, flanked by combination parking-directional lights and air scoops. Accentuating the graceful, flowing lines of the car, a single stainless steel molding sweeps back from above the head lights along the sides of the car and continues in an unbroken line around the rear. Along the sides, this molding serves as a rub-rail to protect the finish from doors of other cars opening against it in tight parking areas.

The new cowl not only enhances the car's lower look, but results also in greater windshield area for improved visibility.

Smart new horizontal-oval tail lights provide illumination to the sides as well as to the rear of the car.

The Lark hardtop with Detroit's skyline and new Convention Hall in the background.

In keeping with the new model's clean, uncluttered, classic design, the hood and deck lid are free of meaningless ornamentation.

The 1959 Studebakers are available with either a brand new six-cylinder or V-8 powerplant, and with either Flightomatic, overdrive or conventional transmission.

Both new engines are designed to operate efficiently on regular gasoline, thus giving a very important plus in economy.

The new, shorter-stroke, 169.6 cubic inch, L-head six with an improved combustion chamber design, a higher compression ratio and new carburetion is designed for smooth, lively performance and maximum economy and durability.

For those desiring the extra power of V-8 performance, Studebaker offers an improved, short-stroke, 259.2 cubic inch, V-8 engine with a higher compression ratio and new carburetion. This powerplant, too, provides exceptional economy of operation and long life.

Chief Engineer E. J. Hardig pointed out that "Studebaker's more efficient 1959 engines, coupled with the elimination of useless pounds of 'dead' weight in the car itself, result in a very marked improvement in both engine performance and gasoline economy."

Among other major engineering advances is a softer, smoother ride resulting primarily from Studebaker's improved variable-rate front coil spring design. These unique variable-rate springs automatically compensate for variations in load and road conditions to provide an exceptionally level, well-controled ride over even the roughest roads. New shock absorber valving and redesigned rear leaf springs also contribute to Studebaker's improved riding qualities.

The new suspension system also results in increased stability with a substantial reduction in body roll on curves.

A new, more efficient steering gear is used on the Lark six-cylinder sedan, station wagon and hardtop models. It provides faster steering response, improved steering wheel "recovery" and requires fewer turns from extreme left to right. And, the effort required to turn the wheel has been so greatly reduced that power steering is not even offered on six-cylinder models. Power steering is available optionally on V-8s.

On the new Studebaker Larks, the turning diameter has been reduced considerably to enhance their sports-car maneuverability.

A new, more rigid frame and body construction results in a quieter ride free of annoying squeaks and rattles.

The new 1959 Studebaker Lark station wagon is shown above. A new "Flight Stream" roof panel accentuates the lower silhouette and provides a lower center of gravity for a better ride and greater stability. The station wagon is available in both Deluxe and Regal trims and with either the new six or V-8 engine.

Studebaker's adherence to functional design is further revealed by the use of removable fender panels. Should a panel become damaged the cost of repair is far less than on conventional cars using integral panels.

A new under-dash heating, ventilating and defrosting unit provides improved heat distribution, faster defrosting and quieter operation. For protection from outside elements, the new heater motor is located inside the passenger compartment. A redesigned front seat permits the heat to flow unobstructed under the seat to the rear. This new seat design also permits greater rear seat leg room.

To prevent tampering with the engine, all 1959 Studebakers feature a new inside-the-car hood release.

On Lark sedan and hardtop models, the gas tank filler door is located more conveniently just to the right of the rear license plate.

Reclining front seats are available optionally on all 1959 Studebakers. Each divided front seat back is adjustable to seven different positions—including a position flush with the rear seat cushion to form a "bed."

Both front seat backs on two-door models can be folded forward simultaneously to permit rear seat passengers to enter and exit with greater ease. Front seats on all models are wider.

The Lark sedan and hardtop seats, as well as the Silver Hawk's, are upholstered in attractive, long-wearing nylon-rayon acetate fabric bolstered with top quality, hair-cell grain vinyl. All-vinyl seats are standard equipment in the Lark station wagon, and are available optionally in Lark hardtop and Silver Hawk models.

Interiors in all models are offered in one of four color schemes—blue, green, gray or tan—to harmonize with the seven new exterior colors—Hawaiian Green, Campfire Red, Alaskan Blue, Tahiti Coral, Silvertone Gray, Velvet Black, and White Sand.

The new Larks feature a newly designed instrument panel with large, easy-to-read dials located directly in front of the driver.

For maximum convenience, the glove compartment is located in the center of the panel, and the door opens out to form a horizontal "table" with built-in cup wells. Safety padding, both at the top and bottom of the panel, is standard on Regal models, optional on Deluxe models.

The exclusive Twin Traction "non-slip" differential is available optionally on all 1959 models, as are power brakes and air conditioning. The unique Automatic Hill Holder is offered optionally on all models except those equipped with Flightomatic transmission.

Optional on the new Studebaker Lark station wagon is the practical Hideaway Third Seat which increases passenger carrying capacity from six to eight. When not in use, the seat folds down in the floor.

★ ★ ★

The new 1959 Silver Hawk is offered on a 120.5-inch wheelbase with either the new six-cylinder or the new V-8 engine. The parking lights have been lowered from atop the fenders to the bumper. A new chrome line accents the fins which are also highlighted by "Silver Hawk" in scroll and the corporate "Hawk" emblem.

STUDEBAKER LARK VI SEDAN LARK VIII STATION WAGON

WHENEVER a new car is introduced, the first task for viewers and reviewers alike is to decide exactly what market the manufacturer is pitching for. After all, it's hardly fair to condemn a pseudo-sports car when the maker is really intending to sell it to tired old businessmen.

Well, there were some businessmen in South Bend, Indiana who were tired alright, tired of watching the sales curve dipping downward. Having their heads screwed on properly, they proceeded to take a good, long look at the state of the car market.

Recognizing that they had gotten an unsatisfactorily small slice of what till lately was the huge market for equally huge cars, they decided it might be better to be a relatively larger frog in a much smaller pond.

With their confidence in a more economical car's prospects bolstered by last year's Scotsman, they set to in a crash program to prepare tooling for the new series. The basic concept was that if a full-sized car which looked economical was successful, then a similar car which augmented these virtues by eliminating the pretense of being a "big" car would be still more successful. Better still if it could be done with a minimum of retooling.

The result is the Lark, and to judge by what we read in the papers, a revival of civic confidence in South Bend. The key words used by the admen to describe the Lark are "compact" and "sensible." They accurately indicate the market being aimed at; city-dwellers to whom space is dear and economy-minded owners who need a six-passenger machine but don't care for juke-box styling, no matter how beautifully proportioned it may be.

We tried two quite different Larks, a light-gray four-door sedan with the six cylinder engine and overdrive (not quite a stark Lark) and a green two-door station wagon with the V-8 engine and automatic transmission. Both were driven to Sebring and back by our stalwart test crew and both have seen lots of urban-suburban

traffic in the New York area before and since. We are quite convinced that the six especially is unsuited for heavy cross-country work as its 90-hp leaves it definitely in the poopy category when trying to overtake at 50-plus mph. No doubt about it, we've been spoiled by the horsepower race and we do not like having to plan our passing maneuvers so extensively.

In town, it's quite another story, and one that snuck up on us unexpectedly. If you pretend it's been mildly souped, with a larger carburetor and a semi-race cam and therefore you hang on in each gear right out past peak power, why, then you find you are running out in front and the Lark VI feels very spirited. Our first ride in a Lark was in a taxi version (there are several hundred of them in NYC now) and the driver treated it as if there were seven or eight liters under the hood and then complained about the poor acceleration. In this respect, it's much like many of the imports, what performance there is isn't world-shaking, but it's always available and easy to use. The gear ratios aren't too close, they can't be when you've got a three-speed box. But Studebaker has spread the ratios as nicely as they possibly could with a 1.6 : 1 step with both shifts. (Third is direct, second is 1.63/1 and first gear is 2.60/1.)

Our six had the Borg-Warner overdrive and accordingly, the rear axle ratio was 3.73/1 instead of 3.54. At any speed above 30 mph, momentarily lifting one's foot off the accelerator pedal permits it to engage automatically. A kickdown switch under the same pedal provides instantaneous shifts back into direct. A hand control lets you lock the device completely out but unless this is used, the car will free-wheel (no engine-braking) in any gear below 25 mph.

The result is much the same as having a four-speed gearbox with automatic shifts between third and fourth, or, since second-overdrive is so similar to third, between second and "third." The latter is rather fun in city traffic, though the free-wheeling may induce you to forget you're still in gear until the car speed drops to corre-

STUDEBAKER LARK VI SEDAN

Suggested List Price, FOB South Bend, $1995
Manufacturer: .... Studebaker-Packard
Corp.,
South Bend 27, Ind.

PERFORMANCE

TOP SPEED:

Estimated .... 80 mph

ACCELERATION:

From zero to	seconds
30 mph	5.0
40 mph	8.5
50 mph	12.7
60 mph	19.0
Standing ¼ mile.........	21.7
Speed at end of quarter ..	63 mph

SPEED RANGES IN GEARS:

	(4300 rpm max.)
I	0-33
II	6-53
III	10-top
III-OD	25-75

SPEEDOMETER CORRECTION:

Indicated Speed	Timed Speed
30	27
40	36
50	45
60	54

FUEL CONSUMPTION:

Lark VI	18-20 mpg
Lark VIII	14-18 mpg

SPECIFICATIONS

POWER UNIT:

Type	In-line, Water-cooled six
Valve Arrangement	side-valve
Bore & Stroke	3.00x4.00 in. (76.2x101.6)
Stroke/Bore Ratio	1.33/1
Displacement	169.6 cu in (2781 cc)
Compression Ratio	8.3/1
Carburetion by	Single-choke downdraft
Max. Power	90 bhp @ 4000 rpm
Max. Torque	145 lbs-ft @ 2000 rpm

DRIVE TRAIN:

Transmission ratios		(optional ratio)
I	2.60	(9.69)
II	1.63	(6.08)
III	1.00	(3.73)
III-OD	0.78	(2.91)
Final drive ratio	3.73	(3.54, 4.10, 4.27)
Axle torque taken by	rear springs	

CHASSIS:

Frame	Box-section, ladder type with 4 cross members
Wheelbase	108.5 in.
Tread, front and rear	57.4, 56.6 in.
Front Suspension	Independent, coil and wishbone
Rear Suspension	Rigid axle, semi-elliptic leaf springs
Shock absorbers	tubular
Steering type	cam and twin lever (V.S. cam and lever with roller stud)
Steering wheel turns L to L	5.0
Turning diameter, curb to curb	37½ ft.
Brake lining area	146.4 sq. in.
Tire size	5.90x15

GENERAL:

Length	175 in.
Width	71.4 in.
Height, loaded	57.5 in.
Weight, as tested	2870 lbs.
Weight, curb	2720 lbs.
Weight distribution, F/R as tested	44/56
Fuel capacity	18 U.S. gallons

RATING FACTORS:

Specific Power Output	0.53 bhp/cu. in.
Power to Weight Ratio (as tested)	31.9 lbs./hp
Piston speed @ 60 mph	2000 ft./min. (1560 in OD)
Braking Area	102 sq. in./ton
Speed @ 1000 rpm in top gear	20.0 mph (25.7 in OD)

Lark six (top left) is Studebaker's '58 flat head de-stroked to increase gas economy. Sedan (left) can be converted into fairly comfortable sleeping quarters. Split seat back makes it possible for passenger to cat nap while underway.

Truncated Lark sedan (top) amazingly does not give away many cubic inches in the trunk department. Center-mounted spare is possible source of suitcase scars. Wagon and sedan (right) very obviously belong to the same family of compact cars. Wagon is fitted with top-mounted chrome luggage rack.

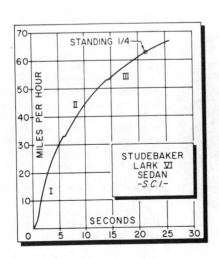

STUDEBAKER
LARK VI
SEDAN
–S.C.I.–

Lark wagon (top) has LST capacity with rear seats down and tail gate open. Spare is stowed under rear compartment floor board. Studebaker V-8 has more than enough muscle to tote spring creaking loads.

spond with engine idle speed and suddenly you find you're lugging the engine and about to stall it.

The column shift is fairly taut, though reverse was still stiff to engage even after 6000 miles had come and gone.

About pretending the engine's been hot-rodded, in a sense it has. But the engineers had one strong limitation on them. The Larks, both VIs and VIIIs (we're fascinated by these Roman numerals), are intended to run on regular gasoline rather than premium or super. And for economy, both of operation and first cost, there is only one carb. So to squeeze out extra power, familiar tricks of the hot-rodding fraternity were used. First they settled on the highest compression ratio suited to current "regular" gas. This turned out to be 8.3/1 compared to last year's 7.5/1. Alterations to the camshaft and carburetor, not to forget the reduction in displacement from 185.5 to 169.6 cubic inches, brought the peak torque down from 152 lbs-ft to 145.

That drop in displacement came from chopping the stroke to four inches even. Though that hardly qualifies it as a short-stroke, it certainly is a step to encourage revving, what with lower piston speeds and increased bearing overlap. And as we've already indicated, the proper way to drive the Lark VI is to use lots of revs.

Just to make the engine's life easier, the weight is reduced some 120 pounds from the '58 models. This came about from the general shortening process that occurred on the drafting boards, but to brush the Larks off as merely last year's models with 8½ inches chopped out of the middle and most of the overhang amputated is to overlook the many detail changes which add greatly to the ease if not joy of owning such a straight-forward, functional car.

The simplicity of the car's lines not only reduces the expense of the stampings but adds considerably to the car's appeal. Some prospective owners have no wish to advertise their social or financial standing—and not because they have none.

Another practical virtue is that cars with clean lines are much easier to keep clean. Some feel that such a car avoids minor traffic dents better than more ornate ones, too. There's no step-down (and clamber-out) frame, so inside the floor is flat and a whisk broom replaces the vacuum cleaner as a how-to cleaning tool. All fenders are attached with bolts which means that if you tear one, you needn't weld the next one on.

There is no doubt that the Lark is intended as a sensible, economical transportation. What then is it like to drive?

Both the sedan and the wagon share the same dashboard styling. Wagon (above) was fitted with Studebaker automatic transmission.

Well, to start with, the engine occasionally was difficult to start, especially in damp weather. We're inclined to blame the automatic choke which would introduce itself into the proceedings even when the engine was fully warm. Though easily eliminated by a heavy blip of the throttle, perhaps another step backwards would be in order, as hand chokes rarely give you trouble.

On slow idle the engine seemed a bit rough, perhaps an inevitable result of the extra high compression ratio. And to cap these minor unpleasantries, the clutch throw-out disc was mis-aligned. Combined with soft engine mountings and a rear axle entirely dependent on the limber leaf springs for longitudinal location, every start was made with a shudder that fed its way back into the throttle pedal.

Light overall weight and an ability to rev past peak power gave the six satisfactory performance away from the traffic signals. At high revs, the engine retains a determined sort of hardness that reminds you that it's working for you. Quite unlike the turbine smoothness of the V-8 which, coupled to the Borg-Warner automatic transmission (dubbed Flightomatic) gives typical American performance — smooth, yet very brisk. Unless the few extra miles per gallon mean a lot, the smoothness of the eight makes it altogether more satisfactory. The six, of course, is noticeably cheaper to buy and maintain.

Under the hood accessibility looks good on the six, though the dipstick is so long and so far to the rear that it must be bent slightly to clear the opened hood. A plain paper air filter traps the dirt but not all the sounds at the carburetor. The battery is far forward on the left fender well in both cars, probably the coolest under-hood location available.

Seat adjustment fore and aft is large enough to raise a complaint from the rear seat passengers, but since the prospective customer rarely rides back there, this should cause no problems for him. A good deal of the decrease in wheelbase seems to have been accommodated by shortening the rear seat cushion, but as long as the front seat is not all the way back, the back one is plenty comfortable.

The backs of the front seats are also adjustable for rake, If the front seat is adjusted to its full-forward position, the backs drop down flush with the rear seat cushion, to make a bed. The passenger can stretch out alone while the driver presses on alone, or both sides can be lowered, converting the Lark into a miniature bedroom. Perhaps a No Vacancy sign may be offered soon as an optional extra.

Our main complaint about the seats is our usual one; no lateral support. Even with the small transmission bulge pushing the pedals to the left of the steering column center line, the driver, more likely than not, eventually is found slouched against the door, his left elbow on the armrest and his hands on the wheel at seven and two o'clock. Not easy to stay alert when you don't even look alert. The accelerator pedal, typically for American cars, has its hinge point about an inch or so back from the floor board. Unless you assume the catty corner seating position just mentioned, you find that either the left foot doesn't quite reach the floorboard or the right leg is inadequately supported by the seat. We're beginning to wonder who shaped these Mr. Averages that are used so much in American design studios.

The Lark has a very pleasant, attractive instrument panel with, thank goodness, a round, yea, even circular speedometer dial. What will they think of next? Warning lights care for oil pressure and amperage deficiencies, with gauges present for fuel supply and water temperature. The latter rises quickly to its operating figure, enabling the excellent heater-defroster to be used within a half-mile or so. Of the four knobs around the instrument cluster, the upper ones operate the headlights (good) and the windshield wipers (two-speed electrical—especially important on low powered cars). A two speed fan for the heater and a combined heater vs. defroster and thermostat control (whose knob fell off) and the ignition key/starter complete the dashboard array. Just under the edge are tee handles and knobs for the hood release, fresh air intakes and the overdrive lock-out. The radio at the center of the dashboard has good selectivity and power and excellent tone. (Not the push button model, incidentally).

Despite the drastic surgery, the trunk seems to have suffered not at all. The advantage of squared off lines is that the flat panels can enclose really useable space. Our only complaint about the trunk is a usual one, those little sharp edges which chomp away at your leather suitcases, mile after mile. The station wagon, on the other hand, features the now-typical American arrangement whereby the second seat folds forward, its two sections providing a flat extension of the rear floor and a protective wall just behind the front seat. The rear floor panel covers the spare and an ingenious but inexpensive hook holds it up when the jack or wheel are being removed.

Brakes, as to be expected on a car of moderate weight, have an easy job to do. Pedal pressure is medium and the brakes are capable of locking the wheels. Studebaker's interesting Hill-holder keeps the brakes on as long as the clutch pedal is all the way down—provided only that the Lark is headed up-hill. When reversing into a parking space under these conditions, it may be disengaged merely by placing the transmission in neutral.

Steering and handling, never exactly Studebaker strong points, seem to vary with the load being carried. Both Larks feel lively when light, becoming increasingly soggy as the load grows. Empty, the sedan maintained mild understeer right up to the ragged edge. Steering forces remained light, yet not so light as to hide the behavior of the front wheels. With heavier loads aboard, the major steering force in the six seemed to be mostly friction in the peg and sector steering box (the V-8 gets a roller and sector box which improves this facet of the problem). Both cars when heavily laden seemed uninspiring, even when just going straight down the turnpikes. Unladen, they were transformed into lively little devils that turned out to be much fun to drive. In this condition, their major drawback is the heavy proportion of unsprung mass involved in the rigid rear axle. Despite very good shock absorbers, the rather light Lark VI would pick up and skitter on some corduroy surfaces.

As the Europeans have shown, when you make a light car, the only way to get big car comfort on all roads is to incorporate independent suspension on all wheels. Easier said than done, unfortunately.

STUDEBAKER TAXICAB, owned by Radio Cab Company in Detroit, has economical stock 107.8-cubic-inch Mercedes-Benz 180-D engine in place of 185.6-cubic-inch Studebaker Champion engine.

DIESEL ENGINE IN A STUDEBAKER

BY JOE H. WHERRY

Will there be a diesel engine in the economy car of the future? Detroit taxicab company's successful experiment lends support to theory of diesel-domination in commercial auto fleets.

SUCCESS by a Detroit taxicab company in the use of a diesel engine in its cabs lends support to the theory that the diesel may one day dominate commercial auto fleets and may find its way into the economy car of the future.

Because several Mercedes-Benz 180-D cars have been sold in various Eastern and Midwestern communities for service as taxicabs, the idea struck Karl Hosten, auto dealer in the Detroit suburb of Grosse Pointe, that a rather happy marriage might result between a Studebaker cab already in service and a stock 180-D engine. Hosten, who sells both Studebaker-Packard and the Mercedes-Benz line, presented the idea to officials of the Radio Cab Company in Detroit, which had purchased Studebaker cabs from him.

The roomy Studebaker cabs were costing less to run than the competitive makes, but because the MB-180-D car is able to consistently deliver upwards of 34 mpg of low-cost diesel fuel, the possibility of achieving 20 mpg or more in rigorous taxicab service was quite appealing.

Removing the stock 185.6-cubic-inch Studebaker Champion 1958 model engine—built on a 120.5-inch chassis—and installing the MB-180-D was not difficult. There was no need to modify the frame in any way. The stock Studebaker radiator core was retained and so were all suspension units, the propeller shaft, etc. After determining the comparative dimensions of the 180-D engine, it was decided that the powerplant should be installed on a slight angle toward the left side of the engine compartment. The front end of the engine had to be slightly higher than the rear or bell-housing end.

The front motor mounts of the diesel engine were used, but it was necessary to fabricate special brackets on which to fasten these mounts. The rear rubber motor mounts were completely hand-fabricated. Hosten says that on subsequent installa-

tions the rear mounts will be soft rubber to eliminate the minor vibration now evident.

The stock 180-D transmission with its four speeds was used, but the column-mounted Studebaker shift linkage was discarded and Hosten's shop made a new linkage set-up which works remarkably well. There was not sufficient space to accommodate the original Studebaker linkage. Drivers of the experimental diesel-Studebaker are favorable to the new cab but said they would prefer to have a floor-mounted shift lever. This is planned on subsequent installations.

Hosten contemplates more diesel-economy installations, unless an engine comes along that occupies less space, weighs less and is more economical to operate. There is a belief that the diesel engine has not yet exhausted its potential for development.

This 107.8-cubic-inch German, fuel-oil engine does not develop impressive power and torque—just 46 hp at 3500 rpm and the torque is on the order of 62 to 76 foot pounds for a spread of 1500 to about 2400 rpm. Installed in its native habitat in the Mercedes-Benz 180-D car, with curb weight of 2,64? pounds, the economical engine is good for about 68 mph a top speed. Acceleration is not impressive—it takes about 3? seconds to reach 60 mph.

The stock Studebaker taxicab, equipped with two-way radic and the meter, weighs about 3400 pounds or more. The weigh? remained the same with the switch to the diesel engine, accord ing to Hosten. The old Packard proving grounds at Utica Michigan, served as a site for running acceleration tests fo MOTOR LIFE. It was apparent that the best point of throttl opening to release the clutch was when the tachometer read 220? rpm. At this engine speed, the clutch load would reduce engin speed to around 1700 rpm; releasing the clutch pedal at an

SMALL DIESEL ENGINE was able to move this 3400-pound Stude-baker cab (left) quite impressively. Fuel consumption figures were upwards of 25 miles per gallon, with little maintenance.

NO FRAME MODIFICATION was necessary to remove the Studebaker engine and install the MB-180-D (center). Special brackets were fabricated for mounting motor; new shift linkage was made.

MERCEDES-BENZ 180-D engine was installed on a slight angle toward the left side of the engine compartment (bottom photo). Front end of engine had to be slightly higher than rear.

other speed resulted in losing effective torque.

An hour of practice acceleration runs revealed that the small diesel engine could move this heavy car quite impressively. Acceleration figures, with one passenger aboard, are listed as the average of at least three runs in each direction:

STANDING TO CORRECTED SPEED	SECONDS
20 mph	5.9 (first gear only)
30 mph	10.6 (first and second gear)
40 mph	22.4 (first and second gear)
50 mph	31.9 (first, second and third gear)

It took a couple of laps around the big high speed test track to attain the maximum speed—68 mph, which should be fast enough for any cab.

The gear speeds for the diesel-Studebaker, as compared to those recommended by Mercedes-Benz for the 180-D sedan, are:

GEAR	DIESEL-STUDE MPH	MB-180-D CAR MPH
First	20	17
Second	32	30
Third	51	47
Fourth (top)	68	68

Rear axle ratios available to owners of the Studebaker cab are numerous, but this particular model had the standard ratio of 4.09. The lighter-weight stock 180-D sedan has a 3.70 rear axle, which accounts for the heavier diesel-Studebaker being able to maintain comparable and even better performance.

The diesel-Studebaker tested had been on the job quite some time and had 14,000 taxicab miles, with only one trip to a shop and that for a minor tune-up. Fuel consumption figures were upwards of 25 miles per gallon, while it had only attained 15 mpg with its own stock engine.

A drive on a busy thoroughfare proved that the cab could keep up quite well with traffic, although the hand-fabricated column shift was a bit slow through the gears. Vibration was evident only when idling, and this was accompanied by the usual diesel noises.

Except for a quick blurp of gray smoke that pops from the tail pipe the instant the engine is revved up, the Studebaker cabs are not too easily identified as being equipped with a diesel engine. The tell-tale smoke vanishes when the car gets under way.

Hosten is not yet prepared to quote a price on switching to the diesel engine. Until details, such as the new motor mounts and the need for a stick floor-shift are worked out, he would rather not set a price. "This installation has been most satisfactory; seems possible it will outlast two gasoline engines with less maintenance, and it will save money," claimed Hosten.

This is probably the first installation of an MB diesel engine in a Studebaker. The lighter-weight '59 Lark cab will probably perform better with the diesel. Whether the Studebaker factory picks up the idea for '61 or '62 is anybody's guess. There could well be a diesel engine in the economy car of the future. ●

Construction was exceptionally rigid with double walls and strong supports. The interior sides were flush with no intruding wheel wells, the widest such box available. The tail gate would open the full width of the box, easing loading operations. The spare tire could be carried outside where it was not in the way of cargo yet was still easy to reach. Finally, in keeping with the Scotsman's theme of economical service, the exterior walls were much less susceptible to collision damage.

Throughout, the design showed attention to functional details.

STUDEBAKER

PRACTICAL engineering is not as obvious as a stylish appearance, making it easy to underestimate the Studebaker Scotsman pickup. Many truck buyers are apt to pass it up because, in their opinion, it looks obsolete.

They may be missing a good bet. The object of a hauling vehicle is to provide reliable service at minimum cost and the test results indicated that the Scotsman was among the best in that respect. It had one of the lowest list prices for a full-sized pickup and it appeared to be very inexpensive to operate even under the most rugged conditions.

The most apparent disadvantage of the older design was the narrower cargo box. At nearly 50 cubic feet, its capacity was equal to most other conventional models though certainly less than recent full-width types. Still, it had several points in its favor.

The taillight, for example, was spring mounted to swing out of the way under impact, thus avoiding breakage. It would then automatically reset to its original position. An important safety feature was the placement of the gas tank underneath the cab instead of inside behind the seat. It was shaped long and narrow to fit between the driveshaft and one of the outside frame rails.

The mounting of the instruments was another piece of ingenuity. The dash itself served as the firewall with the gauges on a separate, detachable panel that permitted all wiring and connections to be made from under the hood. Such an arrangement would not only be easier to service but cheaper to manufacture.

Despite this single wall between the engine and driving compartments, very little heat or noise came into the cab.

The interior was comfortable, if stark looking. Again, func-

TEST DATA

Test Car: Studebaker Scotsman
Body Type: Pickup Truck
Basic Price: $1561
Engine: ohv V-8
Carburetion: Single two-throat
Displacement: 259 cubic inches
Bore & Stroke: 3$\frac{9}{16}$x3$\frac{1}{4}$
Compression Ratio: 7.5-to-1
Horsepower: 180 bhp @ 4500 rpm
Horsepower per cubic inch: .69
Torque: 260 lb.-ft. @ 2800 rpm
Test Weight: 3280 lbs. without driver
Weight Distribution: 58 per cent on front wheels
Power-Weight Ratio: 18.2 lbs. per horsepower
Transmission: Three-speed synchromesh with overdrive
Rear Axle Ratio: 4.27-to-1
Steering: 4 turns lock-to-lock
Dimensions: overall length 198$\frac{3}{4}$ inches, width 75$\frac{5}{8}$, height 69$\frac{5}{8}$, wheelbase 122, tread 60$\frac{13}{16}$ front, 62$\frac{9}{16}$ rear
Springs: Semi-elliptic
Tires: 7.10x15
Gas Mileage: 16 mpg
Speedometer Error: Indicated 30, 45 and 60 mph are actual 27$\frac{1}{2}$, 40$\frac{1}{2}$ and 54 mph, respectively
Acceleration: 0-30 mph in 4.1 seconds, 0-45 mph in 7.5 and 0-60 mph in 12.8 seconds
Ground Clearance: 7$\frac{3}{4}$ inches
Maximum GVW: 5,000 lbs.
Axle Ratings: 2200 lbs. front, 3200 lbs. rear
Cargo Box Dimensions: Nominal length eight feet, inside length 95$\frac{13}{16}$ inches, inside width 51$\frac{1}{2}$, inside height 17$\frac{1}{8}$, tail gate width 51$\frac{1}{2}$, capacity 48.9 cubic feet.

INSTRUMENT CLUSTER is on a detachable panel which has direct wire connections for ease in servicing. Driver's position is upright and comfortable with adequate visibility both front and rear

tion and economy had been placed ahead of style. The door panels were not upholstered but consisted of painted metal panels, while the seat used a simple plastic covering selected for durability rather than design.

The seat was well positioned, with plenty of head and leg room. The window cranks were conveniently placed but the door handle was awkward.

The smaller rear window did not limit visibility as much as it might seem and it did provide better protection from the sun

PICKUP

than some bigger versions.

The controls felt noticeably stiffer than most of the other light trucks tested recently. The clutch and brake pedals operated directly through the floor rather than being suspended. The steering, however, was fairly light considering it took only four turns from lock-to-lock.

The ride, too, felt a bit stiffer than usual, even with a load. The handling on turns was as good as usual for a pickup, better than most cars but breaking away at the rear rather sharply when cornering too fast.

Most trucks, being geared for loads, take practice to start smoothly from a dead stop when no weight is carried. The test Scotsman was an extreme case with its unusually low rear axle ratio of 4.27-to-1.

A common problem with such gearing is driveshaft whip but Studebaker avoids it with a two-piece shaft, similar to those on some recent General Motors passenger cars.

Because of the low ratio, it was practically impossible to avoid wheelspin during the acceleration runs. The gearing also made it necessary to use all three speeds to reach 60 mph. Usually, only first and second are required.

Light overall weight permitted good performance, 0-to-60 taking 12.8 seconds, despite an engine of relatively modest displacement. As would be expected with the gearing, lower speed pulling power was also good. Even with a full load on some rough dirt roads, the truck never hesitated.

The 292-cubic-inch power plant was essentially a modified version of the original Studebaker V-8. Time has proven it to be ruggedly built, requiring very little maintenance, another contribution to the low cost of the Scotsman's operation.

The overdrive incorporated a free-wheeling device that permitted the driver to alternate between second and third gears without using the clutch. It also contributed to lower fuel consumption by preventing compression braking at higher speeds when the accelerator was released.

The overdrive itself did not contribute as much to economical city driving as some other because, in high gear, it did not engage below 40 mph. Still, overall mileage was a respectable 16 mpg.

Another good mechanical device long familiar to Studebaker drivers was the hill-holder. This locked hydraulic pressure in the braking system so that the brakes would not release until the clutch was engaged, saved a lot of tricky footwork when starting on a grade.

Overall, the Scotsman is much more truck than meets the eye. It would be difficult to find one better engineered for really rugged duty. The design was sound enough when first conceived that few changes have been necessary. •

UPPER CAB area is not styled with the bold lines so common to current trucks. This would tend to give the impression that the whole pickup is of small proportions. Actually the Scotsman's real work area, the bed, is the widest without obstructions on the market. While comparing, it is interesting to note that this Studebaker is also the cheapest truck in its field.

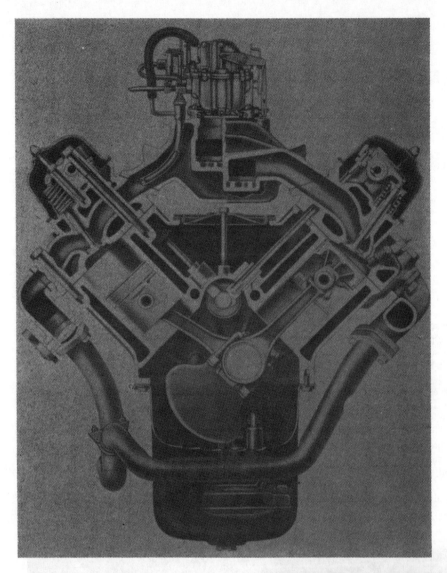

THE
Commander
IN DETAIL

This cross-section of the 4¼-litre Studebaker Sweepstakes V8 engine, with which the Commander is equipped, illustrates well its straightforward design and robust construction. The cylinder banks are set at 90-degrees to each other. A single camshaft, mounted in the cylinder block directly above the crankshaft and supported by five bushings, actuates the valves via push-rods and rocker arms. The crankshaft is supported by five main bearings.

On the right is a front view of the V8 engine, which has a maximum power output of 180 b.h.p. at 4,500 r.p.m. The engines of all Commander Hard-Tops assembled in South Africa have heavy-duty fans and dual exhaust systems. A bore of 90·9 mm. and a stroke of 82·55 mm. provide a cubic capacity of 4,248 c.c. (259·2 cu. ins.). The compression ratio is 7·5 to 1. Maximum torque is 260 lb.-ft. at 2,800 r.p.m.

The STUDEBAKER Commander hard-top

EFFORTLESS high-speed cruising is a forte of the Studebaker Commander. A speed of about 90 m.p.h.—which the Commander will readily attain from a standing start in less than half a minute—may be maintained wherever road conditions permit. When the car is travelling at this speed in overdrive top gear the engine is turning at only about 3,000 r.p.m., the overall gear ratio of overdrive top being 2.611 to 1.

The high gearing also pays dividends in the way of mileage per gallon of fuel. In the course of average motoring, which included a little town driving and a fair amount of high-speed cruising, we obtained an overall figure of 23.3 m.p.g.

High-speed motoring in the Commander is peaceful because the suspension provides excellent riding comfort, the engine is inaudible, there is remarkably little wind noise, and the inherent stability of the car is outstanding.

The Borg-Warner overdrive automatically goes out of engagement when road speed falls to about 18 m.p.h., and the Commander is capable of pottering at as low a speed as 10 m.p.h. in the direct top gear. Therefore, a speed range of 10-100 m.p.h. (the latter being the Commander's maximum speed on a level road) is available without the driver using the gear lever.

The overdrive is engaged at any speed above about 24 m.p.h. by momentarily releasing pressure on the accelerator pedal, and it may be disengaged at any time by momentarily depressing the accelerator pedal to the full extent of its travel. The "kick-down" change from overdrive top to direct top is particularly useful for overtaking and for climbing the steeper type of main-road hill.

Overdrive 2nd gear has an overall ratio of 4.047 to 1 (compared with 5.78 to 1 for normal 2nd); it is thus very similar to the overall direct top gear ratio of 3.73 to 1. For this reason—in our experience—overdrive 2nd is not frequently employed. However, when the driver is in a hurry and is travelling on a winding road (either on the flat or uphill) he may elect to leave the gear lever in 2nd-gear position and to use normal and overdrive 2nd according to circumstances, alternating between the two by means of control exercised via the accelerator pedal.

One more characteristic of the Borg-Warner overdrive needs to be described for the benefit of readers who are not conversant with this unit : a free-wheel automatically becomes operative when the overdrive goes out of engagement at about 18 m.p.h. (A push-pull control enables the overdrive and free-wheel to be put out of action if the driver so desires; this is useful when very steep hills have to be descended.)

Because of the free-wheel, the gear lever may be moved from one position to another at speeds below 18 m.p.h. without the clutch pedal being depressed. Therefore, provided that he engages top gear at under 18 m.p.h., the driver of a Commander need use the clutch only when moving off from rest.

From the foregoing it will be evident that the Commander may be driven in any one of a variety of ways, according to the driver's mood and preference. Each of these is entirely appropriate; the man at the controls chooses according to his taste and the whim of the moment.

Large-engined cars invariably have a versatile performance. The Commander is particularly gifted in this respect because its 180 b.h.p. 4¼-litre engine is mated to a good, quiet gearbox working in conjunction

with the time-proved, silent Borg-Warner overdrive unit.

The V8 o.h.v. power unit is admirably unobtrusive—smooth and very quiet at all times; it is, in fact. frequently inaudible to the car's occupants.

Positioning of major and minor controls is sound. and this fact—together with the very good view-out that is obtained in all directions—helps to make the Commander an easily-driven large car.

A Hill Holder is included in the standard equipment of this model. This excellent device keeps the brakes applied on an upgrade (with the same pressure as was employed on the brake pedal when the car was stopped) for as long as the clutch pedal is depressed. Thus, the driver's right foot is freed from the brake pedal—without the hand-brake being applied—and moving uphill away from rest is merely a matter of depressing the accelerator and allowing the clutch to engage in the usual way. As the clutch engages, the Hill Holder and brakes are automatically released.

The Studebaker Commander Hard-Top provides generous room for six adults (and their baggage) and transports them quietly, comfortably, and as rapidly as they may reasonably desire. These qualities, and the ease with which it is driven, are the car's outstanding virtues; noteworthy, too, are its very moderate thirst for fuel and its handsome lines. Of course, even at a price approaching £1,400, one cannot have *everything* —and it must be admitted that there are cars of similar price that offer less than the Commander in certain respects but can boast a better quality of detail finish and trim. The Commander Hard-Top, handsome as its lines are, is a very much more impressive car on the road than in a showroom.

Inspecting this car in a showroom, a prospective buyer might fail to be favourably impressed by such things as the detail finish around the headlights, the apparent hardness of the seats, the fact that a strut must be employed to hold the bonnet-top open, the lack of windscreen washers. These things, however, lose significance when the car is taken out on the road and they are viewed against the broad background of

The baggage boot is of extremely generous size.

exceptionally powerful, effortless and comfortable motoring that the Commander provides. The quality of the ride that the suspension gives masks the seats' limited resilience, and the other minor complaints are rapidly forgotten.

Our test included about thirty miles of motoring over untarred, corrugated roads. The Commander rode very well over these bad surfaces, and control was at all times easily exercised and certain. A variety of small rattles became evident during this period of the test. but all of these disappeared when the tarred road was regained.

Cornering and road-holding abilities are good for a vehicle of this style; there is little roll and no tyre noise unless corners are taken with altogether inappropriate gusto.

The brakes are powerful and act absolutely evenly, they can be applied with confidence at all speeds up to and including the car's maximum of 100 m.p.h. Brake pedal pressure is moderate during all normal motoring Severe tests showed that the onset of fade is accompanied by a warning smell of hot linings, and that ever such harsh treatment does not make the braking uneven —it does, of course. result in appreciably higher pressure being needed on the brake pedal.

The wrap-around windscreen produces noticeably less distortion of view than most. (This fact may be observed by studying the view through the windscreen as shown in the photograph of the Commander's controls.) The two-speed electric windscreen wipers are contra-acting and, like all of their kind, leave a large V-shaped area in the centre of the windscreen unswept

The twin horns have a power that matches the car' performance, and a gentle tap on their D-shaped control which is set within the circumference of the steering wheel, results in a note of tone and volume appropriate for use in towns.

The maximum speed of 100 m.p.h. was reached in direct top gear (in which ratio that speed is just about equivalent to the engine's power peak of 4,500 r.p.m.) We found that 97 m.p.h. could easily be maintained in overdrive top on a level road—the 3 m.p.h. difference representing the loss of speed due to momentarily releasing the accelerator pedal to allow the overdrive to engage.

On favourable gradients 100 m.p.h. may easily be reached, and exceeded, in overdrive top gear.

A reasonable maximum speed in direct 2nd gear is 70 m.p.h. We did not establish the reasonable maximum speed in overdrive 2nd gear. The "kick-down" change in the car that was submitted for test was so adjusted that it operated immediately the accelerator pedal reached the full-throttle position. This was entirely suitable for normal motoring, but it prevented us from being able to time the Commander's maximum speed in overdrive 2nd, as we felt there would have been a risk of the normal 2nd gear being unintentionally engaged and causing the engine to reach excessive r.p.m.

First-grade (premium) fuel was used throughout our test; at no time was there the slightest suggestion of pinking. Irrespective of whether the engine was cold or hot, starting was immediate.

The engine is capable of pulling strongly immediately

Carburetter, distributor and battery are high-mounted and excellently accessible.

The controls are well positioned to suit a driver of virtually any stature. The test car had a radio, which is not a standard fitting. Standard equipment includes an electric clock, added facia-top, and a cigarette lighter.

after it has been started from cold, and the automatic choke works smoothly and well. We have, in fact, never encountered a less "temperamental" power unit than that of the Studebaker Commander, and much of the considerable charm of motoring in this large car is unquestionably due to the big, powerful, willing and unobtrusive power unit with which it is equipped.

As was mentioned earlier in this report, we obtained an average of 23.3 m.p.g. This was in the course of normal driving. Anyone who was seeking to achieve the greatest possible mileage per gallon would allow the overdrive top gear to engage at a lower speed than we did, and would also treat the accelerator pedal more gently; with such driving it is possible to cover about 29 miles in exchange for each gallon of petrol consumed. This was proved during the 1958 Mobilgas Economy Run when an overdrive-equipped Studebaker Commander won its class by achieving 28.98 m.p.g.

SPECIFICATION AND PERFORMANCE

BRIEF SPECIFICATION

Make ... ... STUDEBAKER
Model Commander Hard-Top with overdrive.
Style of Engine V8. Water-cooled. Overhead valves (push-rods operated by a single high-mounted camshaft).
Bore ... 3·56 ins. (90·49 mm.)
Stroke ... 3·25 ins. (82·55 mm.)
Cubic Capacity 259·2 cu. ins. (4,248 c.c.).
Maximum Horse-Power 180 b.h.p. at 4,500 r.p.m. (Compression ratio 7·5 to 1).
Brakes Hydraulic. Self-centering, self-energising. Hill Holder device for easy starting on hills.
Front Suspension Independent. Wishbones and heavy-duty variable-rate coil springs. Anti-roll torsion bar.
Rear Suspension Long semi-elliptic leaf springs.
Transmission System Clutch and three manually engaged forward gears. Synchromesh on 2nd and top gears. Borg-Warner overdrive.
Gear Ratios ... 1st 2·57 to 1
2nd 1·55 to 1
Top Direct
o/d. 0·7 to 1
Rev. 3·48 to 1
Final Drive Ratio ... 3·73 to 1
Overall Length ... 16 ft. 10½ ins.
Overall Width ... 6 ft. 3¾ ins.
Overall Height (loaded) 4 ft. 9½ ins.
Turning Circle ... ... 39 ft.
Dry Weight ... ... 3,395 lbs.
Price ... £1,361 at Coast Ports

PERFORMANCE

Acceleration 0-30 m.p.h. 4·0 secs.
0-40 m.p.h. 6·2 secs.
0-50 m.p.h. 9·8 secs.
0-60 m.p.h. 12·8 secs.
0-70 m.p.h. 16·9 secs.
0-80 m.p.h. 22·4 secs.
0-90 m.p.h. 29·7 secs.
In top gear from a steady 40 m.p.h. to 60 m.p.h. ... ... 7·5 secs.
In top gear from a steady 50 m.p.h. to 70 m.p.h. ... ... 8·3 secs.
In top gear from a steady 60 m.p.h. to 80 m.p.h. ... ... 10·0 secs.
Maximum Speed ... 100 m.p.h.
Reasonable Maximum Speed in 2nd Gear ... ... 70 m.p.h.
Fuel Consumption ... 23·3 m.p.g.
Test Conditions Sea level. Moderate wind. Dry road. 90-octane fuel.

ROAD TEST STUDEBAKER LARK

Sturdy and unchromed, it rides more softly than imports at its price

HISTORY repeats itself, for it was just 20 years ago that another Studebaker product, the famous Champion, was introduced.

The new and the old have many similarities, particularly in size, weight and power. However, the Champion was a completely new and original concept; the Lark is not. This means that the new car is, in some respects, a compromise. Of course, there is no harm in this; all automotive design is very much a compromise, and the Lark is a good example. Its purpose is to provide sensible, economical motoring, with as little sacrifice as possible in over-all comfort.

Mechanically and technically the Lark has many excellent features. There's absolutely nothing wrong, or unsound, with an L-head (side-valve) engine. The old "Champ" 6 had a good reputation, and the new Lark has the same powerplant with a few worthwhile refinements. Of these the most important is a new crankshaft with larger-diameter main bearings. The stroke, though not down to the original 3.875 inches, is an even 4 in. (the last Champions had a 4.375-in. stroke). There is also a revamped combustion chamber shape (for smoothness) and improved carburetion. In operation these changes pretty well eliminate the old bugaboo of roughness, but for some strange reason there is considerable air intake noise at high revs. Our test car had the standard dry-type air cleaner and a brief run in another car, equipped with the extra-cost oil bath cleaner, showed some reduction in noise.

The old Champion's ability to rev (up to 5000 revolutions per minute) seems somehow to have been lost. The Lark will just touch 60 miles per hour and no more in 2nd gear; this is equivalent to 4500 rpm. Best standing-start performance comes when using shift points equivalent to 4200 rpm, or

Above: the Lark has very little overhang, which gives the car a neat if slightly stumpy appearance. The white square in the side window is an itemized price list, in accordance with the new laws of the land. The trunk is spacious enough but, due to the fact that everything has to come up before it comes out, unloading objects of any weight will require muscle.

*The Studebaker Lark presents
a bland face to the world.
This sort of simplicity in an age
of baubles, bangles and beads
is a rare sight indeed.
We found the return of the grille
to its function (as a hole to admit
air to the radiator) very refreshing,
although such directness is something
that people will applaud or deplore
according to their personal tastes.
We are also happy to see that the
last vestige of the radiator
filler cap, the hood ornament,
has disappeared once more.
Let's hope it's for good.
Despite the dent (not guilty),
the Lark's bumpers are stronger
than those on a number of imports.*

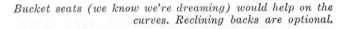

this case maximums of 33 mph in 1st and 55 mph in 2nd.
he clutch is very light but slips a little on the initial start.
ere, for once, we've found a 1st gear which is undoubtedly
little too high at 9.20 over all. (The 1939 Champion's was
).7.) The column shift works nicely and is easy to use for
affic, though a little recalcitrant when forced, as during
e acceleration checks. The transmission gears are extraor-
narily quiet, by the way.

Riding qualities are good by domestic standards, cer-
inly softer than those of any comparable import. Corner-
g roll is considerable and tire squeal easy to induce. There
also a feeling of mushiness or instability when taking
 S bend that may be due to the fact that one sits so high.

Steering also rates good. It takes 4.4 turns lock to lock (a
reless check would indicate 5.0 turns due to spring back).
ypically Studebaker, the steering wheel does not spin
ck after a turn, and this can be a trifle surprising to those
ot familiar with it. The steering characteristic is of course
dersteer, and in the 6 this is not nearly so pronounced
 in the V-8 model with automatic transmission (the latter
s about 58% of its weight on the front wheels).

Fuel economy was disappointing in hard driving (which
e car is not designed for): we got only 16/17 miles per
llon. But steady cruising at 60-65 mph gives 21/23 mpg,
d overdrive should add about 2 mpg to that. Maintenance

costs should be low, for the car is ruggedly built and easy
to work on.

So much for the good points; there are a few areas
which need attention. In the first place, the body design is
not up to modern American car standards. It is restrained,
it is readily identifiable, and many people will like it.
However, some of the old tools and dies had to be used and
the net result is a vehicle which, to us, seems extraordinarily
high (57.5 in. loaded, which does give lofty head room)
and, over all, a trifle stubby looking.

A second area of deficiency lies in the performance. We
felt that it would be most interesting to test the plain-Jane
6 with stick shift, this being a sensible, practical economy
car. As the data panel and acceleration chart show, this
combination gives a performance which may be adequate
but can hardly be called sparkling. Not that we think a car
of this type should be a brilliant performer; we do not. But,
the truth is, we at first thought something was wrong with
the car. Actually, what has happened is simply this: The
original 1939 Champion of similar weight and piston displacement pulled a rear-axle ratio of 4.10:1, or 4.55 if
equipped with overdrive. With 70 brake horsepower it
would accelerate from 0 to 60 mph in 18 seconds, or less
with overdrive ratios. The standard Lark, as tested, uses a
3.54 axle ratio, or 3.73 with overdrive. Although the Lark's

*Hello, down there! This small (2.7-liter) flat-head
6 looks a bit lost in all that room.*

*Bucket seats (we know we're dreaming) would help on the
curves. Reclining backs are optional.*

PHOTOGRAPHY: POOLE

power and torque are up, the gear ratios are poorly chosen for American needs. The engine just doesn't have a chance, and acceleration from 20 or 25 mph in high is so slow that a shift to 2nd gear is almost imperative. For comparison purposes the following data show how the Lark looks beside the original Champion:

	1939	1959
Curb weight	2650	2750
Tire size	5.50–16	5.90–15
Displacement, cu in	164	169.6
Axle ratio	4.10	3.54
Cu ft/ton mile	100	90.2
Engine revs/mile	3110	2795
Tapley pull	200	185
Time, 0-60	18.2	21.0
Top speed	78	80

Obviously the Lark could use an axle ratio of about 3.90 to good advantage. Since only 3.73, 4.10 and 4.27 are optional, we suggest 3.73 and the next larger tire (6.40-15). This should give a 0 to 60 time of close to 18.5 sec, or virtually identical to the 1939 model. With overdrive, the 4.27 ratio would be our recommendation; on a car of this type overdrive is a wise investment if brisker performance is desired (0 to 60 time should drop to about 17 sec). As for the automatic transmission, it should not be considered at all on the 6. If you want a bomb, and luxuries, buy the V-8 Lark, which really moves (Road & Track, December 1958).

The test car was one of the early ones off the assembly line, and the general quality level (body and door fits, etc.) was only fair. The interior is very stark, even by imported economy sedan standards, and the front seat lacks something in appearance, quality and comfort. Rear seat leg room (two-door sedan) is adequate, but wheelhouse encroachment makes it strictly a seat for two; in other words this is definitely not a six-passenger car. The instruments are neat and readable, but plain. The best we can say is that for once (and at last) we found a speedometer that was dead-accurate up to 60 mph. Above that speed the needle wobbled badly but actually was slow.

The summed up and considered opinion of every R&T staff member was the same: it is a good little car, but it is at best an "economy car." Whether the American public will accept this or not is the question. There are several imported sedans of about the same size which offer equal comfort, equal or better performance, better economy; yet these imports do not convey the sternly utilitarian feeling that one gets from the Lark. Fortunately for Studebaker, these imports all cost more than the Lark. Not alone because of this, it will sell in greater numbers than even the No. 1 import (VW), a fact which should shake up the overconfident export managers of any overseas manufacturer you can name.

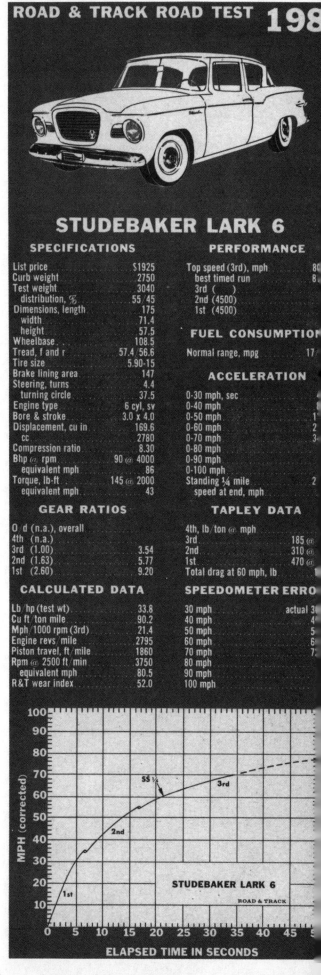

ROAD & TRACK ROAD TEST 198

STUDEBAKER LARK 6

SPECIFICATIONS

List price	$1925
Curb weight	2750
Test weight	3040
distribution, %	55/45
Dimensions, length	175
width	71.4
height	57.5
Wheelbase	108.5
Tread, f and r	57.4/56.6
Tire size	5.90-15
Brake lining area	147
Steering, turns	4.4
turning circle	37.5
Engine type	6 cyl, sv
Bore & stroke	3.0 x 4.0
Displacement, cu in	169.6
cc	2780
Compression ratio	8.30
Bhp @ rpm	90 @ 4000
equivalent mph	86
Torque, lb-ft	145 @ 2000
equivalent mph	43

GEAR RATIOS

O/d (n.a.), overall		
4th (n.a.)		
3rd (1.00)	3.54	
2nd (1.63)	5.77	
1st (2.60)	9.20	

CALCULATED DATA

Lb/hp (test wt)	33.8
Cu ft/ton mile	90.2
Mph/1000 rpm (3rd)	21.4
Engine revs/mile	2795
Piston travel, ft/mile	1860
Rpm @ 2500 ft/min	3750
equivalent mph	80.5
R&T wear index	52.0

PERFORMANCE

Top speed (3rd), mph	8(
best timed run	8.
3rd ( )	
2nd (4500)	
1st (4500)	

FUEL CONSUMPTION

Normal range, mpg	17

ACCELERATION

0-30 mph, sec	
0-40 mph	
0-50 mph	1
0-60 mph	
0-70 mph	3
0-80 mph	
0-90 mph	
0-100 mph	
Standing ¼ mile	2
speed at end, mph	

TAPLEY DATA

4th, lb/ton @ mph	
3rd	185 @
2nd	310 @
1st	470 @
Total drag at 60 mph, lb	

SPEEDOMETER ERROR

30 mph	actual 3(
40 mph	4
50 mph	
60 mph	
70 mph	
80 mph	
90 mph	
100 mph	

STUDEBAKER LARK 6

ROAD & TRACK

ELAPSED TIME IN SECONDS

STUDEBAKER LARK SPECIFICATION			
Cylinders	... ...	Six	V-8
Bore	... ...	76.1 mm.	90.4 mm.
Stroke	... ...	101.5 mm.	82.5 mm.
Cubic capacity	...	2,785 c.c.	4,248 c.c.
Piston area	...	42.2 sq. in.	79.4 sq. in.
Valves	... ...	Side	pushrod o.h.v
Compression ratio	...	8.3	8.8
Max. power (gross)	...	90 b.h.p.	180 b.h.p.
at		4,000 r.p.m.	4,500 r.p.m.
Max. b.m.e.p.	...	129 lb./sq. in.	152 lb./sq. in.
at		2,000 r.p.m.	2,800 r.p.m.
Top-gear ratio (normal transmission)		3.54/1	3.31/1
Wheelbase	...	9 ft. 0½ in.	9 ft. 0½ in.
Overall length	...	14 ft. 6¾ in.	14 ft. 6¾ in.
Width	... ...	5 ft. 9 in.	5 ft. 9 in.
Height	... ...	4 ft. 9½ in.	4 ft. 9½ in.
Dry weight	...	23½ cwt.	26½ cwt.
Turning circle	...	37½ ft.	37½ ft.
Brake lining area	...	147½ sq. in.	147½ sq. in.
Tyre size	...	5.90—15	6.40—15
Top gear m.p.h. at 1,000 r.p.m.		20.8	23.1
Top gear m.p.h. at 1,000 ft./min. piston speed		31.2	42.6

1959 CARS

Neat and unadorned, the Lark which is seen here as the two-door hardtop model is America's most serious attempt yet to build a car that is economical in every way.

The STUDEBAKER LARK

An American Small Car First Announced in *The Motor* Last Week

NEWS from the United States in recent months has made much of the public reaction said to be growing against a constant diet of Longer, Lower, Wider automobiles, a feeling which has so far been met by Detroit's Big Three exclusively with models which are yet Longer, still Lower and even Wider. If the public-opinion testers are correct a healthy revival should be in store for the Studebaker-Packard Corporation in their remote (from Detroit) fastness of South Bend, Indiana, which have been the first to take the plunge on models combining really compact size with very simple decoration.

The Lark series which is the fruit of this bold decision is evidently intended to offer the American public the possibility of all-round economy. Although passenger accommodation is claimed to be rather more liberal than last year, it is enclosed in a smaller body which is hence cheaper to build, less vulnerable to damage and easier to repair (having detachable wing panels), and deliberately undating, to suffer less by depreciation.

Considerable efforts have also been made to provide economical performance. The capacity of the six-cylinder side-valve engine supplied with the cheaper models has been reduced from 3,041 c.c. to a mere 2,785 c.c. by shortening the stroke, while at the same time a re-designed cylinder head allows an increase of compression ratio to 8.3/1 without sacrificing the ability to run on "regular-grade" fuel of about 90 Octane. The power output is given as 90 b.h.p. at 4,000 r.p.m.—the first new American model to have less than 100 b.h.p. for some years— and the maximum torque of 1,740 lb. in. occurs at half that engine speed. A new automatic-choke carburetter has been designed, with economy chiefly in view, in which the enrichment jet for maximum acceleration is opened only by a combination of vacuum and extreme throttle pedal movement. Plainly

indicative of the way the company is thinking is the claim for a 20% improvement in torque and 8% improvement in economy at *35 m.p.h.* For customers in search of performance there is a V-8 engine of 4,248 c.c. developing 180 b.h.p., or 195 b.h.p. when equipped with a four-choke carburetter and dual exhaust. Like the Six it is intended for 90 Octane fuel.

The styling ancestry of the Larks is evident from the Hawk series which is continued as the prestige car of the range, the silhouette being effectively that of the Loewy-designed "sports" models shorn once more of tail fins and drastically trimmed of front and rear overhang. The extent of the trimming can be judged from the comparative overall lengths: 14 ft. 7 in. for the Lark saloon, 17 ft. for the Hawk coupé. A typical family saloon from one of the Detroit Big Three is 14 in. longer still.

Studebaker have never lagged in technical progress, and although there are no outstanding engineering changes in the latest cars a large number of details have been improved to consolidate ground already won. Reduction in weight has led to redesigning of the variable-rate front coil-spring suspension, with new rear springs and modified shock absorbers. This, with a wider track, is said to reduce cornering roll, while the steering has been given a variable ratio to make it more direct, lighter and better at self-centring. Power brakes, a limited-slip differential and air-conditioning are available as extras on all models, as well as power steering on the V-8 cars. An automatic "hill-holder," which traps pressure in the brake system when the car stops on an upgrade, is offered as an option on all models except those with automatic transmission.

Like the Lark, the well-known Hawk model is available with either a 90 b.h.p., side-valve six-cylinder engine or a 180 b.h.p. V-8.

1960 STUDEBAKER

Powered by a bigger-displacement V8 engine, the Hawk for '60 will also have a new heavy-duty transmission and radiator, bigger clutch, better brakes. Hawks will be available with conventional, overdrive or automatic transmission.

by Bill Callahan *Detroit Editor*

A YEAR AGO Harold Churchill, president of Studebaker-Packard, promised prospective buyers of his new Lark series that these new cars were designed for a minimum of year-to-year style changes. This year he has kept his promise. The cars are not changed, but he has added a convertible and a four-door station wagon to his line. The same overall length of 175 ins. is continued for the convertible and sedan models, and wagons continue at 184.5 ins.

As in 1959, all models will be available with six or V8 powerplants. The Lark engines have not been changed except for improvements in carburetion and engine mounting. The 169.9-cu.-in. L-head six is still rated 90 hp at 4000 rpm, with compression ratio 8.3 to 1. The V8, with standard two-barrel carburetor, develops 180 hp at 4500 rpm at 8.8 to 1 compression. Optional equipment, including a four-barrel carburetor and dual exhaust, boost the output of this 259.2-cu.-in. engine to 195 hp at 4500 rpm.

The new V8 engine used in the Hawk series has been increased in displacement from 259 to 289 cu. in. and now develops 210 hp at 4500 rpm. Compression ratio is 8.8 to 1.

Most chassis and engine refinements in the Lark series provide smoother, quieter operation and better gasoline economy. The torque converter has been redesigned to reduce slippage and new air cleaners lower intake air noises. On the V8's, the new distributor location will facilitate servicing and tune-up. Frames, steering and suspension have not been changed.

In the interior, the gasoline pedal has been relocated for greater comfort, and there is a new instrument panel with instruments grouped closely in front of the driver. Rear seat legroom in all models has been increased one in., merely by redesigning the front seat. In all models with split front seat, knee room in the rear has been increased two ins. and headrests will be optional. Reclining seats, non-slip differential and power brakes are also optional.

The new Lark convertible and the two-door hardtop will be part of the Regal line. The four-door station wagons will be in both Regal and Deluxe lines, while the four-door sedan is featured in both lines. The two-door sedan and two-door station wagons are available only in the Deluxe series.

Studebaker kept their word to last year's buyers: no significant changes; however, they did add a wagon and a convertible. Latter has heavy-gauge box-section ladder-type frame with additional beefy X-member. Engine: six or V8.

NEW LARK CONVERTIBLE, WITH CHOICE OF ENGINE AND TRANSMISSION, IS THE ONLY CONVERTIBLE BEING OFFERED IN COMPACT-SIZE LINES.

LARK FOUR-DOOR STATION WAGON HAS SAME OPTIONS. TAILGATE HAS LOTS OF GLASS AREA AND LOCKS TO HOLD OPEN SECTIONS IN PLACE.

CONVERTIBLE LARK

BY STUDEBAKER

In the mid-1950's Detroit's formula for conquest in the market place was embodied in the concept of the "classless car". The differences that had prevailed historically — in size, room, finish, performance, price and general quality — deliberately were narrowed to the vanishing point. What the public was offered amounted very largely to its choice of ad campaigns, its choice of the folklore of "distinct" makes and models that differed little if, essentially, at all.

The utopian manufacturing economies implicit in the classless-car concept spelled paradise to car makers but not to a buying public whose automotive tastes were becoming more sophisticated by the day. The conformist millions passively rebelled, demanded and necessarily were given variety and distinction. In today's broad spectrum of choice, variations are played upon variations. One of the most arresting of these is the Studebaker Lark V8 convertible.

In SCI for June, '59 the Lark V8 station wagon was reviewed and the Lark sedan with six-cylinder engine was the subject of a full-scale road test. Thousands of miles were accumulated on both cars on round trips from New York to Sebring and in the traffic of the metropolis . . . *not* meaning Sebring. Our experience with the Lark V8 also includes driving one car from Los Angeles to Denver, over the high Rockies, plus wringing out a second specimen on our all-inclusive test course in Southern California. This was a Lark convertible with optional four-throat carb, dual exhaust and Borg-Warner torque-converter "Flightomatic" automatic transmission; this car is the one we tested.

The variation on the compact car theme represented by this vehicle has little to do with low purchase price. At this writing the Lark V8 convertible's base price (according to AUTOMOTIVE NEWS) is $2,756, not including transportation cost from factory or the cost of myriad options. Base prices for Chev, Ford and Plymouth convertibles are $2,847, $2,800

and $2,967. Even with six-cylinder engine the Lark convertible is no budget package at $2,621, in the sense that the Lark V8 two-door sedan is, base-priced at $2,111.

Unlike other compacts the Lark V8 convertible is a heavy car; ready-to-go weight was 3580 pounds. Its fuel consumption is not in the compact class. Under maximum-consumption test conditions we averaged 14.7 mpg and in fairly easy-going town driving the average rose to 19.5. Nor is the Lark V8's performance merely "good enough," as it is with most compacts. With one mile to wind up in, our test car streaked through the timing trap at a clocked 106 mph. In spite of a slow-to-take-hold transmission it moved from zero to 60 in just over 13 seconds.

The most striking single feature of the Lark convertible is the combined attractiveness and quality of detail and finish. The handsome, pleated vinyl seats are some of the most comfortable we've encountered in a domestic car in years. Their padding is ideally firm, their height relative to the floor is excellent and they support the back positively all the way to the shoulders. Fingerlight adjustability fore and aft is provided over an unusually useful range. The front seat is split and the passenger can make his leg-room adjustments independently of the driver. Full advantage of this feature can be taken when the optionally-available reclining seat backs are used. These recline all the way to the horizontal, forming a bed that's continuous with the rear seat cushion. Thanks to the chair-height seating and large glass area, vision from the car is very good.

So are most of the controls. The power steering has good feel and is emphatically self-centering. In spite of 4.5 turns from lock to lock, the car we took over the Rockies had no slop in its steering and felt entirely secure. The test convertible, on the other hand, had one-third turn of free play

Continued on page 142

ROAD TEST

STUDEBAKER LARK Regal V8 Convertible

Price as stated:	$2756 basic
Manufacturer:	Studebaker-Packard Corporation South Bend, Indiana

ENGINE:

Displacement	259 cu in, 4251 cc
Dimensions	Eight cyl, 3.56 x 3.25 in
Compression Ratio	8.8 to one
Power (SAE)	195 bhp @ 4500 rpm
Torque	265 lb-ft @ 3000 rpm
Usable rpm Range	550-4500 rpm
Piston Speed ÷ √ s/b @ rated power	2555 ft/min
Fuel Recommended Mileage	15-20 mpg
Range	270-360 miles

CHASSIS:

Wheelbase	108.5 in
Tread, F, R	57½, 56½ in
Length	175 in
Suspension: F, ind., coil, wishbones, anti-roll bar; R, rigid axle, semi-elliptic leaf springs.	
Turns to Full Lock	2¼
Tire Size	6.70 x 15
Swept Braking Area-drum F, R...156, 126 sq in.	
Curb Weight (full tank)	3580 lbs
Percentage on Driving Wheels	39%
Test Weight	3755 lbs

DRIVE TRAIN:

Gear	Synchro?	Ratio	Step	Overall	Mph per 1000 rpm
Rev	Auto	2.00	—	6.14	13.2
L	Auto	2.40		7.38	11.0
			63%		
2nd	Auto	1.47		4.52	18.0
			47%		
D	Auto	1.00		3.07	26.4

Torque converter ratio: 2.15 maximum at 1800 rpm.
Final Drive Ratios: 3.07 to one (auto), 3.31 (manual), 3.54 (overdrive).

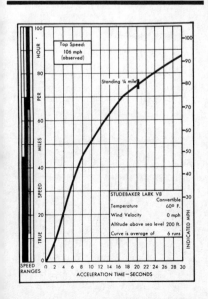

Top Speed: 106 mph (observed)

Standing ¼ mile

STUDEBAKER LARK V8 Convertible
Temperature 60° F.
Wind Velocity 0 mph
Altitude above sea level 200 ft.
Curve is average of 6 runs

SPEED RANGES

ACCELERATION TIME—SECONDS

in its steering and would not have been enjoyable to drive on iced mountain roads. At right or left full lock the tires rubbed against the chassis with noisy protest. The throttle pedal spring is absurdly stiff and the spring load against kickdown takes all you've got. The pedal is located well to the left of the gearbox tunnel almost on the centerline of the driver's body . . . not the handiest position.

The three-speed torque converter transmission has good and bad points. On the good side it is quiet and shifts smoothly and fast. On the other side it takes about four seconds by stopwatch for any significant amount of power to reach the driving wheels when digging out from standstill. This is true in both Drive and Low ranges; over the standing quarter mile we were able to gain only .4 second by starting in Low.

The car's handling generally is quite good, as you might expect of a sway-barred, decently-shocked, short-wheelbase car. An interesting feature here is its breakaway characteristic. It sticks *very* well in the turns. While most cars break away much earlier at the rear than at the front, our Lark convert would merely go into a very gradual outward slide. Its cornering balance is good.

The car's ride is delightful on all normal surfaces and at all reasonable cruising speeds. It's skittery on washboard and from about 90 mph upward it becomes light and hobby-horses palpably but not disturbingly. The car is smooth and exceptionally quiet even on rough (not washboard) roads. The engine is quiet, its exhaust note authoritative.

The convertible top functions easily and conveniently. To lower the vinyl top two large, easily-gripped toggles on the top header bar are released. A lever under the instrument panel is moved and humming electric motors stow the top neatly in a matter of seconds. A vinyl snap-on boot is provided for covering the top-well. The top is erected just as quickly and easily and no unusual gymnastics are required to secure it with the toggles. On our test car a few thousandths of an inch of daylight showed between the top's side rails and the aluminum strips that carry rubber-channel window seals. No wind came through these slight gaps; they were one of the few instances of less-than-fine fit and finish throughout the vehicle.

As we've said, this is a compact-dimensioned big car. It possesses none of the relative austerity that marks most of the compacts, instead it is rather luxurious and definitely *chic*. Priced as it is, it's a sensible choice for anyone who wants the handling ease of a compact, much more than typical compact performance, plus the pleasure of open-air motoring. It's a rugged, strongly-built vehicle that is spirited, untiring to drive and that draws admiring looks wherever it's seen.

—*Griff Borgeson*

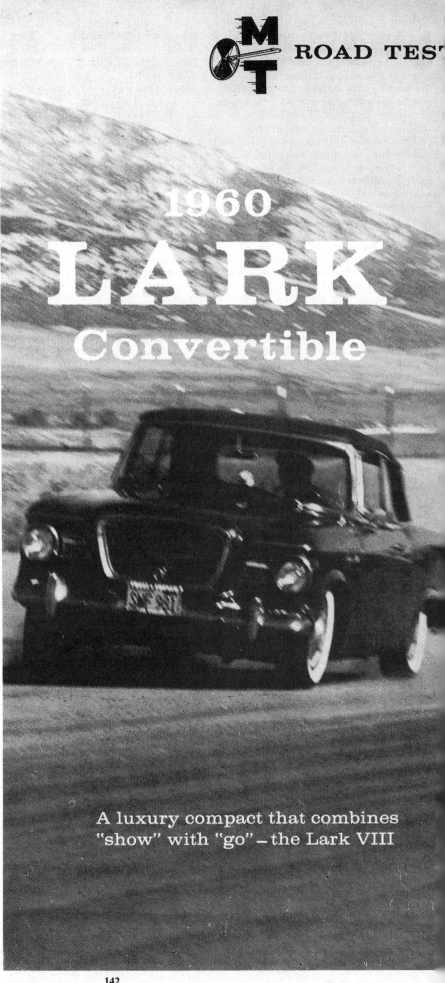

1960
LARK
Convertible

A luxury compact that combines "show" with "go"—the Lark VIII

Power-operated top, standard equipment on all Lark convertibles, folds neatly into compartment behind rear seat. Two rugged latches on upper windshield frame clamp the leading edge of top against grooved rubber sealing strip.

PHOTOS BY PAT BROLLIER

by Chuck Nerpel
Technical Editor

AN EVER-INCREASING NUMBER of imports, most of them economy cars, has led to a new way of thinking among domestic car buyers, and the major Detroit manufacturers have responded with compact cars scaled to American needs and budgets. Economy, low upkeep and modest purchase price are the selling points, but all sorts of optional extras are offered, and customer response to these options may start a new class of car— the luxury compact.

Studebaker's Lark, which debuted in 1959, followed American Motors into the compact field and offers two-door and four-door sedans and station wagons with six- or eight-cylinder engines —and for 1960, a convertible.

For years, soft-topped automobiles known as roadsters were popular but rather restricted to use in warm climates, due mainly to their liberal supply of outside air—even with flapping side curtains. Roll-up windows and snug, well-insulated tops soon made the convertible a desirable year-around car in any climate. Till now, however, this body style has been available only in the larger sporty-type domestic cars or the smaller imports.

The 1960 model year finds a wide variety of American compacts with more coming, but currently the Lark is the only one offering a convertible. Due to the increased amount of hand fitting necessary for soft tops, plus the mechanism involved in folding them down, and heavier frames to add rigidity lost by elimination of the steel top, convertibles have always cost more than conventional sedans of the same model. Add to this all the goodies optionally available for the Lark, such as powerpack 195-hp V8 engine, automatic transmission, power steering and brakes, limited-slip differential, radio, heater, reclining

Big V8 engine loaded with power accessories crowds the engine compartment but has enough hood clearance for deep carburetor air filter. Easy access to plugs, points, carburetor and top-mounted screw-on oil filter reduces tune-up and maintenance service costs.

LARK continued

Head-on, the Lark VIII convertible resembles other hardtop models. Only major front-end styling change for 1960 is new chrome texture for grille and vents.

With its "jewel box" appointments, the Lark VIII adds a plush touch to rugged construction and sparkling performance

Newly designed dash, featuring easy-to-read instrument cluster, center glove box and radio, has non-glare cowl and padded strip on lower edge to protect knees.

seats, adjustable headrests, bumper guards, wheel discs, whitewall tires and several other irresistible items—and you have a veritable jewel box compact convertible, that goes.

Cost has also gone . . . up, as factory-recommended f.o.b. retail of this little package is nearly $3500. We have seen some rather stark imports sell for a lot more, while offering less in the way of options and performance, with the possible exception of better fuel mileage.

The Lark's 259.2-cubic-inch engine is small by present V8 standards and is dragged down on fuel consumption by the power accessories, but the dual-exhaust system and optional four-barrel carburetor make it possible to crank out 195 hp at 4500 rpm, sufficient for over 70 mph in the ¼-mile.

We thrashed the Lark V8 pretty good during our cross-country road tests, slamming the little car into tight corners, taking advantage of the maneuverability of its short 108-inch wheelbase, powering out by holding it in 2nd gear (possible with the use of LOW selector once the gearbox has upshifted into 2nd), and generally driving at or over the maximum speed limits. This is possibly the most fuel-consuming type of driving one can possibly indulge in, yet overall mileage totaled 14.5 mpg. Fuel consumption, however, is not in the economy or compact car range, mainly due to the many power accessories that are using gasoline indirectly to perform their functions. Loaded with these as the test car was, highway mileage at high cruising speeds in the 17 to 18-mpg range is possible.

Handling characteristics vary according to the passenger load. With only the driver and one passenger aboard, lean is very noticeable but stabilizes well below the panic point. With a pair of rear seat passengers, or with about 200 pounds of luggage compartment load, cornering is flat with good resistance to bottoming, even over sharp dips at speed. Much of this stability over dips is due to front springing customized to suit the weight on the front wheels. The Lark V8 is not just a Lark chassis with a bigger engine, as the spring rate on the variable-rate front coil springs is 25 to 30 pounds more for each wheel than the springs on six-cylinder models. Rear springing is by semi-elliptical leaves designed to maintain the car in level position with 700-pound loads. The rear axle is mounted forward of the center of the spring and torque windup is held in check by the shorter and stiffer forward side of the spring.

We mentioned earlier the heavier frames necessary with convertibles, but the Lark goes one better in striving for rigidity and rattle-free operation. A deep box-section frame with an extra-thick "X" cross-member is much stiffer than the box-section, ladder-crossmember type used in the steel-topped Larks. Body sections for the convertible feature built-in sheet metal box sections to provide additional resistance to twist and deformities that loosen hinges, latches, and cause poor fits to develop in doors and trunk lids.

Larger brakes are also supplied with the V8 Lark with 11-inch front drums and 10-inch rear drums—a full inch larger than those supplied on the six-cylinder models. In addition, brake lining widths are greater and give a total of 172.8 square inches of effective lining area. This little convertible really stops on a dime, and repeatedly without fade, despite 3250 pounds of curb weight. With the lining area provided it figures out to about 105 square inches of lining per ton of vehicle, comparable to many of the large domestic cars. Add to this the ease by which added pressure can be attained through the Hydrovac power assist, and we have a sensible, adequate set of brakes.

Cruising through the sweeping curves of a wide highway or threading the congested traffic lanes of a big city requires a steering that is light but quick. The Lark V8's Bendix power unit requires only 4½ turns lock-to-lock, responds to the pressure of one finger, yet gives a positive feeling that the steering wheel is actually attached to the road wheels. The steering box itself, a cam-and-roller unit, is center-mounted in the front of the chassis, which allows tie rods of equal length and provides uniform steering geometry to the full turning range to both left and right.

Quiet and cozy with windows up, the padded convertible top is solid and rattle-free. A flick of the front latches, a touch of the under-dash lever, and the top folds neatly into a recess behind the rear seat. Preferred operation, of course, is with the car standing still. Further finish to the smart convertible lines and as a protector for the folded top is a heavy plastic tonneau cover, with plenty of snap-on buttons to insure a taut fit.

Under the hood, unseen but noticeable changes have been incorporated in the engine, carburetion and engine mountings. Modifications to the combustion chamber to reduce high-compression rumble result in smooth, quiet engine operation at all speeds. Engine and transmission mounts, which are now made of long-lasting, oil-resistant synthetic butyl, are furnished with different rebound rates custom-tailored to the various engine and gearbox combinations available. Studebaker engineers found that one standard for these mounts did not absorb the different vibration frequencies of the V8s, the sixes, and the manual or automatic transmissions. The manifold and automatic choke cam have been altered to shorten warm-up time and reduce the fast-idle period after a cold-engine start.

There are off-the-beaten-path roads and sweeping open highways all over this country that just demand to be driven in a lively, comfortable car. Combine the driving thrills of positive steering and good acceleration with the open-air advantages of a top-down convertible, and you have it in one package in what could be considered a new class of touring car—the luxury compact Lark VIII.

MT | '60 LARK ROAD TEST

Car At a Glance

Things We Like	Things We Don't Like
Compactness	Relatively low gas mileage
Driving ease	for compact car
Good brakes	Noticeable but not uncomfortable
Passenger comfort	body lean on sharp turns
Rugged frame and body	
Lively performance	

Acceleration

0-45 mph 9.0 secs. 0-60 14.9
Quarter-mile 20.6 secs., 71 mph
30-50 5.1   45-60 5.7   50-75 14.9

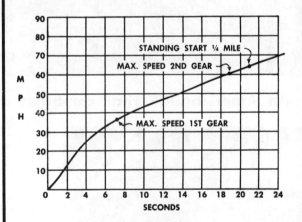

Stopping Distance

From 60 mph to standstill 198 ft.
(In 4.5 secs. with maximum of 0.68-G deceleration)

Stop after maximum acceleration to end of ¼-mile 320 ft.
(In 5.7 secs. with maximum of 0.74-G deceleration)

Gas Mileage

	Mpg
Stop-and-go heavy traffic	13.9
Normal traffic	14.6
Open highway, steady cruise	19.1
Open highway, fast cruise	17.9

Road Test

BIG STUDEBAKER V-8 is the 289-cubic-inch unit last offered in 1958. With a single two-barrel carburetor, it produces 210 hp.

STUDEBAKER'S HAWK is a car of subtle but very solid virtues that are appreciated the moment you get behind the wheel. Lower than most other domestic makes, the car's windshield is raked back sharply and further increases the feeling of being closer to the ground. Wheel position is excellent for both comfort and visibility, but other controls are conventional. In fact, power steering and automatic transmission are just like those of the Lark.

Cruising along the highway, one important characteristic seems different—the ride is relatively firm. And that's the tip-off the Hawk has hidden virtues and is no ordinary car.

Driven hard, it reveals an exceptional degree of stability. Rear end squat under full acceleration, nose dive during sudden braking and body sway in turns are all so slight that the driver is hardly aware of them. Even as the car is snaked through an "S" bend, there is no appreciable roll.

Studebaker Hawk

An American GT that combines comfort and roadability

The Hawk is at least 300 lbs. lighter than any other full-sized V-8, so the springing effect is firmer with modest spring rates. The coils in front actually are variable rate type. They stiffen under increased loads, offer added support to the outside wheels when turning, and reduce bottoming tendencies over dips.

Semi-elliptics are used at the rear, with the axle mounted ahead of the spring centers, to allow accelerating and braking forces to act primarily against a short, stiff spring section and reduce axle wind-up.

How well the suspension is engineered is shown by the way it counteracts a slightly nose-heavy weight distribution. Approximately 58 per cent of the 3420 lbs., as tested, is on the front wheels, yet the car feels extremely well balanced. The weight bias can be attributed mostly to the engine. Though it is mounted well back on the chassis (the front of the block is just about even with the front wheel centers), it is an extremely heavy unit for its size.

On wide turns, the Hawk behaves beautifully. Even a four-wheel drift, executed by a skilled driver, does not betray the slight nose heaviness. In tight corners, though, the feel of con-

PLUSH HAWK INTERIOR is finished in vinyl with reclining seatbacks as an option. Round-dial instruments are easily legible.

trol is less certain. One obvious reason is the 120.5-inch wheelbase, hardly that of a sports car.

But another problem is the power steering. Like too many units of its kind, it has a slow ratio, 4.5 turns lock-to-lock, and virtually no road sensitivity. There is some resistance but it is within the system itself, not from the road. Except for parking ease and slightly less steering effort, a power assist offers no great advantage in the Hawk. The manual system has the same ratio plus the benefit of a natural feel. It would seem the wiser choice for high-speed driving.

Several mechanical changes have been made in the Hawk for 1960, none of them involving really new equipment. The six-cylinder engine has been dropped and the 289-cubic-inch V-8 used prior to 1959 has been revived. Last year, the car was offered with the same 259-cubic-inch unit as the Lark V-8. To accommodate the bigger powerplant, the radiator, clutch and transmission revert to heavier duty specifications. Also brought back from pre-1959 models are finned brake drums.

The engine develops 210 hp with a two-barrel carburetor and 225 hp with an optional four-barrel. Dual exhausts are standard on both versions, as is an 8.8-to-1 compression ratio for operation on regular fuel.

The automatic transmission, called Flightomatic by Studebaker, is the familiar Borg-Warner unit incorporating a torque converter and three-speed planetary gear set. With it, the standard rear axle ratio is 3.07. The conventional and overdrive ratios, 3.31 and 3.54 respectively, are available as options at no extra cost.

Flightomatic has just two forward ranges, marked with the customary "D" and "L" on the shift quadrant. Normally, "D" is limited to second and third gears, starting in first only under full throttle. First is the usual operating gear in "L," though second will engage with a downshift from "D" at speeds above 20 mph. Either first or second can be held from an upshift by applying full accelerator pressure.

The acceleration technique of pushing "L" to the limit and shifting to "D" does not work in the Hawk because it causes a shift from first to third, skipping second entirely. And starting with first in "D" is not too satisfactory because the upshift to second requires a release of accelerator pressure. Either way, power has to be sacrificed momentarily.

Best results are obtained by starting in "L," shifting to "D" as the engine peaks, then immediately dropping back to "L" to get second. Such a technique produced an average 0-to-60 mph time of 12.3 seconds, between 1.5 and two seconds faster than those obtained with the other methods. The controlled downshift is also useful for cornering, allowing second gear torque to reach the rear wheels for firmer traction.

Naturally, taking advantage of the transmission's flexibility has its effects on fuel consumption. During the performance and roadability checks, the car yielded 12 mpg, quite a comedown from the 18 mpg possible with conservative driving.

The Hawk body is a club coupe—a two-door, four/five passenger style with only limited rear seating. No hardtop has been available in the series for two years. Originally introduced in 1953, the car received its only major facelift in 1956. Styling changes this year are confined to minor trim, notably dropping the word "Silver" from the script on the tail fins. It now reads just plain "Hawk."

Upholstered in a pleated, grained vinyl, the seats are high enough from the floor for long-range comfort. Those in front are separately adjustable and can be had with reclining backs.

The basic design of the Studebaker V-8 coupe is in its eighth year but it is still impressive. It has been known at times as the Commander, President, Speedster, various sorts of Hawks and even a Packard. The current model may not have the glamour of some of its predecessors, especially the 275-hp Golden Hawks of 1956 through 1958, but it is a thoroughly seasoned car, distinctive in appearance and functional in operation. ●

—John Lawlor

1960 STUDEBAKER HAWK

Test Car

TEST CAR: Studebaker Hawk
BODY TYPE: Coupe
BASE PRICE: $2650

Maneuverability Factors

OVERALL LENGTH: 204 inches
OVERALL WIDTH: 71.3 inches
OVERALL HEIGHT: 55.5 inches
WHEELBASE: 120.5 inches
TREAD, FRONT/REAR: 57.4 and 56.6 inches
TEST WEIGHT: 3420 lbs.
WEIGHT DISTRIBUTION: 58 per cent on front wheels
STEERING: 4.5 turns lock-to-lock
TURNING CIRCLE: 41 feet curb-to-curb
GROUND CLEARANCE: 6.9 inches

Interior Room

SEATING CAPACITY: Four/five
FRONT SEAT—
 HEADROOM: 35.5 inches
 WIDTH: 59.5 inches
 LEGROOM: 44.0 inches
TRUNK CAPACITY: 11.1 cubic feet

Engine & Drive Train

TYPE: Ohv V-8
DISPLACEMENT: 289 cubic inches
BORE & STROKE: 3.56 x 3.62
COMPRESSION RATIO: 8.8-to-1
CARBURETION: Single two-barrel
HORSEPOWER: 210 @ 4500 rpm
TORQUE: 300 @ 2800 rpm
TRANSMISSION: Flightomatic (Torque converter with three-speed gearbox)
REAR AXLE RATIO: 3.07

Performance

GAS MILEAGE: 12 to 18 mpg
ACCELERATION: 0-30 mph in 4.5 seconds, 0-45 mph in 7.4 seconds and 0-60 mph in 12.3 seconds
SPEEDOMETER ERROR: Indicated 30, 45 and 60 mph are actual 28, 42 and 55 mph, respectively
POWER-WEIGHT RATIO: 16.3 lbs. per horsepower
HORSEPOWER PER CUBIC INCH: .72

ALTHOUGH IT IS NOT very apparent from the outside, 1961 is a year of many important changes at Studebaker. There is a new version of the Lark which, although it is still a compact, has a longer wheelbase and more room on the inside. Another newcomer this year is an ohv six-cylinder engine. There are other relatively important changes—one is a four-speed transmission for the Hawk. Moreover, there is also a long list of refinements.

The new Lark is called the Cruiser. Its overall length is 179 inches, four inches longer than the regular Lark sedan. The wheelbase of 113 inches compares with 108.5 inches on other Lark sedan models. The Cruiser's larger body provides increased interior dimensions. The rear seat has more legroom and a folding center armrest. The rear doors are wide and the floor is level with the door sills, which should make exit and entry easy. Other distinctive Cruiser features include European-type pockets on all four doors, and rear window wing vents.

But Studebaker's most important news this year is under the hood. Gone is the old-fashioned L-head and in its place is a new 170-cubic-inch overhead-valve powerplant. The new Six develops 112 hp at 4500 rpm, compared to the 90 hp at 4500 rpm of the previous flathead design. The compression ratio is now 8.5-to-1 as opposed to the former 8.3-to-1. Studebaker engineers have always been quite ingenious in adapting their

engineering features to new designs. This is probably one of their cleverest projects—not only are several components from the old design incorporated into the new model, but the basic block is carried over.

Performance specifications for the Lark V-8 remain unchanged this year. With standard two-barrel carburetor, the engine develops 180 hp at 4500 rpm. A four-barrel-carburetor option is available that develops 195 hp at 4500 rpm. The changes in this powerplant are mostly refinements, although a new fuel pump with a 15-micron filter element has been adopted.

Along with its new engine the Lark has a new automatic transmission and a new converter. The new unit has a one-way clutch to provide smoother shifting, and the clutch has been increased from 8 to 9⅛ inches.

One 1961 change should eliminate much of the stiffness in the Lark's manual steering. This is a newly designed recirculating-ball-type steering gear. In addition, the caster has been changed from 2½ degrees negative to zero degrees, and the knuckle upper bushing is a new steel-back type, precision ground. What this means is that friction will be reduced. In fact Studebaker engineers claim a 30 per cent reduction on six-cylinder models and 10 per cent on V-8's.

Among the other 1961 changes for the Lark are new bonded

STUDEBAKER

an important new engine plus a roomier body option

Studebaker has a new Lark for '61. The Cruiser, far right, is four inches longer than the regular Lark, above and right, is much roomier inside. The Hawk, far right above, retains its familiar styling but has added a four-speed floor-mounted transmission and bucket seats on the inside.

linings for the brakes. The clutch and brake pedals are now suspended, and pedal pressure has been reduced. Shock absorbers have been given new settings and the front springs have been redesigned.

The Hawk, Studebaker's only standard-sized car, is virtually unchanged in visual appearance this year. It has added more of a sporty flavor, however, by adopting bucket seats and a floor-mounted, four-forward-speed transmission.

The Hawk's 289-cubic-inch powerplant is unchanged from last year. It has a horsepower rating of 210 at 4500 rpm. A four-barrel-carburetor option brings this up to 225 hp at 4500 rpm. Dual exhausts are standard equipment.

In addition to the new optional four-speed transmission with floor shift, Hawks are also available with either standard, overdrive or automatic transmissions. Options that are exclusive for the car are tachometers and deck-lid-mounted radio antennas.

All Studebakers scheduled for California delivery are equipped with forced crankcase ventilation to reduce smog-producing fumes. Gasoline fumes that escape from the rings in the cylinders are piped to the intake manifold to be burned in the cylinders.

Six-cylinder and V-8 Larks will be available as two- and four-door sedans, two- and four-door station wagons, two-door hardtops and a convertible. The Lark Cruiser is available only as a four-door sedan, and the Hawk only as a sport coupe. **/MT**

The Lark's big news for 1961 is under the hood. Gone is the old L-head engine. In its place is a new overhead-valve Six with 170-cubic-inch displacement and 112 hp.

Simple, easy-to-read instrument group is viewed through oval wheel.

S P E C I F I C A T I O N S

Model Tested:	Studebaker Lark Regal 2-door with automatic transmission.
Price:	$3100. (Toronto

E N G I N E

Cylinders:	V-8 watercooled
Bore & Stroke:	3.56 x 3.25 ins
Displacement:	259.2 cu in, 4247.5 cc
Torque:	260 ft/lbs @ 2800 rpm.
B.H.P.:	180 @ 4500 rpm
Compression Ratio:	8.8:1

D I M E N S I O N S

Track:	
Front:	57.4 ins
Rear:	56.6 ins
Wheelbase:	108½ ins
Length Overall:	175 ins
Width Overall:	71.4 ins
Height Overall:	56.5 ins
Weight:	2965 lbs

I N T E R I O R   C A P A C I T Y

Legroom:	
Front:	44 ins
Rear:	40 ins
Headroom:	
Front:	35.25 ins
Rear:	34.75 ins
Hiproom:	
Front:	59.5 ins
Rear:	59 ins
Seating Capacity	6
Trunk Capacity:	12.6 cubic feet

D R I V E   A N D   S U S P E N S I O N

Transmission:	Automatic, mounted behind engine at front.
Final Drive:	Rear axle, 3.07
Suspension:	
Front:	Coil springs with co-axial telescopic shocks.
Rear:	Semi-elliptic springs (4 leaf)
Steering:	37.5 feet turning circle, 4¾ turns lock to lock.
Electrical System:	12 volt

P E R F O R M A N C E

Times:
0-30 mph — 3.5 seconds
0-40 mph — 5.5 seconds
0-50 mph — 7.2 seconds
0-60 mph — 10.1 seconds
Maximum speed (mean of three one-way runs)
105 mph

Speedometer Error:

Indicated	True
30 mph	27.5 mph
40 mph	37.0 mph
50 mph	37.0 mph
60 mph	54.0 mph
Fuel Consumption:	18.6 to 24 mpg
Heater Rating:	Very Good
Timing Equipment:	S. Smith & Sons

Despite square frontal area of Lark wind noise is minimal.

180 hp V-8 under-hood space.

ALTHOUGH ITS PRICE makes the V-8 Studebaker Lark somewhat suspect as an "economy" car, there is no doubt that it comes within the "compact" definition. This year's model, with its improved steering, has only to be driven once through city traffic for the driver to appreciate its external proportions. The overall length of 175 inches is carried on a 108.5 inch wheelbase and measures 71.4 inches across its widest point.

The Lark was one of the first compacts and is currently offered with one of the widest combinations of body styles and engine and transmission combinations in its field. To properly evaluate the modern Lark, Canada Track & Traffic borrowed two cars from W. Ornstein - British Motors Ltd., in Toronto, a V-8 Regal with automatic transmission and a stick shift 6-cylinder model, the latter will be writtten up in next month's issue.

The V-8 Lark chosen for road testing was a Regal, one of three four-door sedans known as the Deluxe, Regal and Cruiser. There is little difference between the first two except that the Regal has superior interior appointments such as foam rubber cushions and floor carpeting. There is also better trim on the Regal ver-

sion. The Cruiser is both larger and more luxurious.

The engine in the test Regal developed 180 bhp at 4500 rpm with torque of 260 ft/lbs at 2800 rpm. This power was transmitted to the rear wheels through a 10-inch clutch and a Borg-Warner automatic transmission and torque converter. For an automobile which weighs 2965 lbs, there is power to spare and with only the driver aboard it was found that the rear wheels lost traction readily with not much more than a moderate stabbing at the gas pedal.

The transmission embodies three forward speeds with the lower ratios being 2.4 in low and 1.47 in second. Reverse is geared to 2.00. Studebaker have retained the steering column selector lever with reverse to the far right of the quadrant next to low and drive which makes rocking simple when the car is caught in loose ground or snow.

With the selector lever at "drive" position the low gear engages only when the pedal is depressed fully when starting the car away from rest. No upshift occurs if the pedal is held to the floor.

The Lark Regal is a simple automobile to operate and requires a minimum of movement by the driver. The

driving position is somewhat upright but it places the driver in an excellent position for controlling the vehicle and gives him a very clear forward view over the surprisingly short hood.

The handling of the Regal, however, is far removed from the characteristics exhibited by larger cars. The steering has been improved in the 1961 models with the recirculating ball type of steering replacing the cam and lever of previous models. Despite the high gearing of 4¾ turns lock to lock, the wheel conveys ample road "feel" and returns freely and rapidly to the centre position.

The car handles very well on the highway at all speeds and is easily controllable in strong cross winds although it exhibits strong understeer tendencies. This understeering can be compensated for in corners by applying some of the excess power to the rear wheels. When the tail end comes out it does so gradually with ample time to correct. On wet surfaces the test car was inclined to let go faster than we would have liked in a family sedan but this can be controlled to a degree with tire pressures and the fitting of good rain tires.

Among other improvements in the 1961 Larks there has been an almost 20 per cent increase in brake lining

Chunky exterior lines of Lark are clue to interior roominess.

area with the Regal now applying a total of 172.8 square inches of brake shoe to conventional drums. The foot brake lever, as well as the clutch lever, are now suspended for better leverage but we found that a very authoritative pressure was still needed on the brakes to bring about any positive stopping action. When applied hard, however, the brakes took hold in no uncertain manner.

The Regal's suspension is among its strong points. There is very little lean on tight corners and nose diving and tail end dip are negligible.

The interior of the Lark is worthy of mention in this report not only because the car is a family car but because a real effort has been made to supply comfortable seating for six adults. The hiproom variation between the front and rear seats varies only by half an inch and there are no uncomfortable protruberances to dig passengers at either end of the seats. Back seat riders are allowed a comfortable 40 inches of legroom but they lose out an inch in headroom. The lowered roof line on later models has also cut into headroom at the front end and this, combined with the high seating position, is something of a drawback.

The heater we have rated as "very good". On the test car itself while the heater was apparently performing, the blower left a lot to be desired, but we have noted that other Larks are fitted with a strong blower. These blowers are two speed units supplying a business-like rush of warm air when required. The air can be channelled either to floor or windshield but no provision is made for rear seat passengers.

Minimum of trim gives Lark clean, functional look.

Luggage must be hefted over high trunk sill but there's plenty of room inside.

STUDEBAKER HAWK

FUN AND PRACTICALITY IN ONE FAMILIAR PACKAGE

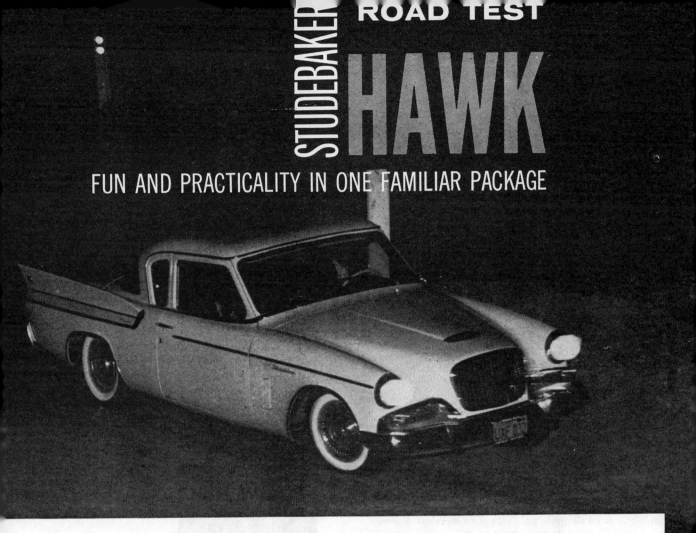

FOR DRIVING PLEASURE with family utility, the Studebaker Hawk is a top choice in its price class. It has good measures of performance and roadability, yet is a comfortable, practical car for everyday use. Further sporting flavor has been added this year with bucket seats and, as an option, a four-speed floor shift.

In basic design, the Hawk V-8 has changed little since it first appeared as the '53 Studebaker Commander coupe. Steady refinement, however, has forged it into a superior highway machine.

The '61 Hawk tested by MOTOR TREND combined a 210-hp engine, the new four-speed gearbox and a 3.31 rear axle to reach 0-30 in 4.5 seconds, 0-45 in 7.0 and 0-60 in 10.6 — above-average figures for a standard V-8 in the lower-priced field. Compared with an automatic transmission, the new stick shows its biggest performance advantage at higher speeds, where a downshift from fourth to third provides a solid jolt for passing.

Because of short valve timing, the powerplant is extremely flexible. It will push the car beyond 50 mph in first gear, yet accelerate smoothly from below 15 mph in fourth. It is an engine that reacts briskly to frequent shifting but does not demand it. In other words, the Hawk tolerates a variety of driving moods, the type of characteristic that gives it its appealing personality.

Fuel consumption was in the 13-to-17-mpg range, with an occasional stretch between 18 and 20 mpg at moderate highway speeds.

The 289-cubic-inch Hawk engine is the same as the current Lark V-8 but with a longer stroke. It has an 8.8-to-1 compression ratio to allow the use of regular fuel, a dual exhaust system and, with normal two-barrel carburetion, develops 210 hp at 4500 rpm and 300 lbs.-ft. of torque at 2800. An optional four-barrel intake advances these figures to 225 hp at 4500 and 305 lbs.-ft. at 3,000.

In addition to the new four-speed transmission, choices include a conventional three-speed with or without overdrive and an automatic three-speed supplied by Borg-Warner. Axle ratios of 3.07 and 3.54 can be ordered in place of the 3.31.

The four-speed gearbox is similar to that used in the Corvette and even has the same ratios, 2.20 in first, 1.66 in second and 1.31 in third, closely spaced for road work in contrast to the somewhat wider spread for drag racing used in the big Chevrolet and Pontiac four-speed units. As fitted to the Hawk this transmission is well within the outputs for which it was designed and should give extremely reliable service.

The Hawk's performance is complemented by very good suspension, one of those rare systems that provide control without sacrificing comfort. Cornering becomes a problem only when a turn is extremely tight. Then, the 120.5-inch wheelbase can be slightly awkward to handle, and a slight nose heaviness causes the front end to plow. Generally, though, the car rates high marks for its stability. A capable driver can get a Hawk down a winding road much faster than he could several makes with much more horsepower.

The steering is adequate, if somewhat slow at 4.6 turns lock-to-lock. Unfortunately, it does not have the refinements incorporated in the '61 Lark for quicker recovery and better feel of the road.

From a comfort standpoint, the relatively long wheelbase is an advantage. There is little fore-and-aft pitching on even the roughest surfaces. Overall riding qualities are firmer than normal but rarely harsh.

Highlighting the interior this year is a pair of bucket seats in front. Carefully contoured, they are padded with foam rubber and finished in vinyl and cloth or, optionally, completely in vinyl. Reclining backs are available and recommended; the normal angle is too erect for some tastes.

Despite the close-coupled layout, the rear compartment offers a fair amount of room for two adults or three children. Skillful modifications have improved it considerably since the first '53 coupe.

The cockpit is comfortable and functional with only a few minor flaws. The steering wheel, slightly oval-shaped, is well placed and the floor gear lever is right at hand without being in the way of anybody's legs. If the car is parked with reverse engaged, however, the lever collides with the emergency brake handle, located along the right side of the steering column.

A more serious problem involves the foot controls. Because of the transmission hump, the pedals are offset to the left, placing the brake left of the steering column. As a result, the driver is apt to trip his toe on the column as he moves from throttle to brake. He soons learns to swing his foot around it, of course, but until he does, he can lose a precious second or two during a panic stop.

The offset pedals, which are not suspended but protrude through the floor, also force the driver to sit at a slight angle, though it is not at all uncomfortable.

The dash is one of the best to be found on a current U.S. car and features a complete set of instruments. Honest, round dials indicate not only speed and fuel level but also replace the silly lights so often used to show temperature, oil pressure and generator charge. Appropriately enough with a four-speed manual shift, a tachometer is available as an extra, placed where it belongs, right in front of the driver. Such completely functional instrumentation is the ideal finishing touch on a car meant for people who really like to drive. And that the Hawk is.

/MT

MOTOR TREND TEST DATA

TEST CAR:	Studebaker Hawk
BODY TYPE:	Club coupe
BASE PRICE:	$2650
ENGINE TYPE:	Ohv V-8
DISPLACEMENT:	289 cubic inches
COMPRESSION RATIO:	8.8-to-1
CARBURETION:	Single two-barrel
HORSEPOWER:	210 @ 4500 rpm
TRANSMISSION:	Four-speed manual
REAR AXLE RATIO:	3.31
GAS MILEAGE:	13 to 17 miles per gallon
ACCELERATION:	0-30 mph in 4.5 seconds, 0-45 mph i 7.0 seconds and 0-60 mph in 10. seconds
SPEEDOMETER ERROR:	Indicated 30, 45 and 60 mph are actua 30, 44.5 and 59 mph, respectively
ODOMETER ERROR:	Indicated 100 miles is actual 97 mile
WEIGHT-POWER RATIO:	15.27 lbs. per horsepower
HORSEPOWER PER CUBIC INCH:	.727

Bucket seats and four-speed gearbox add to the Hawk's appeal. Functional dash arrangement has complete set of instruments, including tachometer as optional.

6

**Studebaker 6
Impressions**

WHEN LAST MONTH CT&T tested the Studebaker compact Lark V-8 equipped with automatic transmission it occurred to us that here was all the power, seating comfort and carrying capacity of a domestic car neatly contained in a compact package. In fact the power developed by the V-8's 180 horsepower motor seemed possitively luxurious and therefore we were curious to find out how this car performed when driven by a 6-cylinder motor of 112 horsepower.

The comparison is an interesting one in that the vehicle is basically similar whether powered by V-8 or 6. Wheelbase, overall length, height and width and the interior dimensions are identical. There is a weight difference of 250 lbs accounted for by the smaller engine and transmission unit in the six.

In performance the Six gives a very good account of itself which will be welcome news to those who were disappointed by earlier Larks which performed below expectations.

The engine in the 1961 Lark 6 has been redesigned to develop more power chiefly through a new cylinder head with overhead valves and with the intake area being boosted by 45 per cent. This unit produces 154 lbs/ft of torque at 2000 rpm with a bhp of 112 at 4500 rpm. The engine is now smoother and snappier.

In direct comparison with the V-8 the chief advantages of the Six are clearly increased fuel economy during city and short run driving. At the low end of the range the Six gives 22.8 mpg compared with 18.6 mpg for the V-8 and while the spread on the cruising mileage is smaller, the Six with 27 mpg is 3 mpg better than its bigger cousin. On maximum speed the Six is about 10 mph slower but still turns in a very respectable 91.4 mph.

The Lark 6 employs a three-speed manual gearbox as standard equipment with the shift lever being mounted on the steering column in the conven-

tional manner. This arrangement precludes very fast shifts but the linkage is smooth and the shifts fast enough to satisfy most drivers.

A higher rear axle ratio, 3.73:1 as against 3.07:1 in the V-8, is partly responsible for the Lark's sharp performance in low gear although there is the inevitable sacrifice in maximum speed. The 0-30 mph and 0-40 figures for the Six, 4.6 and 8 seconds respectively compare favourably with the V-8's 3.5 and 5.5 seconds for the same speeds. In fact the Lark has one of the most lively low gear performances of all the 6-cylinder compacts.

The Lark's low gear with a ratio of 2.71 is good for 33 mph but this is hardly necessary, for second, with 1.63:1, will pull away quite smoothly

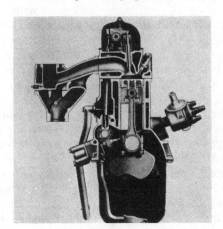

from 15 mph with 360 lbs of testers on the front seat. This middle gear is a true work horse and can be held until an excess of 60 mph (66 mph indicated) is reached.

The speedometer error is one thing which has not improved with the passing of time and in some cases is greater than the earlier models.

One of the handling characteristics that impressed us when testing the V-8 Lark was the ability of the suspension to resist lean when cornering hard. With the lighter Six this is even more noticeable. With less weight on the front wheels there is less understeer with the Six which makes for easier cornering. The steering ratio of 4¾ turns lock to lock is unchanged and a certain amount of "winding" is necessary, but as with the heavier car, the return is fast.

As we noted earlier the interior dimensions of the Six are the same as the V-8 which impressed us for its ability to seat six in comfort. This combined with the same 12.6 cu. ins. trunk and the creditable performance and greater economy make the Lark 6 a very worthwhile choice in the compact field.

SPECIFICATIONS

ENGINE

Cylinders:	6 in line, watercooled
Bore & Stroke:	3.0 ins x 4.0 ins.
Displacement:	169.6 cu. ins. 2780 cc
Torque:	154 ft/lbs @ 2000 rpm
B.H.P.:	112 @ 4500 rpm
Compression Ratio:	8.3:1

TRANSMISSION

Gearbox: 3 forward speeds, reverse, manually operated; column-mounted shift. 1st: 2.6:1; 2nd: 1.63:1; 3rd: 1.00:1; Rear axle: 3.73:1.

PERFORMANCE

Times:

0-30 mph — 4.6 secs.
0-40 mph — 8.0 secs.
0-50 mph — 11.8 secs.
0-60 mph — 15.4 secs.
Maximum speed (mean of three one way runs):
91.4 mph

Fuel Consumption:	22.8 — 27 mpg
Timing Equipment:	S. Smith & Sons

CT&T's Editor tries out the Lark Daytona at South Bend.

THE NEW STUDEBAKERS

Studebaker for '62 Offers More Than Just A Lark . . .

IN 1960, Studebaker-Packard gambled on the compact market with its new Lark series. These stubby, unpretentious cars were a success and few changes were made for the 1961 model year. Alas, the winning combination of 1960 — utility and economy — was unaccountably an also-ran in '61. Faced with declining sales figures, S-P realized a new formula was needed.

The formula for 1962 largely abandons the utility-first concept. Over-all body lengths on all Larks have been increased — as much as 13 inches on four-door sedans — and the top-line Cruiser series measures a decidedly un-compact 188 inches over-all.

Gone is the short rear overhang which lent Larks something of the looks of plump Manx cats. Rear quarters seem more balanced by the addition of several inches' length, and the former deliberately austere body has been extensively tinkered-with to add eye-catching style. In front, slightly more overhang and a glittery, Mercedes Benz-influenced grille contribute to the '62 models' dressed-up appearance.

Interiors in all Larks have been upgraded from the practical, no-nonsense predecessors. Attractive new seat fabrics and a richer-looking instrument panel contribute to the flossier tone dictated for 1962.

A new series has been added to the Lark lineup — the Daytona, available as a two-door hardtop or con-

vertible. Going along with the success of the Corvair Monza and similar, semi-sporting compacts offered by almost every U. S. maker, the Daytona can be had with a 210-hp, 289 cu. in. V-8 engine and either automatic transmission or a floor-mounted four-speed manual shift. This and bucket-style seats plus a special trim package give the Lark line a jaunty, sports-slanted contender in the luxury-compact sweepstakes. The Daytona is kept on a 109-inch wheelbase.

Others in the Lark series are the Cruiser, fitted with a 259 cu. in. V-8 as standard equipment and dolled up with various deluxe features to make it the queen bee of the Studebaker hive; the Regal, fitted with either the OHV "Skybolt" Six or 259 V-8 engines as standard and fitting into the middle range; and the Deluxe, the basic Lark.

Gone is the Hawk. This series was more than a token gesture towards developing a true American Gran Turismo automobile, though not even Studebaker would go so far as to claim the sports car tag for these fast, flashy five-seaters. Replacing the Hawk as Studebaker's prestige item is the sleek Gran Turismo, highly styled (and priced) to do battle on the rarified level of luxury "personal" cars. As such the Gran Turismo is a serious contender, though in fact it is less than Gran Turismo in character and looks than its Hawk redecessors. Equipped with the 210-hp V-8 and either utomatic or manual four-speed transmission, and oasting bucket seats, sports car instrumentation and host of gewgaws calculated to lure the well-heeled port, the Gran Turismo is an ingenious reworking of what is basically the same old Hawk body — and the Hawk in turn was an ingenious reworking of Loewy's 953 coupe. That makes nine years with the same asic body, and the proof of the soundness of Loewy's esign lies in the fact that the 1961 Gran Turismo oesn't look old.

The G.T., Studebaker claims, will sell for consider-bly less than the Thunderbird (about $1,000 less was -P's rough estimate). In connection with the T-Bird, tudebaker counters raised eyebrows over the Gran urismo's similarity in roofline contour to Ford's pride nd joy with bland candor. Back in the early Fifties, seems, Packard introduced a "dream car" known as e Predictor. The Predictor's roofline was later lifted y Ford Styling for its Thunderbird, Studebaker-ackard says, and they have just decided to use it hemselves.

Products of Studebaker-Packard have kept pretty

Without any real opportunity to wring the new Studebakers out under something approaching normal road conditions, it was naturally impossible to formu-late a complete road test report on their capabilities. However, with the 210-hp V-8's it was easily possible to circulate around the oval at over 100 mph (indi-cated) with a sense of complete security. The Daytona model was in high demand with its big 210-hp V-8 and manual shift, and rewarded patience by proving the most fun to drive. Studebaker's bucket-style seats are hardly the kind seen in racing cars but they do offer vastly improved support over the bench type. Brakes could be better. Putting on the anchors from 100 mph led to funny smells and juddering up front and a fair amount of dipping.

Studebaker makes a big point about its quality construction, and the models we saw definitely did reflect above-average care in assembly. And despite our general lack of enthusiasm for useless overhang, we have to admit that with their slight extra length the Larks have become markedly better-proportioned.

The Studebaker name has traditionally stood for solid, dependable cars just as a hundred years ago it

ytona Hardtop features special trim.

Interior of Daytona features bucket seats. Automatic shift in photo can be replaced by optional four-speed floor box.

ell aloof from much association with sports motor-g, however remote. The Lark, though not exactly atherfooted in its handling nor a performance world-ater, was welcomed as a drive in the right direction nd attracted new respect by coming up winner of the cent Trans Canada Rally. Recently we were invited South Bend to look over and drive Studebaker's 62 line.

Studebaker's proving grounds a few miles distant om South Bend itself features a road course, various ecialized testing facilities, and a three-mile oval ack for high speed runs. This track is banked at the rners and the straights are long enough to allow t-out gallops. For reasons known only to Stude-ker-Packard officialdom, our activities were con-ned to the test oval where for a few hours we could ll around and around in any of a dozen new cars.

stood for solid, dependable Conestoga wagons and other horse-drawn vehicles. The President models of the early 1930's were among the best-looking, most durable American cars of that era. Twice in the post-war years Studebaker showed that it was ahead of its public; in 1947 with the "coming-or-going" model and in 1953 with the Loewy-styled coupes. This enter-prising member of the American auto industry has working for it the virtue of not being too big; Stude-baker is flexible enough to move with the times instead of being tied down to billion-dollar programs. Times have been anything but easy for Studebaker-Packard of late, but we feel the 1962 S-P line, with a car for almost every price bracket, is more competitive than any this company has offered for some years and we expect to see a satisfying upturn in sales figures dur-ing the coming year.

UNDER MOST HANDLING CONDITIONS, THE LARK STAYS RIGHT IN THERE WITH MINIMUM LEAN, TAKING A GOOD BITE ON ALL SURFACES.

Studebaker Lark Daytona *continued*

PHOTOS BY BOB D'OLIVC

The well-appointed interior of the deluxe Daytona features a padded center console-armrest and semi-bucket front seats that can be adjusted all the way back.

Traceable to a European influence is a dash of leather padding and simulated wood around the instruments. The wheel is a bit "out-of-round" to aid visibility.

by Jim Wright, Technical Editor

DAYTONA is the name of this latest entry into the growing ranks of the luxury compacts. Basically, the Daytona follows the same formula as do the others in this class. It's a deluxe model (in this case a Regal) to which have been added a pair of bucket seats separated by a console, more expensive upholstery, and different chrome trim. The Daytona doesn't offer any more performance than its lower-priced kin, but it does offer a little more quality and prestige, which is just about all the other cars in this class are offering.

This year the basic Lark body shell has undergone some extensive reworking. This is not so noticeable up front, where the main change has been the addition of a Mercedes-like radiator grille. (We haven't heard any rumors about just what Mercedes' opinion is on this, but they no doubt do have one.) Strangely, this grille treatment is a natural for this car and fits in real well with the short, squared-off front end. We like it. Toward the back is where the big change has taken place. Overall length has been increased to 184 inches, which allowed them to create a lower, slimmer rear-end line. Since the wheelbase has been lengthened only a half-inch, to 109 inches, most of the added length is in rear overhang. Front and rear track remain the same.

The Daytona is offered only as a two-door hardtop or two-door convertible. The latter was selected as MT's test car. Because the Daytona falls into the family-pleasure class, we specified that our car be equipped with the standard 259.2-cubic-inch V-8 engine. This is the same basic engine that they have offered previously and puts out 180 hp at 4500 rpm, and 260 lbs.-ft. of torque at 2800 rpm. Also specified was the three-speed automatic transmission and standard 3.31 rear axle. It was felt that this combination would best represent the car that the average driver would be most interested in.

Frankly, we've always felt that the Lark line has been too heavy. Studebaker-Packard still employs a separate frame and body type of construction, and it shows up on the scales. The convertible is made even heavier by the addition of an X-member to the already beefy four-cross-member, ladder-type frame. At 3305 pounds, unloaded, it is 290 pounds heavier than its companion hardtop, and over 700 pounds heavier than one of its competitors. All this poundage helps give the Daytona a solid, big-car feel, but unfortunately, it also detracts from the performance and handling one expects from a compact-size car (especially one with a fairly good-sized V-8 under the hood). But, as we said before, this is strictly a family-pleasure type auto, and it fills this classification nicely.

Our performance figures, for 0-30, 0-45, and 0-60 mph, logged with two aboard, the usual instrumentation, and a full gas tank, produced times of 5.0, 8.8, and 14.3 seconds. The quarter-mile trap was cleared at 72 mph with a 21.1-second e.t.

There are several options available that are capable of perking up the Daytona's performance. The addition of a four-barrel carburetor and dual exhausts, coupled with a rise in compression ratio from 8.5 to 8.8 to 1, pulls the horsepower up to 195 at 4500 rpm and increases the torque reading to 265 lbs.-ft. at 3000. Also available is the bigger 289-cubic-inch, 210-hp V-8.

The Daytona's odometer registered 1700 miles when we started our tests, and all together we put over 600 miles on it. Again, the heaviness of the car showed up in our fuel consumption figures. Overall average, which included varying types of driving and road conditions, was in the 14-to-17-mpg range.

An optional, at no extra charge, 3.07 rear axle is available that should up the mileage figures a bit. Also available for the Daytona is the ohv, 170-cubic-inch, 112-hp Skybolt Six engine. With the in-line Six and the 3.07 rear axle, fuel consumption should be up in the 18-to-24-mpg range, but the lack of performance would probably be more than anyone would be willing to bear.

The additional length doesn't seem to have had any effect on the Lark's handling characteristics. Suspension is unchanged, with coils at the front and longitudinal leaf springs at the rear. The spring rates and shock settings feel just right—the ride is solid and not at all mushy. Under normal driving conditions the steering is light and responsive—thanks to the well designed recirculating ball type steering gear introduced last year. Cornering ability is not as good as it could be. A lot of the car's extra weight must be concentrated up around the front end, and as a result the understeer becomes very noticeable on tight,

Within the engine compartment, there is easy access to most components, including plugs. There is a two-barrel carburetor on this 259-hp version of Lark's V-8.

Although rear end has been restyled, the high lip on the trunk compartment has not been eliminated. Spare is easy to reach, but its position cuts down on space.

Hydraulically operated top is no trouble to raise or lower. For quick placement of the tonneau, it's always better with four hands instead of two.

twisty roads. One thing we did like—although it might plow a bit in the corners, it takes them with a minimum of body lean, and on the open road you can relax with confidence because the car is exceptionally stable with no tendency to wander. The big-car feel was most apparent on rough roads, and we were able to take these fairly fast without encountering any excessive bounce, vibration or loss of control.

The brakes are big and more than adequate for the size and weight of this car. Eleven-inch units are used at the front, and ten-inch at the rear. During several panic stops they brought the car to a straight-line stop in a minimum distance. Our car didn't have power brakes, but the pedal pressure was light and positive. No fade was apparent after the hard braking test. Due to no fault of the brakes, we did encounter severe rear

In every stopping situation the brakes proved quite adequate, but rear springing caused severe rear wheel judder in harsh conditions. Note proof of rubber marks on pavement below.

heel judder when they locked up. This is a fault that is common to a great many cars that rely solely on the rear springs to locate the axle laterally. They just can't take the severe loads imposed by any but a normal stop.

The automatic transmission seems to allow more engine revs than necessary when getting under way and at low speeds, such as when crawling along in slow traffic. But at normal speeds the coupling is positive and the shifts are smooth. Under full throttle, with the gear selector in "D," upshifts are made at 4000 rpm (36 and 62 mph). By using "L," the transmission stays in first gear and we wound the engine easily to 5000 rpm in this manner without noticing any valve float.

The Lark has always been one of the roomiest compacts on the road, and the Daytona is no exception. The bucket seats

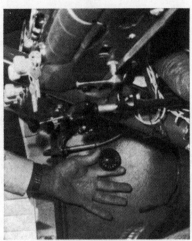

Unique option is manually-operated antenna by means of knob below the dash.

are firm and comfortable. They offer good support to the back but six-footers and over will find the seat cushion too short to offer much support to the thighs. There is plenty of fore-and-aft adjustment available, and the reclining feature will come in handy for driver and passenger on long hauls. Front and rear legroom is better than average for a compact.

The location of the steering wheel provides good over-the-wheel vision and all-around visibility is better than average. Instrumentation is sparse, but what there is is well placed and easy to read. Warning lights are still used for oil pressure and amps. We found the gas gauge a little confusing, because the needle registers full at the left of the dial and empty at the right. Most cars are just the opposite. In the Daytona, after the needle had reached the half-empty mark we always felt as if the gauge were reading almost full.

The trunk is plenty big and should be able to handle the needs of the average-sized family. We liked the fabric boot on the spare tire—it allows items to be placed on and around the spare without them getting soiled. Under-the-hood accessibility is better than average, and you can change the spark plugs without first removing anything else. MT's test car wasn't equipped with an oil filter, but those that are have it mounted on the top of the engine by the oil fill pipe.

As we mentioned, there are a few things about the Daytona that we didn't agree with—namely the weight. A dyed-in-the-wool Lark owner will tell you that the resulting solidness and big-car feel are the main reasons he bought a Lark. There is a large segment of the buying public that shies away from compacts because they feel the cars aren't roomy enough or are too light for comfortable open-road driving. If you belong to this group, you would do well to look in on the Daytona—it could be just the compact for you.   /MT

STUDEBAKER LARK DAYTONA

4-5-passenger convertible

OPTIONS ON CAR TESTED: Transistor radio, automatic transmission, heater
ODOMETER READING AT START OF TEST: 1700 miles
RECOMMENDED ENGINE RED LINE: 5000 rpm

PERFORMANCE

ACCELERATION (2 aboard)
    0-30 mph............................ 5.0 secs.
    0-45 mph............................ 8.8
    0-60 mph............................14.3

Standing start ¼-mile 21.1 secs. and 72 mph
Speeds in gears @ 4000 rpm
    1st..................36 mph   2nd..................62 mph

Speedometer Error on Test Car

Car's speedometer reading	30	45	50	60	70	80
Weston electric speedometer	30	45	50	60	70	80

Observed miles per hour per 1000 rpm in top gear.................21 mph
Stopping Distances — from 30 mph, 43 ft.; from 60 mph, 150 ft.

SPECIFICATIONS FROM MANUFACTURER

Engine
Ohv V-8
Bore: 3.56 ins.
Stroke: 3.25 ins.
Displacement: 259.2 cubic inches
Compression ratio: 8.5:1
Horsepower: 180 @ 4500 rpm
Ignition: 12-volt coil

Gearbox
3-speed automatic (Flightomatic)

Driveshaft
One-piece — open tube

Differential
Hypoid
Standard ratio 3.31:1

Suspension
Front: Coil springs —
    direct double-acting shocks

Rear: 4-leaf semi-elliptics —
    direct double-acting shocks

Wheels and Tires
Steel disc
6.70 x 15 Tires

Brakes
Hydraulic — bonded linings,
self-centering, self-energizing
Front and rear: 11-inch dia.
and 10-inch dia., respectively

Body and Frame
Ladder with 4 cross-members
plus X-member
Wheelbase 109.0 ins.
Track, front 57⅜ ins., rear 56⅞₆ ins.
Overall length 184.0 ins.
Dry weight 3305 lbs.

Photos by Bob D'Olivo

by Jim Wright, Technical Editor

IF THE AMOUNT OF INTEREST generated in and around the Los Angeles area by MOTOR TREND's test car is any indication of what Studebaker-Packard can expect throughout the rest of the country, then we'd say that their new Gran Turismo Hawk is definitely "in."

Whenever we made a gas stop or pulled into the local supermarket, and even while waiting for stop signals to change, the GT was a constant object of inspection and comment. Naturally, a few of the interested parties were already the owners of Silver or Golden Hawks, but the GT attracted more tha[n] its share of motorists who had never owned a Studebaker [in] any model.

Of all the many people who stopped to look, ask question[s] and then offer an opinion, not one had anything but favorab[le] comments to make. In fact, the only remark made that mig[ht] be of an adverse nature was that the top seemed to be copi[ed] after the Thunderbird's. This new hardtop, with its distincti[ve] "earmuffs," is probably the most standout feature of the co[mplete]

162

Studebaker HAWK

Gran Turismo

A bold new approach
to luxury and power —
a man's car all the way

Studebaker Hawk

pletely restyled Hawk. But the truth is, it was originally designed for the prototype Packard Predictor, which pre-dates present T-Bird styling by several years. (For the complete Hawk styling story, see the October MOTOR TREND.)

It seemed that everyone, including the MT test crew, liked the clean, unbroken sweep of the side elevation, the long, tapering hood with its massive radiator grille, and the tasteful, minimal use of chrome trim. With the exception of the deck lid grille, there's not a fancy, unfunctional line in the whole car.

This same straightforward design concept is also apparent behind the wheel and under the hood. It's a car that feels and looks as if it's been engineered instead of just dreamed up. That the Hawk possesses a definite aura of quality and class is attested to by the fact that almost everyone who ventured a guess as to its cost was from $800 to $1000 high. We personally felt the overall result to be an automobile that is completely masculine in character and somehow slightly reminiscent of some of the really great cars of the early '30s.

While we racked up over a thousand miles behind the wheel of the GT and relished every minute of it, we don't think it's a car that the little lady will enjoy driving (our's didn't). But then that's what the right-hand seat is designed for. All she has to do is sit back in that big, comfortable bucket, relax,

keep reasonably quiet, and be secure in the fact that *this* car was designed with her particular man in mind. As several of our friends put it after they had driven the GT, "It looks, feels and drives like a *real* automobile" — which is exactly our sentiments.

Performance-wise, we feel that the Hawk fulfills the promise of its Gran Turismo designation. While not a spectacular performer, it is a willing and able one and definitely in the tradition of the high-speed tourers of Europe.

The MT test car was powered by the same healthy (though small by today's standards) V-8 that S-P has been offering for several years now. With standard dual exhausts, two-barrel carburetor and 8.5-to-1 compression ratio, the 289-cubic-incher puts out 210 hp at 4500 rpm and 300 lbs.-ft. of torque at 2800. Power was geared through the optional four-speed, all-synchro, floor-shift transmission and "Twin Traction" rear axle with standard 3.73-to-1 ratio gears installed. Other performance options included power steering and power-assisted brakes.

The Hawk has an estimated shipping weight of 3230 pounds. With fuel, oil, water, full instrumentation and two aboard, the test weight was right at 3700 pounds and gave the GT a final weight-to-horsepower ratio of 17.5 to 1. Our acceleration figures are the average of one or more two-way runs over a level, measured quarter-mile.

The Hawk was pretty hard to get off the line decently — if we didn't give it enough throttle, it had a tendency to bog, while too much throttle produced wheelspin which, in turn, induced a terrific amount of rear-axle windup. If this were our personal car, we would certainly have a set of rear axle

The Hawk is easy to handle on loose dirt or gravel roads. The suspension is good and allows no bottoming when the going gets rough or when encountering sudden dips in the road surface.

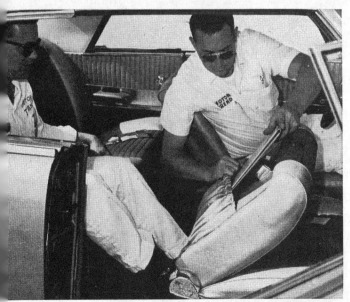

Plenty of head- and legroom is available in front and rear. Optional reclining front buckets are comfortable.

Shift lever for four-speed, all-synchro box is located well and allows for quick, positive changes in all the gears.

stabilizer bars installed, because even in city driving, if we happened to hit a wet spot in the pavement while accelerating normally in the lower gears, the wheels went into their annoying dance. This was probably made more noticeable by the "Twin Traction" axle, but it would still occur to some degree without it.

After finding the quickest way to get off the spot (slip the clutch a bit), we tried a variety of shift points before deciding that our particular gearing and carburetion combination produced the quickest times when winding to a maximum 4500 rpm in the lower three gears. The engine will twist unprotestingly to 5500 rpm in 1st and 2nd, but that last thousand comes up awfully slow, and as it was, we were barely dropping into top gear before clearing the quarter-mile lights. We recorded the 0 to 30, 0 to 45 and 0 to 60 mph speeds in 4.0, 7.1 and 11.7 seconds, respectively. The standing quarter-mile was covered in 19.1 seconds with a top speed of 78 mph showing on the electric fifth-wheel speedometer. The engine was very responsive in all gears up to 4500 rpm and we were more than satisfied with the resulting acceleration figures.

This is the biggest engine that S-P is offering but the 15 extra horsepower offered by the optional four-barrel carburetor would add a lot to performance because you can definitely feel that the two-barrel isn't allowing the engine to draw as big a breath as it would like. The factory spec sheet lists several other axle ratios that would be real sweet for dragging — a 4.1 and a 4.56. These aren't listed as being available for the Hawk (they're actually for the six-cylinder Lark) but we bet that if somebody wanted one badly enough it could be had. With the four-barrel and a 4.56 axle it wouldn't surprise us if the Hawk would be capable of turning in the high 80's, with an e.t. of somewhere between 16.0 and 16.5 seconds.

The gearbox is a Borg-Warner unit with well spaced ratios and just as good as any (and better than many) we've encountered in European cars. The shift lever is located within easy reach and the throws are short and positive. Speeds recorded in all four gears at 4500 rpm were 39, 53, 67 and 101 mph, respectively. The 10.5-inch clutch requires moderate pedal pressure but is more than adequate for the torque it has to transfer, and quick shifts to 2nd, 3rd and 4th produce a satisfying chirp from the rear wheels.

Overall fuel consumption was in the 14-to-19-mpg range, and this included all types of driving and road conditions from city traffic to freeway to mountains. An optional 3.31 axle is

Twisty mountain roads like these offer no obstacle to the Hawk's near-perfect handling characteristics.

Trunk space is wide and long, but not too deep. Lip is low, and lifting things in or out is no problem.

Complete instrumentation and functional layout of the dash are in keeping with masculine character of the GT.

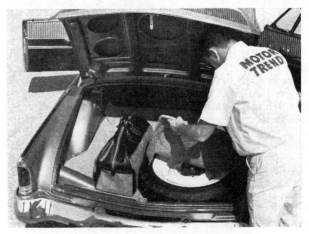

ON THE OPEN ROAD THE HAWK LIVES UP TO ITS GRAN TURISMO DESIGNATION AND WILL ALLOW COMFORTABLE ALL-DAY HIGH-SPEED CRUISING.

Studebaker Hawk

continued

available that would up this figure a bit but at a sacrifice in performance.

We liked the power braking system used on this car. Pedal pressures are a little more than those required in other systems, but the stops are just as quick, with less tendency to lock up. Finned, 11-inch, cast-iron drums are used on the front and 10-inch units at the rear. Repeated panic stops from 30 and 60 mph produced fast, straight-line stops with no indication of brake fade or increase in pedal pressure. Front-end dive under hard braking is at a minimum, and we were surprised that no rear wheel judder was encountered when the rear wheels were locked up.

Optional seat belts were installed in the test car and came in very handy during our braking tests — especially for our co-pilot, who rides with a lap full of instruments and is usually hard pressed to keep them off the floor and himself off the dash when we hit the binders at 60.

Suspension is by the usual control arms and coils at the front, rigid axle and five-leaf semi-elliptic springs at the rear, with dampening action supplied by direct double-action tubular shocks on all four corners. The ride is real firm but comfortable, and noticeable by its absence is that floating feeling one usually associates with contemporary American automobiles. Rough stretches of road can be stormed with confidence — as long as you don't break the rear wheels loose, and very little road shock is transmitted back to the driver. Normal dips were taken without any sign of bottoming or loss of control. On the open road the Hawk is very stable and cross-winds or camber changes have very little effect on its good directional stability.

Even with power assist the steering is a bit heavy (4.6 turns lock-to-lock) but precise. We took the GT through the mountains on several occasions and were favorably impressed with its handling characteristics. On tight, slow corners the Hawk understeers slightly but on the wider-radiused, faster corners it was more neutral, with final oversteer coming on as the limit of tire adhesion is approached. There is very little body roll during fast cornering and the desired line can be easily held. With a little practice we found that the Hawk could be drifted through the faster corners and that any tendency for

the rear wheels to creep out was easily corrected with the steering wheel.

For long trips the well designed interior of the Hawk offers the utmost in comfort. The contoured reclining bucket seats have rather firm springing and padding and are big enough to give excellent support to the back and legs. Fore-and-aft adjustment should handle the tallest drivers. There's plenty of legroom (front and back) and the steering wheel is well placed, allowing good over-the-wheel vision. We did think that with the excellent styling of the interior the Hawk should have a little better-looking wheel. Also the horn bar is a trifle sharp on the ends and could be made safer. The front seats are separated by a padded console, which contains a built-in ash tray and lift-lid storage box. The back seats can seat three comfortably but if the center armrest is down, this is reduced to two.

The safety-padded instrument panel contains all the necessary instruments and can best be described as classic. The dials are large, round, easy-to-read white-on-black units positioned directly in the driver's line of vision against a curved wood grain panel background, and there's not a boob light used for anything. Aircraft-type toggle switches are used for lights and heater controls and are within easy reach of the driver. A hood is incorporated into the fiberglass dashboard and the top of it is finished in flat black to prevent annoying reflections from the windshield. The curved, but not wrap-around windshield offers distortion-free vision. The side pillars are a trifle thick, but all-around visibility is more than adequate.

The interior of the test car was finished in vinyl, with cloth inserts on the seats. All-vinyl upholstery is optional but we liked the cloth, which should be cooler in the summer and warmer in the winter than all-vinyl. The floor, kick panels and bottom halves of the doors are carpeted, which should wear very well. The acoustical vinyl headliner is standard equipment. Sound-deadening materials used in the Hawk do a good job of shutting out wind and road noises, and at cruising speeds normal conversation is possible between front and rear seat passengers. Overall, the interior detail work is excellent and reflects a high degree of quality control work on the part of the S-P factory.

Under the hood, which is still without sprung or counter-balanced hinges and is still held up by a steel rod, we found about as much accessibility as could be expected with power accessories. The replaceable oil filter cartridge is on top of the engine by the oil fill pipe for easy servicing, but it looks as

The big 11-inch finned brake drums and an excellent power brake system allowed fade-free, straight-line stops.

if one or two items might have to be removed before the spark plugs can be reached.

Usable trunk space should be adequate for the average-size family on moderate-length trips. It's not too deep but it is wide and long. The spare is mounted flat on the floor and is covered with a fabric boot to keep luggage and packages from being soiled.

Now that we're through testing the Hawk GT and have almost finished this report, we're kind of sorry to have to turn it back to the dealer. This is one car that has been a real pleasure to drive and one that we think offers the man in the family something quite a bit different in family-pleasure type transportation. And make no mistake about it — the Hawk GT is strictly a man's car and S-P's new president, Sherwood H. Egbert, deserves at least one free round wherever real men congregate for having the guts to buck the frilly feminine-oriented thinking that has crept into American automotive styling during the last decade. /MT

Under-hood accessibility is hampered by power brake and steering units. Long fan shroud shows that the engine is set well back from the front wheels.

STUDEBAKER HAWK GRAN TURISMO
5 passengers

OPTIONS ON CAR TESTED Power brakes, power steering, "Twin Traction" rear axle, transistor radio, heater, tachometer, 4-speed, all-synchro gearbox.
BASIC PRICE: $3095
PRICE AS TESTED: $3695.17, plus tax and license
ODOMETER READING AT START OF TEST: 1221 miles
RECOMMENDED ENGINE RED LINE: 5500 rpm

PERFORMANCE

ACCELERATION (2 aboard)
    0-30 mph.................................4.0 secs.
    0-45 mph.................................7.2
    0-60 mph.................................11.7
Standing start ¼-mile 19.1 secs and 78 mph
Speeds in gears @ 4500 rpm

1st..................39 mph		3rd...............67 mph
2nd..................53 mph		4th...............101 mph

Speedometer Error on Test Car

Car's speedometer reading 31	47	52	63	73	83
Weston electric speedometer 30	45	50	60	70	80

Observed miles per hour per 1000 rpm in top gear................22.5 mph
Stopping Distances — from 30 mph, 37 ft.; from 60 mph, 137 ft.

SPECIFICATIONS FROM MANUFACTURER

Engine
Ohv V-8
Bore: 3.56 ins.
Stroke: 3.62 ins.
Displacement: 289 cubic inches
Compression ratio: 8.5:1
Horsepower: 210 @ 4500 rpm
Horsepower per cubic inch: 0.726
Ignition: 12-volt coil

Gearbox
Manual 4- speed, all-synchro, floor lever

Driveshaft
One-piece, open tube

Differential
Hypoid
Standard ratio 3.73:1

Suspension
Front: Unequal upper and lower control arms; direct, double-acting tubular shocks

Rear: Rigid axle, 5-leaf semi-elliptic longitudinal springs; direct, double-acting shocks
Steering Type—Cam and single lever, with roller stud

Wheels and Tires
5-lug steel disc
6.70 x 15 tubeless tires

Brakes
Finned cast-iron drums; hydraulic, self-centering, self-energizing
Front: 11-inch dia.
Rear: 10-inch dia.
Effective area: 172.8 sq. ins.

Body and Frame
Ladder, with 5 cross-members
Wheelbase 120.5 ins.
Track, front 57⅜ ins., rear 56⁵⁄₁₆ ins.
Overall length 204 ins.
Dry weight 3230 lbs.
Turning diameter 41 ft.

Raising the heavy hood and placing the steel support rod is a cumbersome job, and the addition of a counter-balancing device would be a welcome improvement.

The appearance of the new Lark is a big improvement over the previous model. Grille pattern looks Teutonic.

Studebaker's LARK..

A compact American that sings the tune Australians like to hear, the Studebaker Lark has power to burn the rubber off its back wheels.

Yes, that steering wheel is oval. According to tester Hall, the driver quickly gets used to it. Test car was stick shift job, but automatic is optional.

A GREAT change has come over the Australian car market in the 23 years since the Second World War began.

In the grim days of 1939 when half the world was plunging into war and it was clear that soon the other half would be involved in a terrible struggle, Australians who could afford to buy a motor car were obsessed with American built cars.

And they had good reason to be. With almost the sole exception of Rolls Royce, there were no British manufacturers building motor cars that could stand up to the dreadful roads we had, the long distance driving we had to do and the hard life we gave them. Continental firms perhaps had more rugged products, but they were little known and offered only in small quantities.

Now, our market is dominated by a medium sized car that was designed specifically for our country and made nowhere else. And the next biggest sellers are a medium American car wholly built here, and an enormously tough and basically ugly machine that was designed in the heart of Germany.

British makers, too, are selling cars for which many of us exchange our hard-earned cash (and, generally, a lot of interest, too) and get good value.

And the American car? It has slipped into an exclusive and comparatively small niche in the market, somewhat on a volume par with sports cars where only the moderately rich can look with any real prospect of buying.

Back in the 1930's, a few American makes stood head and shoulders above the common herd in the public mind. They were the quality cars, the machines that politicians, and doctors and managing directors and bookmakers drove. Among their number was the Studebaker.

Even with the front seat adjusted back as far as it will go, there is still ample room for the legs of the back seat passengers.

.. INEXPENSIVE LOW FLYER By PETER HALL

In the first half dozen years after the war, Studebaker retained its aura of exclusiveness, but the changing fortunes of its American maker and the tough conditions of the American market combined with our severe dollar restrictions to put its name slowly out of the car buying public's mind.

Then, in its homeland, Studebaker amalgamated with another famous prestige name—Packard—and changed the public image of its products radically, so it could stay in business.

Australians heard little of Studebaker and nothing of Packard for some years, but in its home country the car was regaining some of its lost popularity— and the company its lost profits—with a new concept in American motoring. Studebaker, never far from the dimensions of the compact car, began to call its models just that and jumped smartly on the bandwagon set rolling by American Motors with their Nash Rambler.

Studebaker-Packard revamped their basic models, called them Studebaker Larks, and began to climb back to solvency.

We still heard little of this old American name, although a handful of Larks were imported at ridiculous prices. Then, late in 1960, the long-established Melbourne firm of Canada Cycle and Motor Company Pty Ltd came to an arrangement with Studebaker-Packard whereby Larks would be assembled for the Australian market in Canada Cycle's small Melbourne plant.

Although the luggage compartment is big, the space is hindered by the flat-mounted spare.

WHEELS FULL ROAD TEST

STUDEBAKER'S LARK . . .
INEXPENSIVE LOW FLYER . . .

Bang came the credit squeeze, and Studebaker in Australia seemed set for a short and profitless run, despite the huge reductions in price that followed the beginning of local assembly.

However, the Larks sold solidly and, even in the depths of the credit squeeze, Canada Cycle managed to keep its assembly line busy.

There were faults in their car—skimpy trim, not-too-perfect finish and a tendency for rattle to develop—but the customers appreciated the great power, reliability, moderate price and, of course, the good name of Studebaker.

Then, late last year, the horizon really began to brighten for Studebaker Lark in Australia. Two Larks performed brilliantly in the second Armstrong 500 sedan car race, coming first and third in their class and second and fourth outright, and the American company released a new range for the home market.

In the early months of 1962, the Victoria Police Force reversed a long standing tradition of using Ford V8s for fast highway work and ordered 14 Studebaker Larks, fitted with the bigger Studebaker Hawk engine and more powerful brakes.

The remaining 1961 Larks sold like hot cakes, especially in Melbourne, and Canada Cycle was able to release the 1962 range within four months of its announcement in the United States.

Apart from detail changes, the complete range of sedans and station wagons was rationalised. Previously, the models were a bit of a jumble with two different wheelbases.

On the new range, the Lark was standardised on a 113 inch wheelbase and exactly the same body was used for the standard and automatic transmission models. The station wagon, with either standard or automatic transmission, was also standardised on the same wheelbase.

The standard model, with a three-speed gearbox, was thereby stretched out 13 inches to an overall length of 15 ft 8 in. The price was also stretched out (by £50) to £1645, including sales tax.

The automatic, however, was slightly reduced (by £16) to £1799. A heater and windscreen washer were thrown into the automatic as standard equipment, but the interior of the gearbox model remained unheated and its screen unwashed—unless you wish to pay extra for these basic necessities of life on Australian roads.

The car provided for my road test was, by choice, a standard transmission model. The automatic is fitted with the familiar Borg-Warner three-speed transmission without benefit of intermediate gear hold and performs fractionally below the standard model.

Although the actual changes are really minor, the exterior appearance of this new model Studebaker is markedly different from the 1961 version.

The stubbiness, the chopped-off look of last year's model, indeed of all earlier Larks, is gone. The new model is somewhat graceful and certainly looks more elegant.

The main points whereby this new handsome appearance is achieved are the front and back ends.

The Lark has a new grille, a protruding finely meshed affair that looks remarkably like a 220S Mercedes-Benz. It is not surprising to learn that Studebaker-Packard have been handling Mercedes-Benz distribution and sales in the United States for the last two years. The influence is obvious, and, I think commendable. If all car makers studied the best features in their opposition products and incorporated them in their own, the drivers of the world would have a breed of immeasurably improved cars.

The bonnet line of the Lark has been lowered and a cheap and tiny, but very effective mascot, placed atop the radiator grille.

The somewhat unsightly dip that occurred in past Larks on the sill of the back door has gone and the car's waist line is now smooth and straight like a Victorian matron's, but much more appealing—at least to the male eye.

The boot lid has been completely redesigned to avoid the chunky appearance of the past, and also to eliminate the excessively high lip that was the bane of Lark owners who carried luggage in their boots.

The lid is now rounded out and "sculptured" (to use an American advertising word) to give it shape.

The fixed lip has been lowered about five inches, and it is hardly any trouble at all to lift the odd case into the big boot. It would be even lower if Studebaker did not persist with the common American idea of having the petrol filler cap right in the middle, above the bumper bar, where service station attendants have to stand on their ear to gas the car.

The changes inside the car are a revelation, especially in view of the fact that they have been carried out with little extra cost to the maker. The trim is smooth and very heavy quality plastic, very attractively and usefully pleated. The padding is thick, and the edges of the seats are rolled to give support to weary thighs.

The doors are covered in the same material, tastefully two-toned, and thick carpets are laid back and front. Apart from a mild transmission hump, the floors are flat and dirt and the inevitable rubbish that accumulates on car floors can be swept easily out, without the impossible hazard of high ridges beneath the doors.

The dashboard is basically the same shape as before, but is now stained in a dark imitation wood color. The dash is attractive without being garish, and liberal quantities of crash padding are provided on the top and along the leading edge.

Instruments are simple, easy to read and right in front of the driver. The foot pedals are comfortably placed and go straight through the floor, making them very easy to use. But it was a pity the designers did not allow for the fact that most people have a left foot — there is nowhere to put it unless you happen to be double-jointed and don't mind resting it on top of the dashboard.

Performance was little different from last year, and was very impressive. The Studebaker's big, smooth V8 engine gave the car a tremendous urge to go forward.

The longer body and consequent change of balance seemed to improve the Lark's handling qualities. While the car basically understeers, its cornering form was consistent and the springing firm enough to keep it on a moderately level keel.

The steering was on the vague side, but not nearly as much as some American offerings, and the turning circle was pleasantly compact. The oval steering wheel took a little getting used to—at first you felt that something was horribly wrong with the steering column—but a few miles behind the wheel and you ceased to be aware of its lack of roundness.

One of the outstanding features of the Lark was its vast interior space. There was ample leg, head and elbow room for six people inside and yet the car was moderate height.

The boot, too, was big, but was spoiled by the spare wheel being plunked right on the floor. Why can't American car makers follow the common British practice of slinging the spare *under* the boot floor?

Finish and workmanship was much improved on the new model, but there were a few annoying squeaks and rattles in the test car. Of course, it is very difficult to get perfect quiet on a comparatively big car fitted with a separate chassis, as the Studebaker is, especially when you have only been in the car assembly business for less than two years.

But overall, the local assemblers have done a very fine job with their Australian reproduction of a model that should regain for Studebaker much of the prestige and warm public following it has enjoyed for most of its car-making life but lost (quite unfairly) because of American public whim in the early 1950's. #

wheels ROAD TEST

TECHNICAL DETAILS
OF THE
STUDEBAKER LARK

SPECIFICATIONS

ENGINE:

Cylinders	eight, Vee formation
Bore and stroke	90.4 mm by 82.5 mm
Cubic capacity	4247 cc
Compression ratio	7.5 to 1
Valves	pushrod overhead
Carburettor	2 barrel downdraught
Power at rpm	180 (gross) at 4500
Maximum torque	260 ft/lb at 2800 rpm

TRANSMISSIONS:

Type	three speed manual
Ratios:	
First	N.A.
Second	N.A.
Top	3.31
Rear axle	3.31

SUSPENSION:

Front	independent coil
Rear	Semi elliptic
Shockers	telescopic

STEERING:

Type	cam and roller
Turns, 1 to 1	5
Circle	39 ft

BRAKES:

Type	drum

DIMENSIONS:

Wheelbase	9 ft 5 in
Track, front	4 ft 9 in
Track, rear	4 ft 8 in
Length	15 ft 8 in
Width	5 ft 11¼ in
Height	4 ft 7¾ in

TYRES:

Size	6.40 by 15

WEIGHT:

Dry	26¾ cwt

PERFORMANCE

TOP SPEED:

Fastest run	97.8 mph
Average of all runs	97.2 mph

MAXIMUM SPEED IN GEARS:

First	50 mph
Second	80 mph
Top	97.8 mph

ACCELERATION:

Standing Quarter Mile:

Fastest run	19 secs
Average of all runs	19.05 secs
0 to 30 mph	3.9 secs
0 to 40 mph	5.4 secs
0 to 50 mph	7.8 secs
0 to 60 mph	12.6 secs
0 to 70 mph	17.4 secs
0 to 80 mph	26.5 secs
20 to 40 mph	6.8 secs
30 to 50 mph	7.5 secs
40 to 60 mph	7.1 secs

GO-TO-WHOA:

0-60-0 mph	16.8 secs

SPEEDO ERROR:

Indicated	Actual
30 mph	28.2 mph
40 mph	37.4 mph
50 mph	46.2 mph
60 mph	55.7 mph
70 mph	64.5 mph
80 mph	73.5 mph

FUEL CONSUMPTION:

Cruising speeds	NA
Overall for test	16.3 mpg

PRICE:

Price	£1645

Pit Car...Tow Car... Spectating Car... "Show" Car

Our new '63 Lark Wagonaire is the nearest thing on the road (or at the track) to being all things to all people.

With its sliding roof section the sky's the limit for loading. And looking. All you need is a pit pass.

With its wide power options—including the Avanti supercharged high performance engine —and axle ratios (your choice at no extra charge) you can haul an "Unlimited" on its trailer from Riverside to Bridgehampton with no sweat.

If you're the Race Marshal you won't be diffident about showing off our Wagonaire around the course, either. It's got the go, the looks—and the stop. Especially if you have those power-boosted caliper disc brakes.

Off the track the Wagonaire does duty as a family sedan, a convertible, and a utility wagon too

What other wagon can make that statement?

Visit your Studebaker Dealer and scrutinize.

'63 LARK Wagonaire

From the Advanced Thinking of  Studebaker CORPORATION

Raymond Loewy gets credit again for advanced styling of fiberglass body, available only as closed coupé. Without any grille, Avanti gets cooling air through a scoop hidden below bumper. Use of single headlights is happy return to simplicity.

Studebaker Springs a Surprise

"Avanti" is Italian for forward, which is Studebaker's intended direction

Luxurious cockpit has console controls ahead of the "stick shift," many gauges, pleated vinyl-covered dash and wood trim. Front seats are "bucket," rear bench.

Studebaker Corporation insists on calling its new GT-styled Avanti a "high-performance personal prestige car," but its behavior may live up to its exciting looks. It has power under the hood (the 289-cu. in. V-8 is available with a Paxton-McCulloch supercharger) and the Avanti design seems intended to get this power to the road. There are three transmission options—three- and four-speed manual and three-speed automatic—all with floor shift. Radius rods help locate the conventional leaf-spring-suspended rear axle. There are anti-roll bars front and rear; body roll should be no problem. The 193-inch length is 11 inches shorter than the Hawk's, as is its 109-inch wheelbase (an inch more than the Corvair's). The Avanti pioneers in this country with British-style disc brakes at the front. The fiberglass body is from the firm that makes the Corvette's.

Different in appearance from any other U.S. car, Avanti suggests Studebaker is again setting a style trend, as in '47 and '53.

LARK

Studebaker Corp.

STUDEBAKER ROLLED BACK the top on its Lark wagon. A larg
sliding metal panel in the rear roof section may be pushe
forward and open. With the tailgate down, this uncovered are
makes it easy to carry trees, barrels, etc. — items that are picku
cargo otherwise. Passengers in the optional third seat bas
under the sunroof, or if they'd rather not bask, can pull it close
without stopping the car.

Other body styles include a convertible, two- and four-do
sedans and wagons, and a two-door hardtop. Series are st
called Regal, Cruiser, and Daytona — the Daytona being bucke
seated and sportier.

Lark's engineering story is fairly straightforward, with
important changes in steering or suspension. Bodies are firm
bolted to frame assemblies, well insulated against noise. Se
energizing brakes, aluminized steel mufflers, and torsion-spri
hood and trunk hinges are among Lark's engineering develo
ments.

Engines offered are an ohv Six with 112 hp, and two V-
putting out 180 or 195 hp in the 259-incher, and 210 hp
the 289-inch version. Three- and four-speed transmissions co
plement an automatic, and overdrive is available.

Minor differences distinguish the new Lark, and the flip-t
wagon is the most easily recognized as a '63.

DAYTONA, SPORTY MEMBER OF LARK LINE-UP, HAS BUCKET SEATS. IN ADDITION TO SEDAN, HARDTOP, CONVERTIBLE, AND WAGON ARE C

SCORES A FIRST WITH "FLIP-TOP" WAGON. SLIDING METAL PANEL IN REAR ROOF SECTION IS PUSHED FORWARD FOR OPEN-AIR RIDE.

HAWK

HAWK'S HANDSOME LINES are changed hardly at all for '63, and the minute differences in grille, mesh, headlight rings, and chrome moldings are indications that South Bend knows enough to let good design stand.

The Hawk Gran Turismo has had a tough time of it these last few years. No one knows precisely why. Its clean styling, good handling, tasteful interior, and ample power would seem to make it much more sought after.

Hawk's standard engine is the same 289-incher optional in the big Lark. In basic form it gives 210 hp, but with a four-barrel carb, horsepower goes up to 225. A three-speed transmission is available with overdrive, or a fine four-speed floorshift gearbox may be had at extra cost.

Ample finned brake drums contain self-centering, self-energizing shoes, which assure stopping power expected in a car of this sort. With a wide range of optional items, including various axle ratios and Twin-Traction, Hawk can please the most demanding driver. /MT

AVANTI

AMONG NUMEROUS DISTINCTIONS, Avanti has enjoyed the advantage of being America's first 1963 car (MOTOR TREND, July, 1962). As everyone knows by now, its body is fiberglass, its performance lively, and its price high.

Raymond Loewy styled the car with several themes in mind. The "jack-rabbit" hindquarter and Coke-bottle side treatment give names to the elements, but despite these tags, the car is pleasing and impressive. Four bucket seats make it rather specialized, but not more so than other semi-sports machines — and a prospective buyer has special things in mind anyway when he considers the car.

The engine offers a basic 280 hp from 289 cubic inches. These figures, though, give way to larger ones, depending on the performance tailoring wanted. Andy Granatelli builds special engines for Avanti, and the variety is almost endless.

Options are mostly in the line of axle ratios, transmissions, and running gear. Standard luxury items are so complete that Avanti needn't offer many options for comfort. /MT

(LEFT) Interior view of Avanti shows air conditioning ducts in the console, with push button controls overhead.

THE HANDSOME DESIGN OF THE HAWK HASN'T BEEN CHANGED FOR '63. ONLY DIFFERENCES ARE IN GRILLE MESH, HEADLIGHT RINGS, MOLDINGS.

THE STYLING OF THE AVANTI BEARS THE DISTINCTIVE RAYMOND LOEWY LOOK. IT IS ONE OF TWO U.S.-MADE CARS WITH FIBERGLASS BODY.

LUXURY ITEMS, SUCH AS FOUR BUCKET SEATS, MAKE AVANTI A SPECIALIZED CAR. PERFORMANCE-TAILORED ENGINES ARE ALSO AVAILABLE.

Studebaker Lark Daytona 2-door hardtop.

INTRODUCING THE '63 CARS

STUDEBAKER

Lark & Cruiser

STUDEBAKER'S MOST INTERESTING Lark for 1963 is easily its new Wagonaire 4-door station wagon. Based on the "long" wheelbase (113 in.—also used for the 4-door sedans) this new wagon has a telescoping panel at the rear of the roof which opens up by sliding forward. This provides a large opening for sunning, ventilation or carrying tall objects. A third seat, facing to the rear, is optional, as is a power-retracted tailgate window and a fold-away step. The Wagonaire is longer and slightly taller than Studebaker's previous station wagons.

The Cruiser models will have the 289 cu. in. V-8 as standard equipment, where other Larks have the inline-6 of 170 cu. in. as their nominal power and a 259 V-8 as first option. All Studebakers in the 1963 line will be equipped with Prestolite alternators.

The simulated hardtop look has been applied to the Lark sedans via straighter windshield posts and squared off rear windows. A notable option for all cars is the power-operated disc brakes originally adopted for use on the Avanti front wheels.

Lark Wagonaire.

MODELS & STYLES

Lark Deluxe	Lark Daytona
2-door sedan	2-door hardtop
4-door sedan*	2-door convertible
4-door station wagon*	4-door station wagon*
Lark Regal	**Cruiser**
2-door sedan	4-door sedan*
4-door sedan*	

GENERAL SPECIFICATIONS

Wheelbase, in.	(*113.0)	109.0
track, f/r		57.4/56.6
Overall length, in.	(*188.0)	184.0
width		71.25
height	(*57.0)	55.75
box volume, cu. ft.	(*442)	422
Luggage capacity, cu. ft.		13.57
Fuel tank capacity, gal.		18.0
Brakes, swept area, sq. in.	(*281.6)	239.2
Tire size	(*6.50-15)	6.00-15
Curb weight, lb.	(2995)	2900

ENGINES

cu. in.	type	bhp/rpm	torque/rpm	carb.	comp.
170	il-6	112/4500	154/2000	1-1 bbl.	8.25
259	V-8	180/4500	260/2800	1-2	8.50
259	V-8	195/4500	n.a.	1-4	8.50
289	V-8	210/4500	300/2800	1-2	8.50
289	V-8	225/4500	n.a.	1-4	8.50
289	V-8 (S)	(Avanti)	n.a.	1-4	9.00

TRANSMISSIONS

	4th	3rd	2nd	1st	t.c.
Manual, synchro 2-3	—	1.00	1.63	2.60	—
Manual, synchro 2-3	—	1.00	1.55	2.57	—
Manual, all-synchro	1.00	1.31	1.66	2.20	—
Manual, overdrive	.70	1.00	1.63	2.60	—
Flightomatic (auto.)		1.00	1.47	2.40	2.15

AXLE RATIOS

Manual transmissions—3.07, 3.31, 3.73, 4.10, 4.56
Automatic transmission—3.07, 3.31, 3.73, 4.10

Studebaker Hawk Gran Turismo.

INTRODUCING THE '63 CARS

STUDEBAKER *Hawk & Avanti*

MODELS & STYLES

Hawk
2-door, 5-pass. hardtop

Avanti
2-door, 4-pass. coupe

GENERAL SPECIFICATIONS
(4-DOOR SEDAN)

	Hawk	Avanti
Wheelbase, in.	120.5	109.0
track, f/r.	57.4/56.6	57.4/56.6
Overall length, in.	204.0	192.4
width	71.0	70.4
height	54.7	53.9
box volume, cu. ft.	457	421
Luggage capacity, cu. ft.	11.15	n.a.
Fuel tank capacity, gal.	18.0	21.0
Brakes, swept area, sq. in.	281.6	n.a.
Tire size	6.70-15	6.70-15
Curb weight, lb.	3500	3350

ENGINES

cu. in.	type	bhp/rpm	torque/rpm	carb.	comp.
259	V-8	180/4500	260/2800	1–2 bbl.	8.5
289	V-8	210/4500	300/2800	1–2	8.5
289	V-8	225/4500	n.a.	1–4	8.5
Avanti					
289	V-8	n.a.	n.a.	1–4	10.0
289	V-8 (S)	n.a.	n.a.	1–4	9.0

TRANSMISSIONS

	4th	3rd	2nd	1st	t.c.
Manual, synchro 2-3	—	1.00	1.55	2.57	—
Manual, overdrive	.70	1.00	1.55	2.57	—
Manual, all-synchro	1.00	1.51	1.92	2.54	—
Flightomatic (auto.)	—	1.00	1.47	2.40	2.15

AXLE RATIOS

Manual Transmissions—3.31, 3.73
Automatic transmission—3.07, 3.31

THE 1963 AVANTI was introduced last spring and thus will have no changes (other than those normally made during production runs) for the 1963 model year. The Hawk, Studebaker's pre-Avanti sporting type car, also has had few changes although the two Avanti engines are now available options. The Hawk (and the Avanti) already had 4-speed and automatic transmissions, both units originating at Borg-Warner.

The Hawk has a restyled radiator grille, side grilles, front moldings and parking lamps. The rear deck trim also has been re-done, along with the interior. A 35-amp alternator is standard equipment (40-amp with the Avanti engines), as are self-adjusting brakes.

Horsepower and torque figures of the "R-1" and "R-2" Avanti engines (289 cu. in., 4-barrel carburetion, 10:1 compression ratio unsupercharged and 9:1 supercharged) have yet to be released. However, these engines, and the Avanti's worthwhile disc/drum brake combination, now may be ordered in the Hawk. Ditto the viscous-drive fan introduced with the Avanti.

Other improvements for 1963 include a new water pump, new single 4-barrel carburetion, a water-cooled automatic transmission for the R-engines and larger shock absorbers.

Studebaker Avanti.

GT Hawk

ENGINE CAPACITY: 289.00 cu in, 4725.15 cu cm;
FUEL CONSUMPTION: 16.6 m/imp gal, 13.8 m/US gal, 17 l x 100 km;
SEATS: 4; MAX SPEED: 108.7 mph, 175 km/h;
PRICE: list £ 1,579, total £ 1,909.

ENGINE: front, 4 stroke; cylinders: 8, Vee-slanted at 90°; bore and stroke: 3.56 x 3.62 in, 90.4 x 91.9 mm; engine capacity: 289.00 cu in, 4725.15 cu cm; compression ratio: 8.5 : 1; max power (SAE): 210 hp at 4500 rpm; max torque (SAE): 300 lb ft, 41.4 kgm at 2800 rpm; max number of engine rpm: 5500; specific power: 44.4 hp/l; cylinder block: cast iron; cylinder head: cast iron; crankshaft bearings: 5; valves: 2 per cylinder, overhead, in line, with push rods and rockers; camshaft: 1 at centre of Vee; lubrication: gear pump, filter on by-pass; lubricating system capacity: 5.0 imp qt, 6.0 US qt, 5.7 l; carburation: 1 Carter downdraft twin-barrel carburettor; fuel feed: mechanical pump; cooling system: water; cooling system capacity: 15.0 imp qt, 18.0 US qt, 17 l.

TRANSMISSION: driving wheels: rear; clutch: single dry plate; gear box: mechanical; gears: 3 + reverse; synchromesh gears: II, III; gear box ratios: (I) 2.57, (II) 1.55, (III) 1, (Rev) 3.48; gear lever: steering column; final drive: hypoid bevel; ratio: 3.31 : 1.

CHASSIS: box-type ladder frame; front suspension: independent, wishbones, coil springs, anti-roll bar, telescopic dampers; rear suspension: rigid axle, semi-elliptic leafsprings, telescopic dampers.

STEERING: cam and robler; turns of steering wheel lock to lock: 4.6.

BRAKES: drum; braking surface: total 172.80 sq in, 1114.56 sq cm.

ELECTRICAL EQUIPMENT: voltage: 12 V; battery: 50 Ah; ignition distributor: Autolite; headlights: 4 front and reversing.

DIMENSIONS AND WEIGHT: wheel base: 120.50 in, 3061 mm; front track: 57.37 in, 1457 mm; rear track: 56.56 in, 1437 mm; overall length: 204.00 in, 5182 mm; overall width: 71.00 in, 1803 mm; overall height: 54.65 in, 1388 mm; ground clearance: 5.12 in, 130 mm; dry weight: 3435 lb, 1558 kg; distribution of weight: 54.7 % front axle, 45.3 % rear axle; turning radius (between walls): 22.7 ft, 6.9 m; tyres: 6.70 - 15; fuel tank capacity: 14.96 imp gal, 18.00 US gal, 68 l.

BODY: coupé; doors: 2; seats: 4; front seat: double.

PERFORMANCE: max speed in 1st gear. 51.6 mph, 83 km/h; max speed in 2nd gear: 85.1 mph, 137 km/h; max speed in 3rd gear: 108.7 mph, 175 km/h; power-weight ratio: 16.3 lb/hp, 7.4 kg/hp; useful load: 706 lb, 320 kg; acceleration: standing 1/4 mile 19.1 sec, 0 — 50 mph (0 — 80 km/h) 7.9 sec; speed in direct drive at 1000 rpm: 24.0 mph, 38.7 km/h.

PRACTICAL INSTRUCTIONS: fuel: petrol; engine sump oil: 4.1 imp qt, 5.0 US qt, 4.7 l, SAE 10W-30 (winter) 10W-30 (summer); gearbox oil: 1.6 imp qt, 1.9 US qt, 1.8 l, SAE 80; final drive oil: 1.2 imp qt, 1.5 US qt, 1.4 l, SAE 80; tappet clearances: inlet 0.026 in, 0.66 mm, exhaust 0.026 in, 0.66 mm; valve timing: (inlet) opens 11° before tdc and closes 54° 36' after bdc, (exhaust) opens 51° 36' before bdc and closes 14° after tdc; tyre pressure (medium load): front 25 psi, 1.8 atm, rear 24 psi, 1.7 atm.

VARIATIONS AND OPTIONAL ACCESSORIES: servo brake; axle ratio 3.73 : 1; front disc brakes, servo; power-assisted steering, 4.6 turns of steering wheel lock to lock; limited slip final drive; V 8 engine, capacity 259 cu in, 4234.65 cu cm, max power 180 hp (see Daytona Hardtop); V 8 engine, max power 225 hp at 4500 rpm, 1 downdraft 4-barrel carburettor, axle ratios 3.31 - 3.73 : 1, max speed 111.8 mph, 180 km/h; overdrive, ratio 0.70, axle ratios 3.73-3.31 : 1; Flight-o-matic automatic gear box, hydraulic torque convertor and planetary gears with 3 ratios (I 2.40, II 1.47, III 1, Rev 2.00), max ratio of convertor at stall 2.15, axle ratios 3.31-3.07 : 1; 4-speed mechanical gear box, fully synchronized (I 2.54, II 1.92, III 1.51, IV 1, Rev 2.61), central gear lever, axle ratio 3.31 - 3.73 : 1.

ENGINE CAPACITY: 289.00 cu in, 4725.15 cu cm;
FUEL CONSUMPTION: 17.1 m/imp gal, 14.2 m/US gal, 16.5 l x 100 km;
SEATS: 4; MAX SPEED: 124.2 mph, 200 km/h;
PRICE: list £ 2,187, total £ 2,643.

ENGINE: front, 4 stroke; cylinders: 8, Vee-slanted at 90°; bore and stroke: 3.56 x 3.62 in, 90.4 x 91.9 mm; engine capacity: 289.00 in, 4725.15 cu cm; compression ratio: 8.5 : 1; max power (SAE): 210 hp at 4500 rpm; max torque (SAE): 300 lb ft, 41.4 kgm at 2800 rpm; max number of engine rpm: 6000; specific power: 44.4 hp/l; cylinder block: cast iron; cylinder head: cast iron; crankshaft bearings: 5; valves: 2 per cylinder, overhead, in line, with push rods and rockers; camshaft: 1, at centre of Vee; lubrication: gear pump, filter on by-pass; lubricating system capacity: 5.0 imp qt, 6.0 US qt, 5.7 l; carburation:

1 Carter downdraft twin-barrel carburettor; fuel feed: mechanical pump; cooling system: water; cooling system capacity: 15.0 imp qt, 18.0 US qt, 17 l.

TRANSMISSION: driving wheels: rear; clutch: single dry plate; gear box: mechanical; gears: 3 + reverse; synchromesh gears: II, III; gear box ratios: (I) 2.57, (II) 1.55, (III) 1, (Rev) 3.48; gear lever: central; final drive: hypoid bevel; ratio: 3.73 : 1.

CHASSIS: box-type ladder frame with X cross members; front suspension: independent, wishbones, coil springs, anti-roll bar, telescopic dampers; rear suspension: rigid axle, semi-elliptic leafsprings, radius rods, telescopic dampers.

STEERING: cam and peg; turns of steering wheel lock to lock: 5.

BRAKES: front disc, rear drum, servo.

ELECTRICAL EQUIPMENT: voltage: 12 V; battery: 50 Ah; alternator: 40 Ah; ignition distributor: Autolite; headlights: 4 front and reversing.

DIMENSIONS AND WEIGHT: wheel base: 109.00 in, 2769 mm; front track: 57.40 in, 1458 mm; rear track: 56.60 in, 1438 mm; overall length: 192.48 in, 4889 mm; overall width: 70.40 in, 1788 mm; overall height: 53.90 in, 1369 mm; ground clearance: 5.12 in, 130 mm; dry weight: 3310 lb, 1501 kg; turning radius (between walls): 20.0 ft, 6.1 m; tyres: 6.70 - 15; fuel tank capacity: 17.60 imp gal, 21.10 US gal, 80 l.

BODY: coupé; doors: 2; seats: 4; front seat: double.

PERFORMANCE: max speed in 1st gear: 48.4 mph, 78 km/h; max speed in 2nd gear: 80.1 mph, 129 km/h; max speed in 3rd gear: 124.2 mph, 200 km/h; power-weight ratio: 15.0 lb/hp, 7.1 kg/hp; useful load: 706 lb, 320 kg.

PRACTICAL INSTRUCTIONS: fuel: petrol, 95 oct; engine sump oil: 4.1 imp qt, 5.0 US qt, 4.7 l, SAE 5W-20 (winter) 10W-30 (summer), change every 6000 miles, 9600 km; gearbox oil: 1.6 imp qt, 1.9 US q,t 1.8 l, SAE 90; final drive oil: 1.0 imp qt, 1.3 US qt, 1.2 l, SAE 90; tappet clearances: inlet 0.024 in, 0.61 mm, exhaust 0.026 in, 0.66 mm; valve timing: (inlet) opens 11° before tdc and closes 54° 36' after bdc, (exhaust) opens 51° 36' before bdc and closes 14° after tdc; tyre pressure (medium load): front 24 psi, 1.7 atm, rear 24 psi, 1.7 atm.

VARIATIONS AND OPTIONAL ACCESSORIES: axle ratio 3.31 - 4.09 - 3.07 : 1; power-assisted steering, 3.5 turns of steering wheel lock to lock; limited slip final drive; overdrive, ratio 0.70; Flight-o-matic automatic gear box, hydraulic torque convertor and planetary gears with 3 ratios (I 2.40, II 1.47, III 1, Rev 2.00), max ratio of convertor at stall 2.25, axle ratio 3.31 : 1 and others; 4-speed mechanical gear box, fully synchronized (I 2.54, II 1.89, III 1.51, IV 1, Rev 2.61), central gear lever, axle ratio 3.73 : 1 and others; 235 hp engine, compression ratio 10.25 : 1, 1 Carter 4-barrel carburettor; engine max power 280 hp at 4800 rpm, compression ratio 9 : 1, Paxton supercharger, max speed 149.1 mph, 240 km/h; tuned engines.

The Avanti for '64 features very minor styling changes. One, however, is quite noticeable consisting of square headlight housing.

AVANTI '64

Studebaker's fairly new prestige package remains untainted by yearly styling changes. Of course, there are refinements to the "jack-rabbit" sports car

Studebaker's Avanti, as predicted, has only minor facelifting in the styling department for 1954. For the specialized buyer who likes something different from the run-of-the-mill transportation which always follows the general trend, the Avanti sports machine is just right.

Raymond Loewy, who designed its high hind-quarter body, certainly came up with a one-of-a-kind styling with the Avanti. But that was to be expected, for he was the stylist who also conceived the original Studebaker hardtop which *did* become quite popular back when it was introduced in 1963. The big Studebaker Hawk still resembles this original design in its '64 model.

Changes on the Avanti for '64, however, involve a new square headlight

Aircraft-type controls are featured on center console between driver and passenger. Gear-shift lever also located on console.

Paxton Products of Santa Monica, California, a Studebaker subsidiary, is responsible for the "R-3" supercharged version of the 289.

housing, replacing the recessed round unit of its predecessor. Otherwise, the exterior retains its original introduction appearance.

On the inside, the four bucket seats still are impressive for an American-built car. And, the rest of the interior is keyed to appeal to the sports-car-enthusiast-type of automobile buyer. It has a center console between the driver and his passenger with aircraft-type of controls. Shift lever is located on this woodgrain top console.

The Avanti is built on a 109-inch wheelbase frame; it has a tread up front of 57 3/8 inches, rear 56 9/16 inches. Its road clearance is comparatively high — 6 3/16 inches — for a car purported to be in the sports car class. Its shipping weight is 3195 pounds.

The basic engine for the Avanti is the Thunderbolt 289-cubic-inch V8, developing 210 horsepower at 4500 rpm. This engine has a two-barrel carburetor and the compression ratio is 8.5 to 1. The Jet Thrust unsupercharged version of this

basic powerplant is equipped with a four-barrel carburetor and runs on a compression ratio of 10.25 to 1. Horsepower is reported to about 280. The supercharged version of the Jet Thrust engine uses a 9 to 1 compression ratio and a four-barrel carburetor.

Transmission choice is either a four-speed manual shift gearbox or an automatic transmission. Incidentally, the "R-3" supercharged engine is practically hand-built by Paxton Products (a Studebaker subsidiary) in Santa Monica, Calif.

Studebaker Avanti's high rear-end or rake styling is evident in side view. Trim is the same as on the '63 car except for the rather unique wheels. These reflect the sports car theme.

by Jim Wright, *Technical Editor*

THIS YEAR, Studebaker is pulling out all stops to make their name as nearly synonymous with speed, performance, and endurance as they can. The reasoning is simple: Today's young drivers have the biggest buying potential the country has ever seen — and these same young buyers just aren't apt to come flocking into a showroom to lay down money for a car that doesn't offer anything more exciting than old-fashioned economy and durability.

Studebaker feels the Commander will be their biggest seller this year, so we ordered one as our test car. We chose a two-door sedan, which is built on a 109-inch wheelbase (all the two-doors are — the four-doors and wagons have 113-inch wheelbases). Since we'd also be testing this car for its performance image potential, we ordered it loaded.

Number one on our personal option list was the complete High-Performance package. It adds $766.70 to the car's base price of $2190 (plus $135 freight), but it's worth every penny. Included are the R-2 Jet Thrust supercharged engine,

twin-traction rear axle with radius rods and anti-roll bar for stability (a front anti-roll bar is standard), heavy-duty springs and shock absorbers (Gabriel adjustables at the rear), disc brakes (power assist included), tachometer, 160-mph speedometer, bucket seats, front and rear carpeting, and four-ply tires. We went a step further on the tires and specified Butylaires ($45), mainly because they offer better adhesion under all conditions than do the straight compounds. A four-speed, all-synchro, floorshift transmission ($189) was also specified, along with a 3.54 rear axle.

The Halibrand magnesium wheels weren't specified but were included, as was the racing stripe, mainly for photographic purposes. The wheels, in addition to being photogenic, do have some functional advantages. They let the brakes cool more quickly, and because they're lighter, mean a reduction in unsprung weight — slightly improving the ride and handling. At approximately $297.50 a set, they're a good item.

The R-2 engine displaces 289 cubic inches and mounts a Paxton centrifugal supercharger capable of supplying 5½ to 6 pounds of pressure — pumping

through a four-barrel carburetor. Studebaker is still a little shy about releasing horsepower figures on any of its hot engines, but we'd guess the output of the R-2 to be at least one horsepower per cubic inch around 4800-5200 rpm.

Our acceleration figures show that in a realistic class, this car could make a good showing at the drags. Set up as it was for the street (3.54 rear axle, street tires, no special tuning), the Commander could consistently turn a 90-mph standing quarter-mile with an elapsed time of 15.8 seconds. The car's 0-60-mph average was a very quick 7.3 seconds. Zero to 30 and 0-45 mph came up in 2.9 and 4.7 seconds. With the proper preparation, this little bomb could easily run in the 108-110-mph bracket, with low-13-second ETs. Several top-speed runs down the Riverside backstretch gave an honest 123 mph, with the tachometer needle showing 5800 rpm (which is pretty close to its 6000-rpm red line). Except for the Corvette, Cobra, and a few others, there just aren't very many cars around capable of pulling to the red line with street rear-axle gears.

You can order the Commander with

1964 Studebaker

even more performance by specifying either the supercharged R-3 engine (304.5 cubic inches) or the unblown, dual-quad-carbureted R-4 version (also 304.5 cubic inches). Also available is a wide range of rear-axle gearsets. These run all the way from 2.87 to 4.89.

The Warner four-speed transmission is smooth and quiet, but our linkage was on the sloppy side. During acceleration tests, there were times when it refused to be shifted any way but slowly. All-out, full-throttle power shifts were impossible. From past experience, we'd say that we could've knocked the car's quarter-mile ET down from the re-

(TOP) *A high-performance car like Super Lark should and does have brakes to match its power. Discs up front are unrivaled.*

(RIGHT) *Heavy-duty suspension makes real tiger out of Studebaker around corners.*

(FAR RIGHT) *Interior space gives no hint of the car's smallish, 109-inch wheelbase.*

Super Lark MT Road Test

1) *A lot of other car owners will be in for a surprise when they come up against any mild-looking Larks wearing this emblem.*

2) *Avanti R-2 engine package uses proven Paxton supercharger to pull some mighty healthy horsepower out of the 289-incher.*

3) *Heavy-duty shocks and springs, as well as big disc brakes, are part of high-performance option. Anti-roll bar is stock.*

4) *At rear, optional parts include springs, adjustable shocks, radius rods, and another anti-roll bar for additional stiffness.*

5) *All the above-pictured performance parts add up to give Lark plenty of go off the line. Quarter-mile acceleration runs are equal to many cars with much larger engines which cost much more. Given little help, this could be sleeper at drags.*

SUPER LARK

corded 15.8 seconds to at most 15 flat if the shift linkage hadn't been so whippy. Standard transmission on this car is a three-speed manual, while a three-speed automatic is optional.

Off-the-line traction was good, with both the Butylaire tires and the heavy-duty suspension contributing. The radius rods effectively controlled any wheel hop during hard acceleration. We had the rear shocks set on FIRM, which is their medium setting. The other two settings are REGULAR and EXPORT.

Fuel consumption was what we'd consider good for a package like this. Our overall average was 13.1 mpg. This figure is based on a total of 1688.5 miles that included all types of driving under all conditions. The around-town average fell in the 10.8-13.2-mpg range, while extended freeway and open-road running (65 to 85 mph) produced 14.4 to 15.8 mpg.

The Skybolt Six is still available for those who want the utmost economy. During the Bonneville record attempts, this engine in a two-door Commander surprised everyone when it set a total of 12 records in the American Class C closed car category. The existing records in this class were set back in 1939 by the late John Cobb at the wheel of a Hudson Six. Top speed set by the Studebaker was the flying one-mile record, with a 102.77-mph average!

The disc front and finned rear drum brakes proved excellent, both in reliability and stopping power. They survived several hard stops from 123 mph without any noticeable fade. During our regular braking tests, all stops were quicker than average, and we made them without a trace of swerve or fade. Studebaker doesn't build in any anti-dive control into the front suspension, so the nose dips more than most of today's cars — but not annoyingly so.

We believe we'd order the heavy-duty suspension parts even on an economy model. They transform what we used to consider a "truck" into a car that's extremely light on its feet, with the handling characteristics of a top-flight sports machine. The only complaint here is that the steering's too slow at 4.7 turns between locks. It really should be

(TOP) Braking view shows that more-than-average amount of nose dive is present. This doesn't interfere with fast, fade-free, full-control, straight-line stops, though.

(RIGHT) All sheet metal has been reworked this year to give Lark a more modern look.

down around 3.5 turns to do justice to the car's character. At highway speeds or even flat out in the 120- to 125-mph range, the test car was completely stable. In hard, short corners, the front end pushes only slightly, and there's plenty of power on tap to make needed steering corrections. The front and rear anti-roll bars give the added roll stiffness that keeps this car fairly flat in hard corners.

The all-new exterior sheet metal was well fitted, and we couldn't find any large gaps or other signs of sloppy workmanship. The top is about an inch lower than previous models, but there's still enough room inside for a six-footer wearing a hat. For a car with only a 109-inch wheelbase, the Commander offers hip-, shoulder-, and leg room unmatched in the industry.

The Commander offers a padded dash as standard equipment. Also standard is a full line of instruments that tell the driver what's going on under the hood. They're big and easy to read. The test car had a 160-mph speedo and a 6000-rpm tachometer. Both come with the high-performance package. Speedometer error was an acceptable five per cent, but the tach needed recalibration quite badly. We checked it out with our test tach and found it 450 rpm slow at 3000 and 800 rpm slow at 6000.

Our test car was also equipped with an air/fuel ratio meter (called a Carbumeter) that'll soon be marketed by Paxton Products Division of Studebaker. The Carbumeter was flanked on its mounting panel by the blower and fuel pump pressure gauges. The function of the Carbumeter is to let the driver know, at any throttle setting, whether the engine is running too rich or too lean an air/fuel mixture. It does this by analyzing the engine's exhaust. The meter is sensitive enough to detect minute variations in altitude or temperature, both of which have an effect on the air/fuel ratio.

An area of annoyance was the carburetor flooding that came on hard cornering and on maximum deceleration. Carb flooding is a pretty common complaint with most cars in corners, so this isn't too important. The flooding on hard stops (and the engine would die) is inexcusable on a car with power brakes and could set up an extremely dangerous situation.

In the past, Studebaker has always had a good reputation for durability and we couldn't find anything in the test car's makeup to indicate it wouldn't live up to it. It's a good, honest car and, with the right selection of options, it should more than meet the demands of the enthusiast driver—no matter what age. /M

STUDEBAKER COMMANDER
2-door, 5-passenger sedan

OPTIONS ON CAR TESTED: High-Performance package (see text), 4-speed transmission, radio, heater, magnesium wheels, Firestone Butylaire tires, seat belts
BASIC PRICE: $2190
PRICE AS TESTED: $3784.10 (plus tax and license)
ODOMETER READING AT START OF TEST: 1601 miles
RECOMMENDED ENGINE RED LINE: 6000 rpm

PERFORMANCE

ACCELERATION (2 aboard)
```
0-30 mph.........................2.9 secs.
0-45 mph.........................4.7
0-60 mph.........................7.3
```
Standing start ¼-mile 15.8 secs. and 90 mph

Speeds in gears @ 6000 rpm
```
1st ................50 mph      3rd ....................83 mph
2nd ................67 mph      4th .........123 (actual clocked
                                        speed) @ 5800 rpm
```

Speedometer Error on Test Car

Car's speedometer reading	30	47	52	62	73	84
Weston electric speedometer ...	30	45	50	60	70	80

Observed miles per hour per 1000 rpm in top gear................21 mph
Stopping Distances — from 30 mph, 38.5 ft.; from 60 mph, 133.5 ft.

SPECIFICATIONS FROM MANUFACTURER

Engine
Ohv V-8
Bore: 3 9/16 ins.
Stroke: 3⅝ ins.
Displacement: 289 cu. ins.
Compression ratio: 9.0:1
Horsepower: NA
Torque: NA
Horsepower per cubic inch: NA
Carburetion: 1 4-barrel (supercharged)
Ignition: 12-volt coil

Gearbox
4-speed manual, all-synchro; floorshift

Driveshaft
1-piece, open tube

Differential
Hypoid, semi-floating
Standard ratio: 3.54:1

Suspension
Front: Independent coil springs with upper and lower control arms, direct-acting, adjustable tubular shocks, and anti-roll bar
Rear: Rigid axle, with 5-leaf, semi-elliptic springs, radius rods, direct-acting, adjustable tubular shocks, and anti-roll bar

Steering
Recirculating ball
Turning diameter: 37.6 ft.
Turns lock to lock: 4.7

Wheels and Tires
Optional Halibrand magnesium 5-lug wheels
Optional Firestone Butylaire 6.70 x 15 4-ply tires

Brakes
Hydraulic; caliper disc front, drum rear; power assist
Front: 11½-in. dia. grey-iron disc
Rear: 11-in. dia. x 2 ins. wide finned, cast-iron drum
Effective lining area: 105 sq. ins.

Body and Frame
Ladder-type frame with separate body
Wheelbase: 109.0 ins.
Track: front, 57.375 ins.; rear, 56.5625 ins.
Overall length: 190.0 ins.
Curb weight: 3260 lbs. (with full gas tank)

---

1) *Large, easy-to-read instruments are standout features that will be appreciated. Cluster under dash contains both fuel and supercharger pressure gauges, plus a soon-to-be-marketed (by Paxton) air/fuel-ratio meter that tells mixture strength.*

2) *Trunk area offers enough room for the average family for weekends. Loading is slightly hampered by a high trunk lip.*

3) *Vigorous cornering failed to show any weaknesses in Super Lark's balance and handling characteristics. Well designed factory suspension modifications offer a great compromise between ride and handling at prices average owners can afford. In fact, the factory price is much cheaper than what it would be for owner to gather parts together on his own — easier, too.*

4) *With a top speed of 125 mph (or even faster with a different choice of rear-axle gears), the Super Lark has to be counted among the fastest production cars in the country — right up there with the Avanti and some models of the Corvette and Cobra. MT tests at Riverside showed Lark stable all the way.*

4
←

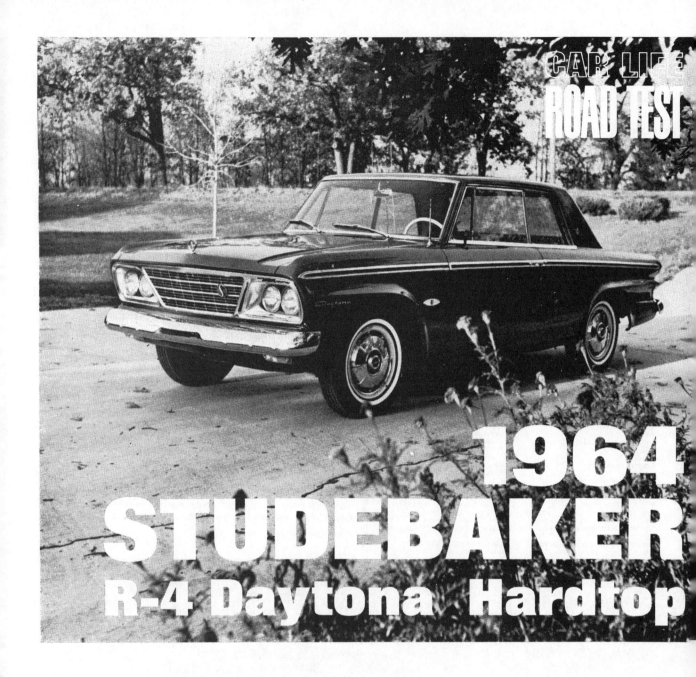

1964 STUDEBAKER
R-4 Daytona Hardtop

A Lark With Class And Calories Turns Into A Bird of Prey

TAKING DELIVERY of our enthusiast's Daytona R-4 hardtop (the bomb that Booth built—see preceding pages) from Studebaker's engineering department, which had (as noted) run in the car for 500 miles and made the thorough, final check in a long sequence of checks, two things immediately struck us. The price sticker, which we were seeing for the first time, totaled $4549.54 and emphasized the performance potential of the car (it is still necessary, Virginia, to pay for what you get). And that potent power, once we slipped behind the wheel for the first taste of driving, was second.

Assured that it was safe to try a few acceleration runs, our first stop was the Studebaker proving grounds for some initial quarter miles. With tires smoking through all three lower gears, the Daytona clocked ¼-mile times ranging from 15.8 to 16.0 sec., which, while not quite up to expectations, were certainly respectable for a street machine. Wheelspin was a serious problem in getting off the line, understandable in view of the car's front-end weight bias, but the throttle feathering used to control this resulted in a more serious carburetion bogging problem.

A few quick laps around Studebaker's antiquated and crumbling 70-mph test track at an indicated 112 mph satisfied our enthusiasm for the moment and in the process scrubbed-in the Firestone treads quite admirably. Then, pointing the Daytona's broad prow westward down the freeway, we started the long journey cross-country to Los Angeles.

Brooks Stevens, known as Kip by the Studebaker brass with whom he works, has produced striking new styling lines for the Lark this year while working within the confines of the long-existent body shell. In appearance, the new Studebakers have taken on a more-pleasing aspect which is best described as "commercial." This was accomplished with a wide horizontal stamped grill piece, new front and rear quarter panels, new hood and deck lids, and a slightly altered contour to the roof panel. It is, as one staff member commented, a better return for Studebaker's styling dollar than, say, Ford got for its. The '64s also justify a remark made (CL, June 1963) by Sherwood Egbert, Studebaker's ex-presi-

190

CRISP LINES of new sheet metal have removed the dumpiness from the Studebaker, added visual lengthening and widening to car.

HEAVY DUTY suspension and front disc brakes are displayed as chassis moves down assembly line.

STUDEBAKER

dent, that there would be something more attractive to "the youth market" in his showrooms that fall.

Inside, however, the Daytona is still all Lark. The instrument panel, with rocker button switches and a trio of large round dials, is virtually unchanged. The steering wheel is still an oddly shaped oval with a flattened bottom, which we found difficult to get accustomed to. There is enough headroom, because of the "old fashioned" body shell, to permit sartorial impeccability for an opera goer. Ample seat padding provides excellent lateral support in the front buckets, which were the reclining option and thus permitted much-needed changes of position during the lengthy drive despite the fact that back rake adjustment had to be limited to the first notch. In that position, a fully extended, arms-out driving posture is possible and, even though it tends to lower eyeball level to the upper rim of the steering wheel, every Walter Mitty immediately becomes a Jimmy Clark or Dan Gurney.

Unchanged mechanically for more than a decade, Studebaker's suspension is considerably improved with the addition of the Avanti components. These are part of the R-4 high performance package—a package that accounts for $1412 of the price. The package includes heavier shock absorbers, stiffer springs (116 lb./in. in front, 136 rear), a 0.75-in. anti-roll bar at the front, a link-type anti-roll bar at the rear and traction bars from the rear axle forward to the chassis. The heavy-duty rear axle is flanged and incorporates a non-slip differential. With such equipment, and 4 lb. more air in the front tires, the normally understeering Daytona becomes quite neutral at speed and body roll is negligible. The enthusiastic driver quickly starts scouting out sweeping curves to drift

around, then just as quickly discovers that a judicious throttle foot is necessary to prevent rear end breakaway when the R-4's excess power is released to the driving wheels. Throttle response is such, however, that this trait soon becomes more an aid to brisk handling than a hazard.

Fuel consumption over the 2330-mile trip averaged 12.66 mpg, with a high on one 40-mile downhill stretch from Kingman, Ariz., of 13.3. A total of 184 gal. of super-premium fuel, necessary because of the 12:1 compression ratio, and 3 qt. of oil was necessary for the trip.

The chrome-encrusted R-4 engine, sprouting no fewer than 5 oil breather caps (but no evidence of a crankcase smog control valve), is available only to specially qualified buyers. It is the non-supercharged version of the 304.5 cu. in. R-3 engine, fitted with a pair of Carter AFB 4-barrel carburetors atop a high-rise manifold and with boosted compression. Mechanical lifters operated by a high-lift camshaft of 308° duration in turn operate valves of 1.875 in. (intake) and 1.625 in. (exhaust). This is about the limit allowed in the present Studebaker cylinder heads and with the normal exhaust manifolding the engine is rated at 280 bhp at a relatively mild 5000 rpm. (The company, after much prodding by NHRA, has now published bhp ratings for the other R-series engines. They are 240 bhp at 5000 rpm for the 289 unsupercharged R-1; 289 at 4800 for the 289 supercharged R-2; and 335 at 5350 for the 304.5 supercharged R-3—all very close to ratings which Car Life had calculated for them some time ago.) The engine winds easily, albeit noisily, right on past the 6000 rpm redline on the 8000 rpm tachometer, but it produces a decidedly stronger power output once the 4000

mark is passed. Despite the listed power peak, there was no apparent dropoff on up to the 6000 mark.

With a total of 13.0 in. of venturi area in the carburetors, there is little wonder that fuel consumption was what it was. Fortunately, the throttle linkage is such that there is a solid stop felt before the secondaries open up, requiring a definite push on the pedal to open the remaining four barrels. Pushing past it seems to affect the fuel gauge needle in inverse proportion to the action of the speedometer needle.

The Warner Gear T-10 transmission makes control of such propulsion somewhat more positive. The gear spacing—2.54:1 first, 1.92 second, 1.51 third and 1.00:1 high—could be improved upon but the R-4 power curve is wide enough to overcome this drawback. In about-town driving, the engine torque develops rapidly enough that direct shifts from low to high are possible. The standard rear axle ratio of 3.54:1, with which our Daytona was fitted, permitted 80-mph cruising with a mild 3500 rpm engine speed. Optional ratios, all with the limited slip feature, of 2.87, 3.31, 3.73, 4.09, 4.27, and 4.55:1 are available and one of the latter two would be a better choice for the drag racing enthusiast, considering the 15-in. wheels upon which the Daytona perches.

Studebaker's vacuum-assisted power brakes, with 11.5-in. discs on front and 11-in. finned cast drums at the rear, are just about the best available for domestic cars. A decelerometer which Car Life editors have been evaluating for use as road test equipment recorded 25 ft./sec./sec., the best retardation for any car so far tested with the device, in stops made without wheel lockup or swerve. The linkage-type power steering, while cutting turns to 4.4, lock-to-lock, and providing greater ease of control for the nose-heavy Daytona, was afflicted somewhat more than usual with road and wind wander, particularly on undulating blacktop roads.

GENE BOOTH PHOTOS

SEWER PIPE carburetors, Prestolite ignition help increase R-4 output.

LARGE DIALS before driver replace all idiot lights.

CAPACIOUS TRUNK has vinyl lining, should carry some sandbags to reduce wheelspin.

Even our car-building editor had to admit, however, that he had done a lousy job with the doors. Both doors developed a sag shortly after the test started. And none of the staff members seemed able to accommodate themselves to the decidedly leftward offset of the hanging brake and clutch pedals. And the driver's sun visor found itself in conflict with the rear view mirror when lowered.

In the final analysis, the R-4 Daytona seemed to be a desirable mount for many an enthusiast were it not for the weight distribution. Given a set of decent exhaust headers, wide slicks on the rear, and the 4.55:1 axle, it still appeared to our slide-rule statisticians that it might begin doing in Class D at drag strips what it has already done on the Bonneville Salt Flats—i.e., set records. ∎

CAR LIFE ROAD TEST

1964 STUDEBAKER
Daytona R-4 Hardtop

SPECIFICATIONS

List price	$2443
Price, as tested	4550
Curb weight, lb	3660
Test weight	3990
distribution, %	60/40
Tire size	6.50-15
Tire capacity, lb	4460
Brake swept area, sq in	377
Engine type	V-8, ohv
Bore & stroke	3.655 x 3.625
Displacement, cu in	304.5
Compression ratio	12:1
Carburetion	2 x 4
Bhp @ rpm	280 @ 5000
equivalent mph	110
Torque, lb-ft	n.a.
equivalent mph	n.a.

EXTRA-COST OPTIONS

High performance R-4 package, 4-speed transmission, power steering, reclining seats, tinted glass, heater, radio, undercoating, vinyl trim.

DIMENSIONS

Wheelbase, in	109
Tread, f & r	57.4/56.6
Overall length, in	194
width	71.5
height	54.8
equivalent vol, cu ft	430
Frontal area, sq ft	21.7
Ground clearance, in	5.25
Steering ratio, o/a	26.5
turns, lock to lock	4.4
turning circle, ft	37.5
Hip room, front	2 x 21.5
Hip room, rear	59.0
Pedal to seat back, max	39.0
Floor to ground	11.5
Luggage vol, cu ft	13.6
Fuel tank capacity, gal	20.0

GEAR RATIOS

4th (1.00) overall		3.54
3rd (1.51)		5.34
2nd (1.92)		6.80
1st (2.54)		8.98

PERFORMANCE

Top speed (6000), mph	132
Shifts, @ mph (manual)	
3rd (6000)	88
2nd (5600)	65
1st (5600)	49

ACCELERATION

0-30 mph, sec	3.3
0-40	4.6
0-50	6.1
0-60	7.8
0-70	10.4
0-80	13.4
0-100	20.2
Standing ¼ mile, sec	15.8
speed at end, mph	88

FUEL CONSUMPTION

Normal range, mpg	10-14

SPEEDOMETER ERROR

30 mph, actual	29.3
60 mph	61.0
90 mph	87.0

CALCULATED DATA

Lb/hp (test wt)	14.3
Cu ft/ton mile	120.1
Mph/1000 rpm	22.0
Engine revs/mile	2730
Piston travel, ft/mile	1650
Car Life wear index	45.0

PULLING POWER

70 mph, (3rd) max. gradient, %	20.0
50 (2nd)	off scale
30 (1st)	off scale
Total drag at 60 mph, lb	185

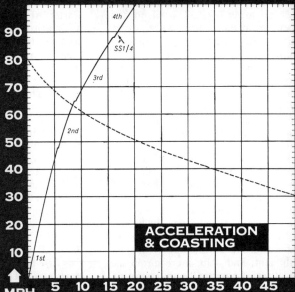

ACCELERATION & COASTING

MPH — ELAPSED TIME IN SECONDS

OPTIONS for Studes include bucket seats, full instrumentation.

FIRST of the '64s

THE newest Studebakers, introduced in America last month, are longer, lower, have new styling and a greater choice of engine powers.

The Lark sedans, as sold in Australia, are six inches longer and an inch lower than the 1963 models. The station wagons are three inches longer.

Higher performance kits are now offered as optional equipment on any of the Studebaker range. The engines consist of the 289 cu. in. R1, a supercharged version of this known as the R2, a big capacity (304.5 cu. in.) supercharged unit designated R3, and an unblown version of this, the R4.

The high performance kits also include suspension and transmission changes to handle the extra power and speed.

Studebakers are having a war against rust. The new primer they are using is applied to the body panels before welding takes place and it is claimed that the bond is not broken by the welding process. In this way it is hoped to eliminate corrosion caused by humidity pockets in the sub-assemblies.

The completed bodies then go through another two anti-rust sections before they are painted.

They are run through a phosphate bath and then into a chromate rinse which is followed by a spray primer.

The final step is an underbody body coating, weighing some 50lb., according to Studebaker's scales.

Although the styling has been greatly changed, the basic appearance is unmistakably Studebaker.

However, four headlamps are obviously on the way out at South Bend, for the frontal treatment of many of the models features two lights, not four.

The Gran Turismo model Hawks have also had their share of changes, one of which is an optional simulated coupe de ville top of vinyl material over the normal steel turret.

Other changes include new wheel discs and a special red badge for the Super versions.

The GTs, like all the new Studebakers, have crash-padded dashboards and recessed instruments. The door locks have been modified for greater strength and chassis lubrication periods have been extended. It is not expected that the new cars will be available locally until well into next year. ● ● ●

STUDEBAKERS for '64 are longer, have high-power engines.

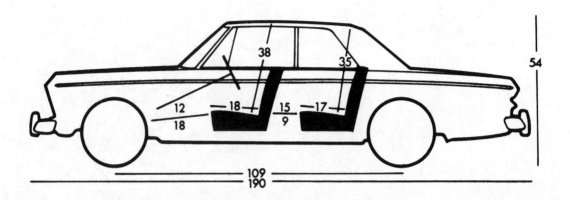

38   35   54

12
18   18   15
9   17

109
190

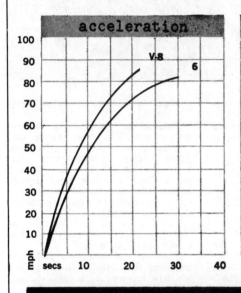

acceleration

100	
90	V-8
80	6
70	
60	
50	
40	
30	
20	
10	
mph	
secs 10 20 30 40	

performance

STUDEBAKER V-8
AUTOMATIC TRANSMISSION

ACCELERATION

0-30— 4.1 seconds
0-40— 5.5 seconds
0-50— 8.1 seconds
0-60—10.7 seconds
0-70—13.6 seconds
0-80—18.0 seconds

PASSING SPEEDS

30-50—3.9 seconds
40-60—5.2 seconds
50-70—6.1 seconds
60-80—7.6 seconds

performance

STUDEBAKER 6
AUTOMATIC TRANSMISSION

ACCELERATION

0-30— 4.7 seconds
0-40— 6.9 seconds
0-50— 9.9 seconds
0-60—13.1 seconds
0-70—18.0 seconds
0-80—26.7 seconds

PASSING SPEEDS

30-50— 4.9 seconds
40-60— 7.2 seconds
50-70— 8.1 seconds
60-80—13.6 seconds

DAYTONA SPORTS SEDAN V-8
CRUISER SEDAN 6

TEST CARS COURTESY
STUDEBAKER OF CANADA, LIMITED

DAYTONA SPORTS SEDAN V-8

ENGINE—
Location: front
No. of cylinders: 8
Head type: OHV
Compression ratio: 9.25:1
Carburetor: 2 barrel Rochester
Cooling: water
Bore: 3.875''
Stroke: 3.00''
Displacement: 283 cu. in.
BHP: 195 @ 4,800 rpm
Torque: 285 lb. ft. @ 2,400 rpm
TRANSMISSION—
No. forward speeds: L-D automatic
Axle ratio: 3.07:1
DIMENSIONS—
Wheelbase: 109'' (2-dr.)
Track f and r: 57⅜''/56 9/16''
Length: 190'' (2-dr.)
Width: 71½''
Height: 54 13/16''
SUSPENSION—
Front: independent coil spring, stabilizer bar-link
Rear: semi-elliptic leaf asymmetric
PRICE AS TESTED— $3,402.15

CRUISER SEDAN 6

ENGINE—
Location: front
No. of cylinders: 6
Head type: OHV
Compression ratio: 8.50:1
Carburetor: 1 barrel Rochester
Cooling: water
Bore: 3.563''
Stroke: 3.25''
Displacement: 194 cu. in.
BHP: 120 @ 4,400 rpm
Torque: 177 @ 2,400 rpm
TRANSMISSION—
No. forward speeds: L-D automatic
Axle ratio: 3.73:1
DIMENSIONS—
Wheelbase: 113'' (4-dr.)
Track f and r: 57⅜''/56 9/16''
Length: 194'' (4-dr.)
Width: 71½''
Height: 54 13/16''
SUSPENSION—
Front: independent coil springs, stabilizer bar-linkless
Rear: semi-elliptic leaf asymmetric
PRICE AS TESTED— $3,554.85

Studebaker Cruiser and Daytona Sports Sedan

coachwork

□ Since Studebaker located all its automobile manufacturing facilities in Hamilton just over one year ago, the company has been making quiet but steady gains and the re-introduction of their heavy duty taxi models should go a long way to ensuring that the name Studebaker appears on the roads in ever-increasing numbers. There have been many skeptics claiming that Stude couldn't make it for very long and skepticism, like a cold, is very catching. However, the patient is doing fine thank you and we — like everyone else in the automobile business — want to see them go on from strength to strength, not only because Studebakers are now made in Canada but because the failure of any car company is bad for the economy and the buyer. This month we tested two examples of the kind of car this over 110 year-old automotive pioneer is producing. They are the Daytona Sport Sedan V-8 and the Cruiser Sedan 6-cylinder cars. Both follow Studebaker's promise of continuity of design and save for the inclusion of two new engines: a 283 cu. in. V-8 and a 194 cu. in. 6, and very minor rear-end chrome trim changes, the main effort has been on improving the basic 1964 model.

The Daytona and the Cruiser are both clean, practical looking cars, in keeping with the current trend towards purity of line, free of frills and gaudy dabs of chrome. The quality of workmanship is high and the high-lustre finish of the cars is as good as anything we've ever seen. The razor-edge roofline of the Daytona is nicely accented by a contrasting vinyl roof cover and last year's 'too-high' look on the rear end has been corrected on the Daytona and Cruiser by relocating the metal trim to give a lower appearance. The solid wrap-around bumpers are continued, but only the Cruiser is fitted with bumper guards. The distinctive grille remains unchanged.

(continued next page)

Studebaker Cruiser and Daytona Sports Sedan

instrument

Studebaker is to be complimented on retaining its excellent direct reading, round dial instruments. Not an 'idiot' light in sight except for the parking brake warning light, which is standard. All instruments are lit by a soft, glare-free, red light. Controls are well-grouped and recessed in a fully padded dash and the oval steering wheel, with a sensibly designed horn ring, allows direct eye-access to every instrument. Standard equipment is a foot-actuated windshield washer, but a hand control would be more convenient.

interior

Wide doors and flat floors make these cars a treat to get in and out of. Interior dimensions compare with virtually all full-size cars except in headroom, where the Studebakers outdo everybody and for really tall drivers this is a real joy. The bucket seats on the Sports Sedan are standard equipment. They are very comfortable and give good support. The conventional bench-type seats on the Cruiser are comfortable and we could find little to complain about them. Studebaker already has one of the industry's best-designed dash and seat combinations and this is continued with little change. The handy console is still there, the glove-box is roomy and courtesy lights here and interior are standard equipment. The overall feeling is one of spaciousness and quality.

engines

The new 283 cu. in. (195 hp) V-8 and 194 cu. in. (120 hp) 6-cylinder are specially adapted GM units from McKinnon Industries. Both cars under test were fitted with automatic and the new V-8 takes a backseat to nobody. The unit is quiet and docile in city traffic, provides effortless high-speed cruising and more than adequate acceleration. It would be nice, though, to have the option of floor-shift. Studebaker's old 6-cylinder never won medals for acceleration but the new 6 is zippy as any we've tried.

handling

Studebaker's Borg-Warner transmission is an ideal mate for their engines with a near-perfect power-to-weight ratio that makes for happier cornering and handling all round. The automatic is a P-N-D-L-R arrangement which we like because you don't go through reverse when placing in it 'Park.' All Stude V8's are equipped with heavy duty finned brakes at the front and their stopping power is excellent; the optional disc brakes are a worthwhile investment. Studebaker has always been a pioneer in engineering developments, though without the attendant fanfare of other manufacturers. They are now the first North American manufacturer to offer transistorized ignition equipment as standard equipment on the Sports Sedan and around a $40 option on all other models. Better performance, economy, longer plug and points life are claimed.

summary

Studebaker of Canada has gone a long way towards producing a near-perfect automobile for the average buyer. Its lowest priced model sells in Toronto for about $2,600 while the top model does not exceed $3,200. Of course, this is basic price and there is a wide range of options available. The 1965 Saudebaker is an excellent all-round automobile; a practical car with practical looks, it does its job efficiently and comfortably. We sincerely hope — for everybody's sake — that the name Stude will be around for another 110 years. Judging by their product there is no good reason why they shouldn't be.

STUDEBAKER

STUDEBAKER has come up with a new ventilation system in its 1966 models that shows great promise. Air for the passenger compartment is taken in at the front of the car and admitted to the interior in the usual way. It then passes to the trunk and from there out through vents designed into the tail lights. These exhaust vents are located in a low-pressure area to get forced circulation at driving speeds.

The object of this new system is to get good ventilation with all windows and vent wings closed, thus eliminating drafts, noise, and buffeting at highway speeds. It's been long recognized that noise contributes to driver fatigue, so the new Studebakers, besides being more comfortable, are safer.

The sporting model of the line, formerly named the Daytona Sports Sedan, is now called the Grand Turismo. It's identified with a GT badge in the center of the grille. Other exterior trim is the same as that of the luxury Cruiser. Low-priced Commanders have different grilles, trim, and interiors, and are offered as 2- or 4-door sedans. A station wagon, called the Wagonaire, completes Stude's list of models. This can be ordered with an optional sliding portion of the rear roof.

A new, higher-performance, 230-cubic-inch, 6-cylinder engine has been added to the list of 6 and V-8 engines (made by Chevrolet) offered in the 1965 models. The manual, overdrive, and automatic transmissions are the same as offered previously. Studebaker continues to offer optional and standard features introduced last year, including Bendix disc brakes, dual master cylinders, and a transistorized ignition system.

Since moving to its Hamilton, Ont., plant, Studebaker has instituted a practice common among European auto makers but almost unheard of this side of the water — running changes. For example, they changed over to a flanged safety axle, improved door latches, and a different accelerator pedal in the spring of 1965 — right in the middle of the '65 model run. This is certainly a logical way of doing things from the engineering and manufacturing standpoints. It's convenient to make changes when they're required or when stocks of the part to be changed become exhausted rather than at some arbitrary time of the year.

Such flexibility in operations is part of the reason Studebaker can break even on around 20,000 cars a year. Most U.S. auto makers use figures considerably higher than this for all-steel cars and somewhat less for fiberglass-bodied ones. The upshot of it all is that the Studebaker buyer can be reasonably sure of being abreast of the times, and sometimes he may even be ahead of the times.   /MT

Walnut-grained trim plus an off-white vinyl interior reveal new luxury of '66 Studebakers.

Louvered vents above tail lights exhaust air from passenger compartment. Back-up lamps wrap around, light sides and behind.

Just facts, ma'am! Full instrumentation on Studebaker dash includes a large clock. Dash padding is non-reflecting material.

Recessed headlights, new grille are "practical changes" for '66. Engines is "283" Chevy.

NEW
AVANTI II
ROAD TEST

Studebaker's great but too-late image
maker rises again, a South Bend phoenix

by Bob McVay
Technical Editor

THEY DO BUILD cars like they used to in South Bend. All those stories about the Avanti's return are . . . *true!*

In an automotive ghost town where several million Studebakers were born, one car a day may seem like small potatoes. But it *is* a car, and it's made with such painstaking care that the quality of each one makes up for the quantity spilled out by most of the others.

The 1966 Avanti II comes as one of a number of cars now being resurrected after several years of dormancy. Others include the Tulsa Cord 8/10 and Indianapolis' Duesenberg. You might also count Brooks Stevens' replica Mercedes. The new Avanti's story hinges on the men who gave it its second chance.

Nate Altman and Leo Newman are, among other things, South Bend Studebaker dealers — the principals in this project. They graduated from high school and Notre Dame together and started out in the car-wash business in 1935. Next year, they leased a used car lot (placing their own personal cars up for sale at the start); then became South Bend Packard dealers in 1937. When Packard and Studebaker merged, Newman and Altman became Studebaker dealers (in 1959). Both men still drive 1955 and '56 Packard Patricians in mint condition.

When Studebaker pulled out of South Bend, a tremendous pool of automotive experts was suddenly put out to pasture. These were men who'd spent most of their lives putting Studebakers together, many of them following in their fathers' footsteps.

Newman and Altman figured there must be a way, if only a small one, to draw on this wealth of technical knowledge and see South Bend once again in the car business. Another natural resource was Studebaker's formidable Avanti, built as a limited-production image-maker during Studebaker's final years before the move to Canada. Leo and Nate bought the plant — lock, stock, jigs, fixtures, tools, parts, and barrel — with 500,000 square feet of space and all rights to the Avanti name. They also latched onto the civilian truck production facilities for possible future ventures into the truck business.

Getting things organized was a mammoth job, but with the tremendous business background of Eugene J. Hardig, Avanti II's vice president of engineering (he held the same position with Studebaker for many years), all the loose ends were finally tied down, and hiring of the cream of former Studebaker technicians began.

First they set up an unconventional assembly line. It's like no other line

We hit speeds of 121 mph on rough straightaways of the former Studebaker test track at South Bend, Ind. The Avanti II was rock-steady at speed, showed good handling traits.

Miniature assembly line ends with manual body drop when finished body and chassis meet. Whether it takes technician one hour or 3 to fit a door, it's perfect when car leaves.

HERB COLLINS, A 30-YEAR STUDEBAKER VETERAN, CAREFULLY FITS CARB AND COMPONENTS TO AVANTI II'S 300-HP CORVETTE ENGINE.

PHOTOS BY BOB D'OLIVO, BOB MC VAY

AVANTI continued

you'll find in this country. Some 30 men work on each car as it passes through various stages of completion.

Men (not machines) are the key to the whole process. Each man has a number of functions to perform in a "bay" setup. He takes as little or as much time as he needs to do the job, but when the car leaves that bay, it's as perfect as man can make it. If any problems crop up, the trouble can be pinpointed immediately and corrected. The men work at their own pace, taking obvious pride in their work. Cars come off this assembly line at the rate of one a day.

Seven bays for the body and 7 for the chassis end in the final hand body drop. Then cars are fitted with hand-sewn interiors selected by customers. They're tuned, aligned, water-tested, and finally

Customers can choose all-vinyl, all-fabric, or a combination of the 2 when they order their Avanti II from their dealer. Even the number of seat pleats is up to the new owner.

Avanti II showed only slight lean on mildly banked track at 95-100 mph. Both stability and controllability were excellent.

Extensive water testing is carried out to make sure every car is watertight before it leaves the factory for dealer showrooms.

inspected, driven and broken in by Master Mechanic Herbert Latzké, a 15-year employee of Newman & Altman.

In Bay #1, the chassis gets its springs, brakes, hubs, drums, anti-roll bar, and gas lines. Bay #2 adds steering assembly, bell cranks, power steering rods and valves, and shocks. As the chassis progresses into Bay #5, Herb Collins, who spent 30 years with Studebaker Engineering, adds the torque-converter or 4-speed transmission, carburetor, air conditioning, oil cooler, generator, and other components to the car's 300-hp, 327-cubic-inch Corvette V-8. Bay #7 is the final body drop, where body meets chassis. Bodies also progress through 7 production bays.

Thousands of interior fabric choices are offered Avanti II buyers, who may choose material, colors, and even the kind and number of pleats they want. Interiors are hand-sewn by Chester Milliken, aged 61, who spent 40 years working for Studebaker in interior trim and experimental engineering. One-half-inch furniture foam, used nowhere else in the automotive business, is used to pad Avanti II seat cushions. Vinyl or leather will also be available in addition to thousands of nylon color and fabric choices. Avanti IIs are truly individually designed and crafted automobiles.

Overseeing the building operation is Luther (Lu) Johnson, for 38 years a Studebaker test driver. Lu drove private and factory-sponsored cars in the Indianapolis 500 when the 336-inch, Straight-8 Studebakers were a real threat on the tracks of this country.

Getting all the parts and pieces was a stupendous job — contacting vendors and making arrangements. This was handled by another key man in the Avanti II operation, John Soelch, vice president and director of purchasing for Studebaker for 45 years. Newman and Altman have nothing but praise for the enthusiasm and cooperation they've gotten from all vendors, large and small.

Molded Fiber Glass Body Co. of Ashtabula, Ohio, supplies the Avanti II's fiberglass body. General Motors furnishes engines; Philadelphia's Budd Co. supplies the reinforced X-member frame, and Borg-Warner turns out the transmissions and gears. Bendix disc brakes are standard on the car's front wheels, with huge, finned drums at the rear. Dana Corp. supplies the rear axles.

Now, finally, what about the car itself? That should be obvious. In our test, run at the old Studebaker proving grounds at South Bend, we drove 2 full equipped, $7200 Avanti IIs on the high

Good-looking dashboard uses round, easy-to-read gauges, is one of best in industry. Cars have adjustable tilt steering wheel.

Lifelong friends and business associates, Nate Altman (left) and Leo Newman bombard McVay with facts about new Avanti II.

speed oval; around twisty, tree-lined, narrow roads; and over the bumpy built-in lumps of the test track.

The original Avanti was an impressive car in its own right, but the Avanti II proves better in every way. A redesigned front end, nearly imperceptible unless an original car is alongside, eliminates the front-end "rake" and gives the car a better balanced look. The extra space also helps accommodate the Corvette engine. This mill gives a considerable weight saving and thus a better power-to-weight ratio. The car handles

better, accelerates faster, and feels better than the old Avanti. A full complement of extras comes standard, and all cars wear Firestone 500 tires, a very good choice and one we'd recommend to other manufacturers of high-performance equipment. You can delete some standard items to bring the price down to $6550. Normal price, though, is $7200.

We found ourselves taking banked curves at 95-100 mph and hitting up to 121 mph on the short straights. In every instance, the car felt solid, steady, and

under control right up to the point of breakaway. Body lean, nose dive, and squat were very well controlled, and the only possible complaint we can come up with is limited rear-seat head room.

Our visit to the Avanti II assembly plant convinced us that this operation is no flash in the pan. Unlike some operations we've seen, where only 2 or 3 cars are made, the Avanti II impressed us as a most serious effort — and an excellent one. They'd built 23 cars before we arrived, and we saw some 30 others in various stages of completion. /MT

AVANTI II

2-door, 4-passenger sports coupe

OPTIONS ON TEST CAR: None (Standard equipment includes: air conditioning, 4-speed manual or automatic transmission, disc brakes, power steering-brakes-windows, twin-traction differential, adjustable/tilting steering wheel, radio, heater/defroster, 4-way "SOS" emergency flasher, electric windshield wipers and washers, hand-sewn interiors with decorator fabrics, tinted glass, seat belts front and rear, built-in roll bar, tool pouch and kit)

BASE PRICE: $7200 f.o.b. South Bend, Ind.
PRICE AS TESTED: $7200 (plus tax and license)
ODOMETER READING AT START OF TEST: 1500 miles
RECOMMENDED ENGINE RED LINE: 5500 rpm

PERFORMANCE

ACCELERATION: (2 aboard)
0-30 mph	3.0 secs.
0-45 mph	4.7
0-60 mph	7.5

PASSING TIMES AND DISTANCES
40-60 mph	3.7 secs., 270 ft.
50-70 mph	4.1 secs., 360.8 ft.

Standing start ¼-mile 16.3 secs. and 89 mph

Speeds in gears @ shift points
1st	52 mph @ 5500 rpm	3rd	121 mph @ 5200 rpm
2nd	85 mph @ 5500 rpm		

Speedometer Error on Test Car
Car's speedometer reading	30	45	50	60	70	81
Weston electric speedometer	30	45	50	60	70	80

Observed mph per 1000 rpm in top gear ... 23 mph

Stopping Distances — from 30 mph, 29.6 ft.; from 60 mph, 110.6 ft.

SPECIFICATIONS FROM MANUFACTURER

Engine
Ohv V-8 (Corvette)
Bore: 4.00 ins.
Stroke: 3.25 ins.
Displacement: 327 cu. ins.
Compression ratio: 10.5:1
Horsepower: 300 @ 5000 rpm
Horsepower per cubic inch: 0.91
Torque: 360 lbs.-ft. @ 3200 rpm
Carburetion: 1 4-bbl.
Ignition: 12-volt coil

Gearbox
3-speed automatic torque converter (on test car) or manual 4-speed, all-synchro; floorshift

Driveshaft
1-piece, open tube

Differential
Hypoid, semi-floating
Standard ratio: 3.54:1

Suspension
Front: Independent, coil springs with upper and lower control arms, direct-acting (adjustable heavy-duty) tubular shocks, and anti-roll bar
Rear: Rigid axle, with 5-leaf, semi-elliptic springs, direct-acting (adjustable heavy-duty) tubular shocks, radius rods, anti-roll bar, and twin-traction differential

Steering
Cam and single lever, roller stud, with power assist
Turning diameter: 37.5 ft.
Turns lock to lock: 3.5

Wheels and Tires
5-lug, 15x5K steel disc wheels
7.75x15 Firestone 500 whitewall tires

Brakes
Hydraulic; disc front, finned drums rear; integral power assist
Front: 11½-in.-dia. grey-iron discs
Rear: 11-in.-dia. x 2-in.-wide drums
Effective lining area: 105 sq. in.
Swept drum area: NA

Body and Frame
Heavy-duty X-member steel frame with molded fiberglass body
Wheelbase: 109.0 ins.
Track: front, 57.4 ins.; rear, 56.6 ins.
Overall length: 192.5 ins.
Overall width: 70.4 ins.
Overall height: 54.0 ins.
Curb weight: 3181 lbs.

THE CAR WITH THE INTERNATIONAL FLAVOUR

Detroit . . . Hamilton, Ontario . . . Madrid . . . Melbourne . . . from all over the world come the bits and pieces that make up Studebaker's Cruiser V8. What's it like? Bryan Hanrahan Reveals All . . .

NOBLESSE oblige. Studebaker Cruiser for 1966 by courtesy of General Motors. Put together in Melbourne by Continental and General Motors from Canadian, American, German, Australian and Spanish bits.

Sounds like the greatest hybrid of all time. But the main components are solid Studebaker, apart from the engine — which is the well-known 195 bhp GM V8 that has powered Chevs and Ponties in Australia for five years. In the Studey it's called Thunderbolt.

Apparently Studebaker, now manufacturing in Canada, found this the solution to the problem of engine production capacity. A good solution, too. Four point seven litres and 195 horses take over from 4.3 litres and 180 bhp.

Perhaps more important in terms of good handling, the bigger engine is some 80lb. lighter — the brutal oversteer of the old car is gone.

The Cruiser is now a genuine ton-topper, and can scorch from 0-50 mph in 8.2sec., from 60-80 mph in 8.2sec.

How To Pick It

In appearance the new model is hard to pick. Only changes outside are a little less chrome trim on the boot, and the word Studebaker set just above the back bumper. Construction is similar: the well-proven combination of a rigid separate chassis carrying stiff panels that mate neatly together.

All is carried on 15-inch wheels, suspended at the front by independent wishbones and coil springs, and at the back by a solid axle carried on leaf springs. Telescopic tubular shocks all round.

But these are not quite the same in action. Back springs are softer and shocker settings slightly stiffer all round. These changes also help to reduce the old arm-breaking understeer.

Transmission on the test car was three-speed Borg-Warner automatic. Manual is available to order — also three-speed. Three well-chosen gears are better than two. The Studey, with a weight advantage, of course, is a much more flexible and a faster car than the current Bel-Air with the same engine and two-speed transmission.

Gear-changing

The extra 15 horses have allowed the engineers to corral a few more to smooth out the gear changes. They're now very smooth, particularly the kickdown under full throttle.

The transmission has no frills — straight P-N-D-L-R. Low is available on the move at 20 mph or below, either by the steering gear selector quadrant or by throttle pedal kickdown.

Second gear, or intermediate, is available by kickdown only at 60 or below. But the speed ranges of the gears and the snappiness of kickdowns do a lot to compensate for such things as second gear holds and dual driving ranges.

This was the quietest big-model Borg-Warner auto I've yet driven. Only time I could get a peep out of it was with the engine running and selector in either park or neutral. It made a sort of high keening noise as if asking for the boot to be spared.

Braking is much improved. For four years the Victorian police have been using Studeys as patrol cars, fitted with 225 bhp engines, manual

> '*Outside, it's the same old Studebaker. But under the bonnet is a 4.7-litre V8, called he Thunderbolt, which takes it over the ton, and from 0-50 in 8.2 sec. The bolt has thunder, all right. . . .*'

FEW outward changes to 1966 Study—but aerial is for radio that's now standard fitting. BELOW: The real change is under bonnet—the lighter, gutsier, 4.7-litre V8 engine from G.M.

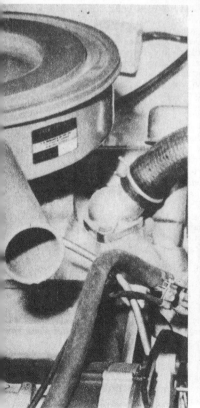

MAIN SPECIFICATIONS

ENGINE: 8 cylinder vee formation o.h.v.; bore 3.875in. stroke 3.0in.; capacity 4673c.c.; compression ratio 9.25:1, maximum bhp 195 (gross) at 4800 rpm; maximum torque 285ft./lb. at 2400 rpm, 2-barrel downdraught carburettor, mechanical fuel pump; 12-volt ignition.

TRANSMISSION: Three-speed automatic Ratios: Low 7.84; intermediate 4.87, drive 3.31; final drive 3.31:1.

SUSPENSION: Independent front by coil springs and wishbones; live rear axle with semi-elliptic springs; telescopic shockers all round.

STEERING: Cam and roller; 4.7 turns lock-to-lock; 40ft. turning circle.

BRAKES: Drum, servo assisted; 172.8 sq. in. of swept area.

WHEELS: Steel disc with 6.40 by 15 tubeless tyres.

DIMENSIONS: Wheelbase 9ft. 5in.; track, front 4ft. 9¾in.; rear 4ft. 8⅛in.; length 16ft. 2in.; width 5ft. 11¼in.; height 4ft. 6¾in.; clearance 7in.

FUEL CAPACITY: 15 gallons.

KERB WEIGHT: 27½cwt.

PERFORMANCE ON TEST

CONDITIONS: Fine, warm, no wind, smooth bitumen, two up, premium fuel.

BEST SPEED: 103.4 mph.

FLYING ¼-MILE: 100.6 mph.

STANDING ¼-MILE: 18.1sec.

MAXIMUM in indirect gears: First 45 mph, second 81 mph.

ACCELERATION from rest through gears in drive range (using full kickdown): 0-30 mph 3.4sec., 0-40 6.1, 0-50 8.2, 0-60 11.8, 0-70 16.5, 0-80 22.4, 0-90 30.2.

ACCELERATION in drive range (using full kickdown): 20-40 mph 3.1sec., 30-50 4.4, 40-60 6.0, 50-70 6.9, 60-80 8.2, 70-90 10.8.

BRAKING: 33ft. to stop from 30 mph in neutral; 175ft. to stop from 60 mph in neutral.

CONSUMPTION: 13.4 mpg over 100 miles, including all tests.

SPEEDOMETER: 1 mph fast at 30 mph, 6 mph fast at 70, 10 mph fast at 100.

PRICE: £2175, including tax.

STUDEBAKER'S interior is neat and tidy. But handbrake twists awkwardly, windscreen wipers are badly set.

THE CAR WITH THE INTERNATIONAL FLAVOUR

transmission and 11in. front brakes with finned drums.

These are now standard on all Cruisers. Total lining area is 172.8 sq. in.

There was hardly any fade on the brake tests. The car always pulled up evenly. They are adequately powerful — no usual thing in an American-style car. Only fault is the high pedal pressures needed to get the best out of them.

This is rather surprising, since the cost of all the Cruiser's new and good things is a price tag of £2175 tax paid — a lift of £185. Why a power booster couldn't be included in this is most puzzling to me.

Braking is the only effortful thing about the car, and all the more irritating because everything else is so much lighter and sweeter. Just this one point, I feel, would put a woman off a car that otherwise she'd likely think very handy.

Equipment

But some of the sting is taken out of the price rise by the Cruiser's very comprehensive equipment. A good radio is standard, so is heater-demister (recirculatory), two-speed electric wipers, screenwashers, reversing lights, boot light, carpets, and folding back seat centre armrests. Four headlights give first-class penetration and spread. An alternator produces the electrical power.

Finish and soundproofing are good, too. Doors close with a nice click, no squeaks or rattles, neat paint and trim. Continental and General can take a big hand for the fine job they do — mating Australian (wheels, tyres and sundries), German (electrical), Spanish (part of toolkit), Canadian (panels), and American (engine and transmission) parts very nicely indeed.

How It Goes

Flogging against the stopwatches, the Cruiser was never ruffled. As usual the figures are a mean of four runs in opposing directions.

The water temperature gauge needle never jiggled; oil pressure stayed constant (almost forgot to mention that the Study has full instruments — for oil, water, amps, fuel, speedo without trip).

It is an utterly sound high performance car that can take it.

Handling is safe and predictable, still with slight understeer. But what of that. Understeer in moderate degree is inherently safe and to the taste of most drivers. You can nearly always shove the tail round with a bit of throttle, if needed. The power is there, all right.

I don't like the steering, though. A giddy 4.7 turns lock-to-lock — and not all that light, either. Perhaps a good power set-up with a few less turns would improve matters. But at least the car points accurately.

Ride is good on most surfaces, particularly over indifferent bitumen.

Plenty of room inside for six people. Driving position is not cramped — nor are passengers.

Two faults for the driver that should really be put right after five years of Australian-produced Studeys: windscreen wipers are set for left-hand drive and leave top right of screen unswept, which is dangerous; the twist-handbrake twists in the wrong direction, which is awkward and irritating.

Boot is ample, well-shaped. Engine accessibility is lousy — buried plugs, distributor hidden at back of block, starter motor looks as if the exhaust manifold would have to be dropped to get at it. A full house indeed.

The Cruiser played fortissimo to the tune of 13.4 mpg. But this was an unfairly short test of only 100 miles. Couldn't be avoided. A few more miles would have improved the figure, and the car was probably still stiff with only 15,000 miles on the clock.

In a Nutshell . . .

I think that fully run-in performance might well improve, too. Whatever, this is one of the most improved cars of the 1966 crop that I've. tested.

It performs well, it handles nicely, and it comes decently equipped and finished — which is a darned sight more than can be said for some more expensive American machinery around.

UNITED STATES OF AMERICA

Commander 2-door Sedan

ENGINE CAPACITY 194 cu in, 3,179.08 cu cm
FUEL CONSUMPTION 21.5 m/imp gal, 17.9 m/US gal, 13.1 l × 100 km
SEATS 6   **MAX SPEED** 92 mph, 148.1 km/h
PRICE IN USA $ 2,215

ENGINE front, 4 stroke; cylinders: 6, in line; bore and stroke: 3.56 × 3.25 in, 90.4 × 82.5 mm; engine capacity: 194 cu in, 3,179.08 cu cm; compression ratio: 8.5; max power (SAE): 120 hp at 4,400 rpm; max torque (SAE): 177 lb ft, 24.4 kg m at 2,400 rpm; max engine rpm: 4,800; specific power: 37.7 hp/l; cylinder block: cast iron; cylinder head: cast iron; crankshaft bearings: 7; valves: 2 per cylinder, overhead, push-rods and rockers, hydraulic tappets; camshafts: 1, side; lubrication: mechanical pump, full flow filter; lubricating system capacity: 8.27 imp pt, 10 US pt, 4.7 l; carburation: 1 Rochester BV 7025087 downdraught single barrel carburettor; fuel feed: mechanical pump; cooling system: water; cooling system capacity: 22.53 imp pt, 27 US pt, 12.8 l.

TRANSMISSION driving wheels: rear; clutch: single dry plate; gearbox: mechanical; gears: 3 + reverse; synchromesh gears: II and III; gearbox ratios: I 3.110, II 1.800, III 1, rev 4.220; gear lever: steering column; final drive: hypoid bevel; axle ratio: 3.730.

CHASSIS box-type ladder frame; front suspension: independent, wishbones, coil springs, anti-roll bar, telescopic dampers; rear suspension: rigid axle, semi-elliptic leafsprings, telescopic dampers.

STEERING recirculating ball; turns of steering wheel lock to lock: 4.70.

BRAKES drum; area rubbed by linings: total 239.20 sq in, 1,542.84 sq cm.

ELECTRICAL EQUIPMENT voltage: 12 V; battery: 53 Ah; alternator; ignition distributor: Delco-Remy; headlamps: 2.

DIMENSIONS AND WEIGHT wheel base: 109 in, 2,769 mm; front track: 57.37 in, 1,457 mm; rear track: 59.56 in, 1,513 mm; overall length: 190 in, 4,826 mm; overall width: 71.50 in, 1,816 mm; overall height: 54.80 in, 1,392 mm; ground clearance: 6 in, 152 mm; dry weight: 2,756 lb, 1,250 kg; distribution of weight: 54.5% front axle, 45.5% rear axle; turning circle (between walls): 39 ft, 11.9 m; width of rims: 4.5''; tyres: 7.35 × 15; fuel tank capacity: 14.1 imp gal, 17 US gal, 64 l.

BODY saloon/sedan; doors: 2; seats: 6; front seats: bench.

PERFORMANCE max speeds: 32 mph, 51.5 km/h in 1st gear; 55 mph, 88.5 km/h in 2nd gear; 92 mph, 148.1 km/h in 3rd gear; power-weight ratio: 22.9 lb/hp, 10.4 kg/hp; carrying capacity: 1,058 lb, 480 kg; speed in direct drive at 1,000 rpm: 20.5 mph, 33 km/h.

PRACTICAL INSTRUCTIONS fuel: 92 oct petrol; engine sump oil: 6.69 imp pt, 8 US pt, 3.8 l, SAE 5W-20 (winter) 20W-40 (summer), change every 6,000 miles, 9,700 km; gearbox oil: 1.94 imp pt, 2.30 US pt, 1.1 l, SAE 80; final drive oil: 2.11 imp pt, 2.50 US pt, 1.2 l, SAE 90; valve timing: inlet opens 62° before tdc and closes 94°

after bdc, exhaust opens 92°30' before bdc and closes 63°30' after tdc; normal tyre pressure: front 24 psi, 1.7 atm, rear 20 psi, 1.4 atm.

VARIATIONS AND OPTIONAL ACCESSORIES 4.100 axle ratio; front disc brakes (diameter 11.50 in, 292 mm), servo, total area rubbed by linings 377 sq in, 2,431.65 sq cm; transistorized ignition; 7.75 × 15 tyres; separate front seats; limited slip final drive; servo brake; 0.700 ratio in overdrive/top, 4.100 and 3.730 axle ratios; Flight-O-Matic automatic gearbox, hydraulic torque convertor and planetary gears with 3 ratios (I 2.400, II 1.470, III 1, rev 2.400), max ratio of convertor at stall 2.1, 4.100 and 3.730 axle ratios; 6-cylinder engine, capacity 230 cu in, 3,769.01 cu cm, bore and stroke 3.87 × 3.25 in, 98.3 × 82.5 mm, 140 hp, max torque (SAE) 220 lb ft, 30.4 kg m at 1,600 rpm, 8.5 compression ratio, only with Flight-O-Matic automatic gearbox, 3.730 and 3.310 axle ratios, max speed 98 mph, 157.8 km/h, fuel consumption 20.3 m/imp gal, 16.9 m/US gal, 13.9 l × 100 km; V8 standard engine, capacity 283 cu in, 4,637.52 cu cm, 195 hp, without transistorized ignition, dry weight 2,950 lb, 1,338 kg, max speed 110 mph, 177.1 km/h, fuel consumption 17.6 m/imp gal, 14.7 m/US gal, 16 l × 100 km (for further mechanical elements see Daytona Sports Sedan) ⱱ Commander 4-door Sedan, wheel base 113 in, 2,870 mm, overall length 194 in, 4,928 mm.

Valiant when buying, with Vauxhall Cresta next, but one in five considered no other car, several saying that they chose this car for caravan towing.

A unique problem emerges under "probable next choice". With Studebaker no longer available, nearly half of owners are undecided, and we can conclude by quoting some typical anguished comments:

● "I have been spoilt by driving the Lark. . . . A great pity that these

STUDEBAKER DAYTONA
V8

* "What can take its place?" is the pointed question from devoted owners . . .

A CAR OWNERS' REPORT

THOUGH Studebaker finally went out of production more than a year ago, the Lark Daytona V8 will continue on South Africa's roads for many years to come and is a car greatly cherished by owners.

This brief summary of owner reports contains some quite unusual features: a very low average monthly mileage, for instance, which is surprising for a car which is popular with farmers (about half of the reports were from country areas).

The most-liked features are revealing, almost every owner mentioning the car's power and overdrive, with fair praise for its compact size, economy, styling and general ruggedness.

DISC BRAKES

While brakes on the pre-1965 models came in for criticism for high-speed fade, owners of 1965 models were unanimous in their praise of the boosted disc front brakes introduced that year as a production "first" from North America.

Criticisms centred on heavy steering at low speed (and the oval steering wheel), the column gearshift, the cramping effect of the spare wheel in the trunk, and ground clearance, with lesser mention for wind noise level and hard-closing doors.

More than half of owners had no trouble with their Stud's, and one in seven reported trouble with brakes (pre-1965 models only) and shock absorbers.

The percentage of approval for dust seal is very low at 38 per cent, with many owners mentioning the luggage trunk specifically.

About half of owners report using dealer service, which averages out as "fair to good", with accolades for the dealerships at Johannesburg, Durban and Kenhardt.

"NEXT CHOICE" PROBLEM

One Stud owner in four considered fine cars are not manufactured any more . . ." (A bank official).

● "Next choice is most difficult — I had been looking forward to the 1966 model. I feel I have lost something irreplaceable, as my Lark converted me to Studebaker for all time . . ."

● A doctor, formerly an Alfa owner: "Having finally found a car to take a family load and still provide motoring pleasure, I face the heavy blow of this lovely car's demise . . ."

● "There is no substitute." (Another medical practitioner).

They have a case. What other car is there with V8 engine, disc front brakes, overdrive, hill-holder and seating six people? ●

REPORT SUMMARY

MAKE AND MODEL:		
Make		Studebaker
Model		Lark Daytona V8
MILEAGES:		
Total		643,208
Average monthly		948·7
FUEL CONSUMPTION:		
About town		18·4
On long trips		23·5
MOST-LIKED FEATURES:		
Power		96%
Overdrive cruising		82%
Compact size		43%
Economy		39%
Hill-Holder		39%
Disc brakes		24%
Appearance		19%
Ruggedness		19%
Overtaking safety		14%
Comfort		14%
DISLIKED FEATURES:		
Column gearshift		34%
Heavy steering		34%
Pre-1965 brakes		29%
Spare wheel position		24%
Ground clearance		19%
Wind noise level		14%
Door closing		10%

TROUBLE REPORT:		
No trouble at all		53%
Shock absorbers		14%
Brakes (pre-1965)		14%
Clutch		10%
Oil seals		10%
BODY SEAL:		
Dustproof		38%
Weatherproof		72%
DEALER SERVICE:		
Use Studebaker service		48%
Quality		Fair to good
No — geographical		29%
No — own service		10%
No — poor service		4%
OTHER CARS CONSIDERED:		
Valiant		38%
Vauxhall Cresta		24%
No other		19%
Ford Zephyr		14%
Ford Fairlane		10%
Volvo		10%
Chevy 2		10%
PROBABLE NEXT CHOICE:		
Undecided		48%
Dodge Monaco		10%
Chevelle		10%

NEW 1952 STUDEBAKER

new Champion ★ The new Commander V-8

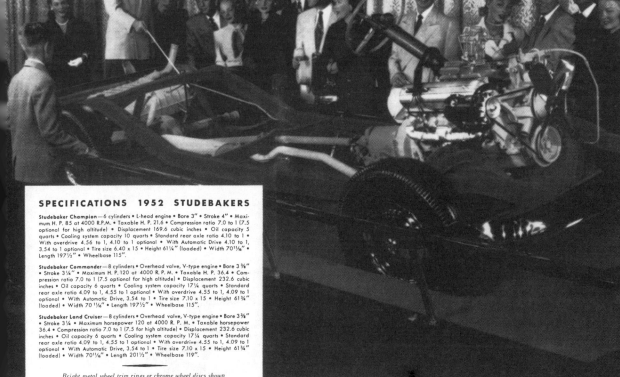

SPECIFICATIONS 1952 STUDEBAKERS

Studebaker Champion—6 cylinders • L-head engine • Bore 3" • Stroke 4" • Maximum H. P. 85 at 4000 R.P.M. • Taxable H. P. 21.6 • Compression ratio 7.0 to 1 (7.5 optional for high altitude) • Displacement 169.6 cubic inches • Oil capacity 5 quarts • Cooling system capacity 10 quarts • Standard rear axle ratio 4.10 to 1 • With overdrive 4.56 to 1, 4.10 to 1 optional • With Automatic Drive 4.10 to 1, 3.54 to 1 optional • Tire size 6.40 x 15 • Height 61¼" (loaded) • Width 70¹¹⁄₁₆" • Length 197½" • Wheelbase 115".

Studebaker Commander—8 cylinders • Overhead valve, V-type engine • Bore 3 ⅜" • Stroke 3¼" • Maximum H. P. 120 at 4000 R. P. M. • Taxable H. P. 36.4 • Compression ratio 7.0 to 1 (7.5 optional for high altitude) • Displacement 232.6 cubic inches • Oil capacity 6 quarts • Cooling system capacity 17¼ quarts • Standard rear axle ratio 4.09 to 1, 4.55 to 1 optional • With overdrive 4.55 to 1, 4.09 to 1 optional • With Automatic Drive, 3.54 to 1 • Tire size 7.10 x 15 • Height 61¾" (loaded) • Width 70 ¹¹⁄₁₆" • Length 197½" • Wheelbase 115".

Studebaker Land Cruiser—8 cylinders • Overhead valve, V-type engine • Bore 3⅜" • Stroke 3¼ • Maximum horsepower 120 at 4000 R. P. M. • Taxable horsepower 36.4 • Compression ratio 7.0 to 1 (7.5 for high altitude) • Displacement 232.6 cubic inches • Oil capacity 6 quarts • Cooling system capacity 17¼ quarts • Standard rear axle ratio 4.09 to 1, 4.55 to 1 optional • With overdrive 4.55 to 1, 4.09 to 1 optional • With Automatic Drive, 3.54 to 1 • Tire size 7.10 x 15 • Height 61¾" (loaded) • Width 70¹¹⁄₁₆" • Length 201½" • Wheelbase 119".

Bright metal wheel trim rings or chrome wheel discs shown on cars illustrated in this catalog are optional at extra cost.

Studebaker
Commander V-8
120 HORSEPOWER
Studebaker Champion
IN THE LOWEST PRICE FIELD

Studebaker again steps out ahead with advanced new styling for discriminating car buyers. Motoring's newest of the new is the swept-back aerodynamic designing that distinguishes the brilliant performing 1952 Studebaker Commander V-8s and the value packed Studebaker Champions of the lowest price field. They are vigorously sleek and beautifully proportioned new Studebakers—and true to Studebaker custom, they're amazingly saving of gasoline. The sparkling power they generate so smoothly is unimpeded by needless excess bulk. Outstanding in eye appeal and drive appeal, this newest Studebaker tells you instantly that it's your kind of car—styled to step up your spirits—designed to thrill you every mile you drive.

Here's the inside story!

Luxury everywhere you look
•
Decorator fabric upholsteries
•

① The Land Cruiser V-8 is luxurious in appointments. Choice of either smart two-tone blue-grey broadcloth illustrated, or rich fawn and tan striped nylon.

② A stunning combination of nylon and vinyl leatherette in the Starliner "hard-top convertible." Leather upholstery optional at extra cost.

③ The State Commander V-8 is upholstered in rich, durable terrace weave nylon over foam rubber cushions. Rich deep pile carpets.

④ The Regal Commander V-8 is attractively styled with pleated door panels. Upholstery is fine quality hickory-beige broadcloth.

FURS, CLOTHING AND ACCESSORIES BY BONWIT TELLER

① The Land Cruiser

② The Starliner "Hard-top Convertible"　　③ The State Commander V-8　　④ The Regal Commander V-8

All over the world...

Studebaker's brilliant performing 120-horsepower V-8 engine is establishing new records for thrift and efficiency

Studebaker's leadership in automobile engine designing is again convincingly confirmed by the tremendous success of this far-advanced new type of V-8. A compact, valve-in-head power plant, this brilliant-performing Studebaker V-8 is so efficient that top automotive authorities point to it as a new-day marvel in the science of gasoline combustion. Without depending upon premium fuel for its amazing zip and pep, the Studebaker V-8 delivers an electric-smooth, whisper-quiet 120-horsepower. Its operating economy is the talk of motorists everywhere.

1952 STUDEBAKER COMMANDER V-8 *State Starliner*

Here's an alluring eyeful! It's Studebaker's excitingly different new "hard-top convertible." The low swung, gracefully contoured body is finished in attractive two-tone colors.

Safe, wide-view vision is another Studebaker contribution to happy motoring. Large one-piece safety glass windshields and expansive windows all around let you see more, assure you peace of mind. One-piece rear windows are standard on all sedan models. Unobstructed vision, fore, aft and sideways, is yours at all times in every new Studebaker.

What a dousing a Studebaker can take! The ignition system has new protection against wet weather stalling. New spark plug caps act as effective "umbrellas" to prevent loss of electrical energy. Doors, windshields and trunk are sealed to keep out moisture and dust. Body insulation protects against heat or cold.

1952 STUDEBAKER COMMANDER V-8 *State Convertible*

There's tour allure aplenty in this dreamlined new convertible—the smartest looking sports car that wheels the highways. Also available in Champion model.

There's unobstructed rear view visibility in convertibles through the large one-piece window. New Orlon fabric natural color top resists staining or fading due to weather or traffic film, keeps its shape and is easily cleaned.

The Studebaker-Philco Automatic Tuning Radio, available at extra cost, is precision built to fit the acoustics of Studebaker cars. Tone is especially fine—comparable to that of your living room console.

Studebaker self-adjusting brakes rarely need servicing. Shoes automatically reposition themselves as lining wears. The firm pedal "feel" of a new car is yours after miles and miles of driving.

① The Regal Champion

Smart new Champion interiors

Superbly fitted and appointed

① Regal Champion interiors feature a smart new decorator fabric of lace striped pattern cloth, tailored over foam rubber seat cushions.

② Leather upholstery with contrasting vinyl trim is optional at extra cost on convertibles. Standard trim is rich, durable nylon.

③ De Luxe Champion interiors are richly upholstered in striped cord and pile Canda cloth. Contrasting leatherette trim on doors.

④ Custom Champion models are smartly tailored in taupe striped Bedford cord fabric. Door trim is contrasting leatherette.

CLOTHING AND ACCESSORIES
BY BONWIT TELLER

② The Convertible   ③ The De Luxe Champion   ④ The Custom Champion

1952 STUDEBAKER V-8 *Land Cruiser*

The special extra long wheelbase Land Cruiser V-8 is truly outstanding in luxury of finish and appointments. No car built, regardless of price, rides more comfortably.

Studebaker's "Miracle Ride" is the most restful in motoring. Car eases itself, and you, over rough spots with delightful ease. Coil-spring front suspension — extra large, extra wide rear leaf springs, direct acting shock absorbers.

Relax in easy-chair comfort. Foam rubber softly cushions the wide, luxurious seats of Land Cruiser, State and Regal models.

The Commander instrument panel has big, sweep-type aircraft dials. The electric clock is standard on Land Cruiser and available on other models at extra cost. Smart, sure-grip steering wheels. Pistol-grip parking brake handle. Large package compartment with easy-to-open lock.

1952 STUDEBAKER COMMANDER V-8 *Regal 2-Door Sedan*

This lowest priced Commander V-8 model has the distinctive out-ahead smartness of exterior design and interior finish that distinguishes all Studebaker cars.

Convenient, disappearing ash trays! Front seat ash trays are standard on all models. Rear seat ash trays in sedans are standard on all Commanders and Regal Champion models.

You won't roll back on upgrades with Studebaker's automatic hill holder. No tap-dancing when you want to go forward after making an uphill stop. Car won't roll back. Standard on Commanders, optional on Champions at added cost.

There's no weave or wander, even when rounding curves. A low center of gravity and scientific weight distribution — a wide, low body and center-point steering — give a reassuring feel of complete control.

1952 STUDEBAKER CHAMPION *Custom 2-Door Sedan*

This lowest priced Studebaker 6-passenger sedan is the popular family car.
Seats are exceptionally roomy—doors are extra wide.

Painstaking craftsmanship keeps Studebaker cars singularly free from wear—fends off repair bills for many miles. Expert craftsmen, many of them father-and-son teams, build enduring quality and wear-resisting soundness into every car.

Plenty of room for luggage in this spacious trunk. Spare wheel stowed at side makes loading easy and may be removed without disturbing luggage.

Easy to park in tight spots! That's one of the joys of owning a 1952 Studebaker—it has an easy-to-turn steering assembly that enables you to edge into and out of tight parking spots with delightful ease. Quick-acting control on the straightaway, too.

1952 STUDEBAKER CHAMPION *Regal 4-Door Sedan*

This exceptionally roomy 4-door sedan comfortably seats six full-size passengers—
and there's plenty of leg room and head room, too.

An easy-acting weather-protected trunk lock is built into the trunk lid handle on all models. Spherical-type handle on Custom Champion. The counterbalanced trunk lid opens and closes with finger-tip ease.

Thrills and thrift with gas-saving overdrive! It goes into action automatically at cruising speeds. Engine effort is reduced about 30% without slowing road speed. Available on all models at extra cost.

Factory approved accessories are custom-styled. Whether you want seat covers or weather lights, a radio, or fender ornaments, you can purchase Studebaker approved accessories with complete confidence.

1952 STUDEBAKER COMMANDER V-8 *State 4-Door Sedan*

This vigorously sleek and beautifully proportioned new Studebaker style star sparkles
with brilliant performance and rides luxuriously.

Built-in directional signal equipment is available as an extra cost accessory. Gives added safety. Front and rear lamps flash intermittently on either left or right hand turns.

Studebaker's resourceful engineering staff has deservedly earned fame throughout the automobile world for its progressiveness and initiative. These men have developed many of the great advancements that increase the efficiency and the economy of motor car engines.

New tail lights faired-in-fenders! They're clearly visible from both side and rear, give extra smartness to the car and increase your safety. Painted bezel on Custom Champion.

1952 STUDEBAKER CHAMPION *De Luxe Starlight Coupe*

Visibility is unlimited in this five passenger "glass-all-around" sports coupe.
Wide doors make it easy to get in and out of the roomy rear seat.

Tinted "green" glass available in windshield and all windows is Studebaker's newest contribution to comfortable motoring. Eye-fatigue, due to glare from brilliant sunlight or strong night lights, is reduced. This glass helps to temper heat from summer sun. Available on all models at extra cost.

Make your climate as you drive. Studebaker's under-seat Climatizer heating, ventilating, defrosting system is available at extra cost.

Glare-proof "black light" illumination. Studebaker dash gauges are "black" lighted. It reduces inside glare, cuts down fatigue, makes night driving safer.

1952 STUDEBAKER CHAMPION *Regal Starliner*

This new Studebaker "hard-top convertible" has the smart style and the unlimited visibility of a convertible with the all-weather comfort of a closed sedan.

Best by test in actual gas mileage! In the 1951 Mobilgas Economy Run, a Studebaker Champion, Commander V-8 and Land Cruiser V-8 finished 1st, 2nd, and 3rd in actual gas mileage to lead a field of 26 cars entered in "standard classifications." The Studebakers used overdrive, optional at extra cost.

Instrument panels of the new 1952 De Luxe and Regal Champion are trimmed in attractive chrome and bright metal. Glare-proof "black light" assures easy-to-read instrument dials. Large package compartment and built-in ash tray. Panel accommodates specially engineered Philco radio, electric clock and cigarette lighter—available at added cost.

Extra marvelous!
STUDEBAKER AUTOMATIC DRIVE
Shifts for itself—No clutch pedal

The new 1952 Studebaker cars offer you the finest "no clutch - no gearshift" driving, available in all models at extra cost. This automatic drive transmission is a combination of torque converter and direct mechanical drive—the brilliant triumph of nearly 15 years' research by the most exacting technicians in the automotive industry.

Drive relaxed all day long! Simply set the selector lever at "D"—that's all. Your Studebaker Automatic Drive "shifts for itself." The gear ratios change automatically, smoothly—in traffic slow-downs and everywhere. Studebaker's Automatic Drive conserves gas at cruising speeds because there's no loss of power due to slippage.

No clutch pedal! The brake pedal is oversize, gives added safety and may be used with either foot. You can't start the engine when car is in gear.

No annoying creep at traffic lights! In fact, even on slight downgrades your car won't move when you brake to a stop. This drive has a special built-in "anti-creep" protection.

No roll-down on downgrades! No roll-back on upgrades! You can park your car safely on a downgrade—it won't budge until selector lever is moved from "park." On normal upgrade stops car won't roll back.

Plenty of extra power when you need it. You boss the drive—it doesn't boss you! Step all the way down on the accelerator and you get an extra burst of power in a flash when you need it for quick, emergency passing.

For down-hill engine braking set the selector at "L." Braking is similar to second gear of a conventional drive car. To "rock" car, flick lever to and fro between "L" and "R."